Poetics of Disturbances

# Narratives and Mental Health



VOLUME 2

The titles published in this series are listed at *brill.com/nmh*

# Poetics of Disturbances

*Narratives of Non-normative Bodies and Minds*

*Edited by*

Deborah de Muijnck
Jessica Jumpertz
Ralf Schneider
Teresa Turnbull

BRILL

LEIDEN | BOSTON

Cover illustration: Abstract painting with dominant red, yellow, and purple tones. By: Steve Johnson.

Library of Congress Cataloging-in-Publication Data

Names: De Muijnck, Deborah, editor. | Jumpertz, Jessica, editor. | Schneider, Ralf, 1966- editor. | Turnbull, Teresa, editor.
Title: Poetics of disturbances : narratives of non-normative bodies and minds / edited by Deborah de Muijnck, Jessica Jumpertz, Ralf Schneider, Teresa Turnbull.
Description: Leiden ; Boston : Brill, 2025. | Series: Narratives and mental health, 2667-0518 ; volume 2 | Includes bibliographical references and index. | Identifiers: LCCN 2024031800 (print) | LCCN 2024031801 (ebook) | ISBN 9789004519879 (hardback) | ISBN 9789004519886 (ebook)
Subjects: LCSH: Mental illness in literature. | Human body in literature. | Literature, Modern–History and criticism. | LCGFT: Essays.
Classification: LCC PN56.M45 P64 2024 (print) | LCC PN56.M45 (ebook) | DDC 809/.93561689–dc23/eng/20240828
LC record available at https://lccn.loc.gov/2024031800
LC ebook record available at https://lccn.loc.gov/2024031801

Typeface for the Latin, Greek, and Cyrillic scripts: "Brill". See and download: brill.com/brill-typeface.

ISSN 2667-0518
ISBN 978-90-04-51987-9 (hardback)
ISBN 978-90-04-51988-6 (e-book)
DOI 10.1163/9789004519886



This book is printed on acid-free paper and produced in a sustainable manner.

# Contents

Acknowledgements

First of all, we would like to extend our gratitude to all contributors to this edition. We would also like to thank the anonymous reviewers for their constructive feedback. We are grateful to the editors of the Narratives and Mental Health series for including our volume in the programme.

Additionally, we want to extend our heartfelt thanks to Anna Klishevich (JLU Giessen) for her proofreading and extensive editorial work on the entire volume.

# Figures and Tables

## Figures



## Tables

# Notes on Contributors

*Simona Adinolfi*
is a PhD student at Ghent University. Her PhD project examines contemporary novels of migration using a critical posthumanities framework, to show how canonical themes usually associated to narratives of migration are being subverted and complicated on a formal level. Her research interests include narrative theory, the critical posthumanities, migration studies, questions of memory and narrative identity.

*Daria Baryshnikova*
recently finished her PhD dissertation at RWTH Aachen University (Germany), in which she investigated the specificity of cut-up-narratives within the different cultural contexts. Her focus is on the representation of mind and mind processes in cut-up-literature. She graduated from the Russian State University for the Humanities (Moscow, Russia). In 2005, she defended her candidate dissertation in the field of history of culture. Since then, she worked as a lecturer at the Russian State University for the Humanities and the University of Witten/Herdecke, as an editor at the art-magazine "Iskusstvo" (Moscow) and as a research assistant at the National Centre for Contemporary Arts (Moscow).

*Marzia Beltrami*
is currently Postdoctoral Researcher in Contemporary Italian Literature at IULM University, Milan. She also held positions as a Postdoctoral Research Fellow in Comparative Literature at the University of Tartu, where she was part of *the Narrative Culture Cognition* research group, and a Visiting Research Fellow at the Medical Humanities in Context Lab (MHiC-Lab) at Sorbonne Nouvelle Paris 3. Her research interests lie in cognitive narratology and the interrelations between narrative and science, with special attention to embodiment, its thematic representations and implications for narrative reception. Her recently completed project focused on the ethical underpinnings of representations of impossible bodies and minds in speculative literature: on this broader topic, she is co-editor of a special issue for 'Marvels & Tales' on *Literary Fairy Tales and the Embodied Mind* (2023), and author of several articles on Primo Levi's and Italo Calvino's science fiction, as well as on A.S. Byatt's fairy tales. Her monograph *Spatial Plots. Virtuality and the Embodied Mind in Baricco, Camilleri and Calvino* (Legenda, 2021) explores the role of spatiality in narrative comprehension

*Sven Van den Bossche*
is a PhD researcher at the University of Antwerp and Ghent University, working on the intersections of literary studies, (trans)gender studies and queer studies. His dissertation project as an FWO fellow is called 'Born in the Wrong Story: An Embodied Approach to Transgender Narratives in Dutch Literary Fiction'. In a corpus of modern and contemporary Dutch novels, he investigates how various transgender embodiments, trajectories and experiences emerge through literary techniques, such as metaphors, temporal ordering and narrative voice. In the Spring of 2023, he was a Fulbright visiting student researcher at California State University Long Beach.

*Laura de la Parra Fernández*
is Assistant Professor in the Department of English at Complutense University of Madrid, where she serves as Academic Coordinator of the MA in North American Studies. She has been a visiting scholar at Birkbeck College, University of London, at Harvard University, and at Project Narrative, Ohio State University, thanks to a Fulbright Postdoctoral Fellowship. Her research focuses on Modern and Contemporary British and American literature by women, life writing, affect theory, and the medical humanities.

*Carolin Gebauer*
is a lecturer of English literature and culture at the University of Wuppertal and a postdoctoral researcher at Wuppertal's Center for Narrative Research. She is part of the Horizon 2020 project "Crises as OPPORTUNITIES", funded by the European Union, which explores representations of migration in the European public sphere, and a member of the executive team of *DIEGESIS*, a bilingual interdisciplinary e-journal for narrative research. Her monograph *Making Time: World Construction in the Present-Tense Novel* (De Gruyter 2021) received the ESSE Book Award for Junior Scholars in the Field of Literatures in the English Language 2022 as well as the Barbara Perkins and George Perkins Prize 2023 of the International Society for the Study of Narrative.

*Liselotte Van der Gucht*
is a research fellow of the Flemish Research Foundation (FWO) affiliated with the Department of Literary Studies at Ghent University. She investigates German/Austrian 19th, 20th, and 21st-century literature by female authors through the lense of neurodiversity, aiming to investigate how non-normative cognition can be experienced and expressed in literary texts. Her most recent publications include a chapter on hypersensitivity as empathy in Marlen Haushofer's autobiographical novel *Nowhere ending sky* (in *Orbis Litterarum* 2023) and an opinion piece on neuronormativity in *De Reactor* (in Dutch).

*Jessica Jumpertz*
is a research and teaching assistant at RWTH Aachen University. She is currently completing her PhD-thesis on the representation and negotiation of highly intelligent female characters in literature from the nineteenth to the twentieth century. In her research, Jessica Jumpertz combines cognitive literary studies and feminist narratology to examine the character construction of brilliant female characters and their effects. She has published articles in the research areas of cognitive narratology and the empirical study of literature, but her research interests further encompass cultural studies, feminist literary criticism, narrative theory, and approaches in first and second generation cognitive literary studies.

*Gunther Martens*
is a Professor of German Literature and a member of the Literature Department at Ghent University. He is also a member of the Centre for the Study of Experimental Literature and the Ghent Centre for Digital Humanities. His research interests include disability studies, neurophenomenology, and rhetorical narratology. He is currently leading a research project titled "Exquisite defects. Detoxing the female literary genius at the crossroads of critical disability studies and neurophenomenology". He has published several articles and papers on topics related to his research interests, including a recent paper on neurodiversity in Ingeborg Bachmann's work.

*Sandra Marzinkowski*
(Ruhr Universität Bochum) holds a B.A. in English/American Studies and Romance Studies (French) and an M.A. in English and American Studies. Her main research interests include queer studies, gender studies, narratology, embodied cognition, phenomenology, affect studies, and critical psychiatry. In her M.A. thesis, she investigated fiction centring around characters whose perception is coded as pathological. Her PhD project builds upon this framework to explore textual (in-/re-)validation strategies as connected with hystericizable femininities as well as the entanglement of deep and surface reading strategies with the (de-)legitimisation of gendered violence and identity materialisation processes in the context of historical fiction.

*Deborah de Muijnck*
is a postdoctoral researcher and academic coordinator of the European PhD Network "Literary and Cultural Studies" at the GCSC, JLU Giessen. She finished her dissertation on cognitive narratological approaches toward post-trauma storytelling at RWTH Aachen University's English Department in 2022. Her research focuses on the medical humanities, (cognitive and embodied)

narratology, and on the reciprocal influence of culture, narration and non-normative life-experiences in literature. Her second monograph explores literary scandals as forms of cultural transgression in British and Irish Literature from the 18th–21st century. In 2023, she was an affiliate at the Institute for World Literature, Harvard University, and a fellow at Graz University's Centre for Cultural Studies in 2024.

*Elizabeth Oakes*
is a salaried doctoral researcher in the English unit at the University of Helsinki. Their dissertation project researches representations of altered consciousness in American science fiction, 1960 to 1979. They use computational methodologies in a stylistic framework to characterise styles of representing altered consciousness in a corpus of science fiction novels. They demonstrate how the fine-grained aspects of these styles generate themes, and how the themes in turn shape and are shaped by contemporaneous socio-cultural currents. They also pursue research interests in the trans-medial formal aspects of impossibilities in new weird novels and comics. They have published on these subjects in Linguistics Vanguard and *Fafnir – Nordic Journal of Science Fiction and Fantasy Research*, where they currently serve as Editor-in-Chief.

*Ellen Peel*
is Professor Emerita in the Department of Humanities and Comparative World Literature and the Department of English at San Francisco State University, who specialises in fiction written in English, French, and German. The author of *Politics, Persuasion, and Pragmatism: A Rhetoric of Feminist Utopian Fiction*, she has published on women's literature, science fiction and utopian literature, and literary theory, especially about "unnatural" narrative, reader response, and feminism. Ellen Peel's contribution to this volume is her larger project on "Frankengenre", which examines narratives about the physical and mental construction of human bodies.

*Ralf Schneider*
is Professor and Chair of English Literature at RWTH Aachen University, and co-founder of the Aachen Center for Cognitive and Empirical Literary Studies (ACCELS). His research and publications cover several areas of British literary and cultural studies, including the relationship between literature and war, literary representations of masculinities, migration and literature, as well as literary constructions of childhood. The main areas of his research, however, have been cognitive narratology and the study of cognitive and emotional processes of response to literature, with a focus on readers' reactions to literary characters.

*Kit Schuster*
is currently pursuing their doctoral degree in North American Literature and Culture at the University of Freiburg, Germany. Their scholarly pursuits center around the realm of trans speculative future fictions, delving deep into how these narratives envision realms beyond the constraints of the cisgender binary. Their dissertation project explores the ways in which such stories shape our understanding of potential futures, particularly concerning notions of ecology, race, identity, and agency. Kit Schuster's research is funded by a Rosa Luxemburg Foundation scholarship. They are currently holding a fellowship position at the John W. Kluge Center at the Library of Congress in Washington, DC.

*Anke Sharma*
is an independent researcher based in Berlin, Germany. Currently, she is working on turning her doctoral thesis on we-narration in post-1968 American literature into a monograph for publication. Anke earned her doctorate through the interdisciplinary program offered by the Graduate School of North American Studies at Freie Universität Berlin. Her contribution to this volume was written while receiving funding from Freie Universität Berlin. Before entering the PhD program, she was awarded an M.A. in North American Studies from Freie Universität Berlin and a B.A. in American Studies and Business Administration from Humboldt-Universität zu Berlin. Her work experience includes roles at McDaniel College (Maryland, USA), at Bard College Berlin and at Humboldt-Universität zu Berlin. Her research interests focus on the tensions between narration and authorship, postcolonial and decolonial embodiment, and queer forms in American literature.

*Christina Slopek-Hauff*
is a doctoral student at Heinrich-Heine-University Düsseldorf, where she also works as research assistant and lecturer in the section of Anglophone Literatures/Literary Translation. Her research interests include medical humanities, queer and gender studies, postcolonial studies, and ecocriticism. So far, she has published on these topics in *Anglia, Gender Forum* and *Storyworlds*. Together with Miriam Hinz, Christina Slopek-Hauff is also engaged in editing a volume on "Participation in Postcolonial Wor(l)ds".

*Jakob Summerer*
is currently an Ussher funded PhD researcher at Trinity College Dublin and part-time lecturer at Maynooth University in Ireland. In the past he taught classes in cultural and literary studies, narratology, and linguistics at University College Freiburg (Germany) and Galway University (Ireland). In his current research, he is focussing on metaphor use in German-language memoirs written

by people with eating disorders, as well as metaphor use in self-help literature with a focus on polyamorous relationships. He is particularly passionate about bringing linguistics and the medical/health humanities into what he believes is a most fruitful dialogue.

*Teresa Turnbull*
is a research and teaching assistant at RWTH Aachen University. Her project concerns the representation of impossible bodies in 21st century speculative literature. Using unnatural narratology, blending theory, gender, and genre theory, she aims at examining reading strategies used by the reader to understand impossible bodies as well as the effects of representing female gendered bodily transformations. Her further research interests include disability studies, gothic literature, and cultural studies. She has recently published an article on "Reading Bodies as Space in Hanif Kureishi's 'The Body'" (2023).

*Xinran Yang*
is an associate professor of Linguistics and English Language/Literature at Beijing International Studies University, China, where she teaches courses including pragmatics, discourse analysis, academic writing, etc. Her major research interests include stylistics, cognitive poetics, narratology, and discourse analysis. She is the author of *A Poetics of Minds and Madness: Fiction, Cognition and Interpretation* (Palgrave Macmillan, 2023), and her publications include stylistic analysis of literary texts, cognitive poetic studies, cognitive narrative studies, and academic writing.

*Henrik Zetterberg-Nielsen*
is a professor at Aarhus University. His research has attempted to contribute to conversations about mainly three areas of narrative theory: first person narration, unnatural narratology, and fictionality. His current project is on human sexuality and the roles of imagination and fictionality in human sexual practices and preferences. Publications in English include "The Impersonal Voice in First-Person Narrative Fiction" *Narrative* (2004), *A Poetics of Unnatural Narrative*, co-edited with Jan Alber and Brian Richardson, (Ohio State University Press, 2013), and "Ten Theses about Fictionality" with James Phelan and Richard Walsh (in *Narrative* January 2015). *Fiktionalitet* (2013) won the prize as Danish textbook of the year across disciplines awarded by Samfundslitteratur. *Fictionality and Literature – Core Concepts Revisited* (edited with James Phelan et al) came out at OSU Press 2023. He heads the research group Narrative Research Lab and the "Centre for Fictionality Studies".

# Introduction – Poetics of Disturbances

*Deborah de Muijnck, Jessica Jumpertz, Ralf Schneider, and Teresa Turnbull*

## 1 Acknowledging the Body-Mind Nexus in History and Narrative Theory

From a historical perspective, mind and body have led a much debated and constantly renegotiated relationship. Aristotle, for example, believed that the body plays a role in human rationality (Newen, De Bruin, and Gallagher 2018, 3). While the relationship between mind and body, or at least moods and the body, was still seen as being in an intricate relationship for instance in medical discourses (such as the assumption of different humors in the body) in the 16th century, Enlightenment philosophers particularly stressed the mind and its abilities. The best-known representative of this understanding is probably René Descartes, who posited a separation of the mind and the body in what later came to be known as Cartesian dualism – a position which has been stressed as underlying the mind-body split in cognitive science and subsequently cognitive literary studies.

However, psychological and philosophical movements in later historical periods have focused on the body as an exhibition of mental characteristics, e.g., personality traits or dispositions. An example is the focus on phrenology and physiognomy as a form of popular science in the Victorian Age. As Sally Shuttleworth explains,

> In its dual role of scientific theory of the mind, and popular social movement, phrenology played a significant part in Victorian scientific, social and economic life. As a scientific doctrine of the materialist functioning of the mind, it established the foundations for later developments in physiological psychology; and in its more popular guise, as the foundations of a widespread social movement, it helped inculcate the tenets of that crucial economic ideology of Victorian England: self-help. (1996, 58)

Thus, phrenology was not only regarded as a scientific attempt to categorise and point out characteristics of a person based on their body but also a political and ideological act in that it spread dominant ideologies of the Victorian Age (cf. Shuttleworth 1996, 59). The study of phrenology and physiognomy can furthermore serve as an example of how understandings of the interrelation of

 | DOI:10.1163/9789004519886_002

mind and body can influence literature as a form of communication embedded in its own specific historical and cultural context. Shuttleworth, for example, claims that Charlotte Brontë had an interest in phrenology and that this knowledge also influenced her work. She points out that phrenology was not a neutral field of science when Brontë encountered it, but rather "one thrust of the phrenological movement was to inscribe psychological questions directly into the domain of politics" (1996, 58). She claims that Brontë used the opportunity phrenology offered for social dissent for the gender politics depicted in her work, simultaneously keeping up bourgeois ideologies and challenging them (cf. Shuttleworth 1996, 58).

Nevertheless, claims about a distinctive link between outer appearances, bodily features, and (seemingly corresponding) personality traits establish normative understandings of people's values. They allow for excuses to exclude individuals who do not fulfil these mind-body norms and further the social divide. These conceptualisations of certain norms are, naturally, not just reflected in real-life interactions but are also mirrored in prose, poetry, and drama. Thus, literature has partially added to strengthening frames of normativity in readers by repeatedly pointing out the connection between bodies which do not correspond to social and cultural norms and immoral or undesirable personality traits.

The beginning of the 20th century, however, partly saw a movement towards the other pole of the mind-body spectrum. Philosophers interested in phenomenology locate the mind as being intricately interrelated with its body. Phenomenologists, such as Merleau-Ponty (1964; 2012 [1962]), point out that the mind is always connected to the environment through the embodied nature of its body and therefore focus on the subjective embodied experience of the world. This situatedness in the world influences the mind – to a degree that in the strongest understandings of embodied cognition, cognitive processes can be considered (partially) "constituted by extracranial processes" and thus to be "essentially based on them" (Newen, De Bruin, and Gallagher 2018, 6). According to Newen, de Bruin, and Gallagher, "Extracranial processes can be *bodily* (involving a brain-body unit) or they can be *extrabodily* (involving a brain-body-environment unit)" (2018, 6).

In this introduction, we argue for an understanding of the mind and body interrelation as a mind-body nexus. In our opinion, the mind cannot be conceptualised without taking the body into account and conversely, the body cannot be thought without its mind. In this understanding, we agree with the weaker forms of embodied cognition which regard both as valid concepts but in a close interrelation and interplay. Thus, we consider cognitive processes and extracranial processes as "non-constitutionally related, i.e., only *causally dependent*" (Newen, De Bruin, and Gallagher 2018, 6). The title of the volume implies a double meaning in this context. On the one hand, it refers to the power of literature to present minds and bodies that do not conform to established criteria of normalcy and may thus disturb our implicit understanding of 'normal' minds and bodies by directing our attention to it. On the other hand, literature has the power to present minds and bodies by using textual strategies that make them appear to lie outside the realm of normalcy, with much the same disturbing effect. As many contributions to this volume show, the representation of 'disturbed' minds and bodies, and 'disturbing' representations of minds and bodies can go hand in hand.

### 1.1 *Narratology: from Representation of Consciousness to Embodied Cognition*

The fact that the mind can be represented in literature preoccupied theorists and practitioners of the novel long before narratology turned cognitive. E.M. Forster famously stated that "in the novel we can know people perfectly, and, apart from the general pleasure of reading, we can find here a compensation for their dimness in life. … They are people whose secret lives are visible or might be visible: we are people whose secret lives are invisible" (2002, 46). Novels, he goes on to say, "suggest a more comprehensible and thus a more manageable human race, they give us the illusion of perspicacity and of power" (ibid.). Much of the visibility of the "secret life" of the characters and the reader's sense of power emerges from the techniques by which authors give us access to the goings-on of the fictional minds (Cohn 1978). In psycho-narration, free indirect discourse, and interior monologue – the latter frequently taking the form of stream of consciousness since the Modernist's attempts to imitate the tendency of human thought to be active in unruly and associative ways – we can watch the mind of fictional beings at work in ways we cannot watch fellow human beings think. Accompanying the growth of the cognitive sciences and the study of the brain from the 1980s on, novelists increased their interest in exploring the diversity of conscious and unconscious processes of the mind, as can be seen in works by, e.g., David Lodge, Ian McEwan, and Mark Haddon that can be labelled 'Fictions of Cognition' (Freißmann 2011). Haddon's *The Curious Incident of the Dog in the Night-Time* (2003) brought an awareness of the workings of a mind on the autism spectrum to a broad readership. Although that notion of autism might have been simplified and popularised, it nevertheless played a role in creating public acceptance of what we now call neurodiversity (see below).

When post-classical narratology turned cognitive in the 1990s, the connections between the mind and narrative began to be more profoundly investigated than in any other approach in literary theory. Two perspectives have dominated this investigation for a long time. On the one hand, narratologists were interested in the way narratives activate the cognitive structures and processes of the readers' minds (cf. Fludernik 1996; Jahn 1997, 2003; Herman 2003a). On the other, cognitive narratology has considered the power of narrative to structure the way we use our minds, or, to use a succinct phrase coined by David Herman, the fact that stories are "tools for thinking" (Herman 2003b, 163). Not only in making sense of our daily experiences, but also in constructing a sense of identity do we employ narrative structures as scaffolds (cf. Bruner 1991, 1993). However, in the last decade, cognitive narratology has witnessed a significant addition through the growing acknowledgment that the mind, which interacts with narrative, is intricately connected to, and its structures and processes fundamentally shaped by, a body. The multidisciplinary research field frequently labelled '4E Cognition' is one of the most lively and fast-growing developments in recent humanities. The mind, according to the major representatives, is embodied, embedded, enactive and extended. "Embodied" refers to the fact that the emergence of the mind is linked to the body as an organism that is in contact with its physical, social, and cultural world; the mind is "embedded" by being always tied to its particular surroundings, and "enactive," since it actively engages with its surroundings rather than passively reacting to external stimuli. Finally, the mind is "extended" when it is also shaped by artifacts and technologies with which humans interact (Shapiro 2014; Newen, de Bruin, Gallagher 2018). 4E Cognition has made an astounding career in cognitive narratology where new approaches have been developed that pay attention to the bodily dimensions of narrative understanding, particularly in the sense of embodied conceptualisations and experiences that are activated by narratives (for a recent attempt at bringing the most important impulses of embodiment theory and narratology together, cf. Caracciolo and Kukkonen 2021). It is safe to say that in current cognitive narratology, the mind is no longer understood as disjointed from the body.

### 1.2 *Experientiality*

As David Herman points out in his seminal definition of narrative, the understanding of what it is like to live through an experience, a storyworld in flux, is crucial to narratives (2009, 9). The assumption that narratives and stories are always about a central experience which is conveyed to a recipient is shared throughout the history of literary studies. In *Poetics,* Aristotle already refers to the representation of a protagonist's fate and the cognitive effects this has for the audience – when well undertaken, a story can thus lead the recipients to experience *catharsis* and feel with the tragic hero (Aristotle 2018, 9; 17–20).

The centrality of qualia, or what-it-is-like, to literature is a phenomenon which has also been investigated under the superordinate term of 'experientiality.' Experientiality, according to Monika Fludernik (1996), is linked to the reader's establishment of narrativity, the central quality which makes a narrative. Fludernik assumes that experientiality is the final step in a four-step model which ends with said establishment of narrativity. She claims that narrative is essentially about an anthropomorphic experiencer whose embodied experiences in the storyworld are transmitted to the recipient through a text and the application of generic, narratological and real-world knowledge by the reader (1996, 30; 43–44, cf. Alber 2021, 8). Thus, her focus is essentially on the character's or character-narrator's embodied existence in the storyworld.

Marco Caracciolo, in contrast, moved the focus from the character and their storyworld experiences to the reader and their prior knowledge and experiences (2012). According to him, readers always bring prior experiences to a text when they read it, experiences which are stored in what he calls the "experiential background" (2012, 180). Through the interaction between the readers' experiential background and the text, readers can "simulate a hypothetical bodily-perceptual experience" (Caracciolo 2014, 104; Alber 2021, 16). The shared common ground of Fludernik's and Caracciolo's model can be found in the centrality and the necessity of experientiality for the reception of literary texts. While both focus on different aspects of the interaction, both claim that the phenomenon plays an important role in our understanding and perception of a narrative. Regarding non-normative representations of bodies and minds, this centrality of experientiality can become essential for the character representation, but also for readers' understanding and reshaping of norms. If non-normative representations of bodies and minds get into the forefront because their experiences are depicted in a narrative, readers will use experientiality to make sense of the characters' experiences, which might lead to a form of perspective-taking. If this perspective-taking has as its consequence a questioning and reshaping of social and cultural norms, much is gained through the reception of this literature in terms of rethinking, but also in terms of comprehensibility and understanding of what has been regarded as 'otherness.'

## 1.3 *Unreliable Narration*

Since the cultural turn in narrative studies and the shift from focusing on structuralist narratology to postclassical narratologies, several areas of literary studies began to question analytical categories and normative depictions in literary texts. Other approaches, such as theories of unreliable narration, have already begun investigating the representation of non-normative minds from the beginning. The seminal definition of unreliable narration, coined by Wayne C. Booth in 1961, establishes unreliable narrators as contradicting the norms and values accumulated in the concept of the implied author ([1961] 1968, 158). Unreliable narration is, from a cognitive perspective, constructed as part of a naturalisation process and based on dramatic irony (Nünning 1999; 2013). Hence, it is based on discrepancies between the narrator's accounts and the reader's understanding of the storyworld, on other characters' behavior and perspectives or textual information which contradicts the narrator's statements, i.e., intratextual factors (cf. Nünning 2013, 27–8 for a list of textual signals). At the same time, readers can recur to schemata of real-world knowledge, cultural models, and generic or literary frames (what Nünning calls 'extratextual factors'; 2013, 30–1).

The schemata of real-world knowledge tellingly include current psychological concepts, morals, and ethics (Nünning 2013, 30), as well as ideas about psychological and moral 'normality' and thus specific sociocultural norms which are applied as a benchmark to ascribe unreliable narration (ibid., 22). From a cognitive perspective, unreliable narration functions as a reading process in which readers try to account for contradictions and discrepancies in a text by naturalising them and thereby making inferences about why the narrator might be contradicting him- or herself (cf. Nünning 2013). The kind of unreliable narration ascribed during the process, however, can give an insight into which normative ideas of (folk-)psychology are applied and which norms and values are taken as a basis for an understanding of morals and ethics. The narrator of Edgar Allan Poe's "The Tell-Tale Heart," for example, has frequently been read as being manic or suffering from a mental illness in various accounts of unreliable narration. As the following passage shows, the narrator of the short story frequently recurs to rhetorical questions, repetitions, and thereby tries to assure the narratee of his sanity. At the same time, the passage indicates the difference between the readers' standards of 'normality' and the narrator's behavior, firstly, through the repeated affirmation of the narrators' sanity, which raises the readers' suspicions, and secondly, through the heightened sensory awareness, which seems unusual:

> It's true! yes, I have been ill, very ill. But why do you say that I have lost control of my mind, why do you say that I am mad? Can you not see that I have full control of my mind? Is it not clear that I am not mad? Indeed, the illness only made my mind, my feelings, my senses stronger, more powerful. My sense of hearing especially became more powerful. I could hear sounds I had never heard before. I heard sounds from heaven; and I heard sounds from hell! (Poe [1843] 2010, 413)

Since many scholars have agreed on ascribing unreliability to this narrator, a shared understanding of psychological but also moral normality seems to be applied – a shared common ground which is based on cultural models. Furthermore, readers frequently apply folk-psychological understandings of human beings to literary texts, which can be grounded in their own experiences but also folk-psychology in general, i.e., the ability for social intelligence. Readers apply this knowledge, for instance, when they construct literary characters (cf. Schneider 2000; 2001; 2013; 2021; and Auyoung 2018). Another area of literary studies, which has shifted the focus to unusual narrative structures, and thus narratives which break with certain literary conventions, is unnatural narratology. As Jan Alber states, unnatural narratives are "humanly, logically and physically impossible" and thus essentially defy norms (2016, 3). Several examples mentioned in studies on unnatural narratives reject normative understandings of the structuring of narrative, e.g., Martin Amis's *Time's Arrow* in which time runs backwards, or *The Lovely Bones* by Alice Sebold, in which the narrator is already dead at the beginning of her story (cf. Alber 2016).

Scholars investigating unreliable and unnatural narration have mostly been interested in the question of how texts construct unreliability and unnaturalness, but also under what premises readers classify a narrator as being unreliable or narrative situations as unnatural. Here the interest in non-normative minds and behavior is, however, still directly linked to an understanding of social and cultural norms and has not always critically questioned the underlying norms themselves. This is one reason why we argue for a narratology of diversity: if narratology does not want to be complicit in perpetuating constructions of normalcy, it must address two questions. First, narratologists must ask themselves which of the concepts and terms they use – such as 'reliability' – are based on an unquestioned import of widespread assumptions about what is 'normal' (or 'reliable,' in this case). Second, narratology needs to investigate whether its strategies of analysis suffice to do justice to the diversity of minds and bodies that are represented in narratives.

## 2 From Deviance to Disabilities and Diversity

Only recently has research in the field of disability/health studies turned its attention toward literary (and cinematic) representations of disabilities, and vice versa. Much of the early research has focused less on disabilities but on its connection to, and nonconformity with, the concept of normalcy (cf. Mambrol 2018; see below for a definition of norm/normalcy and deviance). In *Narrative Prosthesis* (2000), David Mitchell and Sharon Snyder argue that "canonical authors frequently rely on disability as a narrative device both to give their fictions energy and ultimately to reaffirm normalcy in their works" (Mambrol 2018). Additionally, research in literary disability studies has focused on historical contextualisation of disability representations, the use of disability as a metaphor, and the structural power of disability for narratives that are, allegedly, not "about disability":

> [D]isability has a funny way of popping up everywhere without announcing itself *as* disability. Everyone knows Dumbo as the plucky little elephant who can fly; few people think of Dumbo as a child with a disability, even though his ridiculously large ears are, for most of the film, a source of stigma and shame [...]. (Bérubé 2016, 1–2)

The study of some kinds of physical and mental disability in cultural artefacts pre-dates more recent developments in literary disabilities studies, as is manifest, for instance, in feminist criticism's investigations of 'hysteria' as a "female malady" (Showalter 1987), or studies of the long history of representations of blindness and their various cultural functions (cf. Barasch 2001). In the past years, the field of literary disability studies has grown considerably, but much research is still needed, especially regarding postcolonial and indigenous literature. Bolt states that, although "matters of class, gender, race, and sexuality have been considered in relation to representations of disability ... we have barely scratched the surface" (2022, 252).

Although much of the earlier research in disability studies has already focused on deconstructing the concept of the norm, it still serves as a basis against which non-normativity and deviance are measured. By definition (but depending on the context in which it is used – here: social norms), the term 'normativity' refers to a "standard against which behavior is evaluated," based on a set of shared values prevailing in society or culture (Kelly and Setman 2021). The concept of norm is thus a socially constructed binary term necessary for opposing concepts such as "deviation" or "otherness" to emerge. According to Lennard Davis, "the word 'normal' as 'constituent, conforming, not differing or deviating from the common type or standard, regular, usual'" as it is understood today "does not enter the English language until about 1840" (1995, 24). While this means that the concept as we understand it today is a recent one, it also emphasises that normativity is a socially constructed, "fabricated state" that depends primarily on a group or society's shared expectations of what is understood as being 'normal' (Barker and Murray 2018, 3). Thus, the concept does not just appear to be socially constructed in general, but its definition seems to depend also on the particular society in which it is used – similar to other socially constructed concepts such as disability and gender.

Deviance, in contrast, is defined as "nonconformity to a set of norms that are accepted by a significant number of people in a community or society" (Appelbaum et al. 2009, 173). Here, those who do not or cannot follow the socially and culturally accepted norms are marked as deviant. Erving Goffman has described the concept of stigma as a negative departure from expectations that stands in contrast to normativity (1986, 5). The term *stigma*, in its original meaning, "refer[s] to bodily signs designed to expose something unusual and bad about the moral status of the signifier," rendering the stigmatized individual (signifier) as "not quite human" (ibid., 1,5). Goffman differentiates between three types of stigmas:

> First there are abominations of the body—the various physical deformities. Next there are blemishes of individual character perceived as weak will, domineering or unnatural passions, treacherous and rigid beliefs, and dishonesty ... Finally there are the tribal stigma of race, nation, and religion, these being stigma that can be transmitted through lineages and equally contaminate all members of a family. (ibid., 4)

These three types do not only stand for themselves but can intertwine in the moment when more than one identity marker is visible: A black disabled woman, for example, does not only experience stigmatisation for her skin color, sex, or physical difference individually, but also for all three markers combined. As Garland-Thomson argues, "[i]ndividuals are 'markable' because of particular traits, and 'markers' are those who interpret certain traits as deviant" (1997, 31). To "stigmat[is]e describes distinctions among people, their physical traits, what is done to them, who does it, and what it means" (Garland-Thomson 1997, 31). In connection to stigmatising markers, Goffman furthermore distinguishes between people who are discredited and people who are discreditable. The former term describes a person who cannot hide the stigmatising marker (e.g., physical impairment, skin color, etc.), the latter refers to a person whose marker is hidden and who, thus, is "able to pass as normal" (Oliver and Barnes 2012, 45).

Out of the construction of a norm which supports body types that are "untroubled by agedness, physical impairment, gender ambiguity, and racial or ethnic difference" (Covino 2004, 1) furthermore emerges the idea of a perfected, beautiful body, a so called 'ideal' or 'aesthetic' body: "The beautiful is what pleases ear and eye, is associated with ideal proportions in the relation of part to part (good measure, symmetry), and is smooth, clear, white, simple, unified, and regular" (Covino 2004, 7). Covino argues that "the unmodified, unimproved body is always a potential violator of the aesthetic stasis upon which happiness depends" (2004, 1). This implies that only an aesthetically perfect body is desirable while a somehow impaired body is not. Such a notion of the body not only affirms the objectification of bodies in general, but also as a product of power dynamics (e.g., the male gaze; cf. Edwards and Graulund 2013, 32). Contrasting to this understanding of the body is that of the grotesque body – one which is capable of subverting stereotyped conceptions of gender, beauty, and embodiment and thus to "resist absorption into the objectifying gaze that seeks to contain them" (ibid.). In her seminal essay *Powers of Horror: An Essay on Abjection* (1982), Julia Kristeva links the concept of abjection to the female body as something that "disturbs identity, system, order" (1982, 4), especially in form of the maternal body. Hence, Kristeva's theory of abjection is concerned with figures that are in a state of transition or transformation. Barbara Creed states that

> The place of the abject is 'the place where meaning collapses,' the place where 'I' am not. The abject threatens life; it must be 'radically excluded' from the place of the living subject, propelled away from the body and deposited on the other side of an imaginary border which separates the self from that which threatens the self. (2015, 39)

This means that the abject body can be identified as no longer human, which consequently evokes affective reactions such as fear and rejection. In literature, this notion of the abject is well represented in the example of Mary Shelley's *Frankenstein* (1818). Victor Frankenstein assembles his creation from collected body parts, which, despite of his meticulous planning, turns out hideous:

> His limbs were in proportion, and I had selected his features as beautiful. Beautiful! – Great God! His yellow skin scarcely covered the work of muscles and arteries beneath; his hair was of a lustrous black, and flowing; his teeth of a pearly whiteness; but these luxuriances only formed a more horrid contrast with his watery eyes, that seemed almost of the same colour as the dun white sockets in which they were set, his shrivelled complexion, and straight black lips. (Shelley 1818, 39)

Although once planned as a beautiful humanoid created out of carefully collected parts, the creature becomes the definition of what Kristeva describes as the abject: The formerly human parts become an object of horror resembling a cadaver with little to no human features left, causing Victor to reject his creation as soon as it comes to life. But it is not only its creator who is repulsed by the abject state of the creature. Causing everyone it encounters to flee in fear due to its outer appearance, the creature's "deviant body exists outside the framing devices used to contain difference" (Lacom 2005, 549).

### 2.1 *Neurodiversity*

With rising social awareness for neurodiversity in the 20th and particularly in the 21st century, the principle of the 'normal' mind is also necessarily challenged. Neurodiversity is a mindset that questions the assumption that there is only one 'healthy' or 'right' way for the human mind to think and develop. It recognises the natural and valuable, infinite variations between human brains and minds against traditional medical models' interest in causation and cure, including neurodiversity as an inseparable aspect of identity (Kapp et. al. 2013; Stenning and Rosqvist 2021). Neurological conditions such as autism, ADD, and ADHD represent equally valid pathways within human diversity and are regarded as an increasingly normal aspect of the social discourse. With rising awareness for these matters, naturally, literature and its advocates need to address the living reality of individuals living in neurodiverse frameworks. The authors in this volume argue against the pathologising of minority cognitive styles and advocate that our culture(s) benefit from reframing neurocognitive diversity as a normal and healthy manifestation of human diversity.

Neurodiversity proponents have thus far drawn on "social-relational models of disability to challenge the medical model of disability" (Chapman 2021). What society still lacks is an alternative functional analysis to replace conceptions of neurological dysfunction or impairment with a perspective that includes neurodiverse voices. A movement that goes in this direction is 'Mad Studies' (cf. LeFrançois, Menzies, Reaume 2013). In a mixture of activism and multi-disciplinary scholarship that was characteristic also of previous socio-political movements, such as Feminist and Queer Criticism as well as Postcolonial Studies, this new field aims at reclaiming the right to denomination and definition of what it means to be 'mad.' A major aim of Mad Studies is to create an alternative to the dominant conceptualisation of mental disabilities in psychiatry, with its medicalised, i.e., pathologising tendencies, its institutionalised power, and its entanglement with the psychopharmacological industry. This divergent use of the term 'mad' can also be detected in the chapters of this volume. Some contributing authors choose to apply the term 'madness' with inverted commas, thereby highlighting its challenging history, while others reclaim the word without inverted commas, thereby arguing that it has, through Mad Studies, become yet again acceptable in academic discourse.

Literature may also contribute to such impulses of re-definition, as poetics of non-normative bodies and minds naturally challenge the binary conceptualisation of the neurotypical 'normal,' versus the neurodiverse 'non-normal.' Stories and poetry often reflect the (social) world we live in and enrich our understanding of ourselves and others. Confronting readers with disturbances resulting from the evocation of non-normative minds and bodies, the poetics of such texts aim at a broadening of the very foundations upon which widespread conceptions of what is 'normal' rest. Inclusive storytelling that integrates neurodivergent perceptions of reality allows for textual, gendered, and transcultural innovations. Literary studies need to be aware of this diversity. A narratology of diversity is best conceptualised as the scholarly answer to the poetics of disturbances emerging from narrative texts. Within the past decade, (cognitive approaches to) literary studies have slowly witnessed a shift from the language of mind and mentalising to the paradigm of embodied cognition. While cognitive narratologists such as Alan Palmer and Yanna Popova still furnish a more normative understanding of narrative cognition when arguing that it is futile to study narrative in terms of underlying yet invisible neurological mechanisms (cf. Popova 2015, 81), more sustained interaction with disability studies is on the rise. Scholars such as Paul Armstrong (2019; 2020) and Karin Kukkonen (2019) have made a strong case for aligning the study of narrative with neuro-scientifically informed approaches. Hence, in this volume, our aim is to support a critical perspective on the medical and cultural understandings of human consciousness and the mind.

In line with this argument, we should like to mention that the majority of neurodivergent literature and discussions on neurodivergence in the past two decades have focused on depictions of autism (cf. Baron-Cohen 2000; Murray 2008; Price 2011; Silberman 2015; McGuire 2016; Rodas 2018; Kurowicka 2020), specifically on depictions of certain talents and abilities of autistic individuals. As mentioned above, one famous example here would be Mark Haddon's celebrated murder mystery of *The Curious Incident of the Dog in the Night-Time* (2003), in which we follow the fifteen-year-old protagonist Christopher Boone experience the world through the lens of Asperger's autism. While discussions of autism are certainly valuable and necessary, in this volume, all kinds of neurological differences are relevant to our theme. This includes intellectual and developmental disabilities, psychiatric challenges, trauma, cognitive differences, variations in sensation and perception, and neurological impairments. While there are distinct differences between neurodivergent mindsets and the cognitive landscapes of people with mental 'illnesses,' both may work in conjunction with each other. While mental illnesses can be treated through means such as psychotherapy, leading to an overall improvement of life quality, neurodivergent individuals are usually born with this condition. At the same time, societal restrictions and normative behavioural expectations may lead to mental illness in those living with a neurodiverse mind. It also needs to be addressed that many types of neurodivergence, such as Asperger's autism, are currently listed in the Diagnostic and Statistical Manual of Mental Disorder (DSM-5). Therefore, it can be stated that Western medicine regards both states of mind as fluidly feeding into each other, with certain conditions being recommended to be treated, and others being regarded as non-treatable representations of human diversity (Goldberg 2023).

### 2.2 *Mental 'Illness' and Healing through Narrative*

Mental disability (more regularly referred to as 'mental illness') as well as neurodiversity are topics of fast-growing interest in all spheres of Western culture, including popular, governmental, aesthetic, and academic. Narratives of mental illness and of neurodivergence conceptualise diverse experiences and may therefore have both a salutogenic effect (cf. section 3) both for their recipients and for the teller of the tale, hence fostering mental wellbeing. Stories that represent experiences of mental illness in ways that overcome dialectics of mental health and distress and that engage critically with stereotypes surrounding mental health work to deconstruct notions of alterity ingrained in discourses in Western medicine. Fiction may recalibrate the supposed binary between seemingly fact-based medical sciences and subjective human experiences (cf. Whitehead and Woods 2016, 4). The growing field of medical humanities pays attention to the capacities which the arts and humanities may offer in the recalibration of these matters. Furthermore, subsections of the medical humanities testify to the central role of narrative in navigating mental distress and discourses thereof (cf. Pennebaker and Seagal 1999; Charon 2005, 2008, 2014).

This volume highlights the necessary fact that illness models are culture-specific and, especially in the case of mental illnesses and neurodiversity, may not always be translatable across cultural contexts. What may be pathologised by one culture may be regarded positively by another. The subjective experience of diverse mental landscapes can be conveyed only through narratives that share the perspective of individuals living with conditions such as anorexia, schizophrenia, and post-traumatic stress disorder. Yet the nature of the experience itself also poses immense challenges for any author, as "the very faculties required to construct a narrative – perception, memory, and reason – can be profoundly altered by [mental health issues] as well as by treatments such as electroconvulsive therapy (ECT) and psychotropic drugs"

(Jones 1997, 359). Drawing on research in the growing area of mental health narratives, this volume describes not only the disruptions and discontinuities introduced by illness, neurodiversity, and its social and personal consequences, but also the person's efforts to overcome these obstacles, to regain agency, and to create a coherent life narrative of personal self-development. Psychological research suggests that mental illness and diagnosis thereof can threaten identity and sense of self when one's personal story is displaced by dominant narratives focusing on deficit and dysfunction (Roe and Davidson 2005; Carless and Douglas 2008). Narratives of mental health and of neurodiversity may play a pivotal role in this process, as responses such as immersion, absorption, and narrative empathy during the reading process enable readers with an interest in these fields to immerse themselves in new perspectives. These opportunities may not just benefit individuals suffering from mental health issues themselves but may also provide helpful perspectives for those whose loved ones require therapeutic support and those who carry personal or professional interest for the topic. Stories and poetry give cognitive and emotional significance to experiences, as they serve as means of constructing and negotiating a social identity and give moral weight and existential significance to actions and events (Roberts 2000, 435).

This performative quality of narratives is implied in the concept of 'salutogenesis'. Especially relevant in interdisciplinary studies that focus on the role of narrative on health and illness, such as narrative medicine, the term was originally coined by Antonovsky (cf. 1993, 1996, 1998) but has since then been adopted by a variety of narratologists, psychologists, and scholars of literature (cf. Angus and Greenberg 2011; Nünning and Nünning 2017; Kreisberg and Huffaker 2018; Mittelmark, Sagy et. al. 2021; de Muijnck forthcoming). Salutogenesis posits that life experiences help shape one's sense of coherence, supporting individuals in the perception that life can be understood as more or less comprehensible, meaningful, and manageable. While scholars who work in this narrative field have so far mainly explored illness narratives, such as stories told by patients trying to make sense of their experiences, symptoms, and the origins of their health problems (Hydén and Brockmeier 2008, 10), the concept of storytelling for physical and emotional wellbeing shows considerable potential for future research. (Postclassical) narratologists (among them most notably Charon 2008, 2014; Nünning and Nünning 2017) have started to highlight the importance of storytelling for health and well-being, resulting in salutogenic narrative theory, which posits that the reception of certain narratives may help shape one's sense of coherence (cf. Antonovsky 1993, 1996; Nünning and Nünning 2017) – or even further that "narratives and a sense of coherence mutually reinforce each other" (Nünning and Nünning 2017, 174). This translates into the idea that by engaging with certain narratives, life is understood as more or less comprehensible, meaningful, and manageable, fostering an overall sense of health and well-being (ibid.). The general notion that storytelling fosters well-being is not new; verbal therapy relies on the power of autobiographical narrative and on the application of different art forms to support patients on a journey toward their healthy state of mind (cf. Caruth 1996; Richman 2014).

For this volume, one of the most relevant insights from the discipline of narrative psychology is that stories may not only support individuals in making sense of disturbing events and experiences, but that the implementation of these events in storytelling may also provide individuals with a "sense of resolution" (Pennebaker and Seagal 1999, 1248). This leads to an approach to mental health treatment that is referred to as 'bibliotherapy,' which is a form of therapy that involves reading fiction or nonfiction material to improve psychological (and sometimes eventually also physiological) well-being. Some forms of bibliotherapy are used to educate readers about their own condition, encourage them to use self-help materials, or to support them on a spiritual path of self-discovery (Gambrill 2002; Jacobs and Mosco 2008). The most relevant approach to bibliotherapy for this volume is one that invites readers to engage with fictional and non-fictional stories to enable deeper self-awareness and to resonate with the thematic issues addressed in certain stories. This concept is not new; Aristotle's concept of *catharsis* is built on the idea that aesthetic experiences 'purify' recipients from negative emotions (Schaper 1968). Narratives of non-normative bodies and minds hence show promising potential for a variety of salutogenic, bibliotherapeutic reading processes which support individuals in the pursuit to find themselves, foster their own mental and physical well-being, and to engage with storyworlds that represent their psychological and physiological state of being.

## 3 Towards a Narratology of Diversity

The field of post-classical narratology, according to Jan Alber and Monika Fludernik (2010), has undergone a phase of diversification, followed by consolidation. This consolidation does not mean, however, that the development of approaches to narrative has come to an end or should do so. Rather, new areas of social awareness are likely to add questions, concepts, and research strategies to the study of narrative, as they have done over the past decades. Gendered narratologies, mostly in the form of feminist and queer narratologies (Lanser 2014; Warhol/Lanser 2015, Mulhall 2020), as well as narratological investments in post-colonial criticism (Sommer 2007; Dwivedi, Skov Nielsen, and Walsh 2018; Heinen 2021) have paved the way for an even more inclusive narratology. Other categories of social distinction beside gender and ethnicity, such as age and class (or, rather, affluence vs. precarity) have been noted by literary scholars as narrative themes. So far, we have sketched in this introduction that literary texts can follow strategies of presentation of minds and bodies that deviate from socially constructed norms, and we have termed such strategies "poetics of disturbances." A narratology of diversity that investigates such poetics ought to be sensitive to the full range of diverse conditions and manifestations of the lives of bodies and minds, both human and non-human, and the ways in which narratives have the power both to establish or reinforce normative notions about what it means to be human on the one hand, and to work against precisely those norms on the other. Animal Studies and Ecocriticism, for example, have pointed to the importance of reconsidering the anthropocentric world view of (Western) modernity.

Ultimately, we argue that a 'Narratology of Diversity' is called for that both reflects on and tries to overcome notions of normativity, studying narratives as tools for normative and non-normative thinking. It can do so by scrutinising how narratives use the entire toolkit of fictional representation to foreground non-normative minds and bodies. This includes strategies of perspectivisation and questions such as these: Which minds do we get access to through focalisation? Do modes of thinking signal non-normative mental functioning?) What is the relationship between a (non-normative) narrator and (non-normative) focalisers? In addition to that, disturbing deviations from expectable chronologies or perceptions of space may come into play, as do internal discrepancies between events reported by narrators or perceived by focalisers on the one hand, and information on different versions of such events that are either inferable or presented by other agents in the narrative; potentially contrasting characterisations would appear to fall into the same category. As far as experientiality is concerned a (cognitive) narratology of diversity will have to pay particular attention to the way that readers are invited to go to the limits of their experiential backgrounds: With which thematic and linguistic means are minds in distress rendered? Does a narrative try to evoke bodily experiences that most readers are unlikely to have had? Is there a tipping point at which readers' tendency to naturalise (and thus, neutralise) non-normative conditions will no longer work? What is the effect of such reading experiences on readers (e.g., disturbing to different degrees? Scary and off-putting? Cathartic?)? Ultimately, only empirical investigations in inquiring into such effects will shed a light on the conditions under which literature may transform readers' conceptions of normalcy with reference to minds and bodies. Work done on the persuasive power of literature in general and on its awareness-raising potential on current issues, as for instance in empirical ecocriticism, are promising starting points (cf. Hakemulder 2000; Green, Strange, Brook 2002; Love 2003; Schneider-Mayerson, Weik von Mossner, Małecki and Hakemulder 2023). At the same time, a future narratology of diversity needs to be aware of its own potential rootedness in notions of normalcy. Much of what narratologists have said about criteria of unreliable narration rests on the, arguably questionable, assumption that humans are usually rational and honest narrators of their own stories, that they have unhindered access to their own emotions, a full grasp of all events and experiences, and generally a good understanding of themselves, other human beings, and the intricacies of relationships. Once we start asking whether such 'reliable' narration can exist as a backdrop for unreliability in the first place, we begin to suspect that what enters narratological analysis might be an illusory construction of some 'normal' state.

## 4 The Contributions to This Volume

The first part of this collection focuses on *Minds, Narratives and Normativities.* Laura de la Parra Fernández analyses the use of the language of madness in Anna Kavan's *Sleep Has His House* (1948) as an escape from "consenting to femininity," following Teresa de Lauretis (1984). Drawing from Shoshana Felman's idea of women's madness as a "lack of resemblance" (2003), the chapter interrogates how Kavan's representation of the "madgirl" disrupts hegemonic conceptions of post-war femininity, citizenship, and the nation. Xinran Yang explores the intrinsic relationship of tense, focalisation, and mind in *One Flew Over the Cuckoo's Nest.* By mapping a jigsaw pattern of the present and past tenses onto three cognitive facets of focalisation, which she dubs the interactional, concurrent, and evidentiary respectively, she argues that this focalisation strategy is conducive to the representation of both the narrator's sane and insane minds either in juxtaposition or in concatenation. In her chapter, Christina Slopek-Hauff argues that the twin motif and intermedial constellations in Diana Evans's *26a* serve to overcome the dialectic of mental health and distress and thus work to destigmatise the latter. Portraying a British-Nigerian family and especially the twin daughters Bessi and Georgia, her analysis of *26a* engages critically with notions of sameness and difference and explores the potential of postcolonial and black British literatures to bring into dialog various cultural frameworks in an assessment of mental health and distress. Daria Baryshnikova explores the ways of narrativisation of non-normative minds in B.S. Johnson's novel *House Mother Normal* (1971) and in its recent interpretation by digital installation artist Tim Crouch (2021). Drawing on enactivist approaches to cognition she considers the representation of fictional minds in Crouch's installation in a framework, in which minds and their activities are not thought of only as objects of perception but rather as 'the ways in which we perceive.' She demonstrates how the representation of minds can be understood as a relational *process* of sense-making inseparable from the interactions with the world and other minds. Elizabeth Oakes' computational stylistic analysis of a corpus of 1960s American science fiction novels illuminates how styles of representing non-normative minds yield corresponding thematisations, revealing connections between science-fictional speculation and cultural changes during the decade. Two thematic groupings of texts complicate traditional conceptions of 1960s science fiction, demonstrating that novels by popular authors engage with emerging social and environmental concerns progressively through the lens of altered consciousness in contrast to New Wave authors' conservative representations of mental illness.

The second part of this volume explores the body-mind nexus, narratives and normativities. It begins with a chapter by Gunther Martens and Liselotte Van der Gucht, in which the authors discuss neurodiversity in David Foster Wallace's *Infinite Jest* (1996). More specifically, they focus on phenomena like masking, hyperfocus, and eidetic memory to render palpable less visible neurocognitive differences that are usually perceived as shortcomings, and their relation to embodied cognition. The authors argue that the novel exposes the reader to the effects of, for example, severe distraction and hyperlexia to anticipate an enactive understanding of neurodiversity as a mismatch between an organism and its environment. They hypothesise that while Wallace engages in a social critique of American consumerist society, he employs crip humor specifically to transfigure and rationalise what might as well have been a very personal bodily affliction. Simona Adinolfi reconsiders unreliability in the context of Alzheimer's fiction. After a survey of the main theory on unreliable narrators, she examines the novel *Elizabeth Is Missing* (2014), introducing the concept of altered narration, a narrative mode influenced by the presence of a neurological disease affecting the narrator. This chapter is followed by a contribution by Jakob Summerer, who discusses two eating disorder memoirs from the point of view of Cognitive Metaphor Theory and Blending Theory. Specifically, he argues that these autopathographical authors encourage their readers to come to an experiential understanding of their illness experience by using metaphors that have the potential to trigger embodied simulations of physical pain. Henrik Zetterberg-Nielsen's article traces some genealogies to understand the historical reasons behind the fact that sexual preferences which empirically are not unusual and not generally associated with impairment are perceived of as rare mental disorders in the most important psychiatric manuals as well as in colloquial language use. A special attention is given to “sadism” and “masochism,” which as “clinical” terms are constituted from the names of literary authors. The article shows how deeply affected the conceptions of the real-world preferences are by the events and characters in the fiction of these authors. Sven van den Bossche investigates the consciousness of trans child characters in Alain Berliner’s film *Ma vie en rose* (1997) and Marieke Lucas Rijneveld’s novel *Mijn lieve gunsteling* (2020). Through an analysis of cinematic and literary techniques, his article demonstrates how fictional trans child representations can problematise the popular discourse of a child’s (gender) plasticity. Carolin Gebauer’s chapter, which concludes part two, focuses on the depiction of the nexus between (im)mobility and mental well-being in Australian television. Drawing on a new mobility paradigm from the social sciences, Gebauer shows how the mini-series *Stateless* (2020) combines themes of refugeedom and mental health to criticise Australian immigration policies as well as conventional notions of what it means to be a refugee. Thanks to a variety of strategies, Gebauer concludes, the series not only reconceptualises the notion of migration by shifting the focus to mobility, but also encourages viewers to reflect on the perceptual framework that typically informs cultural representations of – and thus influences viewers’ engagement with – humanitarian crises such as forced displacement.

Part 3 highlights embodied non-normativities with contributions by Sandra Marzinkowski, Anke Sharma, Ellen Peel, Kit Schuster, and Marzia Beltrami. Sandra Marzinkowski argues that Clare Allan’s novel *Poppy Shakespeare* (2006) highlights how the adverse effects of psychotropic drugs cut across narrative and embodied levels, thereby disrupting the dominant framing of psychiatric clients as inherently unreliable. The narrator, she suggests, is made to ‘ingest’ poetic disturbance. Reattributing narrative incoherence to the side-effects of the narrator’s drugged embodiment makes it possible for readers to critique the deleterious effects of orthodox biomedical psychiatry. Anke Sharma continues part three with an article that explores how the we-narration of Akwaeke Emezi’s *Freshwater* (2018) expresses the several selves of one ogbanje character, an evil spirit in the regions of Southeast Nigeria that deliberately plagues families with misfortune. The essay argues that *Freshwater*’s we-narration serves as a rejection of transnormativity and binary conceptions of gender, and at the same time ultimately validates the ideal of the integrated self and the narratable self, by staging a journey from a dis-integrated “we” towards an ogbanje “I” which can integrate its multiple selves. When a narrative concerns a body that is constructed (thus, non-normative), that body often houses a non-normative mind, with their interplay creating a non-normative act of narration, as exemplified in Emma Bull’s *Bone Dance* (1991), Stanislaw Lem’s “The Mask” (1976), and David

Brin's *Kiln People* (2002). Using unnatural and corporeal narrative theory, Ellen Peel shows how such texts shake up our sense of "who sees" and "who speaks," and how they defamiliarise more normative bodies, minds, and narration. Kit Schuster investigates the role of embodied empiricism and othering in the creation of a stable subjectivity. In the 2015 modern movie adaptation of Mary Shelley's Gothic literature classic *FRANK3N5T3IN*, directed by Bernard Rose, the body acts as both a site of dehumanisation and a source of identity. Marzia Beltrami's contribution concludes this part and finalises the volume as she discusses the hypothesis that representations of embodiment – that is the irreducible interdependence between the material characteristics of the body and the forms of knowledge, subjectivity and intersubjectivity that ensue – play a central role in Primo Levi's science-fiction narrative. It explores the ethical underpinnings of Levi's science fiction and its explorations of non-normative bodies and minds, also with a view to proposing a broader argument about the potential ethical function of imagination in fiction.

## Works Cited

Alber, Jan, and Monika Fludernik, editors. *Postclassical Narratology: Approaches and Analyses.* Ohio State University Press, 2010.

Alber, Jan. *Unnatural Narrative. Impossible Worlds in Fiction and Drama.* University of Nebraska Press, 2016.

Alber, Jan. "What is Cognitive Narratology?" *Introduction to Cognitive Narratology*, edited by Jan Alber, and Peter Wenzel. WVT, 2021, pp. 1–20.

Angus, Lynne E., and Leslie S. Greenberg. *Working with Narrative in Emotion-Focused Therapy: Changing Stories, Healing Lives.* 1st ed, American Psychological Association, 2011.

Antonovsky, Aaron. "The Salutogenic Model as a Theory to Guide Health Promotion." *Health Promotion International*, vol. 11, no. 1, 1996, pp. 11–18.

Antonovsky, Aaron. "The Structure and Properties of the Sense of Coherence Scale." *Social Science & Medicine*, vol. 36, no. 6, 1993, pp. 725–33.

Antonovsky, Aaron. *Unravelling the Mysteries of Health: How People Manage Stress and Stay Well.* Jossey-Bass, 1998.

Appelbaum, Richard, Deborah Carr, Anthony Giddens, and Mitchell Duneier. *Introduction to Sociology*. WW NORTON, 2009.

Aristotle. *Poetics*. Edited and with a revised translation by Michelle Zerba and David Gorman. Norton, 2018.

Armstrong, Paul. "Neuroscience, Narrative, and Narratology." *Poetics Today*, vol. 40, no. 3, 2019, pp. 395–428.

Armstrong, Paul. *Stories and the Brain: The Neuroscience of Narrative*. Johns Hopkins University Press, 2020.

Auyoung, Elaine. *When Fiction Feels Real. Representation and the Reading Mind*. Oxford University Press, 2018.

Barash, Moshe. *Blindness: The History of a Mental Image in Western Thought*. Routledge, 2001.

Barker, Clare, and Stuart Murray. *The Cambridge Companion to Literature and Disability*. Cambridge University Press, 2018.

Baron-Cohen, Simon. "Theory of Mind and Autism: A Review." *International Review of Research in Mental Retardation*, vol. 23, 2000, pp. 169–84.

Bérubé, Michael. *The Secret Life of Stories: From Don Quixote to Harry Potter, How Understanding Intellectual Disability Transforms the Way We Read*. New York University Press, 2016.

Bolt, David. "Introduction." *Journal of Literary & Cultural Disability Studies*, vol. 16, no. 3, 2022, pp. 249–252.

Booth, Wayne C. *The Rhetoric of Fiction*. The University of Chicago Press, [1961] 1968.

Bruner, Jerome. "The Autobiographical Process." *The Culture of Autobiography: Constructions of Self-Representation*, edited by Robert Folkenflik, Stanford University Press, 1993, pp. 38–56.

Bruner, Jerome. "The Narrative Construction of Reality." *Critical Inquiry*, vol. 18, no. 1, 1991, pp. 1–21.

Caracciolo, Marco. "Note on a(nother) Theory of Experientiality." *Journal of Literary Theory*, vol. 6, no. 1, 2012, pp. 177–194.

Caracciolo, Marco. *The Experientiality of Narrative. An Enactivist Approach*. De Gruyter, 2014.

Caracciolo, Marco, and Karin Kukkonen. *With Bodies: Narrative Theories and Embodied Cognition*. Ohio State University Press, 2021.

Carless, David, and Kitrina Douglas. "Narrative, Identity and Mental Health: How Men with Serious Mental Illness Re-Story Their Lives through Sport and Exercise." *Psychology of Sport and Exercise*, vol. 9, no. 5, 2008, pp. 576–94.

Caruth, Cathy. *Unclaimed Experience: Trauma, Narrative, and History*. Johns Hopkins University Press, 1996.

Chapman, Robert. "Neurodiversity and the Social Ecology of Mental Functions." *Perspectives on Psychological Science*, vol. 16, no. 6, 2021, pp. 1360–72.

Charon, Rita. "Narrative Reciprocity." *Hastings Center Report*, vol. 44, no. s1, Jan. 2014, pp. S21–24.

Charon, Rita. *Narrative Medicine: Honoring the Stories of Illness*. Oxford University Press, 2008.

Cohn, Dorrit. *Transparent Minds: Narrative Modes for Presenting Consciousness in Fiction*. Princeton University Press, 1978.

Covino, Deborah. *Amending the Abject Body: Aesthetic Makeovers in Medicine and Culture*. SUNYP, 2004.

Creed, Barbara. "Horror and the Monstrous-Feminine: An Imaginary Abjection." *The Dread of Difference*, 2nd ed.: Gender and the Horror Film, edited by Barry Keith Grant. University of Texas Press, 2015, pp. 37–67.

Davis, Lennard. *Enforcing Normalcy: Disability, Deafness and the Body*. Verso, 1995.

de Muijnck, Deborah. "Salutogenesis and the Trope of the Dying Girl: Cognitive and Affective Strategies in Contemporary Young Adult Fiction." *New Conjunctures and Directions in Literary and Cultural* Studies, edited by Ansgar Nünning, Magdalena Pfalzgraf, and Anna Tabouratzidis. Narr 2024 (forthcoming).

Dwivedi, Divya, Henrik Skov Nielsen, and Richard Walsh (eds.). *Narratology and Ideology: Negotiating Context, Form, and Theory in Postcolonial Narratives*. Ohio State University Press, 2018.

Edwards, Justin D., and Rune Graulund. *Grotesque*. Routledge, 2013.

Fludernik, Monika. *Towards a 'Natural' Narratology*. Routledge, 1996.

Forster, E.M. *Aspects of the Novel*. Rosetta Books, [1927] 2002.

Freißmann, Stephan. *Fictions of Cognition: Representing (Un)Consciousness and Cognitive Science in Contemporary English and American Fiction*. WVT, 2011.

Gambrill, Eileen. "Bibliotherapy." *Encyclopedia of Psychotherapy*, Elsevier, 2002, pp. 309–15.

Garland-Thomson, Rosemarie. *Extraordinary Bodies: Figuring Physical Disability in American Culture and Literature*. Columbia University Press, 1997.

Goldberg, Hagar. Unraveling Neurodiversity: Insights from Neuroscientific Perspectives. *Encyclopedia, 3* (*3*). 2023, pp. 972–980.

Green, Melanie C., Jeffrey J. Strange, Timothy C. Brook (eds.). *Narrative Impact: Social and Cognitive Foundations*. New York: Psychology Press, 2002

Goffman, Erving. *Stigma: Notes on the Management of Spoiled Identity*. Touchstone, 1986.

Hakemulder, Frank. *The Moral Laboratory. Experiments Eamining the Effects of Reading Literature on Social Perception and Moral Self-Concept*. Amsterdam: John Benjamins, 2000.

Heinen, Sandra. "On Postcolonial Narratology and Reading Postcolonial Literature Narratologically." *DIEGESIS. Interdisciplinary E-Journal for Narrative Research/ Interdisziplinäres E-Journal für Erzählforschung*, vol. 10, no. 1, 2021, pp. 19–30.

Herman, David, ed. *Narrative Theory and the Cognitive Sciences*. CSLI Publications, 2003a.

Herman, David, ed. "Stories as a Tool for Thinking." *Narrative Theory and the Cognitive Sciences*, edited by David Herman. CSLI Publications, 2003b, pp. 163–192.

Herman, David, ed. *Basic Elements of Narrative*. Wiley-Blackwell, 2009.

Hydén, Lars-Christer, and Jens Brockmeier (eds.). *Health, Illness and Culture: Broken Narratives*. Routledge, 2008.

Jacobs, Negar Nicole, and Elizabeth Mosco. "BIBLIOTHERAPY AS AN ADJUNCTIVE TREATMENT." *Evidence-Based Adjunctive Treatments*, 2008, pp. 7–39.

Jahn, Manfred. "Frames, preferences, and the reading of third-person narratives: Towards a cognitive narratology." *Poetics Today*, vol. 18, no. 4, 1997, pp. 441–468.

Jahn, Manfred. "'Awake! Open your eyes!' The Cognitive Logic of External and Internal Stories." *Narrative Theory and the Cognitive Sciences*, edited by David Herman. CSLI Publications, 2003, pp. 195–213.

Jones, Anne Hudson. "Literature and Medicine: Narratives of Mental Illness." *The Lancet*, vol. 350, no. 9074, 1997, pp. 359–61.

Kapp, Steven K., Kristen Gillespie-Lynch, Lauren Sherman, and Ted Hutman. "Deficit, Difference, or Both? Autism and Neurodiversity." *Developmental Psychology*, vol. 49, no. 1, 2013, pp. 59–71.

Kelly, Daniel, and Stephen Setman. "The Psychology of Normative Cognition." *The Stanford Encyclopedia of Philosophy*, edited by Edward N. Zalta, 2021. <https://plato.stanford.edu/archives/spr2021/entries/psychology-normative-cognition/>.

Kreisberg, Joel, and Gary Huffaker. "Narrative Medicine, Healing and Salutogenesis: Contrasting Meta-Narratives." *International Journal of Whole Person Care*, vol. 5, no. 1, 2018.

Kristeva, Julia. *Powers of Horror: An Essay on Abjection*. Columbia University Press, 1982.

Kukkonen, Karin. "Cognition, Good and Bad." *The Cambridge Quarterly*, vol. 48, no. 2, 2019, pp. 167–71.

Kurowicka, Anna. "'Aliens' Speaking Out: Science Fiction by Autistic Authors." *Przegląd Kulturoznawczy*, vol. 3, no. 45, 2020, pp. 261–77.

Lacom, Cindy. "'The Time is Sick and Out of Joint': Physical Disability in Victorian England." *PMLA*, vol. 120, no. 2, 2005, pp. 547–552.

Lanser, Susan Sniader. "Gender and Narrative." *Handbook of Narratology*, edited by Peter Hühn. De Gruyter, 2014, pp. 206–18.

LeFrançois, Brenda A., Robert Menzies, Geoffrey Reaume, eds. *Mad Matters: A Critical Reader in Canadian Mad Studies*. Canadian Scholars' Press, 2013.

Love, Glen A. 2003. *Practical Ecocriticism: Literature, Biology, and the Environment*. Charlottesville, London: University of Virginia Press.

Mambrol, Nasrullah. "Disability Studies." *Literary Theory and Criticism*, 15 Dec. 2018, https://literariness.org/2018/12/15/disability-studies-2.

McGuire, Anne. *War on Autism: On the Cultural Logic of Normative Violence*. University of Michigan Press, 2016.

Merleau-Ponty, Maurice. *Phenomenology of Perception*. Abingdon: Routledge, 2012 [1962].

Merleau-Ponty, Maurice. "The Philosopher and His Shadow". *Signs*, edited by Richard C. McCleary. USA: NUP, 1964.

Mitchell, David T., and Sharon L. Snyder. *Narrative Prosthesis: Disability and the Dependencies of Discourse*. The University of Michigan Press, 2000.

Mittelmark, Maurice B., Shifra Sagy, Georg F. Bauer et al., editors. *The Handbook of Salutogenesis*. Springer International Publishing, 2017.

Mulhall, Anne. "Queer Narrative." *The Cambridge Companion to Queer Studies*, edited by Siobhan B. Somerville. Cambridge University Press, 2022, pp. 142–55.

Murray, Stuart. *Representing Autism: Culture, Narrative, Fascination*. 1st ed., Liverpool University Press, 2008.

Newen, Albert, Leon De Bruin, and Shaun Gallagher. "4E Cognition: Historical Roots, Key Concepts, and Central Issues." *The Oxford Handbook of 4E Cognition*, edited by Albert Newen, Leon De Bruin, and Shaun Gallagher. Oxford University Press, 2018, 3–15.

Newen, Albert, Leon de Bruin, and Shaun Gallagher (eds.). *The Oxford Handbook of 4E Cognition*. Oxford University Press, 2018.

Nünning, Ansgar. "Unreliable, compared to what: Towards a Cognitive Theory of Unreliable Narration: Prolegomina and Hypotheses." *Grenzüberschreitungen: Narratologie im Kontext/ Transcending Boundaries: Narratology in Context*, edited by Walter Grünzweig and Andreas Solbach. Gunter Narr Verlag, 1999, pp. 53–73.

Nünning, Ansgar. "Unreliable Narration zur Einführung: Grundzüge einer kognitiv-narratologischen Theorie und Analyse unglaubwürdigen Erzählens." *Unreliable Narration: Studien zur Theorie und Praxis unglaubwürdigen Erzählens in der englischsprachigen Erzählliteratur*, edited by Ansgar Nünning. WVT, 2nd ed. 2013, pp. 3–39.

Nünning, Vera, and Ansgar Nünning. "How to Stay Healthy and Foster Well-Being with Narratives, or: Where Narratology and Salutogenesis Could Meet." *How to Do Things with Narrative*, edited by Jan Alber and Greta Olson. De Gruyter, 2017, pp. 157–86.

Oliver, Michael, and Colin Barnes. *The New Politics of Disablement*. Palgrave Macmillan, 2012.

Pennebaker, James W., and Janel D. Seagal. "Forming a Story: The Health Benefits of Narrative." *Journal of Clinical Psychology*, vol. 55, no. 10, 1999, pp. 1243–54.

Poe, Edgar Allan. *Edgar Allan Poe: Complete Tales & Poems with Selected Essays*. Createspace, [1843] 2010.

Popova, Yanna B. *Stories, Meaning, and Experience: Narrativity and Enaction*. Routledge, 2018.

Price, Margaret. *Mad at School: Rhetorics of Mental Disability and Academic Life*. University of Michigan Press, 2011.

Richman, Sophia. *Mended by the Muse: Creative Transformations of Trauma*. Routledge, 2014.

Roberts, Glenn A. "Narrative and Severe Mental Illness: What Place Do Stories Have in an Evidence-Based World?" *Advances in Psychiatric Treatment*, vol. 6, no. 6, 2000, pp. 432–41.

Rodas, Julia. *Autistic Disturbances: Theorizing Autism Poetics from the DSM to Robinson Crusoe*. University of Michigan Press, 2018.

Roe, David, and Larry Davidson. "Self and Narrative in Schizophrenia: Time to Author a New Story." *Medical Humanities*, vol. 31, no. 2, 2005, p. 89–94

Schaper, Eva. "Aristotle's Catharsis and Aesthetic Pleasure." *The Philosophical Quarterly*, vol. 18, no. 71, 1968, p. 131.

Schneider, Ralf. *Grundriß zur kognitiven Theorie der Figurenrezeption am Beispiel des Viktorianischen Romans*. Stauffenburg Verlag, 2000.

Schneider, Ralf. "Toward a Cognitive Theory of Literary Character. The Dynamics of Mental-Model Construction." *Style*, vol. 25, no. 4, 2001, pp. 607–639.

Schneider, Ralf. "The Cognitive Theory of Character Reception. An Updated Proposal." *Anglistik*, vol. 24, no. 2, 2013, pp. 117–134.

Schneider, Ralf. "Potential and Actual Cognitive-Emotional Engagement with Characters. A Response to Michael Whitenton and Bonnie Howe & Eve Sweetser." *Biblical Interpretation*, vol. 29, 2021, pp. 530–550.

Schneider-Mayerson, Matthew, Alexa Weik von Mossner, W. P. Małecki, and Frank Hakemulder (eds.). 2023. Empirical Ecocriticism: *Environmental Narratives for Social Change*. Minneapolis: University of Minnesota Press.

Shapiro, Lawrence (ed.). *The Routledge Handbook of Embodied Cognition*. Routledge, 2014.

Shelley, Mary. *Frankenstein: 1818 Text*. Oxford University Press, 2008.

Showalter, Elaine. *The Female Malady: Women, Madness and English Culture, 1830–1980*. Penguin, 1987.

Shuttleworth, Sally. *Charlotte Brontë and Victorian Psychology*. Cambridge University Press, 1996.

Silberman, Steve. *NeuroTribes*. Penguin Publishing Group, 2015.

Sommer, Roy. "'Contextualism' Revisited: A Survey (and Defence) of Postcolonial and Intercultural Narratologies." *Journal of Literary Theory*, vol. 1, 2007, pp. 61–79.

Stenning, Anna, and Hanna Bertilsdotter Rosqvist. "Neurodiversity Studies: Mapping out Possibilities of a New Critical Paradigm." *Disability & Society*, vol. 36, no. 9, 2021, pp. 1532–37.

Warhol, Robyn, and Susan S. Lanser (eds.). *Narrative Theory Unbound: Queer and Feminist Interventions*. Ohio State University Press, 2015.

# PART 1

## *Minds, Narratives and Normativities*

CHAPTER 1

# Through the Looking Glass: Narrating the Madgirl in Anna Kavan's *Sleep Has His House*

*Laura de la Parra Fernández*

## 1 Introduction[1]

Anna Kavan (1901–1968) was born Helen Emily Woods in Cannes, France, to British parents. She had already published six novels under her first married name, Helen Ferguson, when, as Helen Edmonds (after taking the surname of her second husband), she suffered several mental breakdowns and attempted suicide. This led her to being committed to an asylum retreat in Switzerland in 1938, where she became familiarised with psychoanalysis. She then came out of the asylum having her name changed to that of the main character in her novel *Let Me Alone* (1930), Anna Kavan (Callard 1992, 61). From then on, both her writing and visual art changed in an attempt to reinvent herself: her home counties novels turned experimental,[2] going against the grain of her more realist contemporaries, whom she would call "the New Victorians" in the journal *Horizon*, where she frequently wrote (Kavan 1946, 61). This change can be best exemplified by her fourth publication under her new penname, and by far her most experimental one: the novel *Sleep Has His House*. Published in 1947 in the US as *The House of Sleep* and in 1948 in the UK under the title *Sleep Has His House*, this work was both a commercial and a critical failure (Callard 1992, 91). Critics such as Diana Trilling dismissed it as "not worth reading," for it suggested "that madness is a normal, even a better than normal, way of life" (1978, 218). Trilling's second affirmation is not far from the truth, for the text prefigures R.D. Laing's view of madness as a natural reaction toward a dysfunctional society (cf. Laing 1960), something that Anaïs Nin also noticed (1968, 171).

1 The author wishes to acknowledge the support of the research project "Gender and Pathography from a Transnational Perspective," funded by the Spanish Ministry of Science and Innovation (PID2020-113330-GBI00).

2 Middlebrow, realist fiction dealing with the domestic life of a middle-class English family. These novels are set on the so-called "home counties," which are those surrounding London in the South-East of England.

 | DOI:10.1163/9789004519886_003

This chapter aims to provide a reading of *Sleep Has His House* as a counter-bildungsroman, insofar as the story is told by a child, B, who never goes on to grow up and adapt to society, contrary to the traditional bildungsroman. As Sarah Graham posits, "[d]epicting the journey from youth to maturity, a classic Bildungsroman concentrates on a protagonist striving to reconcile individual aspirations with the demands of social conformity" (2019, 1). Thus, the bildungsroman has explored the ability to grow up by integrating the self's subjectivity into the society. Instead, B's decision to remain in the night world, and therefore, to speak the language of madness, implies a rejection of the day world, namely, post-Blitz administered Britain. In order to carry out this analysis, I will consider Kavan's writing of madness as "a failure of translation," following Shoshana Felman, that is, as a break between signifier and signified (2003, 19). This instance of Derridean *différance* turns madness into "an agent of transformation in the text," for it refuses to reproduce "a space exterior to it in order to become an experience that produces its own space" (Felman 2003, 110). The use of the language of madness as the refusal of an exterior space – and, hence, of an outwardly imposed order and logic – has been discussed by Paula Treichler in her reading of Charlotte Perkins Gilman's "The Yellow Wallpaper" (1892) in relation to Anna Kavan's *Asylum Piece* (1940). As Treichler explains, trying to break away from conventional language is also a way to break with the "'sentence' imposed by patriarchy" – that of madness as a medical diagnosis and that of a language that cannot accurately convey women's experience of reality (1978, 67). This reading goes hand in hand with Kavan's view of her contemporaries' realism as an "escapist" and "Victorianist" mode of representation to avoid facing a harsh reality (1946, 63). Kavan preferred, instead, to "abandon realistic writing insofar as it describes exclusively events in the physical environment, and to make the reader aware of the existence of the different, though just as real, 'reality' which lies just beyond the surface of ordinary life and the surface aspect of things" (Kavan in Callard 1992, 122). While experimentalism was retrieved in the 1960s British literary scene, "Kavan's fiction had prefigured this idea since 1940," drawing on surrealist, existentialist and modernist aesthetics (Van Hove 2019, 121). Experimental writing, thus, for Kavan, becomes a challenge to the hegemony and a way to transform the existing reality by looking further into it.

This chapter aims to build on Hannah Van Hove's view of *Sleep Has His House* as a political text, "understood as reflecting and responding to the pressures of British war-torn society in the mid-twentieth century" (2017, 360), by positing Kavan's use of the language of madness as a transformative tool for reimagining national identity and belonging in her counter-bildungsroman. In the novel, the writing of madness accounts for a displaced representation of the feelings of loneliness and alienation from society that arises from refusing to "consent to femininity," in Teresa de Lauretis's words (1984, 133). Thus, the protagonist's wish to remain a *madgirl* at the end of the novel also expresses her refusal to come of age and to partake in the post-war British state, where violence is administered by the State as a "repressive apparatus" (Althusser 1971, 137). This way, the character of B shows how psychiatry is not only used as an ideological state apparatus, following Althusser, but ultimately as a repressive one, enforcing traditional gender roles and compliance with the status quo.

## 2 Undoing the Myth of the Blitz

*Sleep Has His House* deals with the binary division between the day world and the night world. The night world, often posited as negative, embodies in the novel the language of dreams, of possibilities not yet realised, and the language of childhood, as the author indicates in the prologue (Kavan 2002, 5). From the beginning, these two worlds are differentiated both in format and in style: the brief scenes in italics tell more realist (i.e., referential), first-person accounts of the protagonist, called B, and her daily life; whereas the text in roman consists of third-person narrated scenes of a dream-like quality, which unfold from a past life of comfort and memories of B's childhood. By the end of the novel, B learns how to master the language of the night world and decides to stay there permanently, thus refusing to conform to the society of the day world.

As Hélène Cixous explains, dialectic oppositions such as Day/Night, Father/Mother, Logos/Pathos, or Man/Woman are organised hierarchically and maintained through violence, where one of the terms exploits the other on the basis of its given superiority (1996, 63–64). Kavan's text reworks these given assumptions by prioritising the night, the mother, the moon, and pathos; that is, all which does not fall under the patriarchal rule. For this purpose, Kavan subverts the stereotypes that relate the night world with danger and powerlessness by using Gothic tropes in her representation of the day world. The day world is portrayed as threatening, authoritarian, and uncertain—it is the world of the father, of rules and arbitrary conventions—the world of the post-war British welfare state. In doing so, Kavan prioritises the language "of the irrational and subconscious," showing the impact of "rational civili[s]ation" on B's subjectivity (Van Hove 2017, 365). As Van Hove explains, Kavan's psychoanalytic treatment by Binswanger during her internment in Switzerland led her to become interested in the meaning of dreams, particularly Binswanger and Jung's theory of the dream as a place where individual consciousness develops in conversation with collective anxieties (ibid., 367).

In *Sleep Has His House*, the night world progressively becomes a shelter for B, a place where she can express herself and explore her existence in isolation from the violence of the day world. The protagonist, B, is a child who does not understand the rules of the day world, and she is often punished for this. For instance, a scene early in the novel depicts B as a young girl, when she tries to play a game with other children and fails at it: "Perhaps B is nervous, perhaps she doesn't understand the rules, perhaps she just means to introduce an innovation" (Kavan 2002, 32). These rules are immutable and incomprehensible for her, since language, for B, appears to have other referents or uses. These are the rules of a frenzied, highly-administered post-war society threatened by atomic power that hardly sees humans as anything other than a means of production and commodities of exchange, and whose citizens are defined by the following parameters: "AGE; QUALIFICATIONS; CLASS; DESTINATION; ATTITUDE TOWARDS; RESULT" (ibid., 122). In B's day world, human life is not really worth much more than what it can produce, and humanity could disappear in a single second destroyed by war and nuclear power.

In *The Myth of the Blitz* (1991), Angus Calder argues that the making of the so-called "myth" (in the Barthian sense of the word, i.e., myth as ideology presented as though it were innate and immutable (cf. Barthes 1993)) of the World War II bombings of Britain between 1940 and 1941 into a national narrative of belonging and heroic pride erased all complexities of the experience of the war, such as class, ethnicity, or gender. After all, World War II was coined 'the people's war,' since it was the first mass-scale war that directly involved and affected civilians on British ground. But as Alan Sinfield argues, "[t]he blitz was designed to destroy civilian 'morale.' … it signified the people's willingness to go on accepting the government's claim to authority over them" (1989, 8). The myth of the Blitz would be used by both left- and right-wing groups to establish the bombings as a golden moment of community and cooperation to look back to, prompting a kind of nostalgia for a Britain which never really existed except in war propaganda. This fostered conformity to the rules in exchange for reaching a social consensus in the post-war welfare state, such as the Beveridge Report, published by Sir William Beveridge in 1942, which implemented social services within National Insurance and created the National Health Service (NHS). By providing the individual with minimum services, as well as promoting childbearing and employment, the newly established welfare state expected to encourage cooperation between the individual and the state.

In *Sleep Has His House*, post-war society has not only failed its citizens by not providing them with safety from atomic power, but it has also deprived them of their existential freedom: it is a locus of terror for the narrator, where everything is measured, under surveillance and controlled both by her father and the authorities. However, the unintelligibility of language to B and her mother, A, could read as the intricate ways in which death of B's mother, and hence, the dissolution of the normative nuclear family, that is, the lack of referents, allows B to reinvent herself and to break free from the day world. In other words, the trauma of her mother's possible suicide, which she never finds out about (Kavan 2002, 35), provokes a dissociation in B that is at once painful and liberating. The first time that B goes into the night world, "like an embryo prematurely expelled from the womb" (ibid., 8), B feels as though waking up from a nightmare—the nightmare of her mother's possible violent deaths, which she dreams about every night (ibid., 44), and of B's likely subsequent inheritance of her role: "B steps forward, starts after her mother" (ibid., 51). Incidentally, B follows her mother to a place that bears the sign "EXIT TO HELL" (ibid., 52), which B's mother could not read. This woman's consciousness was administered and prescribed as part of the post-war British project. As Elizabeth Wilson contends, the welfare state consists of a set of social policies that make the capitalist state more acceptable, placing in the hands of women the tasks of rearing the workforce and creating spaces of support and social cohesion, in such a way that this free labour is labelled "an act of love" (1980, 7). Wilson corroborates the alienation many women would feel "to discuss these relationships as jobs undertaken for the capitalist State" (1980, 8), that is, putting bluntly that "love" for women in the capitalist State comprises an unpaid job would break the referents upon which love is predicated.

I will now look at how B flaunts these rules, despite never learning—or never wanting to learn—to read them. Hence, she refuses to grow up and fulfil her role as a woman in post-war Britain, where gender conformity is not only linked with sanity in the social imaginary, but also with recognition and endorsement of national values, positing women as "a stabili[s]ing and civili[s]ing force" (Wilson 1977, 2).

## 3 Down the Rabbit Hole

If we consider the Gothic tropes in *Sleep Has His House*, according to Clare Kahane, like in typical Gothic structures, we find dead or displaced mothers, an entrapping structure, and a mystery that the heroine must unravel, "while vague and usually sexual threats to her person from some powerful male figure hover on the periphery of her consciousness" (1985, 334). This threat, of course, is none other than the "consent to femininity": the subordination to male authority and the normative definition of adult womanhood (de Lauretis 1984, 133). In fact, we may wonder if B's mother's unknown death or possible suicide is an expression of the only possible way to escape consenting to femininity in post-war Britain, where the day world is set. In this way, and following Marianne Hirsch's thesis in *The Mother/Daughter Plot* (1989), we can read B's escape into the night world as an attempt to escape identification with her mother: that is, to escape from fulfilling the heterosexual romance plot—to which B's mother gave in, as she was a mother married to B's father—and "to avoid the typically devastating fate of her mother" (Hirsch 1989, 46), which in B's case would be suicide. By flouting the heterosexual romance plot, B does not go through with what is expected from female maturity (ibid., 99), and therefore trumps the narrative expectations of the bildungsroman.

In the Gothic mode of representation underlies what Clare Kahane terms an "ongoing battle with an image who is both self and other" (1985, 337). Halfway through the narrative, when B encounters her mother in the night world, we are told that "B's *doppelganger* [is] … in fact, of course, A" (Kavan 2002, 99). B is, contrary to what other critics have said,[3] not a drug addict or a madwoman, but in fact, a girl: "unmistakably the child of her mother" (ibid., 26). Yet if B does identify with her mother when she decides to stay in the night world, as Jane Garrity concludes (1994, 261), this would be problematic, as Victoria Walker points out (2012, 99), for it would mean that B also commits suicide. For Van Hove, B's "state of introversion into the night-time world … has resulted in a permanent withdrawal from [the daytime world]" (2017, 372). In other words, in order to reject the daytime world, B has become a shadow and hindered her own subjectivity. For Garrity, "B moves gradually toward a greater sympathy for her mother that necessitates her eventual withdrawal—albeit not unproblematic—of paternal control" (1994, 261). This withdrawal signals, for Garrity, B's retreat into her mother's world of the unconscious, which, read in Freudian terms, equals sleep with a liberation of the self from the authority. Thus, Garrity interprets B's journey into the night world as a journey towards pre-Oedipal regression (1994). However, I do not think that B identifies with her mother, but rather that previous understanding of the Other is necessary for disidentification. Therefore, in order not to repeat A's narrative, B needs to understand why she committed suicide—in other words, what the dangers of consenting to femininity are. I argue that B actually manages to refuse

3 Lawrence Driscoll (2001) and Geoff Ward (2001) read *Sleep Has His House* as the narrative of a drug addict, while Sarah Wasson (2010) reads it as that of a child war refugee. On the other hand, Jane Garrity (1994), Victoria Walker (2012) and Hannah Van Hove (2017) read B as a child. Garrity's analysis focuses primarily on the mother-daughter relationship from a Kristevan lens, while Walker reads B's escape into the night world as her becoming a writer (2012, 98), and Van Hove (2017) reads B's night-time language as a way of working through both the collective trauma of war and her personal trauma of parental abandonment.

consenting to femininity through the construction of a language—and thus, a world—of her own.

In this search for a world—a world made by language—we can establish a clear intertextual parallelism with Lewis Carroll's *Alice's Adventures in Wonderland* (1865) and *Through the Looking Glass* (1871).[4] This connection is made explicit in the text: "A nightmare in Alice-in-Wonderland inconsequence"; "whirling through the air like Alice's pack of cards" (Kavan 2002, 102, 190). To start with, Alice and B look alike: "A little girl with fair hair ... peeps in through the open door, unnoticed by the grown-ups; then tiptoes away" (ibid., 26). Both follow a white rabbit: B chases her father on several occasions (ibid., 32, 103), but he is always too busy and alienated by his work to notice her. Both plunge into a seemingly absurd and dream-like world: Wonderland in the case of Alice, and the day world—the world of the father, understood as conventional reality—in the case of B. Both narratives can be considered a different kind of bildungsroman—one that does not represent reality in a conventional way, but, as Kavan would contend, in a more accurate way: in the language of childhood, a language still unforged by convention and restriction.

Alice and B both live in dull, restrictive worlds where they struggle to find their place, that is, to find meaning, among other things, in language. Besides, they are severely malnourished, either physically or emotionally, in a world that does not care about their wellbeing. In the case of Alice, as Christina Nicholson points out, the difficulty in obtaining food in Wonderland, the amount of poison that it contains, and the random changes it provokes, make food a dangerous but necessary means for survival (2003, 366–7). In B's case, her emotional malnourishment is made explicit through the many references to loneliness, lovelessness and abandonment by her fellow peers and parents. It is thus their role in growing up to learn to bargain with these material and affective goods. However, whereas Alice is eventually relegated to her place in society as a woman—"she is not allowed to grow or change through her experiences," as Nicholson argues (2003, 365), for it all ends up being a dream where a terrified Alice grows and changes sizes unwillingly (Auerbach 1973, 35)—B does undergo change wilfully and ends up rejecting her role in society by creating new meaning out of life. This is possible precisely because she acknowledges the existence of the night world.

Furthermore, Alice could be read as B's mother and predecessor, A: since A is B's *doppelganger* and we are told that they look alike, "very similar, with similar

4 Victoria Walker briefly points at this link, but does not analyse it in depth (2012, 88). I would like to gratefully acknowledge that her cue has inspired me to use it as the starting point for my analysis of *Sleep Has His House*.

fair curled hair, discernibly older, wearier, more assured, more disillusioned" (Kavan 2002, 99), and Alice's and A's name begin by the same letter. Thus Alice, or A, represent a failed attempt at liberating themselves from the constraints of femininity: they are B's Victorian predecessors. As Victoria Walker points out, "B must follow A through the looking glass to find her home" (2012, 89). Indeed, Alice only learns the rules of another strange world, and begins to use them to her benefit, in *Alice Through the Looking-Glass* (1871).[5] The fact that B can explore this impossibility is inextricable from her doubly subjected but crucial position as a female child: as Eduardo Valls Oyarzun (2016) contends, following Nina Auerbach (1973), the female child is negated as a subject because she is expected to embody the femininity and innocence demanded both from women and children (36–7), minus the yet unbound and dangerous female sexuality. Thus, a female child is paradoxically expected to learn to submit herself to male authority in order to come into maturity, and this disciplining—of character in general and, particularly, of her sexuality—is key for the future reproduction of society. Unlike a male child's bildungsroman, a traditional female child's bildungsroman would show her disciplining and adapting to the social rules allocated for her gender, epitomised in consenting to marriage and motherhood (Hirsch 1989, 99). Yet this is precisely why B can subvert her position: because she is not a woman yet.

When B realises the trap that her mother had fallen into and even identifies her with stereotypical femininity, that of an "exiled princess" who cannot be helped, she begins to desire disidentification: "*One day when I combed my hair in front of a mirror, my mother looked out at me with her face of an exiled princess. That was the day I knew I was unhappy*" (Kavan 2002, 61; emphasis in original). B reckons that A's past might become her future too, and thus feels unhappy. The shift from childhood to maturity takes place when the child understands the rules of the world—that is, the rules of language, and thereby of power—accepts, and exerts them herself. In this way, language is presented to the child as defining, fixed, and prescriptive. As Beatrice Turner asserts in regard to language and power in *Alice in Wonderland* and *Alice Through the Looking-Glass*:

> The adult creatures of the Alice texts demonstrate, through their mastery of an alien language game and their ability to define Alice at will, that it is the adult who governs and oversees the struggle to generate meaning. The child becomes defined through a language that adults have the power to use, but that child does not possess a reciprocal power to

5 See Valls Oyarzun (2016) on this argument.

> define the adult or the surrounding world according to a corresponding "childish" language. (2010, 248)

Growing up, B, like her mother A, and like Alice, have problems understanding the language of their oppressors: they often cannot read signs which signal danger, as mentioned above. This leads them to unknowingly challenge authority by being oblivious to signs such as "No trespassing" (Kavan 2002, 69). B also has trouble understanding written documents at school or at the doctor or even reading a book, since all the pages seem the same (ibid., 118–9; 122; 107). Language is an unintelligible weapon used against her. Like *Alice in Wonderland*'s "Sentence first—verdict afterwards" (Carroll 1982, 161), or Kafka's Josef K. experience in *The Trial* (1925), B does not know why she is being judged, but she suspects it is because she has given up her place in society, for she does not, and cannot, speak the language of the authorities: "By what judgement am I judged? What is the accusation against me? Am I to be accused of my own betrayal? … Am I to be accused of the untranslated indictment against myself? Is it my fault that a charge has been laid secretly against me *in a different language*?" (Kavan 2002 123; emphasis added). B's impossibility to understand the language used around her situates her in direct opposition to its discursive power, from performing femininity to following the rules. For B, the inexplicability and taboo of her mother's death brings about a "failure of translation," in Felman's terms (2003), a break with language and a loss of the ability to understand how the day world works, and therefore to belong to it, but which in turn frees her from its conventions. Words become useless, senseless except for those in power in an unequal economy of meaning. However, a failure of translation also opens up a space for language "to become an experience that produces its own space" (Felman 2003, 110). This space is, of course, the night world: the realm of the maternal, where language can be reappropriated to rename reality and, according to the forces regulating the day world, the world of nonsense language and, therefore, of madness.

In the night world B learns that the so-called nonsense language, or the language of madness, can become a tool for rebellion against the oppressor, who also often happens to be hold mastery over language, as Humpty Dumpty tells Alice in *Alice Through the Looking Glass* (Carroll 1982, 269). By renaming herself as B and her mother as A, the narrator, as Garrity claims, "convey[s] the possibility of a linguistic revision of the established order, a subversive restructuring of language through women's literary intervention" (1994, 273). Thus, by making language desiderative rather than prescriptive (i.e., by making language name things before they happen or exist, precisely in order to bring them into existence), B can define herself and her world in her own terms. Like children do, she believes that language has a quality of magic which makes things happen by articulating them, in the performative function of language (cf. Austin 1962): "Magical language seeks to establish connections by means of metaphors which occupy the space between the 'real' and the 'not-real' and thus evade those stifling binary divisions" (Nicholson 2003, 364). Both Alice and B use magic: it is not until Alice asserts her needs and reality over others that she is temporarily in command and escapes her sentence in Wonderland; while B also uses magic in order to "*transmute* [...] *flat daylight into* [*her*] *night-time magic and privately made for* [*herself*] *a world out of spells and whispers*" (Kavan 2002 27; emphasis in original). Significantly, in a fragment charged with intertextual references, B remembers going punting with her mother: "And when we drifted in the punt, late, in the backwater, I combed my hair, and I was Orlando, I was not man nor girl, and I was Ariel, drifting between the worlds, and a poem in my hair" (ibid., 133). The literary references—to Shakespeare's *The Tempest* (1611) and Virginia Woolf's *Orlando* (1928)—point to magical characters devoid of gender (Ariel) or whose gender is changeable and therefore have greater freedom throughout different social and historical contexts (Orlando). Besides, both works deal with the creation of new worlds and with changing the present one through language. The narrator highlights that while B is in the realm of literature—that is, of fantasy—she can escape the constraints of the real world: she feels safe. Language and literature, thus, have a kind of magical, powerful quality: creative mastery over language also means mastery to create a different world, which is why Victoria Walker argues that at the end of *Sleep Has His House*, B becomes a writer (2012, 98). In this sense, the magical quality of language means that B is able to make her desires—otherwise ignored—real by acknowledging their existence.

## 4 Becoming a Madgirl: Refusing the State

The difference between *Alice in Wonderland* and *Sleep Has His House* is that Alice does wake up from her dream, unchanged, and goes on with her established Victorian life: at the end of *Alice in Wonderland*, Alice imagines herself recounting her adventures to her children (Carroll 1982, 111). It is therefore implied that Alice will become a woman and a mother, whereas B carries the night world to its ultimate consequences, by escaping the day world and creating a home—and a language—of her own. But refusing the day world comes with a price, as B is constantly reported and scolded for her failure to comply with the rules: "B does not concentrate ... Does not adapt ... Does not cooperate ... Does not compromise ... Not satisfactory ... unsatisfactory ... Does not …" (Kavan 2002, 124). As readers, we are only shown the beginning of the sentences because these are the only written words which B can understand. Yet these 'nots' in the day world become charged with possibility in the night world: by refusing belonging, B is free to create her own identity on her own. According to Elizabeth Wilson, women's achievement of citizenship in post-war British society emphasized the similarity of their role to that of their Victorian counterparts: "Women's traditional role as a stabilizing and civilizing force—the ideology of the Victorians—was made a lynchpin of consensus now that women too were citizens" (1980, 2). Women as carers and agents of reproduction—both biologically and symbolically—of citizenship became therefore central to the post-war project of the British state.

Post-war Britain was built upon the idea of consensus and togetherness, of a welfare state which would benefit everyone and whose social order would be legitimised by all citizens for the first time (Sinfield 1989, 16). However, this does not mean that the state had stopped being repressive and authoritative, only that societies did not function through violence anymore, but through ideology, "by consent, rather than by force" (Sinfield 1989, 16). As Louis Althusser has claimed, it is rather through the private sphere, the sphere of the personal or the everyday (the family, schools, entertainment and the media), that ideology is transmitted in modern societies, since individuals are thus interpellated as free subjects (1971, 219). Nevertheless, ideology can be ultimately imposed, if necessary, through the threat of physical or psychological violence, as is the case of psychiatry (Wilson 1980, 13). In this sense, B's refusal to comply presents a threat to stabilising forces, hence her disobedience is questioned by the medical authorities: "*People started saying how difficult I'd become. Generally they were angry with me … Once a doctor wanted me to tell him what went on inside my head, but I didn't trust him either*" (Kavan 2002, 117; emphasis in original). As Phyllis Chesler argues, "a person is considered mad both by herself and by others when she *acts out* her thoughts and feelings with her body. When a person does this *alone*, without any group support or consensus, she is considered 'mad'" (2005, 149–150; emphasis in original). The labelling of B as mad lays bare the contingent nature of the rules of society, and how these serve the interest of the status quo to mark the different as deviant and prevent their actions from taking on any further political meaning—thus rendering them politically inactive and isolating the deviant subject.

If madness is a "wish to 'step outside' culture," as Phyllis Chesler claims (2005, 87), then B can be defined as mad by conventional representation standards, regardless of medical diagnoses. At the end of *Sleep Has His House*, B chooses to remain in the night world, though she is aware "of both the benefits and the cost associated with a repudiation of the 'day world'" (Garrity 1994,

265). Kavan's protagonist chooses not to replicate the lives of her mother or her father, but to create her own space—to remain a girl, to not follow through the heterosexual marriage plot—which is punished with loneliness: "It's lonely? Sure, it's lonely. That's what you asked for, didn't you?" (Kavan 2002, 54). B's chosen retreat (or madness) may be a "sanctuary, but perhaps also a solitary prison ... The internal incarceration and surveillance of the first-person voice makes the institution a state of mind, and madness itself a confinement," as Victoria Walker argues (2012, 99–100). Although it may seem that *Sleep Has His House* does not contain any change in the social order or a restoration and reunion with the community, to be at home with oneself regardless of a world that is constantly pushing and constraining individuals into very limited definitions of self may be the perhaps the first political step available to B. By refusing the identity imposed on her, B unveils the alienation individuals are subject to and therefore refuses to engage with and reproduce a panoptical society. By deploying the language of madness, B can create her own meaning in a world that makes no sense to her. Narratively, *Sleep Has His House* challenges literary expectations: it is a bildungsroman about refusing to grow up, offering new possibilities for the genre itself while presenting alienation from reality as a form of resistance.

## 5 Conclusion: Resisting Representation

According to Paula Treichler, "[r]epresentation is not without consequences" (1978, 75). It is true that Kavan's deviation from the norm—of the bildungsroman, of the representation of the range of legitimised modes of living and feeling—cost her negative criticism and a loss of audience. Kavan, like B, became "difficult." However, her writing of madness signals alternative possibilities and ways of experiencing reality—of growing up outside of restrictive conventions and imagining instead a different way of living. As Shoshana Felman claims, "[m]adness is there in order to demystify the formidable mystification of our society" (2003, 106). In other words, the writing of madness undoes the apparently fixed logic of the social order, questioning it and fostering the possibility of other alternatives. Indeed, B's madness in *Sleep Has His House* is presented as regaining mastery over language, thus being able to name and to create a different kind of reality. Kavan's protagonist, by choosing to remain mad, although isolated, resists an imposed definition of what being a woman in post-war Britain is supposed to be. Madwomen, and further, madgirls[6] are,

6 My term. As explained above, being a girl can be read as a liminal state where one is not yet a woman, and is able, therefore, to refuse consenting to femininity.

by definition, undefinable because they do not comply with gender roles in society—for madness entails disidentification from the norm. Kavan's madgirls refuse adult femininity and thus the reproduction of the post-war British state, while Kavan's use of language and narrative techniques also refuse to conform to convention and give up traditional logic, thereby creating "its own space" (Felman 2003, 110).

In this sense, Kavan's depiction of madness foreruns that of anti-psychiatrist R.D. Laing: madness is in fact a "breakthrough," liberation from a sick society and existential death (Laing 1960, 7). Although in *Sanity, Madness and the Family* (1964), R.D. Laing and Aaron Esterson explored female madness as an expression of a transgression or rejection of gender roles, these instances were not examined from a structural point of view—of female powerlessness in society—but rather as an attempt to render madness "intelligible" (1970, 12). However, as Elaine Showalter criticizes, Laing's romanticising of madness led him to filter the account of his (mostly female) patients, thus not allowing them to have a voice of their own either and not looking for ways to improve their situation (1987, 222–32). In *Sleep Has His House*, the rejection of the social order is further made explicit not only through the female-child subject's isolation from society and therefore, from fulfilling her role as an adult woman, but also through Kavan's aesthetic choices, which refuse to reproduce the status quo by representing it, opening different ways to experiment with language, and, consequently, to experience reality.

## Works Cited


Althusser, Louis. "Ideology and Ideological State Apparatuses." *Lenin and Philosophy and Other Essays*. New York: Monthly Review, 1971, pp. 126–186.

Auerbach, Nina. "*Alice and Wonderland*: A Curious Child." *Victorian Studies*, vol. 17, no. 1, 1973, pp. 31–47.

Austin, John L. *How to Do Things with Words*. Cambridge, MA: Harvard UP, 1962.

Barthes, Roland. *Mythologies*. Translated by Annette Lavers. London: Vintage, 1993.

Calder, Angus. *The Myth of the Blitz*. London: Pimlico, 1991.

Callard, David. *The Case of Anna Kavan: A Biography*. London: Owen, 1992.

Carroll, Lewis. *Alice's Adventures in Wonderland and Through the Looking-Glass*. Oxford: Oxford UP, 1982.

Chesler, Phyllis. *Women and Madness*. Rev. ed. New York: St Martins, 2005.

Cixous, Hélène and Catherine Clément. "Sorties: Out and Out: Attacks/Ways Out/ Forays." 1986. *The Newly Born Woman*. Trans. Betsy Wing. London: Tauris, 1996, pp. 63–132.

De Lauretis, Teresa. *Alice Doesn't: Feminism, Semiotics, Cinema*. Indiana UP, 1984.

Driscoll, Lawrence. *Reconsidering Drugs: Mapping Victorian and Modern Drug Discourses*. London: Palgrave, 2001.

Felman, Shoshana. *Writing and Madness (Literature/ Philosophy/ Psychoanalysis)*. Palo Alto: Stanford UP, 2003.

Garrity, Jane. "Nocturnal Transgressions in *The House of Sleep*: Anna Kavan's Maternal Registers." *Modern Fiction Studies*, vol. 40, no. 2, 1994, pp. 253–77.

Graham, Sarah. Introduction. *A History of the Bildungsroman*. Ed. Sarah Graham. Cambridge: Cambridge UP, 2019, pp. 1–9.

Hirsch, Marianne. *The Mother/Daughter Plot: Narrative, Psychoanalysis, Feminism*. Bloomington/Indianapolis: Indiana UP, 1989.

Kahane, Claire. "The Gothic Mirror." *The (M)other Tongue: Essays in Feminist Psychoanalytic Interpretation*. Ed. Shirley Nelson Garner *et al.* New York: Cornell UP, 1985, pp. 334–51.

Kavan, Anna. "Back to Victoria." *Horizon* XIII, no. 73, 1946, pp. 61–66.

Kavan, Anna. *Sleep Has His House*. London: Owen, 2002.

Laing, R.D. *The Divided Self: An Existential Study in Sanity and Madness*. Harmondsworth: Penguin, 1960.

Laing, R.D., and Aaron Esterson. *Sanity, Madness and the Family: Families of Schizophrenics*. Harmondsworth: Penguin, [1964] 1970.

Nicholson, Christina. "How to Believe in Six Impossible Things before Breakfast: Irigaray, Alice, and Neo-Pagan Negotiation of the Otherworld." *Feminist Theology*, vol. 11, no. 3, 2003, pp. 362–74.

Nin, Anaïs. *The Novel of the Future*. New York: Collier, 1968.

Shakespeare, William. *The Tempest*. Oxford: Oxford UP, 1987.

Showalter, Elaine. *The Female Malady: Women, Madness & Culture, 1830–1980*. London: Virago, 1987.

Sinfield, Alan. *Literature, Politics and Culture in Postwar Britain*. Oxford: Blackwell, 1989.

Treichler, Paula. "Escaping the Sentence: Diagnosis and Discourse 'The Yellow Wallpaper.'" *Tulsa Studies in Women's Literature*, vol. 3, no. 1/2, 1978, pp. 61–77.

Trilling, Diana. *Reviewing the Forties*. New York: Harcourt, 1978.

Turner, Beatrice. "'Which is to be Master?': Language as Power in Alice in Wonderland and Through the Looking Glass." *Children's Literature Association Quarterly*, vol. 35, no. 3, 2010, pp. 243–54.

Valls Oyarzun, Eduardo. Introducción. *Alicia en el país de las maravillas*. Lewis Carroll. Ed. and trans. Eduardo Valls Oyarzun. Madrid: Escolar, 2015, pp. 11–86.

Valls Oyarzun, Eduardo. Introducción. *Al otro lado del espejo*. Lewis Carroll, Ed. and trans. Eduardo Valls Oyarzun. Madrid: Escolar, 2016, pp. 11–44.

Van Hove, Hannah. "Exploring the Realm of the Unconscious in Anna Kavan's *Sleep Has His House*." *Women: A Cultural Review*, vol. 28, no. 4, 2017, pp. 358–74.

Van Hove, Hannah. "Anna Kavan: Pursuing the 'in-between reality' Hidden By the 'ordinary surface of things.'" *British Avant-Garde Fiction of the 1960s*. Ed. Kaye Mitchell and Nonia Williams. Edinburgh: Edinburgh UP, 2019, pp. 107–124.

Walker, Victoria. "The Fiction of Anna Kavan (1901–1968)." PhD diss. Queen Mary, University of London, 2012.

Wasson, Sarah. *Urban Gothic of the Second World War: Dark London*. London: Palgrave, 2010.

Ward, Geoff. "The Wibberlee Wobberlee Walk: Lowry, Hamilton, Kavan and the Addictions of 1940s Fiction." *The Fiction of the 1940s: Stories of Survival*. Ed. Rod Mengham and N. H. Reeve London: Palgrave, 2001, pp. 26–45.

Wilson, Elizabeth. *Only Halfway to Paradise. Women in Postwar Britain: 1945–1968*. London: Tavistock, 1980.

Wilson, Elizabeth. *Women and the Welfare State*. London: Tavistock, 1977.

Woolf, Virginia. *Orlando: A Biography*. Oxford: Oxford UP, 1992.

CHAPTER 2

# Tense, Focalisation, and Mind: a Triangulate Relationship in *One Flew Over the Cuckoo's Nest*

*Xinran Yang*

## 1 Introduction

The American novelist Ken Kesey (1935–2001), a "West Coast hippy-goy-guru-tribal-leader and sometime-writer" (Widmer 1975, 121), belongs to the cult writers of mental illness narratives of the turbulent 1960s in the West. His first and most successful novel *One Flew Over the Cuckoo's Nest*, published by the Viking Press in 1962, is considered as a canonical work of mental illness (Ohmann 1983, 216–18) and one of the best social and political fictional narratives of the 1960s (Lhamon 1975, 295).

*Cuckoo's Nest* is a first-person narration told by the schizophrenic Native American narrator Chief Bromden about the enclosed world in a state mental hospital. As a novel of psychological realism that depicts life in a psychiatric ward, *Cuckoo's Nest* hosts a rich mine for the exploration of the intrinsic relationships between stylistic and/or narrative techniques and disturbed minds. "I wish to consider the novel as one of the few successful literary treatments of the alteration or expansion of human consciousness", says Hicks (2007, 70).

Kesey's stylistic and narrative innovations are inseparable from his psychological interests. Since its first release in 1962, *Cuckoo's Nest* has attracted a large body of scholarship, including studies on the representation of gender (e.g., Meloy 2009, 3–14) and ethnicity (e.g., Ware 1986, 95–101), and various interpretations of what has been called madness ranging from the causes (e.g., Leise 2018, 63–67), the nature (e.g., Connor 2011, 246), to the cures (e.g., Madden 1986, 203–17), etc. However, somewhat surprisingly, there has been relatively little work on this great psychological novel in terms of recent cognitive, affective, and neuroscientific approaches. Given the few representative cognitive studies, for example, Semino and Swindlehurst's "Metaphor and Mind Style" in 1996, cognitive studies on *Cuckoo's Nest*, especially studies on the junction between narrative and cognition are still limited, a status quo that is both off-balanced and regrettable for this contemporary classic. Therefore, the present research embarks on a cognitive narratological study on *Cuckoo's Nest*, in

 | DOI:10.1163/9789004519886_004

the hope of uncovering the intrinsic relations among the linguistic patterns, narrative techniques and fictional minds in this *chef-d'oeuvre* of verbal art.

## 2 A Jigsaw Pattern of Present and Past Tenses

*Cuckoo's Nest* features itself in a unique tense pattern. It is narrated in primarily two tenses: the present and the past. It opens in the present tense and ends in the past, with frequent shifts in between which form a jigsaw pattern of the present and the past tense.

Some tense shifts in *Cuckoo's Nest* are content based, thus displaying an unmarked pattern of tense shift. In the following example, we may find the tense shifts from the present to the past to reveal the narrator's memory:

> I *remember* real clear the way that hand looked: there was carbon under the fingernails where he'd worked once in a garage; there was an anchor tattooed back from the knuckles; there was a dirty Band-Aid on the middle knuckle, peeling up at the edge. All the rest of the knuckles were covered with scars and cuts, old and new. I *remember* the palm was smooth and hard as bone from hefting the wooden handles of axes and hoes … (Kesey 1962, 25; my emphasis)

By contrast, some other tense shifts seem to be less content-based and more unpredictable, creating a sudden tense shift even within the same event. Such shifts form a marked tense pattern, as exemplified by the following excerpt:

> I'*m* the last one. Still strapped in the chair in the corner. McMurphy *stops* when he *gets* to me and *hooks* his thumbs in his pockets again and *leans* back to laugh, like he *sees* something funnier about me than about anybody else. All of a sudden I *was* scared he *was* laughing because he *knew* the way I *was* sitting there with my knees pulled up and my arms wrapped around them, staring straight ahead as though I *couldn't* hear a thing, *was* all an act. (ibid., 23; my emphasis)

The shifts between the present and the past tense, including both the marked and unmarked patterns, constitute the distinctive linguistic features of *Cuckoo's Nest*. In fact, researchers have long noticed the tense shifts in this novel. For example, Leise finds Bromden's shifts from the past to present tense in narrating his childhood experiences evidence for "the mid-century approaches to processing and treating traumatic loss" (2018, 71). This observation is illuminating. Meanwhile, we also find that Kesey's tense shifts are not just confined to Bromden's narration of his childhood experiences. The tense feature in *Cuckoo's Nest* is far beyond a matter of Kesey's personal taste; it is stylistically significant and merits more comprehensive explanation.

## 3 Windowing of Attention and Focalisation

Two positions of the narrator vis-à-vis the focaliser can be found in *Cuckoo's Nest*: that of the narrator conflating with the focaliser and that of the narrator separating from the focaliser. The former is found predominantly written in the present tense; the latter in both. However, are the modes of focalisation and linguistic patterns inherently connected? And if yes, how?

### 3.1 *A Hypothesis of Attention Windowing in Narrative*

In his cognitive semantic studies, Talmy finds that "languages can place a portion of a coherent referent situation into the foreground of attention by the explicit mention of that portion, while placing the remainder of that situation into the background of attention by omitting mention of it", and accordingly he defines the corresponding cognitive process as "windowing of attention" (2000, 257). By comparing Talmy's windowing of attention with Jahn's definition of focalisation that stresses "the perspectival restriction and orientation of narrative information relative to somebody's (usually, a character's) perception, imagination, knowledge, or point of view" (2005, 173), it is not difficult to see that the two concepts are intrinsically related: in terms of perception, Jahn focuses on who perceives what in a narrative situation, while Talmy on how particular linguistic constituents reflect the focal perception.

According to Talmy's theory of participant-interaction windowing, a participant-interaction event frame consists of "a primary circumstance" and "some participant(s) interacting with that circumstance on (at least) two different occasions" (2000, 282): a participant of the expressed referent event in an indirect interaction or of the current speech event in a direct interaction. In terms of the linguistic devices, the former is expressed in the past tense and the latter in the present tense, as shown below:

a. John met a woman at the party last week. Her name was Linda.
b. John met a woman at the party last week. Her name is Linda. (ibid., 283)

Windowing of attention occurs as a result of the choice of a particular tense:

> In particular, linguistic devices direct an addressee to adopt one of the two participant interaction times as the point at which to locate his

> temporal perspective point, and to place around the interaction there an attentional window that could include such elements of the interaction as the activity, the surrounding scene, or the cognitive content of the participant. (ibid., 282–83)

A quick glimpse at the tense patterns in *Cuckoo's Nest* reveals that Bromden's narration of one story in two tenses seems to correspond to the above-mentioned interactions respectively: a character-participant of the referent event (the event occurring on the ward) and a narrator-participant of the current speech event (narrating the ward experiences). However, this intuitive observation remains to be tested.

Following Barthes's proposition that "a narrative is a large sentence" (1975, 241), the quintessential narrative structure of *Cuckoo's Nest* can be condensed into one sentence: Bromden encounters something in a mental institution. This event, which occurs only once, is akin to Talmy's "punctual event that occurs only once" (2000, 286), albeit in a more complicated manner. We may compare Talmy's punctual event with the events in *Cuckoo's Nest.* In general, the quintessential structure of the events in *Cuckoo's Nest* shares the similar pattern with Talmy's punctual event in the basic structures of their primary circumstances: "Somebody does something at time X" vs. "Something happens at time X" (Table 2.1). Therefore, "what Bromden encounters in a mental institution", can be regarded as, from a cognitive perspective, the primary

TABLE 2.1 A comparison between the punctual events

| **Punctual events** | **Examples** | **Primary circumstance** | **Basic structure** |
|---|---|---|---|
| Talmy (2000, 286) | a. When was her plane going to leave again tomorrow?<br>b. When is her plane going to leave again tomorrow? | Her plane leaves at time X. | Something happens at time X. |
| *Cuckoo's Nest* | a. Bromden told what he encountered in a mental institution.<br>b. Bromden tells what he encountered in a mental institution. | Bromden encounters something in a mental institution at time X. | Somebody does something at time X. |

circumstance in a participant-interaction event frame, and accordingly, the tense patterns in *Cuckoo's Nest* can be examined under Talmy's theory of windowing of attention (2000, 257–309).

Seeing Bromden's narration of his ward experiences as a participant-interaction event frame, we can observe that the initial interaction, i.e., Bromden's ward experiences, while taking place, would have been in the present tense, consisting of "what is happening on the ward". However, Bromden's subsequent narration of the initial interaction may take one of the three forms: 1) I am telling you what happened on the ward; 2) What happened on the ward; 3) What is happening on the ward. Each form activates a window of heightened attention over that interaction, a cognitive process realised linguistically in the form of tense.

Based on the above analyses, the present research hypothesises that Talmy's theory of windowing of attention (2000, 257–309), initially devised for the study of syntactic structures, can be aptly applied to the study of narrative structures, with focalisation in particular. However, this hypothesis remains to be tested.

### 3.2 *Three Cognitive Facets of Focalisation*

The aforementioned three forms of narration can initiate three types of attention windowing around the narrator's interactions with the event frames: the interaction with the reader at present, with the event in the past and at present respectively. In terms of narrative structure, attention windowing as such corresponds to three cognitive facets of focalisation which I propose to call "interactional", "evidentiary", and "concurrent".

#### 3.2.1 The Interactional Facet

In *Cuckoo's Nest* sometimes the same "person" Bromden is separated into two agents: the narrator and the character, and accordingly the text is focalised through the narrator-focaliser or the character-focaliser respectively. The excerpt below exemplifies one instance of focalisation through a narrator-focaliser:

> It's gonna burn me just that way, finally telling about all this, about the hospital, and her, and the guys – and about McMurphy. I been silent so long now it's gonna roar out of me like floodwaters and *you* think the guy telling this is ranting and raving my God; *you* think this is too horrible to have really happened, this is too awful to be the truth! But, please. It's still hard for me to have a clear mind thinking on it. But it's the truth even if it didn't happen. (Kesey 1962, 8; my emphasis)

In this excerpt, the narrator interacts with the addressee, i.e., the reader "you" directly, explaining to his reader the driving forces for him to tell the story. The whole instance is narrated in the present tense. Likewise, the first excerpt cited above also exemplifies a direct narrator-reader interaction, the repeated use of the present tense verb "remember" indicating that the narrator is interacting at the moment with the reader concerning something that happened previously. Like the present excerpt, the narrator uses the present tense to interact with the reader concerning his memory, but in contrast to the present one the content of the memory is narrated in the past tense.

The use of the present tense in the two aforementioned examples realises an interactional facet of focalisation: both are focalised through the narrator-focaliser (interactional focaliser) on the narrator's interaction with the reader at the present moment. This may prompt us to examine focalisation under Talmy's direct interaction in participant-interaction windowing (2000, 283). The switching to the present tense from the past tense in the first excerpt, at the narrative level, typically exemplifies the direct interaction by Talmy as cited above (ibid.), where the addressee may place an attentional window over the speaker's consideration of the woman's name (Linda) at the present moment of speaking. The present tense verb "remember" in the first excerpt enables the reader to place a heightened attentional window over the speaker's, i.e., narrator Bromden's interaction with the reader at the present moment of speaking. In this direct interaction, the windowed subportion is the participant's interaction with the current speech event, namely, narrator Bromden's narration of the primary circumstance and his cognitive state – his memory – at the present moment of interaction with the reader, whereas the rest of the whole event frame remains gapped, namely, remaining in the background. The excerpt above differs slightly from the first one in that it is the constant uses of the present tense rather than the switching from the past to the present that help place an attentional window over the narrator-reader interaction. The present tense in this excerpt windows Bromden's direct interaction with the reader over the primary circumstance – his ward experiences. However, unlike the first excerpt in which the switching between the past and present tense functions as the linguistic device for attentional windows, in the present one only the present tense is available for windowing. The gapped subportions of the whole event frame remain to be activated by the reader in the narrator-reader interaction. Thus, it can be argued that in the second excerpt, like in the first one, Kesey establishes a selective window of attention over narrator-reader interaction through the use of the present tense. Therefore, irrespective of the presence of the primary circumstance, in both the heightened windows of attention are placed on the narrator-reader interaction, linguistically realised by the use of present tense. Instances like the two examples discussed above instantiate at a narrative level Talmy's direct interaction (ibid.) that places an attentional window over the speaker's interaction with the addressee while keeping the rest of the event frame gapped.

A reading of Kesey's idiosyncratic use of the present tense in terms of the interactional facet contributes to the understanding of the interaction in the narrative. Meanwhile, it also foregrounds the interactor's cognitive states while interacting, a key issue in understanding the mental disturbance in *Cuckoo's Nest.* I will discuss the cognitive states in detail in Section 4 after exploring fully the following two facets of focalisation.

### 3.2.2 The Evidentiary Facet

Different from the interactional facet discussed above, in most parts of the novel, however, the events are focalised through the character Bromden while narrated by the narrator Bromden. This exemplifies Genette's distinction between "who sees" and "who speaks" (1980, 186), whereas "who sees" may be extended to "who perceives" or even "who cognises". Cases as such belong to the category in which the narrator and focaliser are separated agents. The prototypical tense pattern corresponding to this category is the past tense:

> … I had to keep reminding myself that it had truly happened, that we had made it happen. We had just unlocked a window and let it in like you let in the fresh air. Maybe the Combine wasn't all-powerful. What was to stop us from doing it again, now that we saw we could? Or keep us from doing other things we wanted? I felt so good thinking about this that I gave a yell and swooped down on McMurphy and the girl Sandy walking along in front of me, grabbed them both up, one in each arm, and ran all the way to the day room with them hollering and kicking like kids. I felt that good. (Kesey 1962, 305)

In the excerpt above, Bromden's post-carnival ecstasy is represented to the reader through the character-focaliser Bromden. From an inside view, the focalised shows Bromden's thoughts and emotions – his reassessment of the Combine and his feeling of drunkenness. From an outside view, the focalised is his actions – a supergiant carrying two persons in his arms. The past tense directs an attentional window over Bromden's interaction with his own thoughts and the people in the event frame at a temporal point prior to the present moment. This instantiates at a narrative level Talmy's indirect interaction (2000, 283), in which the addressee may place an attentional window over the participant's interaction with a past referent event. In the current example, it is exactly the subportion of Bromden's interaction with a past referent that is windowed while the rest is gapped.

This participant-interaction type may support an evidentiary reading.[1] In this type of reading, the narrator Bromden reports faithfully what the character Bromden experienced or witnessed, that is to say, the focaliser's interaction with a past referent event, and nothing else. For this reason, I dub this type of focaliser an evidentiary focaliser and the focalisation involved the evidentiary facet of focalisation.

### 3.2.3 The Concurrent Facet

In addition to the prototypical past tense used in the evidentiary facet of focalisation, a non-prototypical tense pattern – the present tense – is also employed in the category with separated narrator and focaliser. Two reasons contribute to the non-prototypicality of the use of the present tense in this situation: the present tense is used for a narrative about a past experience; this pattern fits into neither of Talmy's two tense forms of a participant-interaction event frame (ibid.), and thus deserves special attention. Scholars have long noticed this special tense feature. For example, Huffman finds the therapeutic value in Bromden's use of historical present tense (1977, 67), and Leise gives an interpretation to the shift from past to present tense in terms of trauma psychology (2018, 62–79). Inspired by these scholars' insights, I seek further to understand the complicated relationships between this linguistic feature and the cognitive activities involved.

The two excerpts below are two instances in which the character-focaliser interacts with the event frame at the present moment:

> I hide in the mop closet and listen, my heart beating in the dark, and I try to keep from getting scared, try to get my thoughts off someplace else … (Kesey 1962, 6)
>
> The new man stands looking a minute, to get the setup of the day room … (ibid., 15)

1 The term "evidentiary" is intended for a general situation, irrespective of the distinction between "normal" and "abnormal" minds. However, in the present study, the use of the word "evidentiary" needs to be relativised to what Bromden believes to be experiencing, be it factual or illusional.

In these two examples, Bromden either participates in the ongoing event or observes as a bystander. In both, the present tense contributes to the placement of a heightened attentional window over Bromden's interaction with the referent at the present moment. This way of windowing of attention creates, on the part of the reader, a simultaneous effect that the event occurs at the same moment when he/she is reading the text. For this reason, I name it the concurrent facet of focalisation and separate it from the evidentiary facet, while both constitute the indirect interaction according to Talmy's definition (2000, 283).

In this type of focalisation, the participant's interaction with the referent event is focalised through the concurrent focaliser. Like the evidentiary focaliser, the concurrent focaliser enables the reader to place an attentional window over the character Bromden's interaction with the referent event whereas the difference lies in the time of interaction: the former in the past and the latter at the present moment. Likewise, like the interactional focaliser, the concurrent focaliser enables the reader to place an attentional window over the participant's interaction at the present moment of speaking while the difference lies in with whom/what to interact: the former being the reader and the latter the referent event. In an interaction focalised through the concurrent facet, the whole event frame is activated, the subportion of the character-participant's interaction with the referent event at the present moment windowed and the narrator-participant's interaction with the reader gapped.

The evidentiary and concurrent facets of focalisation, in a relationship of binary opposition, are the two perspectives to interact with the same event frame, placing a heightened attentional window around two temporal points: a past one and a present one. Kesey's sudden shifts between the past and present tense linguistically materialise the transitions of windowing of attention. The distinction between the evidentiary and concurrent facets of focalisation is conducive to demystifying Kesey's frequent and sometimes even baffling shifts between the two tenses within one event. The differences in attention windowing restrict the perspectives through which the primary circumstance or the events are perceived. The concurrent focaliser provides a view of the participant's present interaction with the referent in the event frame, thus producing a simultaneous effect of "here and now". As for the evidentiary focaliser, it is a view of the participant's previous interaction with the referent in the event frame, all about "there and then".

The interactional, evidentiary and concurrent are three facets of focalisation under the perspective restriction of windowing of attention. One participant-interaction event frame in a narrative context can be focalised through either one, or two or all the three facets, resulting in different windowed temporal points and types of interaction (Table 2.2).

TABLE 2.2 The interactional, evidentiary, and concurrent facets of focalisation

| Linguistic choice | Cognitive basis | Structural property | | |
|---|---|---|---|---|
| | | Focalisation | Focaliser | Focalised |
| Present tense | Attentional window over a direct interaction at present | Interactional | Interactional (narrator) | Narrator's interaction with the reader at present |
| Past tense | Attentional window over an indirect interaction in the past | Evidentiary | Evidentiary (character) | Character's interaction with the referent in the event frame in the past |
| Present tense | Attentional window over an indirect interaction at present | Concurrent | Concurrent (character) | Character's interaction with the referent in the event frame at present |

## 4 The Representation of Mental Illness and Saneness

In *Cuckoo's Nest*, Kesey represents Bromden's two mental states alternatively and/or simultaneously: an unconscious mind and a conscious mind. Technically, he realises the very often subtle alternations and/or simultaneity of the two mental states by his characteristic shifts in tense: the present tense for an unconscious mind and the past tense for a conscious mind. Such linguistic choices, from a narrative perspective, entail two cognitive facets of focalisation by directing the placement of attentional windows: the concurrent facet and the evidentiary facet. By focalising through one facet or another, Kesey not only gives the reader a chance to see the changes of Bromden's mental states at different stages; more importantly, it offers the reader a simultaneous view of his different mental states even within one event.

### 4.1 *Concurrent Facet for an Unconscious Mind*

Generally speaking, Bromden undergoes three mental stages: a severe psychotic Stage I, a recuperating Stage II, and an almost well Stage III. At Stage I, Kesey portrays Bromden as a full-fledged paranoid schizophrenic. With his ingenious medical precision in depicting Bromden's various signs and symptoms, Kesey seems to align with a psychiatric diagnosis of paranoid schizophrenia, whereas on no occasion in *Cuckoo's Nest* has he labeled Bromden as a schizophrenic. This discrepancy may give an ambivalent reading to Kesey's position to mental health issues, which I doubt. This contrast, apart from its social critical value, shows that Kesey considers signs and symptoms more clinically reliable than diagnoses in judging the state of a person's mental health, a position in line with findings in cognitive neuropsychology: "diagnosis remains essentially arbitrary, while symptoms can be reliably assessed" (Frith 1992, 12). Correspondingly, we may find that the concurrent focalisation, linguistically realized in the present tense, is prevalent in this section.

Bromden's characteristic word "fog" lends itself readily for such an observation. Of the 74 occurrences of "fog" in total, 61 of them refer to Bromden's hallucinations. 52 out of the 61 appear in Part 1 where Bromden's schizophrenic state is predominant, with only 6 (3 of which refer to "no fog") in Part 2 and 3 in Part 4. Among the 61 occurrences of "fog" that refer to Bromden's hallucinations, 47 are in the present tense and 14 are in the past tense. Therefore, it can be observed that Kesey tends to choose the present tense in representing the typical symptoms of schizophrenia. As the choice of the present tense enables the reader to place an attentional window over Bromden's interactions with the event at the present moment, the ensuing concurrent focalisation offers the most direct "here and now" view of the content of Bromden's hallucinations and delusions.

From a cognitive neuropsychological perspective, Bromden's hallucinations and delusions are the free-floating notions resulting from his defective cognitive mechanism of metarepresentation. Metarepresentation "is concerned with knowledge about representations" (Frith 1992, 125). The knowledge consists of two components: the form of the representation and its content. For example, in the representation "I know 'X'", the content "X" is represented in the form of "I know 'X'". For some schizophrenics, "metarepresentation fails in such a way that the patient remains aware only of the content of these propositions" (Frith 1992, 126). That is to say, only the content "X" survives in a schizophrenic's representations. For this remaining "X", Frith calls it the "free-floating notion" (ibid.). Take Bromden's hallucinations of the fog as an example: he visualises the fog "snowing down cold and white all over me like skim milk", hearing "Air Raid Air Raid" at the same time (Kesey 1962, 7); he sees the fog "rolling in thicker and thicker" (ibid., 113), etc. For cases as such, as his mechanism of metarepresentation fails, Bromden misattributes his internally generated events, such as mental images and sounds, to external perceptions. With an intact metarepresentation, Bromden would have metarepresented his experience as: "I imagine that the fog rolls in" and "I remember that it says Air Raid Air Raid", etc. However, with a defective metarepresentation mechanism,

Bromden has lost the sources of his metarepresentation, whereas what remains is only the free-floating notions, i.e., the contents of his metarepresentation: "The fog rolls in" and "Air Raid Air Raid", etc. The free-floating notions result in the misattribution of internally generated mental images and sounds to external sources.

Most of Bromden's hallucinations and delusions can be understood as free-floating notions, the very content that indicates his cognitive experiences in the wrong domain of metarepresentation. Thus, the concurrent focalisation, with an attentional window initiated by the present tense over Bromden's interaction with the event frame, is indeed a handy tool that Kesey devises for a vivid representation of the free-floating notions, a basic form of impaired metarepresentation mechanism.

### 4.2 *Evidentiary Facet for a Conscious Mind*

Of the 14 aforementioned occurrences of the word "fog" in the past tense, all are written from a retrospective perspective, revealing the fog experiences as part of Bromden's memory. The past tense helps the reader place an attentional window over Bromden's interaction with the event frame in the past, thus entailing an evidentiary focalisation: Bromden relates what he witnesses as a participant in a past event. The evidentiary focalisation may provide the vantage point from which the psychotic experiences are represented from a mind distanced from that experience. The following excerpt appears in Part 1 of the novel:

> When they first used that fog machine on the ward, one they bought from Army Surplus and hid in the vents in the new place before we moved in, I kept looking at anything that appeared out of the fog as long and hard as I could, to keep track of it, just like I used to do when they fogged the airfields in Europe. (Kesey 1962, 131)

In the first half of the first sentence "[w]hen they first used that fog machine … before we moved in" (ibid.), the focalised is an inside view, focalising on Bromden's thought: his delusional conjectures on the origin of the fog machine. The image of the fog machine deserves some explanations here. Originally an army supply that Bromden first encountered during the war, it resurfaces, in his delusional mind, as an evil accomplice that the Combine uses to control the patients in the ward. This fog-machine-as-a-Combine-accomplice image, from a normativist point of view, reflects a psychopath's "deranged" mental world, while in terms of metaphorical rhetoric, it speaks the political allegory that depicts psychiatric hospital as "a microcosm of societal pressures and authoritarianism" (Lambe 2019, 303). Given the restricted focus of the present study, I will not delve further into the allegorical significance of the fog machine (a subject matter deserving a full-length paper). The psychiatric realities conflated in this image indicate that Bromden is probably still not well when he is telling his experience. Nevertheless, when he says "I kept looking at anything that appeared out of the fog as long and hard as I could" (ibid.), he gives an evidentiary account of his interactions with the past events, namely, his struggles for consciousness. Different from the concurrent focalisation that provides a concurrent reading of Bromden's "here and now" interactions with the event, the evidentiary focalisation places an attentional window over his interactions with the event in the past. Bromden tells his experience in a different mental state: he may not be fully conscious yet, but at least he is out of that intense moment as described.

The excerpt below is taken from Part 4 when Bromden has made great progress in his recovery, and therefore Stage III in my analysis: "And when the fog was finally swept from my head it seemed like I'd just come up after a long, deep dive, breaking the surface after being under water a hundred years" (Kesey 1962, 289). In a conscious state, Bromden recalls his struggle against the devastating Electric Shock Therapy (EST) and gives an evidentiary account of his struggle for consciousness and the subsequent changes that happen to him. The use of the past tense entails an evidentiary focalisation.

By examining the use of the past tense and the ensuing evidentiary facet of focalisation in relation to the word "fog", I presently argue that Kesey employs such a narrative technique to represent Bromden's conscious mind, or at least that part of the mind when he is not having a psychotic episode.

### 4.3 *Simultaneous Representation of Two Mental States*

The above analyses indicate that the shifts between the present and the past tense, initiating the concurrent and the evidentiary facet of focalisation respectively, are very often the indicators of Bromden's shifts between two mental states: an unconscious mind and a conscious mind. In addition to the representation of the two mental states in linear progression, the concurrent and evidentiary facets are also employed in achieving a simultaneous representation of mental illness and saneness. When the two tenses coexist in Bromden's narration of the same event, we often find simultaneous representation of two mental states, as exemplified in the excerpt below:

> They're out there. Black boys in white suits peeing under the door on me, come in later and accuse me of soaking all six these pillows I'm lying on! Number six. I thought the room was a dice. The number one, the snake eye up there, the circle, the white light in the ceiling … is what I've been

> seeing ... in this little square room ... means it's after dark. How many hours have I been out? It's fogging a little, but I won't slip off and hide in it. No ... never again ...
>
> I stand, stood up slowly, feeling numb between the shoulders. The white pillows on the floor of the Seclusion Room were soaked from me peeing on them while I was out. I couldn't remember all of it yet, but I rubbed my eyes with the heels of my hands and tried to clear my head. I worked at it. I'd never worked at coming out of it before. (Kesey 1962, 287–88)

This excerpt is about how Bromden struggles out of the EST. The present tense and the past tense direct the placement of attentional windows around two temporal points respectively. With the present tense, focalised through the concurrent focaliser, the reader gets a chance to see how Bromden struggles on the spot at the present moment. In his dizziness, Bromden sees the black boys urinating on him and relates the number of the pillows – six – to the numbers of the dice. In contrast, in the sentence "I thought the room was a dice" (ibid.), the tense suddenly diverts to the past tense, and correspondingly the concurrent focaliser gives way to the evidentiary focaliser. The switching to the past tense places an attentional window over that temporal point that includes all aspects of Bromden's interaction with the EST, namely a previous experience. This switching of attentional window realised by the switching between the two tenses effectively demonstrates the focaliser's two types of interactions with the primary circumstance: a "here and now" type and a "there and then" type. Many instances of tense shifts in *Cuckoo's Nest* can be readily examined in this way, and the two temporal aspects of the verb "stand" in the sentence "I stand, stood up slowly, feeling numb between the shoulders" in this excerpt makes a handy example (ibid.). Rather than being a confusing tense shift or a sign of Bromden's poor grammar, the slipping of tense here enriches the worlds represented in the novel by windowing two interactions consecutively. By intermingling two tenses in the same event, Kesey simultaneously represents Bromden's two mental states concerning his struggles against the brain murdering EST, thus offering the reader a simultaneous view of both Bromden's mental illness and saneness.

## 5 A Triangulate Relationship of Tense, Focalisation, and Mind

Based on the above discussions on the concurrent and evidentiary facets of focalisation in both the linear progression and the simultaneous representation of Bromden's unconscious and conscious mental states, a triangulate relationship can be observed in *Cuckoo's Nest* that places linguistic patterns, narrative strategies, and mental states into a coherent system (Figure 2.1).

Both the concurrent and the evidentiary facets of focalisation trigger the cognitive processes through which the reader can place an attentional window over the part of the interaction with the event frame that is activated. The corresponding linguistic devices are the present and the past tense respectively. Kesey represents Bromden's two mental states, i.e., an unconscious mind and a conscious mind, either in concatenation or in juxtaposition. Correspondingly, Kesey makes arrangement with the cognitive facets of focalisation: the concurrent for an unconscious mind and the evidentiary for a conscious mind. When Bromden is in a severe state of psychosis, the concurrent facet of focalisation, linguistically realised in the present tense, is prevalent. The present tense enables the reader to place an attentional window over Bromden's "here and now" interaction with the event frame, thus the most direct view of Bromden's disturbed mind. When Bromden's mental state ameliorates, the text is predominantly narrated in the past tense. The past tense initiates an evidentiary facet of focalisation that helps the reader place an attentional window over Bromden's "there and then" interaction with the event frame in the past. This enables the psychotic experiences to be represented from a mind distanced from that experience. The concatenation of the two tenses and the ensuing concurrent and evidentiary facets of focalisation are conducive to the representation of one person in two mental states, offering a contrasting view of "madness" and saneness, whereas the juxtaposition of the two tenses and the two facets of focalisation in one event provides a paralleled view of "madness" and saneness.

The tense shifts, as can often be found in analepsis and prolepsis, are not a new invention by Kesey; neither are the shifts in focalisation. However, Kesey creatively integrates tense, focalisation, and mental representation into a coherent system, and this triangulate relationship of linguistic patterns,

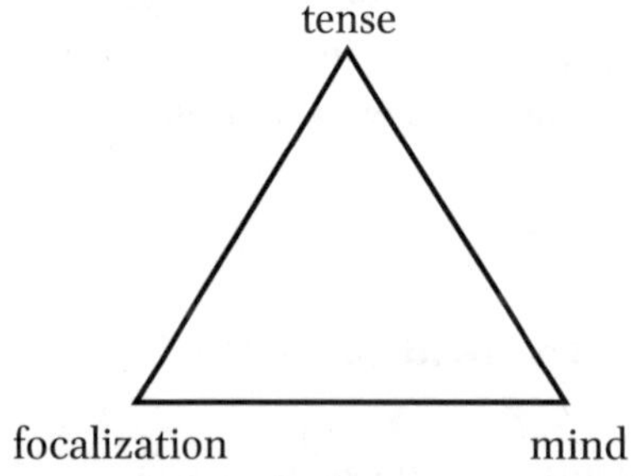


FIGURE 2.1 The triangulate relationship in *Cuckoo's Nest*

narrative strategies and mental states is a unique contribution by Kesey in *Cuckoo's Nest.*

## 6 Concluding Remarks

The present study demonstrates that the linguistic patterns, narrative strategies, and the representation of the fictional minds in *Cuckoo's Nest* coexist in an intrinsic triangulate relationship. The investigation of this triangulate relationship may first offer a technical and objective explanation for Kesey's jerky present-past tense skips – a matter of windowing of attention under the restricted perspectives of different focalisers, thus deepening the understanding of the mental illness in *Cuckoo's Nest*. Besides, the discovery of the three cognitive facets of focalisation may enrich focalisation theory by including the reader's cognitive activity in the study of focalisation on the one hand, and offer a practical tool for analysing the representation of the characters' minds as well as the reader's construal of the fictional minds on the other hand. Accordingly, the present research redefines focalisation as cognitive per se. Finally, it not only offers the opportunity to widen the application scope of Talmy's (2000, 257–309) cognitive semantic theory of windowing of attention in narratives; it may also feed cognitive linguistics with new data. The concurrent facet of focalisation activates the placement of an attentional window over the temporal point of the character-participant's "here and now" interaction with the referent in the event frame. This fits into neither of the two types of Talmy's (ibid., 283) attentional windowing in a participant-interaction frame, for it is logically paradoxical in real-life situations: a same participant-interaction event frame cannot be windowed simultaneously over the participant's interaction with the referent event in the past and at the present moment. However, in a fictional context and by technically switching between the evidentiary focaliser and the concurrent focaliser, it is possible to window a participant's interaction with the referent in the event frame in the past and at present simultaneously.

## Works Cited

Barthes, Roland. "An Introduction to the Structural Analysis of Narrative". *New Literary History*, vol. 6, no. 2, 1975, pp. 237–72.

Connor, Kimberly R. "Reading from the Heart Out: Chief Bromden Through Indigenous Eyes". *Concentric: Literary and Cultural Studies*, vol. 37, no. 1, 2011, pp. 231–53.

Frith, Christopher D. *The Cognitive Neuropsychology of Schizophrenia.* Lawrence Erlbaum Associates, 1992.

Genette, Gerard. *Narrative Discourse: An Essay in Method.* Translated by Jane E. Lewin, Cornell UP, 1980.

Hicks, Jack. "The Truth Even If It Didn't Happen: *One Flew over the Cuckoo's Nest*". *Bloom's Modern Critical Interpretation: Ken Kesey's One Flew over the Cuckoo's Nest,* edited by Harold Bloom, New edition, Infobase Publishing, 2007, pp. 67–80.

Huffman, James R. "The Cuckoo Clocks in Kesey's Nest". *Modern Language Studies,* vol. 7, no. 1, 1977, pp. 62–73.

Jahn, Manfred. "Focalization". *Routledge Encyclopedia of Narrative Theory,* edited by David Herman et al., Routledge, 2005, pp. 173–77.

Kesey, Ken. *One Flew over the Cuckoo's Nest.* Signet, 1962.

Lambe, Jennifer. "Memory Politics: Psychiatric Critique, Cultural Protest, and *One Flew over the Cuckoo's Nest*". *Literature and Medicine,* vol. 37, no. 2, 2019, pp. 298–324.

Leise, Christopher. "Ken Kesey's *One Flew over the Cuckoo's Nest*: Damming the Columbia River and Traumatic Loss". *Interdisciplinary Studies in Literature and Environment,* vol. 25, no. 1, 2018, pp. 62–79.

Lhamon, W. T. Jr. "Break and Enter to Breakaway: Scotching Modernism in the Social Novel of the American Sixties". *Boundary* 2, vol. 3, no. 2, 1975, pp. 288–306.

Madden, Fred. "Sanity and Responsibility: Big Chief as Narrator and Executioner". *Modern Fiction Studies,* vol. 32, no. 2, 1986, pp. 203–17.

Meloy, Michael. "Fixing Men: Castration, Impotence, and Masculinity in Ken Kesey's *One Flew over the Cuckoo's Nest*". *The Journal of Men's Studies,* vol. 17, no. 1, 2009, pp. 3–14.

Ohmann, Richard. "The Shaping of a Canon: U.S. Fiction, 1960–1975". *Critical Inquiry,* vol. 10, no. 1, 1983, pp. 199–223.

Semino, Elena, and Kate Swindlehurst. "Metaphor and Mind Style in Ken Kesey's *One Flew over the Cuckoo's Nest*". *Style,* vol. 30, no. 1, 1996, pp. 143–66.

Talmy, Leonard. *Toward a Cognitive Semantics.* Vol. 1, MIT Press, 2000.

Ware, Elaine. "The Vanishing American: Identity Crisis in Ken Kesey's *One Flew over the Cuckoo's Nest*". *MELUS,* vol. 13, no. 3/4, 1986, pp. 95–101.

Widmer, Kingsley. "The Post-Modernist Art of Protest: Kesey and Mailer as American Expressions of Rebellion". *The Centennial Review,* vol. 19, no. 3, 1975, pp. 121–35.

CHAPTER 3

# Narrating Mental Health and Distress: the Twin Motif and Intermediality in Diana Evans's *26a*

*Christina Slopek-Hauff*

## 1 Introduction: Mental Health and Distress in Literature

Mental illness affects multiple people across many regions and cultures. As the WHO notes, "[m]ental health conditions now cause 1 in 5 years lived with disability" ("Mental Health", online). Tied to historical discourses of insanity (cf. Caminero-Santangelo 1998), mental illness has a lot of stigma attached to it (cf. Hinshaw 2007). This stigma has been variously taken up in literature: Fiction can reinforce anxieties around mental illness or 'madness', as is the case in Charlotte Brontë's (in)famous *Jane Eyre* (1847). Yet, it can just as well contribute to destigmatising mental duress: Narrating experiences with mental distress in ways that overcome dialectics of mental health and distress and that engage critically with stereotypes surrounding mental distress helps to deconstruct notions of alterity ingrained in discourses on mental illness. Importantly, illness models are culture-specific and, especially in the case of mental illnesses, may not always be translatable across cultural contexts. By contrast, the term 'mental distress' can be understood as a more flexible descriptor: it does signify experiences with mental unwellbeing, too, but without pathologising and without privileging one understanding of what exactly constitutes mental health and what classifies as mental illness. Especially in contemporary times, an ever-increasing number of Anglophone pieces of fiction, ranging from trauma novels to autobiographical accounts of time spent in psychiatric institutions, contributes to shaping the perception of mental distress and people living with it by means of the powers of narration. This tendency has also gained currency in contemporary Black British literatures. I am thinking here of, among many others, Derek Owusu's *That Reminds Me* (2019), Leone Ross's *Orange Laughter* (1999), Jackie Kay's *Red Dust Road* (2010), Helen Oyeyemi's *The Icarus Girl* (2005), and the novel this chapter focuses on: Diana Evans's *26a* (2005). All of them *narrate* mental health and/or distress in unique ways, making use of literariness and narrative tools.

What is the surplus value of looking at how mental health and distress are *narrated* in works of fiction? A central point is that fiction can recalibrate the supposed binary between seemingly hard medical science and its soft, fleshy,

 | DOI:10.1163/9789004519886_005

embodied human patients (cf. Whitehead and Woods 2016, 4). Therefore, the burgeoning field of medical or health humanities pays attention to how capacities of the arts and humanities come to matter in this recalibration. From the outset, medical humanities have been defined rather flexibly, allowing a wide range of techniques and dynamics into their midst: In 2001, Deborah Kirklin and Ruth Richardson wrote that the field "can be held to encompass any interaction between the arts and health" (xv). Subsections of the medical humanities testify to the central role of narrative in navigating illnesses and discourses of them.[1] A great variety of narrative forms and strategies is well-suited to reflecting on and shaping images of health and ill-health, mental health and distress being no exception (cf. Gammelgaard 2022, 17). These literary forms can, according to Caroline Levine, "mean all shapes and configurations, all ordering principles, all patterns of repetition and difference" (2015, 3). Concomitantly, literature as form and literary forms can also straddle boundaries between media (cf. Rippl 2015, 1). Furthermore, when different media converge, they are joined "in the production of narrative meaning" (ibid., 7). On these grounds, this chapter analyses how the twin motif and intermedial configurations as literary forms can narrate mental distress.

Diana Evans's contemporary Black British novel *26a* (2005) traces interrelations of mental health and distress with regard to a pair of identical twins, Georgia and Bessi Hunter. The novel tells the story of the Hunter family: A father from Britain, a mother originally from Nigeria and their four daughters (Bel, Georgia, Bessi, and Kemy) live in a house in Neasden, London. When the family spends some time in Nigeria, an employee molests Georgia. This and domestic abuse from her father cause her mental distress. Though they are close, the twins develop very differently, and Georgia ultimately dies from suicide. So far, *26a* has been looked at with regard to "gendered magical realism" (Cooper 2008, 52), "post-racial" positioning (McLeod 2010, 48), "double consciousness" (Cuder-Domínguez 2009), creative use of the *Bildungsroman* (cf. Bastida Rodríguez 2012), diasporic subjectivity (cf. Vogt-William 2015), and, more closely connected to this chapter's focus, "individuality and twoness" (Pérez-Fernández 2013, 292), "mental and social struggles" (Ahmed Rasheed and Abdullah Khalaf 2023, 447), and twin myths (cf. Kaze 2017). Beyond these aspects, *26a* uses the twin motif and intermedial constellations to narrate and challenge the mental health/distress dialectic, which has scarcely attracted scholarly attention so far. In *26a*, both the twin motif and intermedial constellations are entangled with and rethink notions of sameness and alterity

1 A potent example is Rita Charon's "narrative medicine" (2001).

that inform the dialectic of mental health and distress: On the one hand, twin motifs tend to be expressive of sameness and difference (cf. de Nooy 2005, XVIII; Schwanebeck 2020, 1), and have been used time and again to contemplate underlying parameters of the two. On the other hand, intermediality as a means of narration has been discovered to incorporate otherness into an allegedly homogeneous medial framework (cf. Neumann 2015, 517). In *26a*, these narrative strategies jointly navigate the dialectic of mental health and distress. I begin by briefly theorising twinship across 'Western' and 'African' cultures, and then I use this theoretical backdrop to explore how the twin motif in *26a* encapsulates, but also interrogates the mental health/distress binary, and how it constructs and interleaves culture-specific conceptions of twinship to overcome the dialectic. I then continue by outlining central insights from intermediality studies and zoom in on relevant intertextual references in the novel, the novel's engagement with Michael Jackson as an intermedial reference which bizarrely narrates mental distress by and while referring to a singer associated with child abuse, and on a gymnastics scene watched on television that evokes central themes and motifs of abuse and mental distress in Evans's novel. Lastly, I reflect on how the twin motif in conjunction with intermediality undoes dichotomous distinctions between mental health and distress in *26a*, and vice versa, showing that alleged otherness more often than not is already part of what is perceived as sameness.

## 2 The Twin Motif: Exploring the Dialectic of Mental Health and Distress

Twins arouse fascination across many cultures and have been perceived as well as constructed as spectacular, out of the ordinary, for centuries. "Clearly twins are never *not* noticed", Philip Peek notes in his introduction to *Twins in African and Diaspora Cultures: Double Trouble, Twice Blessed* (2011b, 23; original emphasis). Historically, twins have caused sheer wonder in one case and sparked fear of ill omens in another. A statistical anomaly, twins "are eye-catching. The sight of two individuals who look and act so much alike challenges [...] beliefs about individuality and human uniqueness" (Segal 2017, xvii). Nancy Segal here discusses monozygotic or identical twins, but preoccupations with troubling similarities and twins' indistinguishable natures can extend to dizygotic or fraternal twins. Reasons for this hubbub around twins vary, too. To name but a few: Philip Peek points to the fact that multiple births used to be associated with animals in some African cultures (cf. 2011, 2), which may trouble notions of the human and introduce "uncanny" energies into perception of twinship (Bhabha 1994, 192). Juliana de Nooy talks more broadly about dynamics in twinhood perception that can be observed across diverse cultures and mentions "links to the mirror stage, narcissism, the uncanny, separation anxiety, sibling rivalry, the false self, projection of the unconscious, and exteriorisation of inner conflict" (2005, 2). Ultimately, the relationality (cf. Peek 2011, 26) and dis-/similarity of twins convert twinship into something that, culturally speaking, has aroused fascination up to suspicion and anger, and that engenders questions about identity and the self.

Performing culture-spanning fascination with twinship and the mirroring dynamics involved, twins abound in contemporary Black British literatures.[2] Zadie Smith's Magid and Millat in *White Teeth* (2000), one of the most successful Black British novels inaugurating the new millennium, are only one particularly well-known example of a strong tendency across the field to deploy twin characters and resulting twin motifs in order to reflect upon concepts of sameness and difference. Why, though, are twin motifs so especially prolific in Black British literatures?[3] Suzanne Scafe rightly remarks that "'Black British'[…] is leaky and imprecise, serving most usefully to describe how individuals and their work are positioned both in contemporary British society and in relation to their pasts" (2015, 214). Although the label is insufficient and also singles out Black British citizens from among the British population, it has been used as a catch-all. Many 'Black British' literatures address issues and parameters of belonging, often with an eye to race and culture. In the context of Black British literatures, Bénédicte Ledent further observes that "mixed-race twin characters [frequently become] symbols of the ambiguity and inbetweenness that is part and parcel of 'black British' identity" (2009, 5). Ergo, twins like Georgia and Bessi in *26a* bring to the table both the capacity to trouble general concepts of sameness by virtue of being the-same-but-not-quite, and concepts of racial homogeneity versus alterity in particular by means of occupying a liminal position between blackness and whiteness (cf. Vogt-Williams 2015, 137). Considering Britain's colonial past and enduring colonial legacies, coupled as they are with institutional and interpersonal racism both in the country's past and immediate present, it becomes

2 At this point, it is crucial to add that Diana Evans herself rejects labels such as '*Black* British', because they run the risk of essentialising (cf. 2005b, 33). I therefore use the term to broadly contextualise the novel, but without putting any pressure stemming from labels on the writer.

3 This is not to say that twin motifs are irrelevant in other fields of literature: Pakistani British Kamila Shamsie's *Home Fire* (2017) and Nigerian American Chimamanda Ngozi Adichie's *Half of a Yellow Sun* (2006) are but two examples of a farther-reaching interest in twin figures in contemporary Anglophone literatures, an interest that is frequently fuelled by twin characters' potential to stage contrasts on an intimate basis.

clear why twin figures in contemporary Black British literatures often serve the political purpose of challenging notions of identity and alterity.

Alterity, however, is by no means confined to racialised structures, neither in general nor in *26a*. Instead, it is an intersectional issue, involving notions of illness and health. A dialectic of mental health and distress builds on "mentalism" (Chamberlin 1977, xvi), i.e., "dominant contemporary ways of thinking that construct mental illness as the polar opposite of mental health as well as [...] correspondent processes of oppression, exclusion, and belittlement toward individuals with mental differences" (Punzi and Röder 2019). Mentalist structures are countered in *26a* as the novel challenges underlying notions of alterity. Evans's twins have variously been read as an attempt of the author "to stake a claim to Africa as part of [her] heritage" (Cooper 2008, 52), as expressive of the "double consciousness" of the biracial characters in Britain (Cuder-Domínguez 2009), and, generally, as a means to plunge into discourses of "individuality" and difference (Pérez-Fernández 2013, 292; see also Bryce 2008). As Georgia is sexually abused and dies from suicide towards the end of the novel, some scholars have also picked up on the fact that the twins in *26a* are in some way related to how the novel discusses mental distress: Pilar Cuder-Domínguez links the twins to trauma, based on the abuse Georgia suffers and a frightening tale of twin cultures the novel includes (cf. 2009, 8). In a similar vein, Douglas Kaze maintains that "twinhood [...] intersects with other ideas such as identity, coming of age, *trauma* and transnationalism" (2017, 571; my emphasis; see also Boehmer 2018, 131). What I can add to these interpretations is a nuanced analysis of how the twin characters and the twin motif enact and challenge the dichotomy of mental health and distress *in tandem with* an analysis of how Edo conceptions of twins inform *26a* and the depiction of mental distress and health.

The twin motif in *26a* is related to the narration of mental health and distress as Georgia and Bessi are depicted as similar in terms of outward appearance, but as different in the context of a wellbeing/distress dichotomy, or, in terms more germane to this chapter, their differences frequently function as outright signifiers of mental health and distress. Though Georgia and Bessi are very close and form a unit that is not open to other family members, for instance when they contemplate serious matters (cf. Evans 2005, 6–7), they are not interchangeable. Aware of their differences, the twins painstakingly identify where they differ in phenotype, resorting to hard-and-fast comparisons such as "Bessie's eyes are smallist" (42). Concordantly, they develop into different persons as well, Bessi being more assertive and ambitious and Georgia more subdued and dependent on her twin. According to the narrative, some of these differences have their roots in external factors, others do not.

Georgia seems to have been prone to accidents and death from the beginning: "Georgia, who was born first […], refused to breathe for seven minutes. And two and a half years later, still resentful, she was rushed back to St Luke's Hospital with dishcloth, carpet dust, half her afro and tassels off the bottom of the sofa clinging to her intestines" (4). This precariousness seems to attach to Georgia from day one. On the spectrum between wellbeing and distress, Bessi clearly represents the former, which is expressed precisely by the non-articulation of anything extraordinarily distressing concerning her. Wellbeing is posited as the default and Georgia in her deviance from it receives more narrative attention on this matter.

A central component of how the twin motif engages with mental distress and resulting difference within the twin relationship comes from the fact that Georgia is sexually abused as a child when the family lives in Nigeria for some years: One night, an employee of the house, Sedrick, catches her alone in the garden with a kitten, asks her to make cartwheels and then traps her and forces himself onto her (cf. 67–8). This incisive event traumatises Georgia deeply:[4] Back in their shared bed with Bessi, "Georgia tried to think about how she could put the cartwheels and grassfeet and the dark bushes like the evil forest and Sedrick's hands and Sedrick's belt opening into words that were sayable" (69). That trauma complicates speaking and narration of trauma itself has long been recognised by trauma theorists (cf. Caruth 1995, 10). Thus, the facts that Georgia is at a loss for words and that the scene replays itself so incoherently in her mind are indicative of trauma. As a consequence, this traumatising event creates a rift between the twins: "It was the first time ever, *in this land of twoness in oneness*, that something had seemed unsayable" (Evans 2005, 69; my emphasis).[5] Georgia's pain is so big that it at first distances her from Bessi, which narrates a dialectic of mental health and distress.

As Georgia's mental distress gets worse, the twin motif transforms in a way that performs the dichotomy of mental health and mental distress, the latter putting an end to the near-identicality of the twins. Years after the abuse, Georgia regularly suffers from acute mental distress that incapacitates her: "And making [decisions] required, first of all, an assessment of her [Georgia's] current state of mind. Blue would suggest it was mildly feasible. Lilac even more so. Yellow was a good place, but she was not often yellow when it was difficult to buy milk or tomato purée or a new pen. Orange meant it could be dangerous […]. And if she was red, an unforgiving place of chains and confusion, it was out

4 *Trauma* in relation to both twins even goes back to the very beginning of the novel, which starts with a story expressive of the initial trauma of being born (cf. Evans 2005, 3–4).

5 For a detailed analysis of "twoness in oneness" (Evans 2005, 69), see Pérez-Fernández (2013).

of the question absolutely, milk, onions, a walk in the street, everything" (ibid., 149). Her only escape from bad days is Bessi, to whom she still has a strong bond (ibid., 150). Georgia perceiving her emotions in colors and often being unable to carry out mundane tasks is indicative of how her mental health has deteriorated. Yet, at one point, differences between the twins culminate in a confrontation that puts into words the health and distress dichotomy which, up to this point, has largely been implied on the intradiegetic level. On this occasion, Georgia opens up to Bessi: "I needed somewhere that wasn't bad. I wanted to be light and happy like you, and I never wanted for you to see the dark" (ibid., 181). The rhetoric of 'light' and 'dark' translates easily into an evaluative distinction between mental wellbeing and distress. Georgia insinuates that Bessi is her safe space, but that she has also protected Bessi from all the negative emotions. In the heat of the moment, Georgia slaps Bessi in the face. Bessi hides in the bathroom and only comes out several hours later. "[T]here was a tinge of grey in her [Bessi's] face and crimson in one cheek and her eyes were hollow and dim. It frightened Georgia, that look. She had seen it many times before, in the mirror. It didn't belong in Bessi's eyes. [...] I am a thief, [Georgia] thought as she climbed the stairs after [Bessi]. I have stolen from you. But it is also true that you have stolen from me. You are light, I am shade" (ibid., 183). Again, color imagery and 'light' and 'dark' rhetoric give voice to the diffluences between the twins and narrate the dichotomy of mental health and distress.

Yet, as the plot progresses, the twin motif calls into question a clear-cut dichotomy of mental health and distress, along with the latter's alleged alterity. Close to the end of the novel, Georgia dies from suicide: "Georgia climbs the stairs. She throws her head back and shivers and reaches her arm up to the light. The hand is outstretched, the fingers wide apart. Sweep me from my feet. [...] And Bessi feels her face throb. Once" (ibid., 193). Narrative cues as to what Georgia has done remain inconclusive until, after a line break, Bessi's corporeal reaction is narrated. Bessi's automatic bodily reaction to Georgia's moments of pain is known to the reader from the scene of Sedrick abusing Georgia (cf. ibid., 68). To replicate this reaction here as part of the twin motif points to a longstanding bond between the twin sisters and firmly integrates mental distress in the twin motif. *26a* uses Georgia's twin to affirm that Georgia has died, and it does so to highlight how deeply connected the twins are and that they *share* Georgia's experiences of distress. If Evans's novel at first seems to set out to reinforce a dichotomous distinction between mental and distress through twins as a marker of sameness that becomes difference, instances of visceral connection and *shared* pain of mental distress like the one under discussion attest to the fact that the dichotomy of mental health and distress is not absolute. This, in turn, deconstructs mentalist notions of alterity.

The dialectic of mental health and distress is further exposed as untenable through the twin motif as the motif incorporates an Edo view of twin personality, which complicates the distinction between the twins as clear individuals, and, by corollary, calls into question binary oppositions of mental health and distress. As Wieland Schwanebeck writes, Georgia and Bessi are entangled in "a spiritual world of joint wandering" (2020, 6). When their family goes to Nigeria and visits Ida's family, Ida's father reveals to the twins that Edo people used to associate twins with witchcraft and to kill them (cf. Evans 2005, 61–2). One particular story the twins' grandfather tells them is the story "of a woman who once had two girl twins who were best friends from the very beginning, even before they were inside their mother's womb, when they were spirits. Their names were Onia and Ode. Onia was first, Ode was second – they set her on fire". The story further has it that "[w]hen Ode was burnt [...], Onia got sick and wouldn't eat at all until Ode's ghost entered her body. [...] But Ode could only stay for one year" (ibid., 63). The passage reveals Edo belief in spirits and underlines the close connection Edo culture ascribes to twins, a closeness that overcomes boundaries of the body and of the individual (cf. Pérez-Fernández 2013, 292). Although the twins' British father is very sceptical of the story (cf. Evans 2005, 64), *26a* affirms that it applies to Georgia and Bessi, and step by step re-enacts the story of Ode and Onia: When the twins turn 21, they celebrate at a dance-club and take acid together. Under the influence, Georgia starts to see things: "In the distance, she saw two little girls moving towards her. They were doing cartwheels down the hill. [...] When they arrived they stood on the dance floor. [...] Georgia could see clearly now, their white dresses and the same face, holding hands. One of the hands was burnt" (ibid., 171).[6] The little girls who are so much alike stand in for Georgia and Bessi, which their cartwheeling, formerly a hobby of Bessi and Georgia's, also points to. As Georgia was abused right after doing cartwheels, Georgia's vision here intertwines her trauma and twinship, the burnt hand standing in for Georgia's psychological damage (cf. Kaze 2017, 573). Then one of the little twins swallows the other one, the one with the burnt hand. Georgia identifies the twins as Ode and Onia and asks the visible girl: "'Are you Ode now, or Onia?' 'Yes,' said the little girl" (Evans 2005, 172). As the story of Ode and Onia plays itself out, it allows the twoness of twins to merge into oneness – a form of togetherness that dissolves

6 Brenda Cooper cautions us not to explain away experiences which do not concur with Eurocentric epistemologies by seeing them as "mental disturbances" (2008, 53). By contrast, this chapter argues that such a reading does not explain away or 'rationalise' such experiences but rather pays close attention to how *26a* incorporates Edo knowledge in order to narrate and undermine the dichotomy of mental health and distress.

boundaries and binaries which has been important to Georgia from the beginning and which she was saddened to lose after her abuse (ibid., 69). When Georgia dies, the story of Ode and Onia reaches fruition in the lives of Georgia and Bessi: Georgia in her spirit form enters Bessi's body (ibid., 209) and the twins converse with each other inside the body and share parts of it. Bessi's body even develops a rash (ibid., 221), reminding the reader of the initial Ode being set on fire: "Bessi somatizes the death of her sister in her own body, in the form of a rash, and retrieves Baba's story of Ode in Onia and the belief that her sister has entered her body" (Pérez-Fernández 2013, 300). The cohabitation consumes Bessi's body until Georgia's spirit leaves it close to the very end of the novel. But while they share Bessi's body, Georgia and Bessi confirm the story of Ode and Onia, validating the related vision of twinship. Bessi even starts seeing colours in the way Georgia did (cf. Evans 2005, 218), further dissolving boundaries between the two of them and what it seemed they started out standing for: mental health and distress. By these means, *26a* first challenges culturally constructed alterity of those living with mental distress through the twin motif, and in a second step uses Edo concepts of twinship to further contest the dichotomy often ascribed to twins, and, by inference, the dichotomy of mental health and distress.

## 3 Narrating Otherness: Subversive Intermediality in *26a*

Aside from the twin motif, *26a* makes use of another central strategy to narrate and reflect upon the dialectic of mental health and distress: intermediality. "Generally speaking, the term 'intermediality' refers to the relationships between media and is hence used to describe a huge range of cultural phenomena which involve more than one medium" (Rippl 2015, 1). These relationships between media are of miscellaneous nature: Tracing intermedial constellations in literature, one will see that literary texts can make references to, replicate, or incorporate other media and/or their structures, such as pictures and videos. A plethora of contemporary Black British literatures exhibit a proclivity for intermedial references. Andrea Levy's *Never Far From Nowhere* (1996) mentions a multiplicity of songs and song artists in passing, packaging political messages in these references by evoking specific historical sequences of events that shaped Black British life at the end of the 20th century. David Dabydeen's *A Harlot's Progress* (1999) takes up William Hogarth's famous 18th-century paintings and imbues them with narrative life, bringing to the fore what the paintings relegate to the background, such as Black servant figures (cf. Neumann and Rippl 2019, 60–84). Zadie Smith's *Swing Time* (2016) adds rhythm and brio to its narrative by incorporating manifold references to dance and music, fashioning "a variety of worldmaking strategies in and across media, forms and genres" (Pirker 2022, 279). And Evans's *26a* makes use of intermedial references to narrate and simultaneously interrogate the dialectic of mental health and distress.

So far, intermedial constellations in Evans's novel have received comparatively little attention. Christine Vogt-Williams mentions "intertextual echoes" of Robert Louis Stevenson's *The Strange Case of Dr. Jekyll and Mr. Hyde* (1886), but concentrates on how this intertextual link relates to issues of race (cf. Vogt-Williams 2015, 138) and Brenda Cooper (2008) and Elleke Boehmer (2009) pay attention to how *26a* alludes to precursors of Nigerian literature. An *expansive* analysis of intermediality in *26a* and its enmeshment with discourses of mental distress remains to be carried out. This analysis concentrates on intermedial narration of mental health and distress with an eye to the following aspects: Firstly, intertextual references position the novel within literary traditions and implicitly ponder twinship and its connection to mental distress. Secondly, vague intermedial references to Michael Jackson and a concert he gives in London approach the topic of child abuse through an intermedial move and invite readers to draw conclusions about mental distress as a result of sexual abuse. Last but not least, an intermedial scene that involves gymnastics shown on television thematises the power involved in looking at bodies and ligates this to abuse suffered as a possible consequence of objectification, approaching acts and structures that can have a causal relation to mental distress through intermedial narration.

Firstly, *26a* uses intertextual links to narrate mental health and/or distress: The novel nods courteously at a number of other literary texts to situate the novel *vis-à-vis* its precursors: Brenda Cooper suggests that the beginning of *26a* alludes to Ben Okri's *The Famished Road* (1991) (cf. 2008, 57), Elleke Boehmer hears echoes of Wole Soyinka's *The Road* (1965) in the same opening (cf. 2009, 147). By alluding, however obliquely, to these narratives, *26a* positions itself in a tradition of Nigerian storytelling, both in verbal and written form.[7] What is more, Elleke Boehmer traces intertextual relations between *26a* and Chinua Achebe's classic *Things Fall Apart* (1958).[8] She "investigate[s] a set of powerfully *generative* images [which] have to do with modes of reproduction

7 Though I refer to 'Nigerian storytelling', I am aware that the nation-state of Nigeria is a remnant of colonisation and groups together culturally diverse communities. However, with Igbo Wole Soyinka, Chinua Achebe, and Urhobo Ben Okri, there is no African culture to which *26a* exclusively ties itself through intermediality.

8 Chinua Achebe continues to impact on much African and African-diasporic writing. For instance, I have recently identified how Akwaeke Emezi's *Freshwater* (2018) builds on Achebe's *oeuvre* (cf. Slopek-Hauff forthcoming, n. pag.).

that are traditionally cursed or tabooed". Boehmer further explains that these images "are expressed in the shape either of twins [...] or of the ogbanje, abiku or fatefully returning child" (2009, 143). She bases an interpretation of twinship in *26a* on this observation, namely that "the pressure of Georgia's depression" complicates the twins' visceral bond. Boehmer subsequently muses: "It is as if the novel is conceding something to the old Igbo taboo about twins – that nature does not like to allow this kind of mirror-image replication" (ibid., 147). Crucially, Boehmer thus exposes links between intermediality and the twin motif in *26a*. Given the weight Evans's novel attaches to Georgia's mental distress, it becomes clear through Boehmer's intertextually attuned reading of the novel that twinship is connected to intermediality, that both participate in narrating mental health and distress and that an intertextual reading uncovers layers of narration that shape the mental health and distress dialectic in *26a*.

Secondly, an important dimension of intermediality that narrates and navigates mental health and distress in *26a* by showing how media and, hence, intermedial references are sutured to abuse and mental distress engages music and the 'King of Pop' Michael Jackson. Already successful in the timeline of *26a*, Jackson gives a concert at Wembley in London, which the twins, now young adults, attend from afar, while Kemy is actually in the audience: Not having gotten tickets, they try to listen to Jackson from the apartment of two boys. During the concert, at the boys' flat, Bessi sleeps with one of the boys and Georgia with the other. Their first 'voluntary' sexual experiences are thus glued to Michael Jackson's performance: "Michael stepped on stage in black leather and zips and Kemy had love and passion all over her face. He sang. Kemy cried. While Bessi held her breath and tried to sigh" (Evans 2005, 123). Kemy's enthusiasm with Michael Jackson contrasts starkly with Bessi's deflating first experience of sexual intercourse, which is emphasised by the full stop separating the two last sentences that, grammatically, could have been one: For Bessi, sex here is not passionate, but she tries to do what she thinks is expected of her, namely sigh with (feigned) pleasure. This evidences sexist structures in heteronormative intercourse and Bessi's first experience of it. Georgia's experience is even worse: When she and the other boy sleep together, this hurts Georgia: "But the pain. The blood. On the sofa. Is there blood?" (ibid., 123). Her rambling thoughts turn back to the concert: "I can hear Michael singing and people screaming (*Kemy, I wish I was there with you, I wish I was still new and young like you*). I can hear, very faint, a kitten in the bushes and there's heat all around me but how I feel cold" (ibid., 123; original emphasis). Georgia feeling damaged and old on the one hand and the kitten and the heat on the other serve as pointers which ligate this sexual experience to the garden in Nigeria and her being sexually abused. Having sex as a young woman forces Georgia to relive what traumatised her in the first place. The moment of the twins' first time having sex is thus constructed around the intermedial reference to Michael Jackson's concert. This reference as well as the twins' interest in and their sister Kemy's teenage obsession with the famous singer are not unusual, but all the more bitter in the light of Jackson's reputation: In 1993 and 2005, Jackson was accused of and tried for child abuse. Though he was acquitted of all charges, echoes of these trials and allegations (as well as others that have come to the fore after his death in 2005 and long after the publication date of *26a*) accompany his figure. This background makes the intermedial reference uncanny and cynical as it evokes a concert of a pop icon tried for molesting children. Rather than a background symphony, Michael Jackson's concert here is a disconcerting force that stands in for pervasive layers of abuse and for how abuse may be countenanced by the public. Though the scene does not engage specific sounds or lyrics, it uses Jackson as the backdrop against which to narrate mental distress and possible factors by way of an intermedial reference that in its vagueness attests to the encompassing and far-reaching power of abuse: That Bessi thinks she should 'perform' and lend unfelt passion to the act is one result of sexist norms, that Georgia has been abused as a child and that the sexual act here replicates this trauma are consequences of even more pervasive patriarchal structures and male power. These entanglements of structural sexism and abuse are substantiated by the narration in this scene, which has focalisation shift rapidly between the three sisters. With an eye to how intermediality narrates mental health and distress in *26a*, we might say that it here brings to the fore Georgia's mental distress and trauma from being sexually abused and displays links between the private, microcosmic abuse she has suffered and macrocosmic allegations of sexual abuse against Michael Jackson as well as omnipresent patriarchal structures, which in one way or another can cause mental distress for women.

Thirdly, while the intermedial constellation discussed above works through evocation of a pop music icon and centers on music, another strand of intermedial narration in *26a* is more interested in visual cues, the act of watching, and how it re-members abuse and trauma and thus mental distress. After Georgia has died and begun to inhabit Bessi's body, Bessi watches TV with her nephew at her older sister Bel's house. What she watches is narrated as follows:

> A little girl from Romania did three somersaults in a row and landed in the splits. A man in tights flew off the bars and twisted in the air. A girl from Russia who was only thirteen years old hopped up on to the beam. She stuck out her chest and stood straight and proud and ready with outwards feet. Her balance was perfect. […] Then, with her hands

> outstretched, she did a cartwheel. The cartwheel happened slowly. And inside the cartwheel, there were grassfeet memories and a cockroach army and a scream. (ibid., 224)

The gymnastic performances are summarised from a dissociative distance, the narrative, lacking a clear focaliser, does not divulge the feelings of the onlooker. Nonetheless (or precisely because of this), the scene has an unsettling atmosphere: Although words like 'twists' and 'splits' are common in gymnastics parlance, coupled as they here are with the distant, non-committal description of the scene as such, a grotesque subtext accrues to them. 'Splitting' and 'twisting' come to sound dangerous, as if the bodies on display were twisted unnaturally. Furthermore, the sober description of gymnastics performances changes once cartwheels are mentioned: Has the girl's balance, which can be read as a figurative expression of the girl's mental health, been 'perfect' before doing cartwheels, this seems to end abruptly with the cartwheel. Of course, the cartwheel on TV evokes Georgia's being abused, which happened after she had been doing cartwheels in the garden. Cockroaches, here presented as a threatening army, signify pollution, dirt, and taint. They refer back to a cockroach Sedrick once brushed off Bessi's chest, the cockroach giving him license to touch the little girl in a way that would otherwise have been deemed indecent (ibid., 53). Ever since the abuse, Georgia has seen cockroaches in moments of acute mental distress, for instance after having sex (ibid., 123). Over the course of the narrative, cockroaches have thus come to signify abuse and mental distress. In this scene, the cockroaches foreshadow that the girls who are doing gymnastics, their young and small bodies being filmed and thus objectified by the camera and consumed by the viewers, are in a way already being abused in a male-dominated world, and that more abuse is likely to happen. The experience and farther-reaching structures of abuse become the organizing principle of the scene, narrated by means of an intermedial construction. "Bessi felt very itchy indeed. There was a jolt in her ribs, she fell back onto the floor, and burst into tears" (ibid., 224). The itching and the jolting in her ribs may point to Georgia moving in her body, and it is likely that Bessi cries because she or her body know now what Sedrick did to Georgia.[9] Intermediality in this scene reflects upon the power inherent in acts of looking (cf., a.o., Mirzoeff 2011), upon how looking is implicated in patriarchal power structures and abuse, and on how

9 Readers who do not accept the novel's claim that a spectral version of Georgia indeed lives in Bessi might think that Bessi cries because the cartwheels remind her of her sister. Still, intermedial dynamics in this scene would at least bring up Georgia's abuse for the reader in this case, too.

one form of abuse and another are entangled and produce mental distress. *26a* weaves its narration of mental health and distress around intermedial strategies, undoing mentalist binaries.

## 4 Conclusion: Intermediality and Twinship as Twoness in Oneness

This chapter has teased out how the twin motif and intermediality in *26a* narrate the dialectic of mental health and distress and that the two techniques regularly upset mentalist dialectic distinctions, showcasing the power of narrative to engage critically with discrimination. *26a*'s gestures and ties to other media and their reception might fuel future research, too: For instance, at the beginning of the novel, the Hunter family watches Princess Diana and Prince Charles get married on television. The publicly consumed story of royal happiness and luxury is pitted against the family's discontents. Throughout the novel, Diana and Charles's marriage and their separation are mentioned time and again, in a way mirroring hardships of the Hunter family (cf. Evans 2005, 15–23, 109, 155, 225). Thus, Evans's novel continually refers back to this initial intermedial constellation and destabilises the narrative of the happy family, possibly also alluding to colonial exploitation in which British royals were implicated by means of narrative mirroring of the two families. Ordeals of the Hunter family include abuse from the father, which further adds to Georgia's trauma and also affects Bessi (ibid., 123). The father's aggressive disposition is verbalised through an intermedial reference to Mr Hyde from the film *Dr Jekyll and Mr Hyde* (Mamoulian 1931), based on Stevenson's classic novella from 1886. Like Dr Jekyll's vile alter ego, Mr Hunter becomes a Mr Hyde persona who controls and beats his children when he drinks (cf. Evans 2005, 94–108). Generally, intermedial references in *26a* narrate mental health and distress, alluding to abuse and trauma and expressing the two by means of semiotic difference.

Semiotic difference is furthermore relevant both with an eye to the novel's Black British context and its concern with mental health and distress. Why are intermedial references of special importance in Black British and other postcolonial contexts? Anderson illustrates how nations as "imagined communities" are consolidated by literature as part of print culture (1983). However, literature also frequently unsettles narratives of national homogeneity. As semiotic difference, intermediality in Black British fiction is a crucial formal instrument for destabilisation. Tracing an ample array of intermedial constellations possible in literature, Gabriele Rippl stresses that intermediality is immanent to all media and that media are never homogeneous (cf. 2015, 2). Building on this, Birgit Neumann demonstrates that intermediality can be very productive in postcolonial contexts in ways unique to postcolonial negotiations of power structures: As movements between and across medial domains straddle boundaries between media, they perform in-betweenness and incorporate otherness into an *allegedly* homogeneous framework (cf. 2015, 517). Thus, intermediality in postcolonial literatures frequently countervails notions of sameness and, in turn, otherness, deconstructing concepts of alterity in its stride.

Given the potential of intermediality to narrate otherness, it becomes evident why intermediality in *26a* serves as a viable means to narratively explore the dyad of mental health and distress in Evans's Black British novel. In her introduction to Black British literatures, Ledent identifies intertextuality, one form of intermedial relation between texts, as characteristic of many pieces of Black British fiction. Right after pinpointing how twin figures can perform reflections on sameness and alterity, she writes: "This focus on the other as a means of identifying oneself also finds expression in intertextuality" (2009, 5).[10] Eminent Black British cultural critic Stuart Hall likewise acknowledges that "what it means to be 'British […]'" can be an "intertextual [relation]—mediated, through a variety of other 'texts […]'" (1996, 170). From this follows that links between media in Black British fiction attest to the relational character of the narratives. The assertive intermediality of *26a* contests visions of diaspora and hybridity focused on struggles with belonging (Ahmed Rasheed and Abdullah Khalaf 2023, 447) and challenges related binaries.

If "semiotic and material in-between-ness" (Neumann 2015, 513) is a means by which *26a* narrates and overcomes the dialectic of mental health and distress, on a more abstract level, intermediality in tandem with the twin motif in *26a* labors to chip away at the alleged, mentalist 'otherness' of mental distress. Drawing on Homi Bhabha's concept of the in-between space of cultures as a plural and productive site of indomitable frictions (cf. Bhabha 1994, 321), Neumann foregrounds "the often disruptive presence of an*other* medium (2015, 513; my emphasis). As media are always connected to 'other' media, otherness inheres in sameness – which is what *26a* suggests regarding the dialectic of mental health and distress. Boundaries between the two are overcome irrevocably when Georgia enters Bessi's body. This "twoness in oneness" (Evans 2005, 69), which has been explored both in this chapter and in an article by Irene Pérez-Fernández (2013), is characteristic of how *26a* understands twinship and constructs the twin motif. Showing that mental distress is

10 Another link between several sections of this chapter, the one on the twin motif and the one on intermediality, is how prone twins are to being photographed, to being made a spectacle of. The hype around twins can necessitate intermedial constellations (cf. Renne 2011, 311; original emphasis).

not the polar opposite of mental health, just as Bessi and Georgia are neither completely identical nor polar opposites, intermediality *performs* twoness in oneness. Hence, *26a* generatively aligns one of its dominant formal strategies with what it takes up on the level of content, thus reaching ultimate and non-dialectic confluence with regard to the narration of mental health and distress.

## Works Cited

Achebe, Chinua. *Things Fall Apart*. Heinemann, 1958.

Adichie, Chimamanda Ngozi. *Half of a Yellow Sun*. 4th Estate, 2006.

Ahmed Rasheed, Lamia'a, and Noor Abdullah Khalaf. "Non-Belonging as a Psycho-Social Dilemma in Diana Evans' *26a*". *Journal of Namibian Studies*, vol. 33, 2023, pp. 445–57.

Anderson, Benedict. *Imagined Communities: Reflections on the Origin and Spread of Nationalism*. Verso, 1983.

Bastida Rodríguez, Patricia. "El Doble *Bildungsroman* en la Narrativa Británica Contemporánea: Transformaciones desde la Escritura Diaspórica Femenina". *Oceánide* 4, 2012, n. pag.

Bhabha, Homi. *The Location of Culture*. 1994. Routledge, 2004.

Boehmer, Elleke. "Achebe and his Influence in Some Contemporary African Writing". *Interventions: International Journal of Postcolonial Studies*, vol. 11, no. 2, 2009, pp. 141–53.

Boehmer, Elleke. *Postcolonial Poetics: 21st-Century Critical Readings*. Palgrave Macmillan, 2018.

Brontë, Charlotte *Jane Eyre*. 1847. Scholastic, 2013.

Bryce, Jane. "'Half and Half Children': Third-Generation Women Writers and the New Nigerian Novel". *Research in African Literatures*, vol. 39, no. 2, 2008, pp. 49–67.

Caminero-Santangelo, Marta. *The Madwoman Can't Speak: Or Why Insanity Is Not Subversive*. Cornell UP, 1998.

Caruth, Cathy. Introduction. *Trauma: Explorations in Memory*. Ed. Cathy Caruth, The Johns Hopkins UP, 1995, pp. 3–12.

Chamberlin, Judi. *On Our Own: Patient-Controlled Alternatives to the Mental Health System*. 1977. Hawthorn Books, Inc. Publishers, 1978.

Charon, Rita. "Narrative Medicine: A Model for Empathy, Reflection, Profession, and Trust". *JAMA*, vol. 286, no. 15, 2001, pp. 1897–902.

Cooper, Brenda. "Diaspora, Gender and Identity: Twinning in Three Diasporic Novels". *English Academy Review*, vol. 25, no. 1, 2008, pp. 51–65.

Cuder-Domínguez, Pilar. "Double Consciousness in the Work of Helen Oyeyemi and Diana Evans." *Women – A Cultural Review*, vol. 20, no. 3, 2009, pp. 277–86.

Dabydeen, David. *A Harlot's Progress*. Jonathan Cape, 1999.

*Dr. Jekyll and Mr. Hyde*. Directed by Rouben Mamoulian, Paramount Pictures, 1931.

Emezi, Akwaeke. *Freshwater*. Grove Press, 2018.

Evans, Diana. *26a*. 2005. Vintage, 2006.

Evans, Diana. "Diana Evans in Conversation. Interview with Bernadine Evaristo". *Wasafiri* 45, 2005b, pp. 31–5.

Gammelgaard, Lasse Raaby. "Introduction: Madness and Literature and the Health Humanities." *Madness and Literature: What Fiction Can Do for the Understanding of Mental Illness*. Ed. Lasse Raaby Gammelgaard, U of Exeter P, 2022, pp. 1–19.

Hall, Stuart. "New Ethnicities". *Black British Cultural Studies: A Reader*. Ed. Houston Baker, U of Chicago P, 1996, pp. 163–72.

Hinshaw, Stephen. *The Mark of Shame: Stigma of Mental Illness and an Agenda for Change*. Oxford UP, 2007.

Kay, Jackie. *Red Dust Road*. Picador, 2010.

Kaze, Douglas. "Ode in Onia: Reading the Use of Myth and Twinhood in Diana Evans' *26a*". *Journal of English Language and Literature*, vol. 8, no. 1, 2017, pp. 571–74.

Kirklin, Deborah, and Ruth Richardson. "Editors' Preface". *Medical Humanities: A Practical Introduction*,. Ed. Deborah Kirklin and Ruth Richardson, Royal College of Physicians of London, 2001, xv–xvi.

Ledent, Bénédicte. "Black British Literature". *The Oxford Companion to English Literature*. Ed. Dinah Birch and Margaret Drabble, Oxford UP, 2009, pp. 6–22.

Levine, Caroline. *Forms: Whole, Rhythm, Hierarchy, Network*. Princeton UP, 2015.

Levy, Andrea. *Never Far From Nowhere*. London: REVIEW, 1996.

McLeod, John. "Extra Dimensions, New Routines". *Wasafiri* vol. 25, no. 4, 2010, pp. 45–52.

"Mental Health". *World Health Organization*. https://www.who.int/health-topics/mental-health#tab=tab_2. Accessed 21 July 2024.

Mirzoeff, Nicholas. *The Right to Look: A Counterhistory of Visuality*. Duke UP, 2011.

Neumann, Birgit. "Intermedial Negotiations: Postcolonial Literatures". *Handbook of Intermediality: Literature – Image – Sound – Music*, Ed. Gabriele Rippl, De Gruyter, 2015, pp. 512–29.

Neumann, Birgit, and Gabriele Rippl. *Verbal-Visual Configurations in Postcolonial Literature: Intermedial Aesthetics*. Routledge, 2020.

Nooy, Juliana de. *Twins in Contemporary Literature and Culture: Look Twice*. Palgrave Macmillan, 2005.

Okri, Ben. *The Famished Road*. Jonathan Cape, 1991.

Owusu, Derek. *That Reminds Me*. #Merky Books, 2019.

Oyeyemi, Helen. *The Icarus Girl*. Bloomsbury, 2005.

Peek, Philip. "Introduction: Beginning to Rethink Twins". *Twins in African and Diaspora Cultures: Double Trouble, Twice Blessed*. Ed. Philip Peek, Indiana UP, 2011, pp. 1–36.

Peek, Philip. *Twins in African and Diaspora Cultures: Double Trouble, Twice Blessed*, Indiana UP, 2011b.

Pérez-Fernández, Irene. "Embodying 'Twoness in Oneness' in Diana Evans's *26a*". *Journal of Postcolonial Writing*, vol. 49, no. 3, 2013, pp. 291–302.

Pirker, Eva Ulrike. "Intermedial Ways of Worldmaking: Zadie Smith's *Swing Time*". *Tulsa Studies in Women's Literature*, vol. 41, no. 2, 2022, pp. 267–83.

Punzi, Elisabeth, and Katrin Röder. "Challenging Complicity in the Context of Mentalism: Mental Distress Autobiographies and Performance Art". *Complicity and the Politics of Representation*. Ed. Cornelia Wächter and Robert Wirth, Rowman, 2019, pp. 195–215.

Renne, Elisha. "The Ambiguous Ordinariness of Yoruba Twins". *Twins in African and Diaspora Cultures: Double Trouble, Twice Blessed*. Ed. Philip Peek, Indiana UP, 2011, pp. 306–26.

Rippl, Gabriele. Introduction. *Handbook of Intermediality: Literature – Image – Sound – Music*. Ed. Gabriele Rippl, De Gruyter, 2015, pp. 1–31.

Ross, Leone. *Orange Laughter*. Angela Royal Publishing, 1999.

Scafe, Suzanne. "Unsettling the Centre: Black British Fiction". *The History of British Women's Writing, 1970–Present*. Ed. Mary Eagleton and Emma Parker, Palgrave Macmillan, 2015, pp. 213–28.

Schwanebeck, Wieland. *Literary Twinship from Shakespeare to the Age of Cloning*. Routledge, 2020.

Segal, Nancy. *Twin Mythconceptions: False Beliefs, Fables, and Facts about Twins*. Academic Press, 2017.

Shamsie, Kamila. *Home Fire*. Bloomsbury Publishing, 2017.

Slopek-Hauff, Christina. "Multiple Psychiatries: Re-membering Psychiatry in Contemporary Anglophone Novels". *The Cultural Heritage of Psychiatry and Its Literary Transformations: Middle Ages to the Present*. Ed. Katrin Röder and Cornelia Wächter. Brill, forthcoming.

Smith, Zadie. *White Teeth*. Hamish Hamilton, 2000.

Smith, Zadie. *Swing Time*. Hamish Hamilton, 2016.

Soyinka, Wole. *The Road*. Oxford UP, 1965.

Stevenson, Robert Louis. *The Strange Case of Dr Jekyll and Mr Hyde*. Longman, 1886.

Vogt-William, Christine. "Meeting Mr Hyde and Dr Stone: Mixed Race Twins and White Fathers in Diana Evans' *26a* and Abraham Verghese's *Cutting for Stone*". *Diaspora, Memory and Intimacy: Diasporas, Cultures of Mobilities, 'Race'*. Ed. Sarah Barbour, Thomas Lacroix, and Judith Misrahi-Barak, Presses Universitaires de la Méditerranée, 2015, pp. 135–54.

Whitehead, Anne, and Angela Woods. Introduction. *The Edinburgh Companion to the Critical Medical Humanities*. Ed. Anne Whitehead, Angela Woods, Sarah Atkinson, Jane Macnaughton, and Jennifer Richards, Edinburgh UP, 2016, pp. 1–31.

CHAPTER 4

# Whose Story Is That? Experimental Narrative Strategies in Rethinking Normality and Age

*Daria Baryshnikova*

## 1 Introduction

Commenting on his experience of writing the novel *House Mother Normal* (1971), B.S. Johnson (1933–1973) stated that he was planning to take "an evening in an old people's home and see a single set of events through the eyes of not less than eight old people. [...] The idea was to say something about the things we call 'normal' and 'abnormal' [...]" (1973, 26–27). This essay pursues a similar goal: to explore Johnson's text and its recent interpretation by Tim Crouch, a UK playwright and theatre director based in Brighton whose works often invite audiences to actively participate in the environments his plays create and explore. Crouch's plays include *An Oak Tree* (2005), *The Author* (2009), *I, Malvolio* (2010), *I, Cinna (The Poet)* (2012), *Total Immediate Collective Imminent Terrestrial Salvation* (2019), and many others. As an experimental theatre director, Tim Crouch collaborates with many companies and various art forms. For instance, his *ENGLAND – a play for galleries* (2007) deals with the world of contemporary art and was written to be staged in white-walled art galleries. This paper examines the ways in which non-normative bodies and minds are presented in Crouch's digital installation produced for the Brighton Festival in 2021.[1] Crouch's installation reconstructs Johnson's novel exactly, word by word. It has the same title as the novel, moreover, all the words of the novel are reproduced precisely as they were written by Johnson. This digital remastering could be viewed on site, as well as online. The screen is divided into nine segments in which nine actors are permanently present and they are talking all together. It may look like a (weird) Zoom conference with nine windows in which nine participants act together. Actors are shown frontal, head and shoulders against the neutral black background. In an interview, stating his deep affinity with Johnson Crouch explains:

1 I would like to thank Tim Crouch for sharing and letting me explore the video materials of his installation.

 | DOI:10.1163/9789004519886_006

> [Johnson] pushed at the edges of the form, constantly reinventing the possibilities of the written word. He was hugely ambitious in what he was trying to do and struggled to get the recognition he deserved. This is an opportunity to revisit his work and recognise its importance. As a theatre-maker, I've never worked on an existing novel before. Theatre is not a literary form. But I think that what we're doing with House Mother Normal is actually honouring the reach of Johnson's book. (Crouch 2021)

My aim is to show that the representation of fictional minds here can be understood as a relational *process* of sense-making inseparable from the interactions with the world and other minds.

I start with an examination of B.S. Johnson's novel and the ways it narrativises non-normative minds combining the formal analysis of the modes of storytelling with the exploration of the dialectics of discourse and cultural conventions. In his discussion of the novel focused on its narrative and cognitive modes, Lars Bernaerts convincingly shows that the conceptions of the extended, embedded, and embodied mind can be reconciled with a narrative analysis that recognises the artificial nature of fictional minds (Bernaerts 2014, 294). To extend this discussion, the emphasis in the present paper will be directed to the emergence of a collective mind through the interaction of the performance's discourses and the audience.

In the second section, on the example of Tim Crouch's digital installation I investigate the sense-making processes in complex multimodal narratives. Drawing on enactivist cognitive approaches that stress that (fictional) minds function in constant interaction with the world, I consider Crouch's installation in a framework, in which minds and their activities are not thought of only as objects of perception but rather as 'the way in which we perceive', contextualised and dynamic processes (Gallagher 2005, Thompson 2007, Hutto 2000). I reveal how Crouch's artwork enables an access to simultaneous experiences and recontextualises Johnson's novel through the various perspectives on perception and mind functioning. My comparison of the novel written in 1970 and its 'digital remastering' produced during the covid-19 pandemic aims at the question of how representations of impaired (that refers to a physical limitation), disabled (referring to social non-inclusion), and 'normal' (mostly indefinitely) minds change throughout various media and cultural contexts.

## 2 The Mind's Work (and No Play) in B.S. Johnson's Novel

B.S. Johnson belonged, together with Ann Quin, Alan Burns, J.G. Ballard, Brigit Brophy, and others, to the group of British experimental writers who, as Julia

Jordan asserts, "requisitioning non-linear and fragmented forms of narration, [...] actively attempt to repair their ability to represent the 'truth' of experience with mimetic fidelity" (2015, 147). In his experimentation, Johnson was quite concerned with the ways the contemporary novel developed formally. His idea was that the evocation of 'truth' in a literary work could be achieved by the detailed exploration of lived experience. Joseph Darlington argues that "Johnson's innovations have the political intention of disrupting traditional reading patterns" (2019, 36). He considers Johnson's novels as dynamic objects that encourage active readership and "exist as potential narrative experiences. [...] The 'novel' proper emerges as the accumulation of relevant interpretations" (2019, 41).

Before writing *House Mother Normal*, Johnson had already started to experiment with truthful representations of the mind's processes and with their adequate 'translation' into words. In his previous novel, *The Unfortunates* (1969), he explored the form of an unbound book-in-a-box as a metaphor for randomness in the working of the narrator's mind and the fragmented nature of reality. The novel was also not so much about the single experience of a loss but rather contemplated on general processes of mental functioning.

*House Mother Normal* continues his exploration of the constructedness of the novel's form that still allows to consider the 'truth' of how the mind may work. The novel is set in a residential care home and explores dementia, abuse, and elderly age. Thematically, it is centred on a social evening which is presented from nine points of view. Properly speaking, the novel was not absolutely Johnson's formal invention, it took much from Philip Toynbee's *Tea with Mrs. Goodman* (1947), not to mention Kurosawa's *Rashomon* (1950) that reported the same event from different points of view. Toynbee's novel is constructed around a grid consisting of several narrators on one axis and action divided into twelve 'time units' on the other. Each 'time-unit' lasts about a page and a half, has the same descriptive details and fragments of dialogue occurring at roughly the same point on each page (cf. Coe 2004, 296). Johnson described his composition as follows:

> Due to the various deformities and deficiencies of the inmates, these events would seem to be progressively 'abnormal' to the reader. At the end, there would be the viewpoint of the House Mother, an apparently 'normal' person, and the events themselves would then be seen to be so bizarre that everything that had come before would seem 'normal' by comparison. (Johnson 1973, 26–27)

Each chapter in *House Mother Normal* starts with the characters' name on the top of the page, their physical and psychic characteristics that should provide a frame through which the fictional minds can be constructed and interpreted by the readers. The text is rigorous in structure, it has nine internal monologues,

21-pages long each, occurring in the same place and covering the same time range. Every monologue is structured so that the same page of each takes place in the same moment in time. To unravel the novel's plot readers must construct the event themselves from the fragments which are often devoid of coherency but full of gaps and incongruency of thoughts, speeches, and action descriptions of the nine characters. Thus, the question asked by Sarah Lamson on the page seven, "Do you want me to keep the labels?" (Johnson 1984, 13), gets the answer from the House Mother on the next line on her page seven: "No, I don't want the labels kept for anything [...]" (ibid., 189). Such composition prompts the reader to go back and forth in the book to grasp all the parts of an interaction and to reconstruct the context of an event, a strategy that Bernaerts characterises as a "3-D reading experience" (2014, 298). Johnathan Coe suggests the musical analogy for the book as "richly polyphonic, fugal, a novel that can be read 'vertically' as well as 'horizontally'" (Coe 2004, 24).

Descriptions of events – a dinner, singing together, working together, playing the 'pass the parcel' game, a tourney competition, an 'entertainment' by the House Mother – are disintegrated into different pages so that readers are meant to assemble them in order to narrativise the story. In the text it can be a representation of multimodal experiences: visual, aural, sensori-motor. There are series of perception/affective perception (feeling pain), actions with some references to bodily activities (breathing), evaluation, or goal-directed actions. For instance, when House Mother explains how to play the game:

> Stay where you are, sitting round the long table, and we're going to play Pass the Parcel. You pass the parcel from one to another, and when the music stops whoever has it tries to open it. When the music starts again, the parcel must be passed on. And so on. And what a lovely surprise the last one's going to get, the winner! Here we go then. You start off with the music, Sarah. (Johnson 1984, 195)

Another example is when Sara Lamson comments, many pages before, on her plans and actions and assesses the object she deals with: "Me to start? Off. Pass it to Charlie. What is it? Brown paper, soft." (ibid., 20).

*House Mother Normal* was written in the years when disability was mostly analysed medically or sociologically, for instance in research of interactions of people who differ from the expected norm. Erving Goffman (1963) pointed out that disability and its meanings were socially formed and contextually varied but stressed that disability was often being equate with being broken or impaired. Later, Lennard J. Davis in his book *Enforcing Normalcy* (1995) showed that the contemporary concept of normality appeared in the mid-nineteenth century concurrently with the Industrial Revolution and the development of statistics and eugenics. He suggested that literary novels of that time often reinforced the idea of the norm featuring ordinary, non-heroic protagonists, 'the average men,' while disabled characters (one of his examples was Hippolyte in *Madame Bovary*) typically had a marginal role. In the same vein, David Mitchell and Sharon Snyder argue in *Narrative Prosthesis* (2000) that writers often make use of the representation of disability as a narrative device that can reacknowledge normality on contrast, as a binary opposition in their works. In Johnson's novel, the attention goes back to the subjective experience of non-normative minds instead of the more common question of how society treats disabled or non-normative people. Therefore, these minds are mostly performed or enacted, and not so much described.

Each successive character in the novel is graded by their level of physical and mental disability, which structures their narration and participation in the plot. So those monologues become more fragmented, partial, and incoherent up to a few disconnected words appearing apparently at random on the page. Thus, Johnson suggests the way to represent first-person experience and the fragmentary nature of perception of a collective event. These sequences are brought together by the final section in which House Mother explains the activities that the monologues of previous characters have suggested. "The House Mother is credited with an almost metaphysical degree of control over the lives of her charges [...], but the most important instrument of her power is a discursive one" (Mengham 2014, 123).

The movement of the story that is thematically focused not only on the development of the social evening but also on the nature of mind/consciousness as well. From the first lines of Sarah Lamson's monologue, the reader is presented with a fragmentary but still relatively continuous stream of recollections of her past experiences closely intertwined with highly involved commentaries on her actual experiences:

> ... not like this muck, they give us muck, here, I made him a proper dinner, gave his belly a treat after all that Gas, but he could hardly eat, the poor boy, what I put before him was faggots in a lovely gravy, it was something special I made, for him, just for him, then, not like this slimy brown muck they slosh on everything here, can't think why they do it, what the point is, not on my life, no. (Johnson 1984, 8)

In the case of Ron Lamson, careful description of experience is diffused through the acts of perception and bodily sensation. Permanent laments in his narrative can be characterised through his persistent pain: "How I think about anything else, it's constant, the pain, what else is there to think about, it goes round and round in circles, my mind, off it, on it, not very often off it' (ibid., 82) and strong emotional responses as, for example, during the 'Pass the Parcel' game: "It's stopped, it's me, I can get it undone, I'll win, what is it? SHIT! It's a parcel of shit! Is that what I've won? Is that all? Stinking shit! shit shit shit shit shit shit shit shit shit shit shit shit shit shit shit shit shit shit shit shit shit!" (ibid., 86).

Ron's monologue brings together various combinations of basic embodied (pre-conceptual) experiences that are often represented graphically through blank spaces: "aaaaaaaaaah, the pain shoots, shoots!

I can't Ivy, it's my arse. I'm in constant pain

from it. There's no words to describe it." (ibid., 79–80), repetitions, descriptions of visual or audible signs of that experience, and linguistically mediated conceptual experience.

Gloria Ridge is another character who experiences strong mental confusion, her mind often goes repetitively: "[…] and I was always the most special favorite, I was, I was, I was, I was, I was, I was, I was, I was, I was, I was, I was, I was, I was, I was, was, was,

was!" (ibid., 109). These repetitions may additionally draw readers' attention to questions like: What perceptual experience (of a non-normative mind) is like, and then how such perception is structured. In the novel, it is all rendered in a first-person approach, in terms of meaning it has for the experiencing subject. Gloria's memories, implausible and inconsistent, hold the readers' attention with their familiar commonplace motifs. They turn around her 'one true love', which she remembers several times, and every time as a different person. She constantly uses verbal cliches and conventionality formulas: "[…] blue hair he had with his long black eyes, four foot three in his bloomers, I remember him so clearly […] He was my first, it was raining at the time" (ibid., 98), or later in her monologue: "[…] his hair was golden, his eyes were blue, he stood six feet two in his bare socks, the first one. My one true. […] It was a frosty morning. Frost clears away the flu and does good for England" (ibid., 103). Representation of non-normativity in Johnson's narrative often draws on literary conventions and norms that make communication possible, but at the same time devalue and rule out some possible and actual utterances. In this process, Johnson's exploration of the power relationship in an old people's care home corresponds with contemporary cultural criticism. Nancy Fraser in a thorough analysis of Foucault's genealogical investigation of the notion of power demonstrates that Foucault's genealogy approaches culture not so much as a sign system but rather as practices, being concerned with processes, procedures, and apparatuses whereby truth and knowledge are produced with what Foucault calls the "politics of discursive regime" (Fraser 1981, 274). In modern society power is "capillary" and operates in everyday social practices, rather than through belief systems (ibid., 272). Fraser analyses Foucault's claim that functioning of discursive regimes involves forms of social constraint which typically include such phenomena as "valorisation of some statement forms and the concomitant devaluation of others; the institutional licensing of some persons as being entitled to offer knowledge claims and the concomitant exclusion of others […]," etc. (ibid., 274) These everyday social practices are thoughtfully explored in Johnson's novel.

The last inmate is Rosetta Stanton, her monologue is extremely disjointed. Readers are presented with only several disconnected words in Welsh in which she may try to communicate, therefore, suggesting to the readers the direction of her recollections. These scattered words are followed by the short intelligible English phrases that can be read as parts of a dialogue with Ivy Nichols who (on her pages) had asked Rosetta how she was (Johnson 1984, 65):

> I a m
> T e r r i b l e, I v y
> N o w I c a n e v e r y
> W o r d y o u. s a y I am a prisoner in my
> self. It is terrible. The movement agonises me.
>
> Let me out, or I shall die
> (IBID., 175–76)

After this, Rosetta talks again for the last time, answering Ivy's question if she didn't get any lighter: "Push, how she's a weight. 'DON'T GET ANY LIGHTER, DO YOU, MRS STANTON?'" (ibid., 66) Rosetta answers and the quality of her words is emphasised by the graphic features of the text:

> No, I do
> n o t g e t a n y
> l i g h t e r, I v y,
> I. i n-
> t e n d
> n o t
> t o g e t
> a n y-
> t h I n g
> a n y
> m o r e
>
> n o
> m o r
> (IBID., 176)

And after these words there are six entirely blank pages which may imply that Rosetta has gone into an absolutely unnarratable unconscious state.

It is not quite possible to read such a text consequently, to perceive it as a container of meanings that is ready to be consumed. The reader is supposed to actively collaborate, looking closely at every word and word-combination, immerse into the graphic form of the layout. Instead of linear progression the above fragment emphasises thematic associations, spatio-temporal juxtapositions, simultaneity, and disorder. It liberates the narrative from conventional predictability. Associative meanings are not pre-given, but are enacted by interactions, they may arise when the text in the process of reading engages into its socio-cultural environments.

From the very beginning, in the Introduction by the House Mother, readers are involved into the narrative by the participatory formal dynamic used with the second-person narratee: "You shall see into the minds of our eight old friends [...]" (Johnson 1984, 5). House Mother directly addresses the readers, metaleptically involving them into the novel's disturbing fictional world as if in a mimetic representation of face-to-face communication. This transgression between narrative levels involves the actual audience as the implied addressee of the textual you. Therefore, it provides more reasons for empathy and imaginative immersion and bridges the boundaries between intra- and extra-fictional reference. The you-referent is clearly being addressed on the extradiegetic level as a target of discourse directed at them as the text has an imperative function (Fludernik 2011, 110). At the same time, readers are confronted with metafictional devices seeming to hint at an authorial viewpoint behind the scenes, presented from House Mother's perspective: "You shall see into the minds of our eight old friends, *and you shall see into my mind*: You shall follow our Social Evening through nine different minds!" (Johnson 1984, 5, my emphasis). This strategy draws attention to the fictionality of the text. It becomes even more distinct at the end of the novel, where a text's metaleptic move multiplies the voices, and 'the writer' comes to the front of this multi-layered word-texture:

> And here you see, friend, I am about to step outside the convention, the framework of twenty-one pages per person. Thus you see I too am the puppet or concoction of a writer (you always knew there was a writer behind it all? Ah, there's no fooling you readers!), a writer who has me at present standing in the post-orgasmic nude but who still expects me to be his words without embarrassment or personal comfort. So you see this is from his skull. It is a diagram of certain aspects of the inside of his skull! What a laugh! (ibid., 203–04)

Thus, metalepsis undermines the ontological stability of the protagonist's discourse and emphasises the constructedness of the narrative shifting from intra- to extradiegetic levels. House Mother refers to her own discourse as a projection of "certain aspects of the inside of [the writer's] skull," or affectively exclaims: "Oh, Ralphie! Faster! We're getting near the end of the page, Ralphie! oooooh! oh! iiiiiihl! oooooh! nearly! YES!" (ibid., 202) Minds are evoked mimetically, but metafictional comments undermine the illusion of authenticity associated with mimeticism, draw attention to the fictional status of the text and disrupt readers' immersion.

## 3 Tim Crouch's *House Mother Normal*: Dematerialised Bodies, Embodied Minds

Crouch's *House Mother Normal* suggests an interpretation of Johnson's novel representing people with a variety of impairments on screen. But what does Crouch accentuate in his interpretation? Is it the question of normality? Are those people on the screen tragic, damaged, inferior? Are they bad, broken, or wrong? Are they pitiable persons? There are almost no visible or audible signs of disability by them, the audience is presented mostly with just words and rhythm: disability is being constructed exclusively discursively. In this section I focus on the ways in which Crouch's installation evokes minds using visual aspects of simultaneous characters' representation on screen alongside the audible deployment of voices, pauses and sounds, words, and music: "nine voices orchestrated into a spoken-word symphony of old age and absurdism" (Brighton Festival, online).

The installation presents monologues of all the characters, happening simultaneously on nine screens. The characters speaking the monologues are all played by elderly actors, to stress visually the theme of old age. Monologues are predominantly performed unemotionally, actors distance themselves from the characters' minds. Actors represent the narrative of Johnson's novel, rather than experience it or immerse in the characters' consciousness, so that the audience is hindered from identifying with characters in the artwork. Crouch has filmed each monologue separately and then mixed them together. Thus, the viewer simultaneously experiences characters' perceptions, evaluations, dialogues with others, memoirs, associative thinking that interact with their environments. The viewers can also watch every individual monologue separately, these are subtitled, the words by Rosetta Stanton (who mostly utters disconnected Welsh words) are translated.

As Lloyd Evans from *The Spectator* wittily observed: "Tim Crouch has directed a Zoom version of B.S. Johnson's satire *House Mother Normal* […]" (2021). The characters' heads and shoulders appear on screen against a plain black background so that nothing can distract the viewer from the monologues. The grievances, complaints, and reflections of the characters overwhelm the viewer's attention, overstimulating it with the fluxes of utterances, exclamations, and emotions so that speeches are often inaudible. A viewer needs to invest considerable efforts to focus on the characters' trains of thoughts, mind wanderings or recollections. Harvey Bassett from the *Exeunt Magazine* (2021) assessed Crouch's digital installation as a form of a 'deluge' of voices from a nursing home. Lloyd Evans endorsed this attitude: "Perhaps the aim is naturalism, but it makes for stressful viewing." (2021) At the same time, Crouch occasionally increases or lowers the loudness to emphasise some elements of speeches which fade in and out giving the audience some hints of the plot movements or frames for interpretation.

According to Alva Noë, experience itself is not only something we undergo, but something that happens to us: "perception is action" (2004). If to assume, following Noë, that an access to something is more important than a representation of this something in full detail, then we can suppose that the way Johnson enacts the narrators' mind processes in his novel was the most relevant to convey these understandings to the readership. The narrators in the novel set the puzzle of various fragments which on their own do not have so much importance – they are rather simple events or descriptions: a dinner, a memoir, a play, etc. But set together they give access to the process of mind functioning. Therefore, we may see Johnson's fragmentariness in *House Mother Normal* as a relevant development of artistic research into understanding of human cognition. Following these ideas, Crouch's *House mother Normal* may be regarded as a passage from relative statics of representation of separated or connected events and states of affair to the dynamics of representation of actual mental processes in which conventions of 'normality' appear to be rather insignificant and provisional. Using literary conventions, Johnson constructs the 'story' of the novel and explores (on the story level) power relationships in the care home. Crouch's installation is a research into the understanding of the human cognition; for the representation of fictional mental functioning the meanings of the literary conventions as used by Johnson are not very significant. The meaning of the whole here emerges (discursively) in a different way.

Monologues in which the characters' minds wander remembering past events and experience, or they comment on the ongoing events, or share their plans and action-oriented thoughts, are performed in a relatively detached manner with minimal gestures and movements of the performers. Only rarely do they demonstrate feelings or strong emotional reactions (disgust, or fascination). For instance, the viewers hear sighs, fast or heavy breathing, or can see visual signs of pain by Ron Lamson: his tense and anguished but at the same time detached face. This juxtaposition generates the contrast between highly emotional narratives of Johnson's characters and their 'stage' representations.

Crouch, for whom theatre is "closer to being a conceptual artwork than a figurative or representational form" uses this form (of the digital installation) as a kind of sub-plot to Johnson's story (2014). In an interview to the *Aesthetica Magazine* Crouch states that "form is a uniquely contemporary expression. Form talks about 'now' – about how we are and how we communicate to each other. It can speak more forcefully than the stories it contains" (2014). Building on the ideas of conceptual art, Crouch breaks the primacy of the perceptual in a work of art in favour of the compositional and formal structures of language. Through the rhythmical qualities of the monologues, he composes a soundscape beyond representation.

And what is represented in the installation? I suggest that it may represent a specific *way* of grasping reality – perceiving reality, the *processes* of perception of an object rather than specific objects or subjects themselves. The more 'non-normative' the minds of the house's elderly inmates become, the less 'content' is represented in their words. Content in the representational picture is something mental that underlies and supports what it is possible to say in language, to respond to the world. It is always *about* something; it may give clues but may remain almost inconceivable. This form and method of cultural production may reveal how our understanding and sensory experiences of being in the world are shaped. And if to follow the idea that enactive intentionality is not conceived in terms of representation, but as a kind of action-oriented responses to worldly events and to other agents, these responses can be treated as dynamically unfolding interactions with worldly offerings, as in the case of George Hedbury when the readers have just a few words and lots of blank spaces:

> Package
> for me pass,            parc
> what?.
>
> (JOHNSON 1984, 152)

I contend that the installation formally emphasises a collective voice of a group experiencing an event. Characters in the installation speak all at once, making possible a collective identity. What does it mean? Tim Crouch also suggests that in his video installation "the power of the group transcends individual stories. This is an orchestra of voices, not a series of solos. I hope the audience can release themselves into this extraordinary polyphony" (Brighton Festival, online).

Monika Fludernik discusses the representations of collectives from a narratological perspective, exploring the collective at the levels of agency, mind, and narration. She studies groups that function as agents, narrators, focalisers, and traces the collective in three narratological dimension: action – on the plot level, thought or attitude – consciousness, and narration – group engaged in collective storytelling (2017, 141). In Johnson's novel various characters show different degrees of involvement into 'we'-narration. There is an alternation between collective 'we' and individual agency. House Mother in her introduction exaggeratedly uses 'we'-narration, giving the story the direction of the communal storytelling of shared experience: "[…] these are also *our* friends. *We* no longer refer to them as inmates, cases, patients, or even the clients. […] You may if you wish join our Social Evening, friend" (Johnson 1984, 5, my emphasis). Sarah Lamson also starts with the collective identification at the centre: "… not like this muck, they give *us* muck, here […]" (ibid., 8). As her mind moves into memoirs she switches to her singular pronoun. Charlie Edwards in his monologue uses mostly first-person singular, starting almost every sentence with 'I.' Only some shared actions as, for example, singing (ibid., 33) or in the conversation with other inmates (ibid., 43, 45) are narrated with 'we.' Ivy Nicholls remembers her old days and friends using 'we' (ibid., 52), signalling that she still includes herself in that life experiences and they have the same significance as the actual 'we' that includes her care home company. So does Sioned Bowen, remembering her work colleagues as she worked as a servant (ibid., 118). Thus, 'we' narration is used to characterise inmates' degree of involvement in actual events or their rootedness to the past life.

The composition of the installation discloses the performative aspect of Johnson's narration more prominently. Instead of a consecutive demonstration of different ways of experiencing the world by the characters with progressing dementia, it constructs a single discourse by a heterogeneity of a collective mind in the processes of various experiences. But still, the installation may represent 'fictional mental functioning', narrating experience as it is being experienced (perceived, or recalled, or imagined) by a range of minds installed in various (outer) information streams and (inner) conscious and non-conscious processes, and it conveys the shared ways of thinking – rather collective than individual experience. It involves the viewers in processes of communicative interactions and constantly switches the frame of reference from the content to the ways it is represented.

In Crouch's interpretation, *House Mother Normal* comes out of the constraints imposed by the textual form and represents vividly the simultaneity of multiple projections of different minds and their experiences. Although a problem may appear with the issue in question – 'representation' of mind in the installation – enactivist ideas may providc a solution. We represent things but it is not the only way to think. Thinking is not a manipulation of representational items within a 'container' of the mind. Understanding relates to language skills and cultural backgrounds – the 'what' is being understood *and* the way, 'how' it is going. Additionally, we are immersed in shared cultural and linguistic participatory everyday practices, common-sense assumptions about the world. Daniel Hutto and Erik Myin argue that there can be intentionally-directed cognition and perceptual experience without content: "our most elementary ways of engaging with the world and others – including our basic forms of perception and perceptual experience – are mindful in the sense of being phenomenally charged and intentionally directed, despite being non-representational and content-free" (2012, 13). They stress that not all activity requires individuals to construct representations of their worlds. This argument is based on the ideas claiming that the perceived world is constructed through complex patterns of sensorimotor activity (Varela et al. 1991, 164).

## 4 Conclusion

In this paper, I juxtaposed a literary novel and its interpretation in a multimodal installation. B.S. Johnson stands as a one of the principal precursors of current trends of fragmentation, giving voice to marginalisation and displacement. Crouch's work contributes to the recontextualisation of Johnson's text. As a conceptual work, Crouch's *House Mother Normal* favours words (written in the novel) as substituting for the object itself (social evening in a care home). The audience perceives the narratives given in the installation, partially and contradictory (because monologues occur in simultaneity), and fills in the informational and emotional landscapes through a personal investment of contextualising and sense-making. The task of the audience is no longer the reconstruction and retracing of any pre-given story, but rather the mobilisation of their own ability to actively experience the processes offered to them. The story projected on the screens turns out to be extremely fictional. If Johnson's novel stresses its fictionality, Crouch's interpretation exaggerates it because it is aimed not at the wholeness of an aesthetic composition of words, gestures, and sounds. On the contrary, it draws attention to the fragmentariness and the incomprehensibility of the monologues. Hans-Thies Lehmann points out in his *Postdramatic Theatre*:

> Once the formerly 'glued together' aspects of language and body separate in theatre, character representation and audience address are each treated as autonomous realities; once the sound space separates from the playing space, new representational chances come about through the autonomi[s]ation of the individual layers. (2006, 51)

Thus, Crouch deconstructs dramatic elements of the novel (disintegrates them and then puts together in a different way). Though he does not offer a representation of Johnson's novel, he provides the audience with the opportunity for the shared lived experience occurring in the interaction between Johnson's text (as a main protagonist), actors, and the viewers.

My analysis suggests that the text's rhythmical constructions together with the possibilities for the reader's free associations and bodily feelings that may emerge in response to the multimodal stimulation that thematises bodily practices, can participate in audience's engagement with the text. Drawing upon enactivist approaches in cognitive narratology and cultural analysis, I argue that Crouch's artwork not so much presents to the viewers the interpretation of the Johnson's story but rather enacts the experimental discourse of the novel. Under these circumstances Johnson's text shows a way of breaking through limitations of verbal narrative forms with their conventions and clichés. Being mostly incoherent in the stories it tells, being simultaneously a piece of literature, a work of visual art, and a performance, Crouch's installation does not illustrate, narrate, or present events occurring on the social evening in a care home for the elderly. Instead, the installation artistically mediates the processes of perceiving, remembering, or imagining occurring in a contemporary cultural situation. The latter can be described as including such relevant for the present study characteristics as globalisation with its overwhelming fluxes of information, diversity and inclusiveness, and the impact of the pandemic on art practices.

Fictional non-normative minds are represented in the novel as well as in the digital installation as a relational process of sense-making occurring in constant interactions with the world and other minds. Thus, these minds are mostly performed or enacted, and not so much described. Moreover, as there are almost no visible or audible signs of disability by the actors performing the Johnson's characters in Crouch's installation, the audience is presented mostly with 'just' words and rhythms: non-normativity is being constructed discursively.

## Works Cited

Bassett, Harvey. "Review: House Mother Normal at Brighton festival (online)." *Exeunt Magazine*, 09.05.2021. http://exeuntmagazine.com/reviews/review-house-mother-normal-brighton-festival/

Bernaerts, Lars. "Minds at Play: Narrative Games and Fictional Minds in B.S. Johnson's *House Mother Normal*." *Style*, vol. 48, no. 3, 2014, pp. 294–312.

Brighton Festival. https://brightonfestival.org/whats-on/house-mother-normal-online-3112/. Accessed 16.05.2022.

Coe, Jonathan. *Like a Fiery Elephant. The Story of B.S. Johnson*. Picador, 2004.

Crouch, Tim. Interview. *Aesthetica Magazine, 05.05.2014*. https://aestheticamagazine.com/interview-with-tim-crouch-writer-and-director-of-royal-courts-adler-and-gibb/

Crouch, Tim. "5 Minutes with Theatre-maker Tim Crouch." *New Perspectives Theatre Company*. 2021. https://www.newperspectives.co.uk/?idno=1170&p=88&s=Tim%20 Crouch Accessed 16.05.2022.

Darlington, Joseph. "B.S. Johnson: The Book as Dynamic Object." *British Avant-Garde Fiction of the 1960s*. Ed. Kaye Mitchell and Nonia Williams. Edinburgh UP, 2019, pp. 36–53.

Davis, Lennard J. *Enforcing Normalcy: Deafness, Disability, and the Body*. London: Verso, 1995.

Evans, Lloyd. "A Last Hurrah for the Zoom Play." *The Spectator*, 22.05.2021. https://www.spectator.co.uk/article/a-last-hurrah-for-the-zoom-play

Fludernik, Monika. "The Category of 'Person' in Fiction: *You* and *We* Narrative-Multiplicity and Indeterminacy of Reference." *Current Trends in Narratology*. Ed Greta Olson. Berlin, New York: De Gruyter, 2011, pp. 101–42.

Fludernik, Monika. "The Many in Action and Thought: Towards a Poetics of the Collective in Narrative." *Narrative*, vol. 25, no. 2, 2017, pp. 139–63.

Fraser, Nancy. "Foucault on Modern Power: Empirical Insights and Normative Confusions." *Praxis International*, vol. 1, no. 3, 1981, pp. 272–87.

Gallagher, Shaun. *How the Body Shapes the Mind*. Oxford: Clarendon Press, 2005.

Goffman, Erving. *Stigma: Notes on the Management of Spoiled Identity*. New York: Simon, 1963.

Groes, Sebastian. *British Fictions of the Sixties: the Making of the Swinging Decade*. London: Bloomsbury, 2016.

Hutto, Daniel. *Beyond Physicalism*. Amsterdam: John Benjamins, 2000.

Hutto, Daniel and Erik Myin. *Radicalizing Enactivism: Basic Minds Without Content*. Cambridge, MA: The MIT Press, 2012.

Johnson, B.S. *Aren't You Rather Young to Be Writing Your Memoirs?* London: Hutchinson, 1973.

Johnson, B.S. *House Mother Normal. A Geriatric Comedy*. London: Bloodaxe Books, [1971] 1984.

Jordan, Julia. *Late Modernism and the Avant-Garde British Novel. Oblique Strategies*. Oxford: Oxford UP, 2020.

Lehmann, Hans-Thies. *Postdramatic Theatre*. Transl. Karen Jürs-Munby. London and New York: Routledge, 2006.

Malicka, Joanna. "Mapping Multiple Voices in B. S. Johnson's 'House Mother Normal.'" ANGLICA - *An International Journal of English Studies*, vol. 21, no. 1, 2012, pp. 41–60.

Mengham, Rod. "Antepostdated Johnson." Ed. Jordan, Julia and Martin Ryle. *B.S. Johnson and Post-War Literature Possibilities of the Avant Garde*. Basingstoke: Palgrave Macmillan, 2014, pp. 121–35.

Mitchell, David, and Sharon Snyder. *Narrative Prosthesis: Disability and the Dependencies of Discourse*. Ann Arbor: U of Michigan P, 2000.

Noë, Alva. *Action in Perception*. Combridge, MA: The MIT Press, 2004.

Sayer, Andrew. *Why Things Matter to People: Social Science, Values and Ethical Life*. Cambridge: Cambridge UP, 2011.

Tew, Philip and Glyn White, eds. *Re-reading B. S. Johnson*. Basingstoke: Palgrave Macmillan, 2007.

Thompson, Evan. *Mind in Life: Biology, Phenomenology, and the Sciences of Mind*. Harvard UP, 2007.

Varela, Francisco J., Evan Thompson, and Eleanor Rosch. *The Embodied Mind*. Cambridge, MA: The MIT Press, 1991.

CHAPTER 5

# Altered Consciousness in 1960s American Science Fiction: a Corpus-Stylistic Analysis

*Elizabeth Oakes*

## 1 Introduction

As early as 1969, ecologist Paul Shepard described human beings as parts of an environmental whole, capturing our embeddedness in the environment through the arresting image of our porous skin as a blurred boundary with bacteria, soil, air, and the basic materials of the natural world (2015, 63). This image would not feel out of place among present day 4E and posthuman philosophies. Already in 1961, science fiction author Daniel F. Galouye thematised the same interrelation with the natural world, depicting altered states of consciousness as particularly capable of connecting both mind and body with the environment. In his novel *Dark Universe* (1961), the protagonist renews his whole society through the self-understanding and connection with others created by environmental embeddedness enabled by altered consciousness. If science fiction does not always directly inspire the future it imagines, perhaps its speculations echo quieter cultural trends already underway, part of a process of magnification and promulgation.

Galouye is hardly unique among 1960s science fiction authors in construing altered consciousness as a vital perspective into social issues and a tool for speculating on alternate routes into the future. Roger Zelazny, for example, portrays the fallibility precipitated by altered consciousness as nevertheless leaving the sufferer's humanity intact, proposing a more humane view of the mentally ill in his 1966 novel *The Dream Master*. At the time, "[c]onsciousness, subjectivity, and hallucination" became central concerns in the genre "matched by a new self-consciousness in style" (Stockwell 2000, 9). Indeed, the styles in which these authors depicted mental disturbances, irregularities, and alterations in consciousness are deeply entwined with the thematics of their texts, thematics in interplay with contemporaneous cultural currents. Understanding the style of altered consciousness, then, can reveal something about the connection between science fictional speculation and the cultural changes of a tumultuous decade, changes that still ripple in current day society.

 | DOI:10.1163/9789004519886_007

This article explores a corpus of Hugo and Nebula winning and nominated science fiction novels published in the 1960s that contain depictions of focalising characters experiencing altered states of consciousness, namely through dreams, drug use, and madness. During this particular decade, many authors centred altered consciousness in their works. Authors use it to take different perspectives on a variety of themes, to present in fresh ways issues in close connection to the psychological interior of characters, the inner space formulated by James Ballard and central to SF of the time (Gordon 2014). Altered consciousness provides a site melding the psychological interior of characters with issues like environmentalism and community building in ways that feel immediate and fresh even half a century later. Algis Budrys' *Rogue Moon* (1960), Daniel F. Galouye's *Dark Universe* (1961), Harry Harrison's *Planet of the Damned* (1962), Phillip K. Dick's *The Three Stigmata of Palmer Eldritch* (1964), Fritz Leiber's *The Wanderer* (1964), Andre Norton's *The X Factor* (1965), Frederik Pohl's *A Plague of Pythons* (1965), Samuel R. Delany's *Babel-17* (1966), Roger Zelazny's *The Dream Master* (1966), and Thomas M. Disch's *Camp Concentration* (1968) comprise the corpus.

Analysing the corpus with two categorical dictionary programs, statistical methods on the dictionary data with R, and lexically focused stylistic methods, two groups of texts emerge. The distinct thematic groupings uncovered by the corpus analysis complicate traditional conceptions of 1960s science fiction. While New Wave authors have been considered as intimately linked to the 1960s counterculture and the bleeding edge of experimental style (Latham 2014), in fact, a group of novels by popular authors, many unassociated with the New Wave, engages with emerging social and environmental concerns through the lens of altered consciousness in a way that suggests a different kind of avant-garde. Their particular brand of social engagement would expand during the 1970s and in certain respects even appears fresh in light of thematic trends in science fiction today.

## 2 Computational Methods and Text Groupings

I applied two categorical dictionaries to the corpus, Colin Martindale's Regressive Imagery Dictionary (RID) and David Kaufer and Suguru Ishizaki's DocuScope. The RID detects and characterises altered states of consciousness in texts through sorting individual words into nested categories and giving percentages of the total word count that belong to each category. It is designed around the schematisation of mental processes as polarised into conceptual, rational processes versus dedifferentiated, primordial processes

(Martindale 2008, 234).[1] Examining the RID data, two groups emerged based on the Primary – Secondary summary category percentage difference and the Icarian Imagery and Regressive Knowledge categories. Galouye, Dick, and Pohl's novels form one group, and Zelazny, Disch, Leiber, and Harrison's form another. The remaining three texts in the corpus did not share any researcher-detectable stylistic pattern in the dictionary data and are not considered in the following analysis. K-means cluster analysis of the complete dataset supported this grouping without completely replicating it, suggesting that if a researcher could simultaneously take into account all 43 categories of the RID, a slightly modified concept of styles might emerge. While seeking computational support for the findings presented, this approach prioritises researcher interpretation of the data over statistical interpretation as such features are demonstrably accessible to readers and capable of extending their influence beyond the text.

Similar to the RID, DocuScope sorts individual words into nested categories; however, the dictionary is built on rhetorical principles.[2] DocuScope primarily detects sentiment, register, and rhetorical effects. DocuScope's category percentages suggested the same grouping of authors based on the most frequent categories occurring in the altered state passages: Descriptive, Character, and Subjective Register Clusters.[3] Principle component analysis of the DocuScope with R confirmed the groupings.[4]

Computational analysis offers the benefits of being quick, consistent, and replicable while also facilitating a scalar approach capable of linking fine-grained textual specifics to corpus level generalisations (Martindale and West 2002, 377). However, only a researcher's interpretation can make computational data relevant. (Piper 2018, 11). Because this particular style of computational analysis focuses on the lexical level of the text, I take a lexically focused stylistic approach as the starting point of interpretation. I interpret each group

1 The referenced article contains a list of theories constructed around similar frameworks and upon which Martindale structures his Regressive Imagery Dictionary. See also Martindale and West (2002) for detailed description of the dictionary structure and evidence of the validity of the dictionary construct.

2 A detailed account of the underlying principles and structure is given in Kaufer, Ishizaki, Butler, and Collins (2004). Although DocuScope is not explicitly referenced, the dictionary is firmly based on the catalogue described.

3 DocuScope is organised into a nested structure of categories. The dictionary terms the highest, or roughest-grained level Clusters, mid-level are referred to as Dimensions, and the lowest level are LATS, or language action types.

4 All levels counted, DocuScope sorts texts into 172 categories. This proved difficult to process as many of the LATs, the finest grained level, contained no words. To facilitate the statistical analysis, only Dimensions and Clusters were included in the PCA dataset.

of texts demonstrating how themes arise from stylistic elements, and then discuss the thematic groupings in terms of social and cultural forces. Along with Piper, I agree that "paying attention to quantity reveals the grooves and channels of cultural expression, the deep connections among words, ideas, and forms" (ibid., 3).

## 3 Connection and Communication Group

The Connection and Communication Group comprises Daniel F. Galouye's *Dark Universe*, Philip K. Dick's *The Three Stigmata of Palmer Eldritch*, and Frederik Pohl's *A Plague of Pythons*. These popular science fiction authors, already well recognised in the 1950s, continued to command sizable audiences through the 1960s and after. Examining the RID data for this group, in altered state passages in relation to default passages, the percentage of Secondary summary category words stays the same while the percentage of Primary summary category words increases. The result is a Primary – Secondary percentage difference greater in altered passages by one to four percentage points as compared to default state passages. There is an increase in Regressive Knowledge category words in altered passages relative to default passages. In the DocuScope data, these authors use higher percentages of Character and Subjective Register Cluster words in altered state passages relative to default state passages.

A point of thematic note, in the novels by this group of authors, altered consciousness arises from the loss of control resultant of a shared mind space. Altered consciousness is a form of dream-facilitated mental communication in *Dark Universe*. Similarly, in *The Three Stigmata of Palmer Eldritch*, the focalising characters ingest various drugs that allow them to share mental landscapes with other users. In *A Plague of Pythons*, Pohl depicts a kind of possession that results in two minds sharing a body. In all these novels, altered consciousness expands the self by first blurring the boundaries between self and other. Focalisers generally experience this weakening of boundaries as initially terrifying, but as time spent in the altered state progresses, the experience becomes less negatively valenced, perhaps even positive. Altered consciousness is a gateway to knowledge that enables personal transformation.

This understanding of altered consciousness is a clear reflection of developments in clinical psychiatry beginning in the 1950s and spilling out of the lab and into popular culture by the end of the 1960s. From the early 1950s over a thousand papers had been published on the clinical uses of psychedelics, and the results had been put into practice in the treatment of conditions such as depression and schizophrenia (Pollan 2018, 141). LSD therapy garnered highly publicised praise from celebrities as a method of ego reduction and self-discovery that improved the ability to relate to others, and by the end of the decade, the drug began to see use outside of the clinical context (ibid., 157).[5] Texts in the Connection and Communication Group portray altered consciousness in line with the initially positive attitudes toward psychedelics.

Galouye styles altered consciousness as a place of perception rather than action, but the inward perception of the focaliser's own body is projected outward into the environment. *Dark Universe,* a mixed *Bildungsroman* and adventure, depicts a young man attempting to expand his society's understanding of their world. Centuries after nuclear war, the shelters to which humanity retreated have failed. People have mutated, developing echolocation and other adaptations to survive in the complete darkness of a cave system. In the following quotation, the focaliser, Jared, in a dream-like state as a result of injury, perceives the surroundings of his mixed telepathic dream state as mirroring the struggling condition of his body. The RID's Regressive Knowledge words are in italics.

> He had stood *beside* it many times, running his *hands over* its slick moistness and listening to the beauty of the drops.
>
> Yet, even as he aimed his clicks directly *at* it now, it changed like a living thing, growing until its *tip* actually touched the water, then shrinking *back* into the ceiling. *Nearby*, the mouth of a pit *opened* and *closed* menacingly. And the *passage* itself contracted and expanded as though it were a giant's lung. (Galouye 1961, 30–31)

The Regressive Knowledge category contains words indicating a focus on the body and its location in horizontal space that is common to the group. The Regressive Knowledge words in the opening of the passage describe the location and motion of Jared, but as he runs his hands over the rock, these words begin to appear describing the location and movement of the natural environment as though it were a living being.

Galouye uses mainly active verbs and verbal forms in his altered passages, but of the twelve active verbal forms in the first quotation, the focaliser, Jared is the subject or actor of only four. The other verbs describe actions of the

5 Martin A. Lee and Bruce Shlain (1985) thoroughly document the spread and reception of psychedelics in America in chapters two through five of *Acid Dreams: The Complete Social History of LSD: The CIA, the Sixties, and Beyond.* See also Tom Wolfe's *Electric Kool-Aid Acid Test* for documentation of the 1960s counterculture's relationship with LSD.

environment. The environment seems contiguous with Jared yet acts on its own. He recalls contact with, and perception of his environment followed by two verbs of transformation, "changed" and "growing." Then, six of the active verbs depict a rhythmic fluctuation mirroring Jared's struggling breath and perhaps the turmoil of his sickened insides. The verbal progression depicts sympathetic contact, transformation, and finally identification with the environment.

The DocuScope categories capture this progression from a different viewpoint. The Clusters that most strongly characterise the Connection and Communication Group are Reporting (underlined with blue in the following quote), Character (purple), and Subjective Register (red), and all three characterise the passage.

It opens with four Character words belonging to the Personal Pronoun *Dimension*. The dictionary description document describes such words as creating a sense of "[t]he text as a stream of persons, referenced and re-referenced as topics that can persist throughout the discourse" ("DocuScope LAT List" 2012, 14). The focus on Jared as an individual, self-contained person that these words create flips as the passage continues. Subjective Register words belonging to the Personal Register Dimension replace the Personal Pronouns. The dictionary description outlines Personal Register words as "the leaking of private information … or of inner being … creat[ing a] feeling of nearness and proximity to the action … perceptions [that] tell us as much about the perceiver as the perceived" (ibid., 2). Such words also depict a character, but rather than as a discrete person, as a mind in contact with its surroundings, the interrelation of the perceiver and the perceived are foregrounded. The shift from Personal Pronouns to Personal register accomplishes a shift from self-contained character to environmentally entangled character. Both Dimensions appear among a steady flow of Reporting Cluster words, which "functions as a window-on-the-world, making known states, events, processes, and change," creating a "mental model of a world that is both steady and changing, fixed and dynamic, routine and subject to historical change" (ibid., 11). Such words encompass the profound shift depicted in Jared's consciousness, creating a stable backdrop, a mental model for what could otherwise be a disorienting transformation of

below with melodious monotony, for instance. He had stood beside it many times, running his hands over its slick moistness and listening to the beauty of the drops. Yet, even as he aimed his clicks directly at it now, it changed like a living thing, growing until its tip actually touched the water, then shrinking back into the ceiling. Nearby, the mouth of a pit opened and closed menacingly And the passage itself contracted and expanded as though it were a giant's lung. "Don't be afraid, Jared. "A gentle, feminine voice stirred the deep silence."

FIGURE 5.1 Galouye 1961, 30–31, highlighted by DocuScope. The Character Dimension is underlined with purple, Reporting with blue, and Subjective Register with red.

perception and experience. Notably this backdrop is world-oriented rather than character-oriented, emphasising the whole rather than the individual as the persistent, if fluctuating, location of identity and interrelation.

Not only does the environment commingle with Jared, but it extends also into the physical being of others. Yet later, Jared observes another person while in a dream-like state.

> Had it not been for the movement of his *hand*, he might easily have been mistaken for a skeleton. The *head*, trembling with an affliction of senility, was like a *skull*. And the *beard*, unkempt and sparse, *trailed* to the ground, losing itself in the inaudibility of its thinness.
>
> Tap-tap-tap … drip-drip …
>
> Jared was *back* in the *corridor*. And, like commingling sounds, the straggly *beard* had metamorphosed into the moist hanging stone. (Galouye 1961, 87)

Similar to the first passage, an old man's body is described using italicised Regressive Knowledge words, but as the passage continues, these words link and then transmute him into the stone corridor. The old man's beard becomes the stone which Jared's hand had been touching. This circular movement from the body, into the environment, into another character, into the environment, and back into the body is typical of the altered passages. Although Jared remains the focalising character, his point of view disperses through his surroundings, physical and interpersonal.

Analysis of the DocuScope data for this passage suggests a complementary extension of interpretation. Again, in Figure 5.2, Personal Pronouns (Character Cluster, purple) shift to Subjective Register words (red), and as the passage returns to Jared as an embodied, discrete character, the Personal Pronouns appear again. As in the first passage, Reporting words appear throughout.

Altered consciousness provides a site for connection with the environment and with others. As Jared slips into this telepathic dream state, categories of

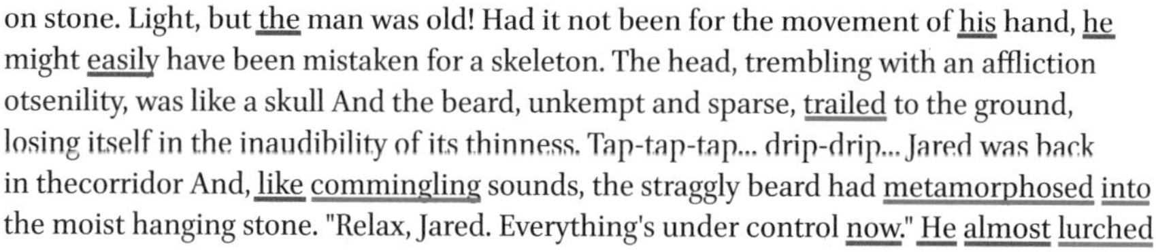
on stone. Light, but the man was old! Had it not been for the movement of his hand, he might easily have been mistaken for a skeleton. The head, trembling with an affliction otsenility, was like a skull And the beard, unkempt and sparse, trailed to the ground, losing itself in the inaudibility of its thinness. Tap-tap-tap... drip-drip... Jared was back in thecorridor And, like commingling sounds, the straggly beard had metamorphosed into the moist hanging stone. "Relax, Jared. Everything's under control now." He almost lurched

FIGURE 5.2 Galouye 1961, 87, highlighted by DocuScope. The Character Dimension is underlined with purple, Reporting with blue, and Subjective Register with red.

spring where he might fashion steaming poultices and tend their wounds. He struck a rock, bounced off , stood swaying for a while, then staggered on. Around the next bend he waded through an arm of the river and collapsed when he reached dry land again. The stream flowed off through the wall and before them stretched a broad, dry passage. Pulling himself forward with the hand that still clutched the spears, he dragged Della along with him. Then he paused, listening to a drip-drip that came with a melodious monotony. His spear point touched rock and the thunk provided him with a composite of the passageway. It was a strangely familiar corridor, with its slender hanging stone dripping cold water into the puddle below, not too far away from a single, well-defined pit. He felt sure he had been here many times before; had stood beside that moist needle of rock and run his hands over its cool, slick contours.

FIGURE 5.3 Galouye 1961, 86, highlighted with DocuScope. Character words are underlined with purple, Reporting with blue, Subjective Register with red, and Sensory Language with yellow.

words suggestive of a bodily anchored ego reduce in frequency,[6] replaced by words that depict an interrelated viewpoint. It is not a complete suspension of ego, as Personal Register words reoccur to distinguish Jared from the others that he meets in this altered state. Yet the Subjective Register words reoccur with higher frequency, attenuating the ego and creating a close connection, though not complete identification, with these other characters.

Let me briefly illustrate the contrastive effect of default state consciousness passages, where Jared struggles with the environment and relation to other characters.

The passage in Figure 5.3 contains nine Character Cluster words occurring fairly evenly throughout, but only two Subjective Register words, neither of them from the Personal Register Dimension. Jared perceives the world as separate from within himself in a pattern of Character words interspersed with Sensory Language Cluster words. This Cluster relates the five senses "to specific features of a person or object [and] to the perception and orientation of objects" ("DocuScope LAT List" 2012, 3). Rather than the interrelation with the environment created by Personal Register words, the combination of Character and Sensory Language words portray Jared perceiving the environment through his senses as external. He has arrived again at the pillar of stone and the pit described in both altered state passages as contiguous with himself. Contrastively, in the default state passage he finds them unfamiliar. In the altered state passages, the Reporting cluster words created a world-oriented backdrop, describing movements, transformations, and states of the environment.

6 By ego, I refer to Thomas Metzinger's phenomenal self-model (PSM). In Metzinger's words, "The content of the PSM is the Ego" (2009, 6). In other words, the PSM can be described as a phenomenal ego, "the content of an inner image – namely, the conscious self-model [...] by placing the self-model within the world-model, a center is created. That center is what we experience as ourselves, the Ego" (ibid., 7). See chapters one and two of Metzinger's *The Ego Tunnel: The Science of the Mind and the Myth of the Self* for a detailed description of the structure and function of the PSM.

In the default state passage, the Reporting words "tend," "stood," "collapsed," "reached," and "dragged" focus on Jared struggling in relation to the environment and the other character in the passage, Della. His containment within a firmly bounded ego communicates as difficulty. Still, many of the Sensory Language words indicate an appreciation of the environment as beautiful or useful. Jared knocks his spear against a rock to hear his surroundings, working with the environment to navigate it. He notices again the "slender hanging stone dripping cold water" from its "cool, slick contours" (Galouye 1961, 86), imagery suggestive of beauty. However, the portrayal of the environment as part of an extended self in the altered passages clearly contrasts with the environment perceived as external to a bounded, defined self in the default state.

Galouye, along with the other authors in the Connection and Communication Group, link altered consciousness to themes of environmental and human interrelatedness. This theme of communion rises directly out of elements of style such as use of Regressive Knowledge words to describe elements of the exterior world as though internal to the character and a pattern of Subjective Register and Character Cluster words that allows a character to focalise without fixing the viewpoint to an ego. At the lexical and thematic level, altered consciousness is relaxation of the ego and communion with others. In all three novels, altered consciousness affords a place of personal development. Characters must renegotiate their relationship to the body, to others, and to the environment, and they emerge with more self-knowledge. Indeed, this connection with a deeper self shapes the plot arc and governs the outcome in all three novels. Altered consciousness is a type of embodied interrelation that fosters change. However, this is not the case in the depiction of altered consciousness in the Void and Disorder Group.

## 4 Void and Disorder Group

In the computational analysis, the style of depicting altered states in Roger Zelazny's *The Dream Master* bears similarity to that in Thomas M. Disch's *Camp Concentration* and Fritz Leiber's *The Wanderer*. More surprisingly Harry Harrison's *Planet of the Damned* also falls into this first grouping of authors. While Disch, like many contemporaneous American science fiction authors, rejected the New Wave appellation, both he and Zelazny engaged in the kind of literary experimentation and preoccupation with inner space that typifies the subgenre. Evident in both novels, patterns of reference signal an identification with "high" literature rather than "genre" or "popular" literature. That pattern of reference is responsible in part for the style in which altered states are depicted. Leiber is also sometimes classified as New Wave due to his association with authors in this group and inclusion in several key anthologies although his writing shifts in style between New Wave experimentation and popular science fiction (Latham 2014).

The inclusion of a popular author, Harry Harrison, appears to disrupt the interpretation of the Void and Disorder Group as aligned with the New Wave, until the stylistic moves made in the altered consciousness passages are examined. Harrison included one short passage of altered consciousness in *Planet of the Damned*, and its style exceeds most New Wave texts in experimentality. Harrison structures this passage like concrete poetry and makes heavy use of poetic effects such as alliteration, onomatopoeia, and rhythm. Considered as a complete text, *Planet of the Damned* reads as a popular novel, yet the altered passages considered in this study offer a moment of New Wave stylishness. In terms of representation of altered consciousness, it is not then surprising that these four novels group together upon closer reading.

Additionally, these novels thematise altered consciousness as a state that estranges the undergoer from a shared reality or from others through intoxicants or experimental technology. This understanding of altered consciousness reflects experiments in dream research as well as the CIA's research with LSD. Dream and sleep research received increasing attention through the 1960s after the identification of REM sleep with dreaming in 1957 instigated the experimental awakening method of dream retrieval (Foulkes 1964, 236). This method moved dream research decisively into sleep labs, and institutes devoted to the scientific study of dreams multiplied over the decade as researchers such as Hall and Van de Castle developed quantitative methods for the study of dreams in the late 1950s and early 1960s (Domhoff 2002, 25). Over the same period, science fiction increasingly featured dream research as a source of novums, for example in Ursula K. Le Guin's *The Lathe of Heaven* (1971). Simultaneously, a darker strand of LSD research also influenced science fiction. During the now infamous Operation MK-ULTRA, the CIA dosed American citizens without their knowledge or consent (Lee and Shlain 1985, 24–25, 285). Agents who considered LSD an inducer of psychosis interacted with subjects, which led to negative experiences and sometimes lasting consequences. Although the operation was officially classified, the final stages were conducted with dubious rigor (Lee and Shlain 1985, 32). Psychedelic drugs as associated with inimical government forces certainly appeared in science fiction of the time, perhaps most famously in Phillip K. Dick's *A Scanner Darkly* (1977).

To characterise the Void and Disorder Group in contrast to the Connection and Communication Group, however, I now focus on a central and representative text. Zelazny structures *The Dream Master* on reference to Arthurian legend and grail mythology while also drawing images from Norse epic, Kabbalistic tradition, and Hellenic mythology. The novel is focalised by the psychiatrist Charles Render, who has agreed to train a blind psychiatrist, Eileen Shallot, in dream therapy. Mastering the therapeutic technique is difficult for even the most stable individual, and Shallot's blindness creates inherent instability when she becomes sighted in the dream state. Render, while initially appearing to be a very solid, rational character, is revealed to be hiding a personal trauma that has left him with repressed psychological instability.

While hints of Arthurian imagery appear in default passages, most notably in the name of the character Eileen Shallot and the suit of armor at the diner club, altered passages contain extended Arthurian metaphors and imagery. These increase in frequency until the final two altered passages in which the therapeutic dream state slips into madness. Indeed, in the final passage the characters reenact the tale of Tristan and Isolde. The shift from specific to metaphoric replaces the particulars of the characters and the story with a void. As the net of references tighten, Render and Shallot transform from characters unique to *The Dream Master* into the archetypical vessels of Arthurian legend, empty as foreshadowed by the recurring and foreboding image of the suit of armour.

On the lexical stylistic level as well, Zelazny increasingly creates void as the novel progresses. I draw the following quotation from late in the novel, but from a point before the characters completely fossilise into Arthurian archetypes. The RID's Icarian Imagery words are in bold, and Concreteness words are in italics.

> Then there came a howl from **high** in the **mountains**, a great wailing cry – half-human, all challenge, all loneliness and all remorse. He saw it then, treading upon the **mountains**, its tail brushing the snow from their **highest peaks**, the ultimate loupgarou of the North – Fenris, son of Loki – raging *at* the **heavens**.
>
> It **leapt** into the air. It swallowed the moon.
>
> It landed *near* him, and its great eyes **blazed** yellow. It stalked him on soundless pads, *across* the cold white fields that lay *between* the **mountains**; and he *backed away* from it, up **hills** and down **slopes**, *over* **crevasses** and rifts, through **valleys**, past stalagmites and pinnacles – **under** the edges of glaciers, *beside* frozen **riverbeds**, and always **downwards** – until its **hot** breath **bathed** him and its laughing mouth was *opened* **above** him. (Zelazny 1966, 245–246)

Of the quotation's 134 words, nineteen belong to the Icarian Imagery category and nine to the Concreteness subcategory. The Icarian Imagery words in the first two thirds of the passage all connote height while those in the last third are neutral or suggestive of depth. Alternation between height and depth is common in altered state passages in Zelazny's novel, and the movement between the two happens at a rapid pace in the early altered passages. In altered passages later in the novel, such as the one from which the quotation has been selected, movement between height and depth slows in pace and is sustained across longer series of Icarian Imagery words. This is paired with proximity to distressing thoughts, memories, and feelings. The above quotation occurs shortly before Render's forced encounter with the embodied memory of his dead family. The earlier passages in which the Icarian Imagery words create a ceaseless swooping sensation are, by contrast, focused on beautiful scenes of nature and the pleasant feeling of exploring a fresh interior world, with control of the mental landscape. As motion slows its pace, Render draws proximal to the thing that has been denied. Motion is required to maintain the void Render desires.

The first half of the passage is devoid of Concreteness words, but the second half contains a high density. These words relate the proximity of the monster to the main character. The downward movement brings the thing, which the main character has been trying to avoid, down on him, and he is forced to negotiate space with it. Subsequent to the quote, the monster chases him, forcing him to confront an image of the aftermath of the car accident that killed his family. The monster then eats at the dead bodies, forcing Render to interact with the whole scene though he has been trying to hide behind his hands. This following scene has only 10 Icarian Imagery words out of 336 words total, but 20 Concreteness words. Rather than swooping about the vertical axis of denial, Render inhabits the horizontal axis of the grim reality he longs not to perceive. Once perceived, the abnegation of self and ossification into empty Arthurian archetypes begins, an alternate method of escape that leads to the climax and denouement of the novel.

The DocuScope data reveals much the same aspects of style. A high percentage of Descriptive Cluster words in the altered passages characterises the Void and Disorder Group. In the above quoted passage, the Space Movement Dimension words of the Descriptive Cluster, which create both "the feeling of extended space in relation to other people or objects" and "the feeling of movement across spaces" ("DocuScope LAT List" 2012, 3–4) describe movement from high to low on the vertical axis. While abundant Sensory Language Dimension words describe the exterior environment, Personal Pronoun words are evenly interspersed with Subjective Register language unlike in the Connection and Communication Group. The effect is a consistent, ego-based viewpoint that views the environment as a separate entity. Although it is profusely described, it lacks stability, shifting and changing through various unreliable landscapes as the viewpoint dances along the vertical axis.

Ultimately, disorder and void are two facets of chaos. The altered states of consciousness in the Void and Disorder Group speak to entropy and annihilation at the levels of story, theme, and style. Elements of style such as an increasing shift from specific to metaphoric within the altered passages and Icarian Imagery words that maintain a void through constant motion along a vertical axis thematise altered consciousness as a lack or refusal. The authors in this group achieve their effect through a channeled, structured prolixity of Primary category words. As Felman observes, "to create the tempest of a madness, or the madness of a tempest, through a riot of writing, an intoxication with hyperbole, an orgy of language – isn't that precisely to create the illusion of plentitude in the void?" (2003, 92) This "illusion of plentitude in the void" appears also in the DocuScope data. The Description Cluster and two of its Dimensions, Sensory Language and Space Movement, characterise the altered passages of the Void and Disorder Group. Through a style of movement and sensory prolixity, the Void and Disorder Group portrays altered consciousness as absence or chaos.

## 5 Discussion and Conclusion

Hinted at in the analysis, the themes that characterise the two groups relate closely to contemporaneous social and cultural concerns. The 1960s were a time of social upheaval and change in America. The science fiction of the time reflects this, and perhaps the speculative played its own part in shaping the changing culture. The Connection and Communication Group reimagines environmental embeddedness as a source of strength at a time when pollution and environmental degradation were peak concerns (Duffy 2003, 45) and climate change was beginning to be recognised (White, Jr. 2015, 40). The Void and Disorder Group opens a window into the cultural resonances of mental illness. This group of texts echoes both the scepticism about psychiatry as complicit in the disease (Laing 1960, 34) and the negative assessment of mental illness common in the 1960s and 1970s. Yet, the portrayal of altered states is more sympathetic than many contemporaneous depictions. These texts depict characters experiencing altered consciousness as nuanced persons whose humanity is emphasised and who are deserving of care as members of a community rather than as othered and separated from society.

The Connection and Communication Group also portrays altered states in a sympathetic light. The positive valuation in this group results from the perception of altered states as a way of learning about the self, others, and the environment through embodied interrelation. Alan Watts (1966) articulates the conceptualisation of the self as one part of a system of people and nature that forms a whole, an idea current and spreading in 1960s counterculture. He posits "the organism, including its behavior, is a process which is to be understood only in relation to the larger and longer process of its environment" and "if the behavior of an organism is intelligible only in relation to its environment, intelligent behavior implies an intelligent environment" (Watts 1966, 90). This sense of arising from the world and remaining interconnected through it was perhaps one response to negative aspects of technological progress such as nuclear weapons, overpopulation, and destruction of the wilderness and croplands with chemicals as well as disorientation caused by rapid advancements in technology (ibid., 7–8).

The novels in the Connection and Communication Group engage with these concerns directly at the level of plot and setting. The characters in *Dark Universe* live underground alongside monstrous, mutated animals and suffer a low birth rate because of nuclear warfare. Key scenes in *The Three Stigmata of Palmer Eldritch*, take place in farming settlements on Mars as Earth has become overpopulated and climatically unsuitable for most crops. Most of society has been subjugated and exploited due to a rapid and bewildering technological advancement in *A Plague of Pythons*. In the default state passages of these novels, characters react to these pressures to cope with daily existence; however, the altered state passages create a space in which characters access an embodied way of being that deepens their knowledge about these conditions and opens avenues to counter and divert them. As demonstrated in the analysis, altered consciousness affords ego relaxation wherein characters redefine their relationship to the body, to others, and to the environment, a process which affords personal growth. The ecologist Paul Shepard expressed a similar view of environmental embeddedness, imagining skin, the traditional boundary of a person as "a delicate interpenetration. It reveals the self ennobled and extended rather than threatened as part of the landscape and the ecosystem, because the beauty and complexity of nature are continuous with ourselves" further maintaining that "oak trees, even mountains, have selves or integrities too" (2015, 63). In balancing integrity and relation, he argued "[w]e must find the faith and force to affirm [nature's] metabolism as our own – or rather, our own as a part of it" (ibid., 64). Along with Shepard, the authors in the Connection and Communication group do not depict altered consciousness as a loss of the self. The movement into the environment and others always results in a return to an expanded and ennobled self whereby interrelation is achieved without sacrifice of integrity.

This particular conception of the self in relation to others and the environment was not the predominant view at the time, but rather part of a set of shifting, complex attitudes held by Americans in the 1960s towards the environment and environmental movements. At the time, environmental groups enjoyed the support of most Americans and brought specific plans of action to bear on specific problems, such as clean air and water or legislation on toxic chemicals, which induced strong sentiment in the public. They used the media to amplify these campaigns with support from celebrities and appealing narratives that pit symbols of innocence and purity against corporate evil (Duffy 2003, 55, 64–65, 67). Yet there was tension between growing environmental awareness and Cold War conformity, which celebrated the chemical industry among other scientific and technological advancements. When Rachel Carson published *Silent Spring* in 1962, it met with intolerance before slowly feeding into and energizing America's growing grass-roots environmental consciousness (Lear 2002, x–xi). An image of American wilderness as a desert that existed in opposition to scientific advancement appealed to attitudes encouraged in the Cold War society, which imagined wilderness as "another field for the exercise of power [to] rehearse the perils and purposes of the community" (Marx 2015, 7) a conception well suited to consolidating the aggressive and conformist mindset.

Concurrent with the mixed attitudes in the mass culture, the counterculture embraced a nuanced relationship with the environment, varied and lively but undergoing consolidation over the decade. A predominant strand of thought disbelieved in a necessary split between environmentally friendly living and technology and instead sought to blend "environmental research, new technologies, ecological thinking, and environmental advocacy to shape a social revolution based on alternative lifestyles and communities – alternatives that would enable future generations to live in harmony with one another and the environment" (Kirk 2007, 19). While responding to the fears and concerns of the masses, Science fiction of the era often shaped its hopeful speculations along these lines. Along with the New Left they depicted environmental degradation as the result of a corrupt system intent on curtailing rights and grabbing resources. The scarcity feared by the mainstream environmental movement was merely the result of corrupt capitalist systems, without which the potential for an ecological society supported by ecologically appropriate technologies already existed thanks to, rather than in conflict with, technological advancement (ibid., 29).

The novels in the Connection and Communication group do not ally themselves with a single strand of this complex web of attitudes. Each draws a unique blend of environmental assumptions that underpin the theme of embodiment as a form of connection and a source of knowledge. However, they perhaps react against the isolating capitalist system, depicting altered states of consciousness as community forming, sometimes in concert with supporting technology or scientific advancements as in Pohl and Dick's novels. This trend continues through the 1970s, and indeed many contemporary novels, such as the work of Jeff VanderMeer engage with similar concerns through similar means of embodied connection to the environment.

Depiction of mental illness in science fiction has followed a similar arc. During the 1960s, negative representations of mental illness were not a given. Stories, such as Ursula K. Le Guin's "Nine Lives" (1968), thematise mental illness as a painful but sometimes necessary path to healing and strengthening the psyche, and her novel *The Left Hand of Darkness* (1969) imagines an integrated and valued position in the community for the mentally ill. Samuel R. Delany's *Babel-17* (1966) arguably depicts mental illness simply as one way of being, a way that opens unique perceptions and relationships as the main character leads a productive, if idiosyncratic, life with the backgrounded support of her therapist and little direct comment on her condition. The novels in the Void and Disorder Group, however, certainly characterise mental illness as a negative state. A common enough attitude in the contemporaneous society generally, this is a seemingly conservative standpoint for the science fiction of the time, especially in a subgenre understood to have been allied with the avant-garde. Yet, both lexical and thematic analysis indicates that this group locates negativity in the vulnerability of the mentally ill rather than in the supposed dangers they pose, a marked shift from the concurrent norms of representation.

In the 1950s, under pressure to reduce cost by transitioning as many patients as possible to community care, psychiatrists sought alternatives to the debilitating treatments of earlier decades, such as aggressive electroshock regimens and lobotomy, which necessitated continuing care in an asylum. After the introduction of Thorazine in 1954 lessened reliance on such treatments, neuroleptics underwent feverish development, becoming extremely profitable for pharmaceutical companies by the end of the decade (Whitaker 2002, 142–155). The profitability of the drugs created a market for the diagnosis of schizophrenia that resonated with the upheavals of the 1960s. In the intolerant atmosphere bred by the Cold War, a wide variety of nonconformist behaviours were quick to be judged as symptomatic of schizophrenia. Scepticism towards psychiatric diagnostics, spread (ibid., 169). Further, while preferable to the extreme treatments of previous decades, early neuroleptics nevertheless were of debatable therapeutic efficacy (ibid., 181) and could have permanent neurological side effects such as tardive dyskinesia (ibid., 204). Such medicated patients treated outside asylum walls in community care made mental illness increasingly visible throughout the 1960s, spreading a thoroughly othered image of the mentally ill along with a scepticism towards the efficacy of psychiatric treatment.

While some science fiction broke with these ideas to reimagine mental illness completely, the novels in the Void and Disorder Group engage with the depictions and valuations of mental illness current at the time of their publication. With the anti-psychiatrists, they see mental illness as a construct that prevents understanding of a person, who should be listened to as a human in order to "see and hear in [...] radically different ways" (Laing 1960, 33). In *The Dream Master*, Render's retreat into madness is a retreat into metaphor, constructs that imprison his personality within the armour of a socially constructed narrative. Along with Cooper, this depicts mental illness as, in fact, self-alienation created and reinforced by poor family and social dynamics (124, 36–37). Render's association with Shallot encourages dynamics, on the quite literal level, of rapid movement and eventual collapse into mental illness thematised as void, a complete alienation from the self.

There is perhaps a resistance to anti-psychiatry here; the experimental technique does not heal. Yet, the mentally ill are depicted in full personhood. The same can be said of other texts in this group including Thomas M. Disch's *Camp Concentration*. Similar dynamics of rapid motion unmask a void in the attempt to disguise it, that is, the protagonist Louis' attempts to avoid recognition of his sickened self. Disch's portrayal of Louis in a humane, sympathetic light invites readers to share in a radically different view on the contiguity of madness and the mentally ill with "normal" society from inside the viewpoint of altered consciousness. As in *The Dream Master*, *Camp Concentration* depicts mental illness as a liability while interrogating normative treatments, both traditional and the experimental approaches of the anti-psychiatrists. This group does not offer a speculative solution for the treatment of the mentally ill, however, it does engage with such persons in a sympathetic way, witnessing them in depth rather than reducing them to a stock type. While the themes of void and disorder may seem harsh and the upshot of these books fashionably despairing, this group offers a gentle take on reshaping attitudes towards the mentally ill.

From the level of style in which theme is grounded, both groups of texts comment on social currents through altered states of consciousness. Although New Wave science fiction has traditionally been associated with serious themes, popular authors also engaged with similar concerns, dividing the subgenres on positive or negative portrayals of altered consciousness rather than seriousness of theme. In both positive and negative portrayals, altered consciousness has a vital role in depicting social realities while imagining social change. Some of these changes took place, influenced by cultural shifts on the whole, of which science fiction was a lively part. In many ways the changes taking place in attitudes towards mental health and the environment advanced in these novels and continued to expand in the 1970s, becoming the roots of how these issues are framed today. Understanding how authors used altered consciousness to speculate these changes into being suggests the fruitfulness of exploring the role of altered consciousness in speculating on similar issues in science fiction today.

## Works Cited


Budrys, Algis. *Rogue Moon*. London: Gollancz, 1960.

Cooper, David. *Psychiatry and Anti-psychiatry*. New York: Routledge, 1967.

Delany, Samuel R. *Babel-17*. New York: Vintage Books, 1966.

Dick, Phillip K. *A Scanner Darkly*. 1977. *Five Great Novels*. London: Gollancz, 2004, pp. 649–841.

Dick, Phillip K. *The Three Stigmata of Palmer Eldritch*. 1964. *Five Great Novels*. London: Gollancz, 2004, pp. 1–157.

Disch, Thomas. *Camp Concentration*. New York: Vintage Books, 1968.

"Docuscope LAT List." *DocuScope*. V. 3.21. PC. 2012.

Domhoff, G. William. *The Scientific Study of Dreams: Neural Networks, Cognitive Development, and Content Analysis*. Washington, DC: American Psychological Association, 2002.

Duffy, Robert J. *The Green Agenda in American Politics: New Strategies for the Twenty-First Century*. Lawrence: UP of Kansas, 2003.

Felman, Shoshana. *Writing and Madness (Literature/Philosophy/Psychoanalysis)*. Palo Alto: Stanford UP, 2003.

Foulkes, David. "Theories of Dream Formation and Recent Studies of Sleep Consciousness." *Psychological Bulletin*, vol. 62, no. 4, 1964, pp. 236–247.

Galouye, Daniel F. *Dark Universe*. New York: Bantam Books, 1961.

Gordon, Joan. "Literary Science Fiction." *The Oxford Handbook of Science Fiction*. Ed. Rob Latham. Oxford: Oxford UP, 2014.

Harrison, Harry. *Planet of the Damned*. New York: TOR, 1962.

Kaufer, David, Suguru Ishizaki, Brian Butler, and Jeff Colins. *The Power of Words: Unveiling the Speaker and Writer's Hidden Craft*. New York: Routledge, 2004.

Kirk, Andrew G. *Counterculture Green: The Whole Earth Catalog and American Environmentalism*. Lawrence: UP of Kansas, 2007.

Laing, R. D. *The Divided Self*. London: Penguin Classics, 1960.

Latham, Rob. "Countercultures." *The Oxford Handbook of Science Fiction*. Ed. Rob Latham. Oxford: Oxford UP, 2014.

Le Guin, Ursula K. "Nine Lives." *The Wind's Twelve Quarters*. New York: Harper & Row, [1968] 1975, pp. 129–160.

Le Guin, Ursula K. *The Lathe of Heaven*. New York: Scribner, 1971.

Le Guin, Ursula K. *The Left Hand of Darkness*. New York: Ace Books, 1969.

Lear, Linda. Introduction. *Silent Spring*. By Rachel Carson. New York: Mariner Books, [1962] 2002.

Lee, Martin A., and Bruce Shlain. *Acid Dreams: The Complete Social History of LSD: The CIA, the Sixties, and Beyond*. New York: Grove Press, 1985.

Leiber, Fritz. *The Wanderer*. New York: TOR, 1964.

Martindale, Colin. "The Laws Governing the History of Poetry." *Directions in Empirical Literary Studies: In Honor of Willie Van Peer*. Ed. Sonia Zyngier, Marisa Bortolussi, Anna Chesnokova, and Jan Auracher. Amsterdam: John Benjamins, 2008, pp. 229–242.

Martindale, Colin, and Alan N. West. "Quantitative hermeneutics: Inferring the meaning of narratives from trends in their content." *Thematics: Interdisciplinary Studies*. Ed. Max Louwerse and Willie Van Peer. Amsterdam: John Benjamins, 2002, pp. 377–395.

Marx, Leo. "Shakespeare's American Fable." *Ecocriticism: The Essential Reader*. Ed. Ken Hiltner. New York: Routledge, [1964] 2015, pp. 39–46.

Metzinger, Thomas. *The Ego Tunnel: The Science of the Mind and the Myth of the Self*. New York: Basic Books, 2009.

Norton, Andre. *The X Factor*. New York: Fawcett Crest, 1965.

Piper, Andrew. *Enumerations: Data and Literary Study*. Chicago: University of Chicago Press, 2018.

Pohl, Frederik. *A Plague of Pythons*. New York: Ballantine Books, 1965.

Pollan, Michael. *How to Change Your Mind: The New Science of Psychedelics*. Great Britain: Penguin Books, 2018.

Shepard, Paul. "Introduction: Ecology and Man – A Viewpoint." *Ecocriticism: The Essential Reader*. Ed. Ken Hiltner. New York: Routledge, [1969] 2015, pp. 62–69.

Stockwell, Peter. *The Poetics of Science Fiction*. Harlow: Pearson Education Limited, 2000.

Watts, Alan. *The Book: On the Taboo Against Knowing Who You Are*. New York: Vintage Books, 1966.

Whitaker, Robert. *Mad in America: Bad Science, Bad Medicine, and the Enduring Mistreatment of the Mentally Ill*. Perseus Publishing, 2002.

White, Jr., Lynn. "The Historical Roots of Our Ecologic Crisis." 1967. *Ecocriticism: The Essential Reader*. Ed. Ken Hiltner. New York: Routledge, 2015, pp. 39–46.

Wolfe, Tom. *The Electric Kool-Aid Acid Test*. New York: Picador, 1968.

Zelazny, Roger. *The Dream Master*. New York: ibooks, 1966.

# PART 2

## *The Body-Mind Nexus, Narratives, and Normativities*

CHAPTER 6

# All to No a Veil: Crip Humour and Neurodiversity in David Foster Wallace's *Infinite Jest* (1996)

*Gunther Martens & Liselotte Van der Gucht*

## 1 Introduction

Critics have not failed to note that David Foster Wallace's *Infinite Jest* (1996) is full of disabled bodies (Sloane 2019; Russell 2011). Yet, its thematic content may seem at the furthest remove from any serious type of disability studies concern. Its humour concerning bodily malfunctions seems widely off the mark, and its depiction of a tennis academy for geniuses may seem to brandish able-bodiedness. However, we argue that the novel operates via crip humour, which is a type of sarcasm that aims to shock the reader into a renewed awareness of harsh realities that might otherwise have become opaque and shrouded. Important discussions about disability rights and representation are often hijacked by nomenclature debates overshadowing the focus on actual needs. Through crip humour, Wallace redirects that focus still via the emphasis on physical able-bodiedness at the tennis academy – an emphasis that is reflected in the ways that societies have dealt with disabled bodies as well – which is offset by the characters' psychological vulnerability.

Disability was long understood to imply, by default, bodily defects that are visible, whereas invisible disabilities – both bodily and mental – have come to both scholarly and public awareness only recently.[1] At the same time, many are still struggling for recognition and understanding through activism and research in the field of Crip Theory. Crip Theory is often used synonymously to disability studies, which is generally understood as a field of "interdisciplinary scholarship that considers disability a socially constructed identity category, like race, class, gender, and sexuality" (Sandahl 2003, 52). Crip Theory, which takes its name after queer theory, adds a "radical edge" (ibid., 53) to the field of disability studies and can be understood as the intersection of queer theory and disability studies: "Cripping spins mainstream representations or practices to reveal able-bodied assumptions and exclusionary effects" (ibid., 37). In

1 "The term crip has expanded to include not only those with physical impairments but those with sensory or mental impairments as well" (Sandahl 2003, 27).

 | DOI:10.1163/9789004519886_008

this regard, crip humour has been adopted as a strategy to expose "the arbitrary delineation between normal and defective" and to "disarm what is painful with wicked humor" (ibid., 37). Such alternative forms of humour, like camp,[2] work opposed to disabled people's sense of humour that is often necessary to relieve nondisabled people of their discomfort. Garland-Thomson argues: "Those of us with disabilities are supplicants and minstrels, striving to create valued representations of ourselves in our relations with the nondisabled majority" (Garland-Thomson 1997, 13).

Growing increasingly relevant to disability studies and Crip Theory in recent years, concepts from the neurodiversity movement will be more central to our argument. The neurodiversity movement aims to reconceptualise neurodevelopmental and cognitive differences previously termed "disorders" as a natural variation among human brains, with unique experiences of the world as a result. Neurodiversity relates to various conditions or learning differences like e.g., autism, AD(H)D, Tourette, or dyslexia. Neurodiversity may be compared to other types of diversity such as gender diversity, biodiversity, or cultural diversity. But whereas the latter are often cherished, cognitive differences in areas like perception, sensory processing or learning are either largely unknown or stigmatised as deviations from medical or social norms. Neurodiversity differs from anti-psychiatry approaches in that it seeks to draw on neuroscientific research. Similarly, over the past few years, literary studies have witnessed a shift from the language of mind and mentalising to the paradigm of embodied cognition, which has enabled a more sustained interaction with disability studies as well. Scholars like Karin Kukkonen and Paul Armstrong in particular have made a strong case for aligning the study of narrative with neuroscientifically informed approaches (Armstrong 2019; Kukkonen 2019). The impossibility of prying apart nature from nurture as a source of caricature and humour is at the centre of section 2 of our chapter. In section 3, we single out dyslexia and its precursor hyperlexia as a case in point to illustrate the embodied view promoted in this chapter, as dyslexia is a case in which cognition is both thoroughly "determined by neural processes", but also contingent on "the embeddedness of such processes in a living body and a social world" (Popova 2015, 82). In addition, Armstrong's aim is not only to transfer this terminology to the study of narrative, but also to take into account disturbances of cognition, such as dyslexia. Towards the end of our chapter, we will take a closer look at the novel's stylistic strategies to convey the experience of

2 "Something so outrageously artificial, affected, inappropriate, or out-of-date as to be considered amusing". "Camp". *Merriam-Webster*, www.merriam-webster.com/dictionary/camp#h3.

such neurodivergence: literary techniques that evoke distraction, hyperfocus, or hyperlexia are paramount to constituting the reading experience. As such, readers are forced to update normative understandings of what counts as communication to be able to arrive at the novel's message.

David Foster Wallace's 1996 novel *Infinite Jest* can barely be paraphrased, as the main plotlines are hard to distinguish from the massive amounts of information that are fired at the reader. The novel depicts a future North American superstate, in which years are named after the highest bidding corporation. The narrative brings together wheelchair assassins planning a coup, addicts progressing through AA and NA recovery programmes,[3] and elite tennis academy students by the overarching motif of the film *Infinite Jest*, which is so entertaining that its viewers lose interest in anything else and watch it repeatedly – hence the title – until they die. The novel is steeped in the language of neuroscience and can be considered a so-called "neuronovel". In addition, several expressions of neurodiversity are featured, though typically in such a casual way that they have failed to attract critical attention so far. Despite all the physical and intellectual capacities ascribed to the protagonist, Hal Incandenza,[4] as section 4 will show, is actually a textbook example of a neurodivergent condition called "twice exceptionality". A twice-exceptional profile is attributed to gifted individuals who at the same time experience one or more disabilities, e.g., learning disabilities, speech and language disorders, coordination, emotional, or behavioural disorders (Filmer 2024). Some critics have argued that Wallace promotes a certain kind of neurobiological determinism deep down at the level of neurochemistry and trauma (Owen 2018). The novel's rather scathing depiction of the futility of (psycho)therapy adds to suspicions towards such determinisms. At the same time, Wallace himself has objected to "a purely neural account" because it leaves out many other factors: "This *within* is what's important here" (Wallace 2012, 21; our emphasis). We follow this line of argument and propose that the embodied approach allows us to revise the question of nature and/or nurture as one-sided and to encompass attention to non-standard brains.

3 Alcoholics Anonymous and Narcotics Anonymous.

4 One of the story lines revolves around three brothers, Hal, Orin, and Mario Incandenza, all three of whom are discussed in our chapter.

## 2 Nature or Nurture? Parental Neglect vs. Neurology of Addiction and Neurodiversity

Critical interest in *Infinite Jest* continues to focus on the novel's myriad intertextual and stylistic echoes in the fields of literature, philosophy etc. But, as the novel has become a locus classicus in the study of mental health, interpretations have also veered off in directions more intricately related to the topic of this paper, to wit the representation of psychiatric conditions like attention regulation issues (Bennett 2022), depression (Mayo 2021), personality disorders (Jackson 2020) and addiction (Miller 2016), Medical Humanities (Charon 2020), the narratological structure of maximalist, encyclopaedic novels (Letzler 2017) and neuronovels (Redgate 2019), as well as the return of the age-old edifying function of literature in the domain of therapeutic or self-help writing (Blum 2023). So far, however, little attention has been paid to the presence of invisible, cognitive disability in the novel. In addition to the relative limited renown of neurolinguistics within literary studies, this lack can also be explained on methodological grounds: so far, narratology has actively precluded access to what are often considered to be "automatic neuronal responses" (Popova 2015, 81). In doing so, cognitive narratologists like Alan Palmer and Yanna B. Popova cater to a somewhat normalising and normative understanding of narrative cognition when they argue that it is futile to study narrative in terms of underlying yet invisible neurological mechanisms. Palmer contends that narrative can only be about what is cognitively mediated and conscious. More recent studies have pointed out the "neurological materiality" (e.g., Henneberg 2020, 134) thematised in neuronovels penned by D. F. Wallace and Don DeLillo. The actual regimes of rendering cognitive differences visible and palpable in representation, however, continue to be poorly understood (e.g., Whitney and Hardin 2022). Crip humour is in fact a fairly traditional strategy (akin to gallows humour) in that it takes recourse to existing, stigmatising discourses for the sake of undermining them. Physical disability lends itself more readily to crip humour,[5] but it needs to be noted that the novel does not discriminate between visible and non-visible disability as both are shown to have crippling and incapacitating effects. Although Mario is most visibly in

5 While there is a plethora of research on the usage of cringe, shame and self-deprecative humour concerning physical disability (especially in stand-up comedy, see: Schweik 2010; Milbrodt 2018; Lindfors 2022; Wegner 2021), there is a dearth of research on impious treatment of invisible disability (which ties in the strong taboo still extant in this area. It will be noted that Hannah Gadsby, when breaking the taboo on neuroqueer identity on stage, was reported to have "broken comedy" rather than to engage in it).

need of external support and although the sheer scope of his physical deformities and cognitive differences turns him into the novel's prime example of crip humour, readers are likely to slowly detach themselves from the description of Mario's bodily posture as grotesque, monstrous, ludicrous, or idiotic by attending to the intricate cluster of underlying neurological differences (e.g., dysautonomia). The pointedly affective quality of gallows humour has the effect of rendering readers aware of their own body schema. By pointing out Mario's capacity for empathy, it is shown that neurodiversity is about hyperempathy rather than about lack of empathy and that it is misleading to think of a specific "wiring" in the brain as a stable, localised given. The expression of neurodiversity is, at least to some extent, elicited and mitigated or aggravated by the environment.

Wallace's use of crip humour in *Infinite Jest* has already been touched upon by Sloane, who calls it "a literary device [employed] in order to facilitate a more empathetically rewarding connection not simply between disabled character and (dis)able [*sic*] reader, but between communities of readers figured as forming a universal in-group whose uniting shared characteristic is an embodiment that is by definition disabling" (2019, 96). The underlying nature vs. nurture debate hinted at in the introduction is central to the novel's crip humour strategy: the novel seems bent on explaining neurodiversity through nurture rather than nature. It posits the internal, cognitive, and emotional consequences of the abundantly featured developmental disorders as having a palpable, external cause: abusive environments, dysfunctional families, toxic parents, etc. are to blame. Steeply's father is so obsessed with the television series MASH that it incapacitates him and his family to participate in ordinary life (Wallace 1996, 638–647); Mario Incandenza's disabilities and neurodevelopmental issues, it is strongly hinted at throughout the novel, are caused by his mother's incestuous relation with his uncle Charles;[6] Gately's stepfather comes across as particularly cruel because there is a method to his madness: he "beat her [Gately's mother] with measured blows, [...] timing the blows" (ibid., 447). The exact nature of this abuse and parental neglect is depicted with gory detail and covers a broad spectrum ranging from rampant alcoholism over parental neglect at all social levels to sexual abuse.

A letter written by Marlon Bain, one of Orin Incandenza's friends, summarises the novel's preoccupation with emotional incest (ibid., 1051): it propounds that trauma can be inflicted also by parents

6 At the same time, however, Mario's premature birth may account for his disabilities. Pitching nature against nurture, the novel's real concern seems to be emotional rather than sexual incest.

> loving and supportive and concerned and involved in their children's lives, profligate with compliments and diplomatic with constructive criticism, loquacious in their pronouncements of unconditional love for and approval of their children, conforming to every last jot/tittle in any conceivable definition of a good parent. (ibid., 1050)

The letter goes on to evaluate the alleged psychological violence exerted by the mother figure, also called "the Moms", as more destructive and disabling than overt physical abuse: Bain presents Orin's deformation (his proneness to lying) as the outcome of his mother's masking strategies. In addition, "Orin had characterized the Moms to Hal [his brother] as a kind of contortionist with other people's bodies, which Hal's never been able to forget" (Wallace 1996, 285). Similarly, the main character Hal is depicted as rationalising his drug abuse as a reaction to his mother's "total unconditional support" (ibid., 68) which he experiences as a confusing mixture of compulsive control and conditional regard:

> [He had visited] interschool range-of-reading-and-recall spelling-beeish competitions called 'Battle of the Books', which these were for Hal pretty much of a public turkey-shoot and approval-fest – when he'd extracted what was desired from memory and faultlessly pronounced it before certain persons, he'd felt almost that same pale sweet aura that an LSD afterglow conferred, some milky corona, like almost a halo of approved grace, made all the milkier by the faultless nonchalance of a Moms who made it clear that his value was not contingent on winning first or even second prize, ever. (ibid., 999)

Hal's mother tries to avoid the impression that her esteem of Hal's worth should depend on his achievements. Yet, this reassurance is repeated throughout the novel so frequently and in such an emphatic way that it ceases to be plausible. Moreover, while the Moms denies exerting pressure on her son, the denial itself is self-defeating, because its elaborate diction ("not contingent on") sets a very high standard for linguistic performance. Differentiation of self as outlined by Murray Bowen's family systems theory (Bowen 1978) becomes tenuous when it is revealed that Hal's linguistic skill is strongly predicated on his mother's hovering presence and perfectionism. But Hal clearly does seek praise: "as if Hal were trying as if his very life were in the balance to please some person or persons" (Wallace 1996, 999), the plural form implying his mother, the Moms. In addition, the association with an LSD afterglow is ominous: the approval that Hal craves from his environment, and the Moms specifically, can be interpreted as some form of addiction. Hal craves his mother's praise but perceives her double identity as mother and school director as conditional regard. While his drug abuse is placed within a genealogy of rampant alcoholism stretching multiple generations, Hal himself engages mother-blaming with such parodistic overtones that psychoanalysis comes into sight as the butt of the irony. Indeed, the psychoanalytic conception of the hovering, meddlesome mother is a very fraught notion in the history of neurodiversity, queerness, and gifted education.

Avril Incandenza, the Moms, is a further case in point for the way in which the novel's crip humour concerning non-visible disabilities operates. She is rendered a caricature in line with Wallace's strategy of using grotesque bodily deformities (Avril is said to be "over two meters tall", Wallace 1996, 755) as externalisations of mental,[7] i.e., non-visible, potentially genetically determined, innate traits. We could look for the cause of Avril Incandenza's seemingly unconcerned parenting style in her Obsessive-Compulsive Disorder, which encompasses much more than the stereotypical compulsive hygiene or panic fear of bacteria. More broadly, OCD can be understood as a regulation mechanism for lack of control over outside influences, where a person's actions become involuntary. Many characters in the novel display compulsive tendencies in their search for drugs and entertainment (reflected in the novel's title, *Infinite Jest*, and its fictional counterpart).

Wallace's crip humour angle on OCD allows for the insight that conditions have an impact on the environment and that potentially anyone can get affected through codependency: "The thing about people who are truly and malignantly crazy: their real genius is for making the people around them think they are crazy" (Wallace 1996, 1041). The psychodynamics of the Incandenza family are highly reminiscent of the "family dance" as described in Murray Bowen's transactional psychology. The multigenerational scope and dynamic nature of transactional psychology may seem to fly in the face of the individualising tendency of the "neurohorror" that Wallace, in the wake of the neurocentric turn

7 One might accuse Wallace of transgressing moral boundaries by grotesquely portraying the so-called "Hideously and Improbably Deformed" (Wallace 1996, 187), but the grotesque contributes to exactly that part of crip humour which subverts and *crips*. Coogan explains how crip humour is reminiscent of a Bakhtinian "grotesque realism" and even "contamination" from oppressive discourses of normality. He argues, however, that these impure strategies are always accompanied by an emancipatory goal. Disability or crip humour reveals boundaries of tolerance and operates by failing to meet norms or expectations (Coogan 2013, 8–9; Corker 1999, 81) and by liberating us from these norms.

of the 1990s, engages in; less so if we assume that cognitive differences are to a large extent inherited (Schiff 2006). Even though Bowen stresses the importance of differentiation of the self, coping with disability necessitates lasting interdependence and support systems beyond the age where these are considered normal or 'healthy'. Externalisation, as a strategy of rendering visible the invisible through hyperbole and exaggeration, thus counters the internalising side-effects of OCD, depression etc. Wheelchair users hover ominously in the back of many of the novel's scenes, yet not much has been made of the Quebec terrorists being physically disabled. The ONAN[8] interdependence and experialism[9] plot is, amongst many other things, about ecology or ecosickness. On a macro-level, the global ONAN-constellation embodies a gigantic externalisation of more invisible psychological family mechanisms like parentification and codependency. In the particular case of disability, some degree of dependence or interdependence (and their stigma) is inevitable. Even Hal is at times unable to refrain from taking this condescending attitude towards Mario ("everybody sort of looked down like they were laughing at somebody with a disability", Wallace 1996, 592). The involvement of visibly disabled assassins can also be seen as a revenge fantasy, a screen memory for the lack of understanding of hidden disabilities such as those inherent in twice-exceptionality and a plot device that turns disability into a political issue.

## 3 Hyperlexia and Dyslexia as Counterparts of a Twice-Exceptional Profile

The question of nature or nurture is even more relevant to one of the novel's most palpable concerns: language. In the case of linguistic giftedness, Wallace's oeuvre seems inclined to come up with various types of (even ludicrous) environmental triggers. Most clearly so with regards to Hal, who has eidetic/photographic memory and displays savant-like skills: a character refers to this ability "not [to] take notes and wait and like inscribe [*sic*] it anytime in the next week and get it verbatim" (Wallace 1996, 1023). But the exact source of this linguistic bravado is once more deferred to external causes that, however, fail to convince readers well-versed in psycholinguistics: "It was Mario, not Avril, who

8 Organization of North American Nations, referring with tongue in cheek to onanism as a nod to the novel's quest for never-ending pleasure.

9 Experialism, as opposed to imperialism, refers to the state of ONAN forcibly donating its northern territories such as Maine, Vermont, and New Hampshire to Canada, and flinging "all its hazardous waste into it" (Leith 2016).

obtained Hal his first copies of the unabridged O.E.D. at a time when Hal was still being shunted around for the assessment of possible damage, [...] months before Hal tested out at Whatever's Beyond Eidetic on the Mnemonic Verbal Inventory designed by a dear and trusted colleague of the Moms at Brandeis" (ibid., 317). A diagnosis or profile of Hal's exceptionality is provided with remarkable detail in the novel. At the same time, its exact aetiology requires a closer look,[10] as Hal's excessive language skill is first thought of as a disability:

> Hal Incandenza had been thought for a while as a toddler to have some sort of Attention Deficit Disorder – partly because he read so fast and spent so little time on each level of various pre-CD-ROM video games, partly because just about any upscale kid even slightly to port or starboard of the bell curve's acme was thought at that time to have A.D.D. – and for a while there'd been a certain amount of specialist-shuttling, and many of the specialists were veterans of Mario and were preconditioned to see Hal as also damaged, but thanks to the diagnostic savvy of Brandeis's Child Development Center the damage assessments were not only retracted but reversed way out to the other side of the Damaged-to-Gifted continuum, and for much of the glabrous part of his childhood Hal'd been classified as somewhere between 'Borderline Gifted' and 'Gifted'. (Wallace 1996, 998–99)

This passage is particularly telling, because it shows that savant skills can be (mis)diagnosed as a disability and vice versa. Moreover, clinical testing is unable to discern to what extent these excessive skills are due to nature or nurture:

> [...] part of this high cerebral rank was because B.C.D.C.'s diagnostic tests weren't quite so keen when it came to distinguishing between raw neural gifts and the young Hal's monomaniacally obsessive interest and effort, as if Hal were trying as if his very life were in the balance to please some person or persons, even though no one had ever even hinted that his life depended on seeming gifted or precocious or even exceptionally pleasing– and when he'd committed to memory entire dictionaries and vocab-check software and syntax manuals and then had gotten some chance to recite some small part of what he'd pounded into his RAM for a proudly

10 Aetiology is "the study of the causes of a disease". "Aetiology". *Cambridge Dictionary*, www.dictionary.cambridge.org/dictionary/english/aetiology.

> nonchalant mother or even a by-this-time-as-far-as-he-was-concerned-pretty-much-out-there father […]. (ibid., 999)

Hal's lexical prowess may seem like a terrific asset, but actually, his eidetic memory is the bane of his existence, which makes him a textbook example of twice-exceptionality. One expression of Hal's exceptionality can be identified as hyperlexia, which designates "the early and extreme development of word recognition skills developing in advance of reading comprehension. As a decoding-comprehension discrepancy, this precocious ability to decode words apparently has a neural basis: hyperlexic reading is brought about by simultaneously drawing upon both the left hemisphere's phonological and the right hemisphere's visual processing systems" (Randi, Newman, and Grigorenko 2010). Given this ambidextrous inclination, which predates the actual acquisition of literacy, the more abstract skills of reading comprehension do not develop along with their word recognition skills. Characteristics of hyperlexia include an obsession with letters and numbers, arranging them endlessly, but in a non-pragmatic, autotelic way. In the novel, this obsession culminates in Hal's memorisation of the Oxford English Dictionary, which facilitates effortless extraction from his memory (Wallace 1996, 999). However, being good at spelling bees does not necessarily reflect phonic decoding competence, which is central to spelling proficiency, but may simply confirm Hal's photographic memory.

What seems like a terrific asset at first glance, incapacitates Hal for normal life, the novel suggests: if the Discursive O.E.D. does not mention the social lower class, then this part of reality is inaccessible to Hal (ibid., 245). Even though readers of *Infinite Jest* tend to take a positive view of those able to command polysyllables, they are probably less acquainted with hyperlexia's commonly co-occurring conditions, such as dyspraxia: dyspraxia is a Developmental Motor Coordination Disorder that may affect mundane skills like tying one's shoelaces, "knifework […] at table" (ibid., 314) or overall cleanliness. Once more, the blame for this neurological condition is put on the mother in crude psychoanalytic terms: "Maybe in like psychic opposition to their Moms's compulsive cleaning thing, both Orin when he was at E.T.A. [Enfield Tennis Academy] and now Hal are horrific slobs" (ibid., 1000). In addition, the novel points out in various instances that these hyperliterate people are also at risk of living too much in their heads. Geoffrey Day "used to think in long compound sentences with subordinate clauses and even the odd polysyllable" (ibid., 271). In keeping with this profile, Hal Incandenza is portrayed as having a rigidly logical mind that seemingly lacks emotional intelligence. However, *Infinite*

*Jest* challenges our assumptions that literate people have better mental health, or that either higher IQ or literacy itself vouchsafe for mental health, as "it is statistically easier for low-IQ people to kick an addiction than it is for high-IQ people" (ibid., 203). There is more than a whiff of competitiveness attached to hyperliteracy.

Hyperlexia counts as a precursor of dyslexia. It is surprising that one of the most verbose, baroque texts can bring us so close to the experience of processing differences and not just dyslexia, but even alexia. Alexia designates word blindness, often caused by cerebral damage, resulting in the inability to read or recognise written letters or words. Throughout *Infinite Jest*, this inability is evoked in the reader multiple times, e.g., through unknown acronyms and abbreviations. "E.W.D"., for instance, is short for "Empire Waste Displacement", as can be derived from page 539. By then, the acronym has already been used (without explanation) on pp. 25, 26, 48, 56, 217, 242, 288, 301, 311, 411, 467, 475, 478. The "ATHSCME" acronym never gets explained and continues to be the object of speculation (asthma? Ask me? A pun on the fictional Acme Corporation featured in the Road Runner cartoons?).

In line with his twice-exceptional intelligence profile, Hal is also considered a tennis prodigy:

> Although Wallace establishes Hal's tennis prowess early on, he curiously quarantines that prowess from Hal's other physical limitations. We're told during the admissions scene that Hal is a great tennis player, "gorgeous. Possibly a genius" who has reached the semifinals of the "prestigious WhataBurger Southwest Junior Invitational [...] as of this morning". This evidently means that Hal's capacity to play tennis has not been affected by the change in his condition. (Hayes-Brady 2013, 140)

However, Stephen J. Burn finds it hard to reconcile the tennis results with the fact that Hal's gestures in the interview room [during his admission interview] are animalistic, and that he is avowedly incapable of typing or writing clearly but instead produces "some sort of infant's random stabs" (Wallace 1996, 9). If Hal is so gifted a tennis player, how can he be unable to govern his movements sufficiently to write clearly? Perhaps this discrepancy reinforces the mystery of Hal's condition by adding a bewildering and implausible symptom: that Hal's disability extends only to communication, spoken, written, or nonverbal, but does not affect his performance in any other sphere (Burn 2013, 75). The apparent contradiction of athletic genius alongside linguistic shortcomings, e.g., the fact that Hal is unable to write clearly (which points to dysgraphia), continues to puzzle scholars. However, this co-occurrence is not a "mystery" or "implausible" at all; it is a common occurrence in neurodivergent people. Hal's photographic memory results in extreme verbal skills, but these skills are the flip side of the logographic, "preverbal" way in which Mario deals with language (Wallace 1996, 590). The novel summarises this conundrum by means of a somewhat "lame", yet aptly crip-humorous joke, which details the lesser-known co-existing burdens of neurodivergent dyslexic thinking: "'Mario, what do you get when you cross an insomniac, an unwilling agnostic, and a dyslexic'. […] 'You get somebody who stays up all night torturing himself mentally over the question of whether or not there's a dog'" (ibid., 41).

Exceptional skill and exceptional dependence on one's environment become interchangeable, as also illustrated by Madame Psychosis' ambiguous membership of the "Hideously and Improbably Deformed, an agnostic-style 12-step support-group deal for what it calls the 'aesthetically challenged'" (ibid., 187). The AA adheres to principles of behaviourist psychology in that it does not delve into invisible psychological causes, but restricts itself to recipes and rituals that depend on strong social control, "shaping" of behaviour and active condemnation of specific conditions as a failure to fulfil moral obligations towards the community. The neurodiversity movement is critical of the deficit model of disability and of treatments that aim to fix these so-called deficits, especially regarding mental conditions. Specifically, a neurodiversity approach is aware of the wide variety of symptoms, be they visible or invisible, mental or physical, and common or uncommon by employing the iceberg model.[11] Behaviourist treatments are strongly focused on reinforcing socially desirable behaviour through external (also aversive) stimuli. Both E.T.A. and Ennet House are shown to be "conditioning" people (ibid., 110). In taking a critical view of the behaviourism underpinning the diagnostic and medicalised agenda, the novel manages to counter the spectacularised representation of neurodiversity that, unfortunately so, continues to dominate in popular media:[12] during a lengthy exposition by Pemulis,

---

11 By way of example, the iceberg model of Tourette syndrome lists vocal and motor tics as the tip of the iceberg, and learning disabilities, AD(H)D, handwriting difficulties, depression, behavioural issues, disinhibition, anxiety, sleep issues, social communication deficits, sensory processing issues, transition issues, and executive functioning deficits among others as its (possible) "underwater" characteristics and co-occurring conditions. "Iceberg Illustration Poster". *Tourette Association of America,* www.tourette.org/resource/iceberg-illustration-poster/.

12 A widespread prejudice against disability as minority identity is that e.g., wheelchair users or neurodivergent people continue to be perceived as childish, lazy, immature,

who "has the highest Stanford-Binet of any kid on academic probation ever at the Academy [...] two of the kids squeeze tennis balls; two rock and bob Hasidically to stay alert" (ibid., 67). In the behaviourist definition of the *Diagnostic and Statistical Manual of Mental Disorders*, these gestures would qualify as types of stimming (self-stimulating) or repetitive behaviours that need to be replaced by other, more socially acceptable ones. In view of the circumstances (the kids are just tired), however, these behaviours are perfectly understandable, so that the difference between normal and abnormal gets blurry.

It would be the easy way out to turn Hal Incandenza into a "freak", but his profile is much more detailed than that. His hyperlexia is accompanied by various other common traits of neurodivergence, like time blindness and proneness to addiction. In addition, just like Christopher Boone from *The Curious Incident of the Dog in the Night-Time* (2003), Hal is judged not to have shown enough grief upon the death of his father. One could say that the inability to mourn, although contradicted by Mario (Wallace 1996, 41), points to the character of Shakespeare's *Hamlet* rather than questions of neurology. As we will analyse more closely in section 4, Hal's senses are so acute that he cannot help but notice that the smell coming from the microwave oven, which his father used to commit suicide, actually smelled "delicious" (ibid., 256).

The novel does not just have neurodiversity as its hidden core – not every reader is familiar with twice-exceptional profiles –, it also anticipates an enactive understanding of neurodiversity as a mismatch between an organism and its environment. Ultimately, Hal may feel so hollow because he acutely feels how his own level of attainment and skill is transfused and wired to the dysfunctional environment of his family. The grammar and pronunciation nitpicker in his head echoes his mother's perfectionist cognition, and it kicks in involuntarily from the first[13] to the last[14] page of the novel. In addition, Hal goes about experiencing his emotions in relation to others to such a large extent that he rationalises his emotional response by reading up on it in ludicrous ways. He does so, for instance, when trying to guess his grief therapist's

self-centered, requiring unfair accommodations or posing excessive demands. Whilst it cannot be said that *Infinite Jest* combats this perception squarely, it addresses the issue by turning disability into the default mode of existence for most of its characters.

13 "I presume it's probably *facilitate* that the tennis coach mistook for *accentuate*, though *accelerate*, while clunkier than *facilitate*, is from a phonetic perspective more sensible, as a mistake" (Wallace 1996, 6; original emphasis).

14 "Gately thinks *sadism* is pronounced 'saddism'" (Wallace 1996, 981; original emphasis).

expectations after having found his father at the scene of the latter's suicide. Hal describes:

> The whole thing was nightmarish. I just could not figure out what the [therapist] wanted. I went down and chewed through the Copley Square library's grief section. Not disk. The actual books. I read Kübler-Ross, Hinton. I slogged through Kastenbaum and Kastenbaum. I read things like Elizabeth Harper Neeld's *Seven Choices: Taking the Steps to New Life After Losing Someone You Love,* which was 352 pages of sheer goo. I went in and presented with textbook-perfect symptoms of denial, bargaining, anger, still more denial, depression. I listed my seven textbook choices and vacillated plausibly between and among them. I provided etymological data on the word acceptance all the way back to Wyclif and 14th-century *langue-d'oc* French. [...] [The therapist] was my worst nightmare. Talk about self-consciousness and fear. Here was a top-rank authority figure and I was failing to supply what he wanted. He made it manifestly clear I wasn't delivering the goods. I'd never failed to deliver the goods before. (Wallace 1996, 253)

Not being able to distinguish his own needs from those of others, Hal tries to deduce what others expect from him from what he does know and is able to do: to absorb (written) knowledge.

Another character in whom motifs of abuse and neurodiversity are brought together is Gately, who is described as "academically ambivalent and A.D.D.-classified" (ibid., 905). Gately's issues in adulthood primarily emerge from his abusive environment; it is strongly suggested that his learning and attention disorders stem from his upbringing in a dysfunctional family. To some extent, he even seems to halt his academic progress in order not to make his mother feel inferior. The summary of his school career once more highlights the susceptibility of AD(H)D to addiction.

> Quaaludes and QuoVadis and Percocets are lethal in terms of homework, especially washed down with Hefenreffer, and extra-especially if you're academically ambivalent and A.D.D.-classified and already using every particle of your self-discipline protecting football from the Substances. And – unhappily – high school is totally unlike higher education in terms of major-sport coaches' influence over instructors, athletes-and-grades-wise. Kite got Gately through math and Special Ed. Science, [...] But English just fucking killed him, Gately. All four of the English teachers the Athletic Dept. tried Gately on had this sieg-heil idea that it was somehow

> cruel to pass a kid that couldn't do the work. And the Athletic Dept. pointing out to them that Gately had an especially challenging domestic situation and that flunking Gately and rendering him ineligible for ball would eliminate his one reason even to stay on in school–these were to no, like, a veil. English was his sink-or-swim situation, what he then termed his 'Water Lou'. (ibid., 905)

This passage quips on the practice of admitting student-athletes based on their athletic prowess rather than their academic achievements. Less directly mentioned, the reader can infer from the description filtered through Gately's perception that the latter is also dyslexic and dysgraphic, as he errs on the spelling of "to no avail" and "Waterloo". The quote expresses sympathy for the idea that Gately's life would have been different if school had not just focused on cognitive skills, which reminds us of current debates regarding education and its priorities. Attentive readers will notice that this passage mirrors Hal's admission interview, during which all parties involved precisely aim to avoid the bad impression that athletic admissions would involve lowering academic standards. In the specific case of Hal, it is suggested that he is effectively home-schooled and trained for competitive sports to shield his cognitive differences. It is one of the novel's profound structural ironies that it manages to highlight the similarities between the socially remote contexts of inhabitants of the posh E.T.A. tennis academy and the halfway house. The comic effects engendered by this crass juxtaposition enable the insight that neurodivergence, contrary to popular opinion, is *not* simply due to disadvantaged socio-economic circumstances.

David Foster Wallace spells out for his readers sensorimotor activities that are supposed to go unnoticed. Mario is "leptosomatic, so damaged he can't even grip a stick, much less flail at a moving ball with one"; he is bradykinetic (slow-moving); and has congenital analgesia and familial dysautonomia (Wallace 1996, 313, 589), a neurological deficiency that makes it impossible for him to experience physical pain. His sensorimotor difficulties are extended to his language and communication skills, which are areas that are often associated with one another: "[motor coordination and sensory responsivity] difficulties could affect the necessary sensorimotor skills involved in non-verbal language and communication such as gesture and imitation, consequently leading to what is perceived as idiosyncratic behaviors i.e., eye gaze aversion, limited non-verbal communication and restricted facial gesture" (Hannant et al. 2016, 3). For all its extravagance, *Infinite Jest* provides us with a very good grasp of the practical aspects of various neurodevelopmental differences, while also disrupting their negative image. While Mario is the most disabled character in the novel, he is also the only one who is portrayed as *able* to show empathy and in a way he is the novel's only likeable character.

Once more, it is interesting to have a look at how such neurodivergence is rendered in narrative via crip humour (Wallace 1996, 590): in this case, humour operates via the scabrous and grotesque of a primal sense like smell (cf. Hal being susceptible to the smell of his microwaved father); Mario's numbness to pain "wasn't even discovered until Mrs. Clarke thought she smelled her eggplant overcooking" (ibid., 589). Mario is also the only character whose utterances are untainted by the desire to 'mask' in a non-committal way one's quirks and deformations in order to comply with ableism. Mario's preference for 'single entendre' is also at the core of the narrator's sardonic situational humour concerning prostheses, as in the scene when Poor Tony Kraus robs a woman of her artificial heart which she carries around in her purse: "Stop her! She stole my heart!" (ibid., 143).

## 4 Hypo- and Hypersensitivity in Proprioception

One of the conundrums of neurodiversity is that overstimulation is not antithetical to, but in fact the flipside of "being divorced from all stimulus" (Wallace 1996, 112). Hyposensitivity goes hand in hand with (hyper)sensitivity. This section is devoted to a detailed analysis of the novel's famous opening scene in order to show that a crip approach to disability is a central concern of the novel from its very first pages onwards. With its allusions to Kafka's *Metamorphosis*, the scene showcases society's prototypical reaction to neurodivergence: it demonstrates how, in a context of close monitoring, any visible or invisible difference can be turned into a grotesque impairment:

> [...] the others sit, stand and stand, respectively, at the periphery of my focus. The tennis coach jingles pocket-change. There is something vaguely digestive about the room's odor. [...] My chest bumps like a dryer with shoes in it. I compose what I project will be seen as a smile. [...] 'Is Hal all right, Chuck?' Athletic Affairs asks. 'Hal just seemed to ... well, grimace. Is he in pain? Are you in pain, son?' [...] I do the sage thing, relaxing every muscle in my face, emptying out all expression. (ibid., 3–5)

This scene portrays Hal's multi-sensorial experience of his college admission interview: we have insight into how *he* experiences the moment, not how it really takes place. We are led to experience the scene through Hal's senses – sight ("the periphery of my focus"); sound ("the tennis coach jingles pocket change"); and smell ("the room's odor") – all establishing a strongly sensory experience accompanied by corporeality. In the same scene, especially limited motor skills are thematised: his "high-traction sole" sneakers insinuate bodily instability (ibid., 3), which is later picked up again when Hal is described as "asymmetrically hobbled" (ibid., 269). Thus, Hal Incandenza is characterised by both a lack of grip on the ground as well as, and especially, his own body: he seems to live in a permanent state of unbalance, referring again to dyspraxia. At the same time, as Hal also excels as a tennis prodigy, he knows exactly how to command his body, albeit unconsciously – or hyperconsciously? –, when playing a match of tennis.

Another element that surfaces in the opening scene is Hal's hyper*awareness* of his body, its position in its environment, what it does and how it feels, despite not being able to command it: "I have committed to crossing my legs I hope carefully, ankle on knee, hands together in the lap of my slacks. My fingers are mated into a mirrored series of what manifests, to me, as the letter X" and a bit later: "My chest bumps like a dryer with shoes in it" (ibid., 3, 5), which seems to be a very odd way of describing either the bodily function of respiration or heartbeat. At the same time, not just the body itself, but also the interpretation thereof is both over- and underdeveloped. We again notice these traces of twice-exceptionality in the sense that even though Hal seems to be hyper-aware of what exactly he is doing, he has no sense of how others perceive him, which the opening scene exemplifies: "*I believe I appear* neutral, maybe even pleasant, [...] I have committed to crossing my legs *I hope* carefully, [...] I compose *what I project will be seen as* a smile" (ibid., 3–5; our emphasis), despite the fact that he has "been coached to err on the side of neutrality and not attempt what would feel to me like a pleasant expression or smile" (ibid., 3). Verbs like "believe", "appear", and "hope" are used to emphasise the discrepancy between how Hal thinks he acts and how his actions are ultimately perceived by others. But in the end, the people interviewing him interpret his intentions differently: "'Is Hal all right, Chuck?' Athletic Affairs asks. 'Hal just seemed to ... well, grimace. Is he in pain? Are you in pain, son?'" (ibid., 5). Hal thinks he is showing off a smile, which is not his own idea of a smile, but what he has learnt others are likely to interpret as one. However, it is this conversion that fails: the others perceive his execution as a grimace that expresses pain. Finally, Hal positions his body the way he has learnt to: "I do the safe thing, relaxing every muscle in my face, emptying out all expression" (ibid., 5). Consequently, there exists a large gap between what Hal himself is inclined to do, what others expect him to do, and how his ultimate actions are perceived despite his intentions.

However, it must be stated that Hal is painfully aware of this inconsistency in his own perception and that of others: "I would yield to the urge to bolt for the door if I could know that bolting for the door is what the men in this room would see" (ibid., 8). Here, he explicitly states that he does not know for certain that his own interpretation of his actions is what others would understand. In addition, Hal questions not only his visual sense but also his perception through touch: "what I feel to be a hand over my sportcoat's biceps (surely not)" (ibid., 9).

The intense sensory perception that Hal demonstrates throughout the opening scene is commonly linked to the suspicion that he might be high on DMZ, an incredibly powerful and mysterious hallucinogenic drug in the world of *Infinite Jest*. One of the drug's effects is the transformation of communication. This hypothesis does not preclude our assumption that Hal experiences more non-intermittent communication issues during the interview. The novel intertwines the motif of addiction with (numbing of) hypersensitivity and synaesthesia: "a kind of semi-sleep-like trance with visions, elation, sensations of physical lightness and increased strength, heightened sensual perceptions, synaesthesia, and favorable distortions in body image" (Wallace 1996, 66). In reality, a link between neurodivergence and susceptibility to addiction can indeed be established: untreated AD(H)D, for instance, may lead to attempts to self-medicate by engaging in high-sensation or high-risk activities. In the novel, "Le Jeu du Prochain Train" is a game of chicken played by male offspring of Canadian asbestos workers. Given its lethality, it is a particularly wry nod to the extremes to which those with an all too efficient dopamine depletion or reward discounting system will expose themselves in order to activate neurons. The *crippling* effect of AD(H)D on day-to-day life is illustrated by the fact that this novel is haunted by the presence of people in wheelchairs, but also by the fact that research has not paid much attention to the unexplored parts of the human cortex which these elements of the plot are about. While risk-proneness is a feat of adolescent behaviour (and of supply-side economics) in general, this feature of the novel has increasingly fallen out of grace with critics, as it is often deemed juvenile, reckless, outré.

The college admission scene is also a case in point for a central tenet of the enactive approach to neurocognitive diversity: the "audience effect"[15] is a well-established effect in social psychology, and its effect on performance is central to both the tennis academy (which fosters visibility on 'the show' but has strict policies concerning excessive media attention) and Boston AA (which advocates helping behaviour and gratitude through group sessions). Yet, experimental research has shown that the audience effect is diminished

15 The audience effect refers to "the influence on behavior of the presence of bystanders". "Audience effect". APA *Dictionary of Psychology*, https://dictionary.apa.org/audience-effect.

in the neurodivergent population and may even work to the detriment (Chevallier et al. 2014). Hence, the neurotypical gaze can be said to aggravate Hal's condition and to turn his body into a freak show at the beginning of the novel. Hal shows how developmental coordination issues, even under adverse, high-stakes circumstances, can be compensated for by turning one's explicit attention to every gesture that is supposed to go without notice. As the focalisation sticks with Hal exclusively, the reader is made to experience the maximal rift between Hal's self-perception of his stimming gestures as soothing and comforting and the extreme othering to which his stimming (meant to enable focus and attention) is subjected.

In addition, it should be noted here that neurodivergent individuals like Hal – whether officially diagnosed or not – are subjected to the scrutiny and surveillance of neurotypical society in all its facets, all the time. Institutions like the tennis academy and the university Hal is applying to in the opening scene contribute to the discursive construction and regulation of normativity in a Foucauldian sense. As some kind of panoptic machine, they function to keep both norms and individuals in place. The novel chimes in with Foucault's emphasis on a plurality of seemingly innocuous, subtle techniques that contribute to subjugation and normalisation. While the institutions (the tennis boarding school and the halfway house) present themselves as anti-authoritarian, inclusive and benign, they reinforce regimes of extreme synchronisation that tend to backfire and render non-typical bodies and minds even more asynchronous. Central to the "humour" inherent in Wallace's descriptions of neurodiverse and/or neurotypical is the emphasis on the machine-like, mechanical nature of the (addicted) brain at the cortical level, which was identified by Bergson as a source of humour (Hamon 1996, 66).

Dialing back to Hal's neurodiversity, he is explicitly labelled as autistic in the opening scene: he is named an "athletic savant" (Wallace 1996, 15), which conceptualises his giftedness ("balletic athlete", "reads like a vacuum" (ibid., 15)) as splinter skills. The scene can indeed be read as an approximation of an autistic meltdown, a failure of automatisation. This holds true even when one holds the view that Hal's composure crumbles because of the negative attitudes and expectations of those that refuse to treat him with compassion and empathy. "His arms were [...] flailing. This sort of awful reaching drumming wriggle. Waggling" (ibid., 14). The objections raised by the members of the board will sound familiar to anyone who has attempted to put a neurodivergent person through a neurotypical institution that can only objectify and express a wish for more firm control ("various grips designed to transfer that control to him", "get a grip, son" (ibid., 13)). Such institutions tend to attribute stubbornness and a fixed mindset to those who are perceived as non-productive or non-functional ("Hal here functions, you ass. Given a supportive situation" (ibid., 15)). But the challenge arises from e.g., the work situation or in this case the school system when it is based on competition ("compete", "inject him into all the rigors of college life" (ibid., 14, 15)) without accommodations and "support system" (ibid., 14).

Whatever may have caused Hal's body schema[16] to disintegrate (he is possibly still under the influence of DMZ), he is able to command an outrageous amount of attention to his body image, activating all senses in a truly memorable density. This process requires a conscious and purposeful distribution and attribution of energy: "I expend my energy on remaining utterly silent in my chair, empty, my eyes two great pale zeros" (ibid., 8). Bringing himself to remain utterly silent requires a lot of mental capacity: a state of total stillness demands of him all the energy he can muster, which draws a parallel to AD(H)D and other types of neurodivergence. In current terminology, the activity of consciously directing one's body image is called 'masking'. Elsewhere in the novel, Wallace discusses the emergence of "High-Definition Masking" as a reaction to so-called "Video-Physiognomic Dysphoria" (Wallace 1996, 147), presumably induced by a sci-fi imagination of videoconferencing. While this is obviously a (prophetic) riff on the alienation caused by technological interfaces, the reference to masking as compensating for the lack of automaticity in mirroring body language specifically carries strong neurodivergent overtones. Instilling in neurotypical audiences a heightened sense of presence and continuity, possibly because 'normal' standards of fluency do not apply, is what makes art by writers and directors read (or readable) as neurodiverse (Kubrick, Fassbinder, Godard …) so compelling. But *Infinite Jest* shows that this hyperreflexivity is not only extremely tiring; it is ultimately also maddening. The novel does so in keeping with enactivist premises, moving away from a restriction to biological nature: "the philosophical stance of enactivism makes it unlikely that we will find a single neurological basis for autism"(Stenning 2020, 110).

As illustrated by the opening scene, the energy that Hal invests in self-talk affects his social proprioception. In this respect, the novel demonstrates that neurodiversity is intimately tied up with a complex range of sensorimotor differences, rather than with the simple absence or presence of a Theory of Mind. It is hard to ignore that proprioception at the level of the body schema is pervaded by social norms: "We gain a sense of the relative position of our

16 We understand Hal's body schema and image here in the sense of Shaun Gallagher's conceptual clarification (1986). Thus, the body schema refers here to the operative performance of Hal's body as it actively attempts to integrate its positions and responses in the environment (e.g., posture/movement), but clearly fails to do so (Gallagher 1986, 548).

body parts and the effort required for movement through resisting and complying with the built world (e.g., uncomfortable classroom chairs) and learning social and cultural techniques for controlling our bodily orientation to that environment (e.g., sitting still because we are told to do so by teachers)" (Alper 2018). As James Savarese summarises, "our motor systems create an essential continuum by constantly anticipating – we might even say, by constantly remembering – the future" (Savarese 2018, 83). In terms of predictive processing, neurodivergent minds have been described as minds with too much precision in an imprecise and uncertain world (Constant et al. 2018).

In line with the novel's thematic concern with disability, its narrative form is equally geared towards making the reader aware of the (dis)orienting nature of a proprioceptive system overwhelmed by various types and amounts of sensory input. Our reading shows how the novel makes us experience neurodiversity and sensorimotor activities that are supposed to be self-evident and to go by unnoticed,[17] just as the intensely sensory experience showcased in the opening scene. Readers who may find themselves struggling to deal with the balance between text and footnotes are exposed to both distraction and its flip-coin, hyperfocus. Readers whose eyes cannot fixate the meaning of lavishly technical terminology packed in cantilevered sentences that are literally out of balance also experience the side-effects of hyperlexia and dyslexia.

Finally, readers need to update their "prior assumption" that abstract language and proto-narratives are "non-experiential" or deficient types of narrative: lists of seemingly random information (like James Incandenza's Filmography at the end of the novel) and the extensive digressions on neurochemistry and neurophysiology are part of the experience; it is the extended cognition, if not of the addicts themselves, then certainly of the readers who need to wade through a jumble of unsorted (or overly sorted) information in order to arrive at important details of the plot. This information is packaged in a type of cerebral and syntactically challenging language that can be said to be part of the "problem" rather than of the solution. As Wallace himself argues with regard to Kafka, this type of visceral humour is "not only not neurotic but anti-neurotic, heroically sane" (Wallace 2007, 64), more inclined to unsettle than to amuse and entertain the reader.

---

17 Cf. Russell 2011, 170: "[…] its weight or endlessly flipping back to the endnotes, reading this book becomes a curiously physical task. These excessive qualities call attention to the body consuming the text, but the novel also announces the extraordinary bodies between its covers. At a distended 1079 pages, the most obvious anomalous body is perhaps the text itself".

## 5 Conclusion

Crip humour is used in *Infinite Jest* to unmask, pace Sandahl, the delineation between normal and defective or disabled, as it turns out that precisely the instantiations of physical able-bodiedness (as exemplified by the Tennis Academy) or cognitive (hyper)ability (as instantiated in the novel's polysyllable intellectualism) are no less marked by compulsiveness than so-called maladaptive coping strategies or neurodevelopmental deficiencies. Crip humour hinges on various strategies of hyperbolic and sarcastic externalisation, which extend to both the societal cultivation of stigma and theoretical framings of disability (as implied in e.g., psychoanalysis). *Infinite Jest* could be accused of glorifying or exploiting trauma because of the excess of dismal or straightforwardly abusive circumstances piled on top of insightful descriptions of neurodevelopmental differences. In this contribution, we argued that the novel thus may profit from being read from the intertwined points of view of Crip Theory and neurodiversity. The idea of the extended mind comes naturally to the study of neurodiversity, mainly by problematising Theory of Mind. With regard to crip, *Infinite Jest* does not revel in disrespectful designations for mental health problems ('crazy', 'semi-retarded', 'crippling') for the sake of having a laugh at the expense of little-known minorities. The novel engages tactically in crip humour because the lopsided way in which it introduces and describes serious neurodegenerative conditions allows it to question society's disregard for hidden, invisible disabilities and raise awareness of their impact. Through strategies like information overload, *Infinite Jest* simulates experiential qualities of neurodiversity. At the same time, the often vulgar and uneven treatment of complex conditions echoes the way in which characters attempt to explain away or cope with the severity of their afflictions, as could be seen most clearly in the case of Gately.[18]

## Works Cited

"Aetiology". *Cambridge Dictionary,* www.dictionary.cambridge.org/dictionary/english/aetiology.

Alper, Meryl. "Inclusive Sensory Ethnography: Studying New Media and Neurodiversity in Everyday Life". *New Media & Society* 20.10, 2018, pp. 3560–79. doi.org/10.1177/1461444818755394.

18 Liselotte Van der Gucht wishes to acknowledge financial support by the FWO: Flemish Research Foundation (PhD Fellowship 1128122N). During proofreading, we noticed that Brick (2024) corroborates many of our findings.

Armstrong, Paul B. "Neuroscience, Narrative, and Narratology". *Poetics Today*, vol. 40, no. 3, 2019, pp. 395–428. doi.org/10.1215/03335372-7558052.

"Audience effect". *APA Dictionary of Psychology*, www.dictionary.apa.org/audience-effect.

Bennett, Alice. "David Foster Wallace and Attention". In *David Foster Wallace in Context*, edited by Clare Hayes-Brady, Literature in Context. Cambridge: Cambridge University Press, 2022, pp. 109–18. doi.org/10.1017/9781009064545.013.

Blum, Beth. "Polypharma Fiction". *American Literary History*, vol. 35, no. 3, 2023, pp. 1259–79. doi.org/10.1093/alh/ajad142.

Bowen, Murray. *Family therapy in clinical practice*. New York, Aronson, 1978.

Brick, Martin. "Narrative Voice and Autism in David Foster Wallace". *Autistic-Coded Representation and Autism Stereotypes: Looking for the Spectrum*. London, Lexington Books, 2024, pp. 103-116.

Burn, Stephen J. "'Webs of Nerves Pulsing and Firing': Infinite Jest and the Science of Mind". *A Companion to David Foster Wallace Studies*. Ed. Marshall Boswell and Stephen J. Burn, New York, Palgrave US, 2013, pp. 59–85. doi.org/10.1057/9781137078346_4.

"Camp". *Merriam-Webster*, www.merriam-webster.com/dictionary/camp#h3.

Charon, Rita. "Spoken Body: An *Infinite Jest* of Life, Death, and the Medical Tongue". *Poetics Today*, vol. 41, no. 2, 2020, pp. 261–79. doi.org/10.1215/03335372-8172570.

Chevallier, Coralie, Julia Parish-Morris, Natasha Tonge, Lori Le, Judith Miller, and Robert T. Schultz. "Susceptibility to the Audience Effect Explains Performance Gap between Children with and without Autism in a Theory of Mind Task". *Journal of Experimental Psychology. General*, vol. 143, no. 3, 2014, pp. 972–79. doi.org/10.1037/a0035483.

Constant, Axel, Jo Bervoets, Kristien Hens, and Sander Van de Cruys. "Precise Worlds for Certain Minds: An Ecological Perspective on the Relational Self in Autism". *Topoi*, vol. 39, 2018, pp. 611–22. doi.org/10.1007/s11245-018-9546-4.

Coogan, Tom. "'Usually I love The Onion, but this time you've gone too far': disability humour and transgression". *Journal of Literary & Cultural Disability Studies*, vol. 7, no. 1, 2013, pp. 1–17. doi.org/10.3828/jlcds.2013.1.

Corker, Mairian. "'Disability' The Unwelcome Ghost at the Banquet … and the Conspiracy of 'Normality'". *Body & Society*, vol. 5, no. 4, 2019, pp. 75–83.

Filmer, Rhonda: *Neurodiversity and the Twice-Exceptional Student. A Comprehensive Resource for Teachers*. New York, Routledge, 2024.

Gallagher, Shaun. "Body Image and Body Schema: A Conceptual Clarification". *Journal of Mind & Behaviour*, 15, 1986, pp. 541–54.

Garland-Thomson, Rosemarie. *Extraordinary Bodies: Figuring Physical Disability in American Culture and Literature*. New York, Columbia UP, 1997.

Hamon, Philippe. *L'ironie littéraire, essai sur les formes de l'écriture oblique*. Hachette, 1996.

Hannant, Penelope, Sarah Cassidy, Teresa Tavassoli, and Francesca Mann. "Sensorimotor Difficulties Are Associated with the Severity of Autism Spectrum Conditions".

*Frontiers in Integrative Neuroscience*, vol. 10, no. 28, 2016, pp. 1–14. doi.org/10.3389/fnint.2016.00028.

Hardin, Whitney, and Julia E. Kiernan, eds., *Adaptations of Mental and Cognitive Disability in Popular Media*. Lanham: Lexington Books, 2022.

Hayes-Brady, Clare. "'…': Language, Gender, and Modes of Power in the Work of David Foster Wallace". *A Companion to David Foster Wallace Studies*. Ed. Marshall Boswell and Stephen J. Burn, New York, Palgrave US, 2013, pp. 131–50.

Henneberg, Julian: *Subjects of Substance: Recent American Literature and the Materiality of Mind*. Bielefeld: transcript-Verlag, 2020.

"Iceberg Illustration. Poster". *Tourette Association of America*, www.tourette.org/resource/iceberg-illustration-poster/.

Jackson, Edward. *David Foster Wallace's Toxic Sexuality: Hideousness, Neoliberalism, Spermatics*. London: Bloomsbury Publishing, 2020.

Kukkonen, Karin. "Cognition, Good and Bad". *The Cambridge Quarterly*, vol. 48, no. 2, 2019, pp. 167–71. doi.org/10.1093/camqtly/bfy031.

Leith, Sam. "Infinite Jest at 20: 20 things you need to know". *The Guardian*, 26 February 2016, https://www.theguardian.com/books/2016/feb/26/infinite-jest-david-foster-wallace-20th-anniversary-20-things-need-know. Accessed on 6 May 2022.

Letzler, David. *The Cruft of Fiction: Mega-Novels and the Science of Paying Attention*. Lincoln: U of Nebraska Press, 2017.

Lindfors, Antti. "Awkward Connections. Stand-up Comedy as Affective Arrangement". In *Punching Up in Stand-Up Comedy*, edited by Richa Chilana and Rashi Bhargava. London: Taylor & Francis, 2022, pp. 181–196.

Mayo, Rob. *Depression and Dysphoria in the Fiction of David Foster Wallace*. London: Routledge, 2021.

McCaffrey, Tony. *Incapacity and Theatricality: Politics and Aesthetics in Theatre Involving Actors with Intellectual Disabilities*. London, Routledge, 2019.

Milbrodt, Teresa. "'Today I Had an Eye Appointment, and I'm Still Blind': Crip Humor, Storytelling, and Narrative Positioning of the Disabled Self". *Disability Studies Quarterly*, vol. 38, no. 2, 2018. doi.org/10.18061/dsq.v38i2.6163.

Miller, Adam S. *The Gospel According to David Foster Wallace: Boredom and Addiction in an Age of Distraction*. New York: Bloomsbury, 2016.

Owen, M. M. "David Foster Wallace and the Horror of Neuroscience". *The Millions* (blog), 13 March 2018. www.themillions.com/2018/03/david-foster-wallace-david-lynch-and-the-horror-of-neuroscience.html. Accessed on 10 May 2022.

Popova, Yanna B. *Stories, Meaning, and Experience: Narrativity and Enaction*. London, Routledge, 2015.

Randi, Judi, Tina Newman, and Elena L. Grigorenko. "Teaching Children with Autism to Read for Meaning: Challenges and Possibilities". *Journal of Autism and*

*Developmental Disorders*, vol. 40, no. 7, 2010, pp. 890–902. doi.org/10.1007/s10803-010-0938-6.

Redgate, Jamie. *Wallace and I: Cognition, Consciousness, and Dualism in David Foster Wallace's Fiction*. London/New York: Routledge, 2019.

Russell, Emily. "Some Assembly Required: The Disability Politics of Infinite Jest". *Reading Embodied Citizenship*. Ed. Emily Russell, New Brunswick, NJ, Rutgers UP, 2011, pp. 170–97. doi.org/10.36019/9780813549903.

Sandahl, Carrie. "Queering the Crip or Cripping the Queer? Intersections of Queer and Crip Identities in Solo Autobiographical Performances". *GLQ: A Journal of Lesbian and Gay Studies*, vol. 9, no. 1–2, 2003, pp. 25–56.

Savarese, Ralph James. *See It Feelingly: Classic Novels, Autistic Readers, and the Schooling of a No-Good English Professor*. Durham, N.C., Duke UP, 2018.

Schiff, Sarah Eden. "Family Systems Theory as Literary Analysis: The Case of Philip Roth". *Philip Roth Studies*, vol. 2, no. 1, 2006, pp. 25–46.

Schweik, Susan. "Marshall P. Wilder and Disability Performance History". *Disability Studies Quarterly*, vol. 30, no. 3/4, 2010. doi.org/10.18061/dsq.v30i3/4.1271.

Sloane, Peter. *David Foster Wallace and the Body*. New York, Routledge, 2019. doi.org/10.4324/9780429286483.

Stenning, Anna. "Understanding Empathy through a Study of Autistic Life Writing". *Neurodiversity Studies: A New Critical Paradigm*. Ed. Hanna Bertilsdotter Rosqvist, Nick Chown, and Anna Stenning, London, New York, Routledge, 2020. doi.org/10.4324/9780429322297.

Stock, Robert. "Singing Altogether Now: Unsettling Images of Disability and Experimental Filmic Practices". *Documentary and Disability*. Ed. Catalin Brylla and Helen Hughes, London, Palgrave, 2017, pp. 227–41.

"Twice-Exceptional Students". *National Association for Gifted Children*, http://nagc.org.442elmp01.blackmesh.com/resources-publications/resources-parents/twice-exceptional-students.

Wallace, David Foster. *Both Flesh And Not*. London, Penguin UK, 2012.

Wallace, David Foster. *Consider the Lobster: And Other Essays*. Boston, Little, 2007.

Wallace, David Foster. *Infinite Jest*. Boston, Little, 1996.

Wegner, Gesine. "'Kill the Puppies!': Cringe Comedy and Disability Humor in the Live Performances of Laurence Clark". *Humanities*, vol. 10, no. 3: 105, 2021. doi.org/10.3390/h10030105.

CHAPTER 7

# Altered Narration: Unreliability in Narrators with Alzheimer's Disease

*Simona Adinolfi*

To Alessandra Benedetti

## 1 Introduction

In recent years, contemporary literature has increasingly been engaging with the human mind and its processes. The neuro-novel (Roth 2009) is, for instance, one of the most interesting examples of this trend. In particular, a specific thematic turn in contemporary fiction which lays in between, on the one hand, the aforementioned interest in the workings of the mind and, on the other, in raising awareness about specific neurological conditions[1] is the "Alzheimeri[s]ation" (Adelman qtd. in Zimmerman 2022, 56), or Alzheimer's epidemic (Burke 2018, 88), a boom in the literary – and more in the general artistic – portrayal of Alzheimer's Disease.[2]

Alzheimer's Disease, "a progressive, degenerative disease characterised by the death of nerve cells in several areas of the brain" (Turkington 2003, 14), affects around 35.6 million people in the world today and this number is expected to "double by 2030 and triple by 2050" (Hartung 2016, 174). For years, the term 'Alzheimer's Disease' has labelled rare cases of early onset dementia, until the 1960s, when medical research started claiming that Alzheimer's also influenced later stages of dementia (ibid., 173). Today, "early onset Alzheimer's" labels the illness affecting patients from forty to sixty years of age and is

1 See for example the works of Lisa Genova, neurologist and best-selling author whose novels all deal with neurological diseases and shed a light on the hardships of living with them.

2 Lucy Burke is, to my knowledge, the first to link the neuro-turn and fiction on Alzheimer's Disease in her 2018 essay "Missing pieces. Trauma, dementia and the ethics of reading in *Elizabeth is missing*".

 | DOI:10.1163/9789004519886_009

understood to be genetically transmitted. Alzheimer's Disease is grouped under the umbrella term *dementia*, which designates all the cognitive impairments appearing in old age, specifically memory loss.[3]

Some scholars identify this literary trend in the anxieties about the end of the "era of the witness" (Wieviorka 2006), hence, a fear linked to collective memory. Others relate it to the spread of the disease in recent years (Garrigós 2022, 2). Lucy Burke praises dementia fiction, and in particular, literary works with a first-person narrator affected by dementia, for its ability to give an insight, albeit speculative, into the *subjective* experience of living with Alzheimer's Disease and raise "ethical and epistemological questions" (Burke 2018, 88).

If we focus on the literary aspect of this topic, we may look at Alzheimer's as a neurological condition which hinders the very basic process of narrating. It undermines the essential tools of narration, above all memory of course, but also language, and consequentiality, thus depriving us of one of our most instinctual and human traits, that of telling a story.

It is indeed challenging for an author to conceive a work where the narrative is entirely in the hands of a narrator suffering from Alzheimer's Disease. And yet, more and more novels – starting from Mordecai Richler's *Barney's Version* (1997), Alice LaPlante's thriller, *Turn of Mind* (2011), as well as films – with the award-winning *The Father* (2020) as a brilliant example thereof – embark on this demanding task and generate new discourses about the strategies people living with Alzheimer's employ. Typical features of novels where the narrator has Alzheimer's Disease are, to name a few, non-linearity in the progression of the plot; the importance given to written sources; physical objects as milestones in the narrative; the pivotal role played by spaces such as the house, the eldercare, the hospital; a focus on the caregivers – whether they are family members of the patient or specialised nurses in an institutionalised home.[4]

In his work *Strange Narrators in Contemporary Fiction*, Marco Caracciolo highlights the popularity of contemporary novels narrated in first person (2016, 28) by *strange narrators*. A strange narrator is, in his definition, one whose strangeness "can be explained in terms of a real – world category (e.g., autistic people) and when his or her mental condition is perceived as impossible in the real world" (ibid., 21). One of their main and most interesting features, which contributes to the feeling of strangeness, is their unreliability (ibid., 28). This is also what makes them so appealing to contemporary audiences because

3 In this essay, I will use the term Alzheimer's Disease and dementia interchangeably.

4 In my Master's dissertation, I explore themes and narrative strategies of four contemporary Alzheimer's Disease novels. http://dspace.unive.it/bitstream/handle/10579/11737/841528-1213096.pdf?sequence=2

unreliability both challenges readers' worldviews and requires them to engage more actively with the text in order to decipher it. I contend that narrators affected by Alzheimer's Disease are also *strange narrators* in Caracciolo's terms and, in this essay, I want to focus on the complexities of deeming such narrators as simply unreliable.

To do so, it is important to have an overview of the main theories of unreliable narration which may apply to a narrator with Alzheimer's Disease, both from classical and cognitive narratology. My approach for this chapter will be to look at the textual cues for unreliability, while simultaneously speculating on the reading experience of such texts. Through the analysis of Emma Healey's novel, *Elizabeth Is Missing*, we will see what can be defined as an instance of altered narration and how it differentiates from unreliability. Before we start, however, it is important to stress that this essay investigates purely literary structures: the portrayal of a character with Alzheimer's Disease does not correspond to the actual experience of living with dementia. It is a literary experiment which however, as we will see, may help us make some considerations on the socio-cultural perceptions of this illness.

## 2 Unreliability: Text Oriented Approaches

Whenever we encounter a first-person narrator – or more precisely an autodiegetic narrator (Nünning 2008, 119)[5] – we must take into account the possibility that she or he will be unreliable. Unreliability has undoubtedly been one of the most debated and controversial aspects of classical narratology, and more recent discourse on the topic has also involved cognitive studies. The first definition of the term which also enjoys a notable longevity up to today is Wayne Booth's: a narrator is *reliable* if he or she "speaks for or acts in accordance with the norms of the work" and *unreliable* when he "does not" (1983, 158–59). This approach, which focuses on the text and on its (implied)[6] author's intentions has dominated the discourse on unreliability but has also often been criticised for its broadness. Hence, many attempts have been made to narrow down the definition and specify particular cases of unreliability.

5 Namely "a narrator who is identical with the main protagonist and narrates his or her own life story, instead of being just an observer or a witness" (Nünning 2008, 119).

6 For reasons of brevity, I will not go into detail as to the debate over the implied author. Extensive contributions to the topic areJames Phelan's *Living to tell about it* and Ansgar Nünning's essay "Reconceptualizing the Theory, History and Generic Scope of Unreliable Narration: Towards a Synthesis of Cognitive and Rhetorical Approaches" (2008).

Among taxonomical works, James Phelan's model, which distinguishes between six kinds of unreliability, subdivided into "reporting" and "interpreting" categories, is perhaps one of the most prominent attempts at situating unreliability under more precise terms (2005). Another approach, which is worth mentioning in this context, is Greta Olson's distinction between *untrustworthy* and *fallible* narrators, whereby the former are "*dispositionally* unreliable" (2003, 102), because their inconsistencies seem to stem from their behaviour or an interest in lying. The latter, on the other hand, misinterpret a narrative event because their world knowledge is limited (Olson gives the example of *Huckleberry Finn*) or they simply lack a reliable source of information (2003, 201).

The analysis of character types has been central to William Riggan's seminal work *Picaros, Madmen, Naïfs, and Clowns: The Unreliable First-Person Narrator* (1981), in which he looks at unreliability as stemming from mentally unstable characters. Drawing on Riggan's book, Per Krogh Hansen (2007) claims that unreliability may derive from a character being a specific type, such as a madman, but also distinguishes between four kinds of unreliable narration, namely intranarrational, internarrational, intertextual, and extratextual. The first regards situations where the narrator gives contradicting statements which make the reader question their reliability. Internarrational unreliability can be detected when a character undermines the narrator's statements – and many are such cases in my case study, as we are about to see. The third has to do with cases where the cues for unreliability rely in the paratext. The last typology lies in the discordant worldviews between the narrator and the reader, in other words emphasis is put on the reader's perception of the narrator's accounts. Monika Fludernik has lamented a lack of studies on "the most typical case of narratorial unreliability: the narrator who [...] suffers from a patent epistemological distortion regarding the fictional world" (1999, 77) and has proceeded on to analyze the unreliable narrator of "The Yellow Wallpaper" as a case study.

Moving closer to the object of this paper is Stephan Freißmann's study of the autistic narrator in *The Curious Incident of The Dog In the Night-Time*. Freißmann defines the autodiegetic narrator Christopher as a "limited narrator" (2018, 396), arguing that his experience and perception of reality is limited by autism, an aspect that cannot be ignored when debating on his narrative strategies.

These approaches may all very well apply to narrators with Alzheimer's Disease. We can argue that they often *misinterpret*; there's no doubt they are *fallible* – although there are exceptions to the rule[7] – and they surely can be

7 See my reading of Alice LaPlante's *Turn of Mind* in my dissertation.

accounted for as limited, if we agree that Alzheimer's Disease, like autism and other neurological impairments *limits* one's perception. But what I would like to contend here is that the textual features of a narrative entrusted to a narrator with Alzheimer's Disease are very specific and have to do with time-space perception as well as with speech impairment and a sense of awareness about one's altered sense-making of reality.

To my knowledge, the only work of research focusing on narrators living with Alzheimer's Disease is Maria Vaccarella's study on graphic novels with cognitively impaired narrators. Here, Vaccarella asks "how do authors manage narrative unreliability when it stems out of the narrator's (maybe temporary) cognitive impairment?" (2014, 88). And she examines, among others, Sarah Leavitt's *Tangles*, a graphic memoir on her mother's Alzheimer's. This graphic memoir strongly relies on the visual cues and on the carer's interventions to support the narrative and bridge its gaps (Vaccarella 2014, 91). But what about a novel in which the only one in charge of the narrative has Alzheimer's Disease?

## 3 Unreliability: Cognitive Approaches, Nünning's Model and Altered Narration

To look into this, I would like to briefly turn to the contribution of cognitive narratology to the matter. The cognitive approach has tried to detach itself from the notion of the implied author and has focused on the reader's perception of unreliability. Cognitive theorists use frame theory to conceptualise unreliability. Frame theory is a sociological theory which implies that people's sense-making of reality falls back on the frame in which a specific entity is being understood. This is thought to influence decision making and is also used in political and media studies. In the context of narratology, a concept from frame theory, naturalisation, can be helpful to understand the reader's response to unreliability (Nünning 2008, 45–47). Each reader's frame of reference in making sense of a text will be different: consequentially, each reader's perception of a narrator's (un)reliability will be different, too.

In the case of dementia fiction, for instance, a reader whose background life experience includes having met, having cared for, or living with someone affected by Alzheimer's Disease will clearly be different from someone who has only ever heard of the condition or read about it. We can argue that the former may be more attentive to spotting when a narrator is contradicting his or her former statement, or when a worsening of the illness is detectable in the narrator's stances. It is worth noticing here that many of the authors who have written dementia fiction have been influenced by direct experience with the illness.[8]

However, we must not simply dismiss the importance of the textual cues when looking into unreliability issues. In this regard, Ansgar Nünning has sustained that the two approaches, cognitive and textual, must merge, because, both "world experience and literary conventions" contribute to our understanding of unreliability (2008, 47). My model for unreliability in novels narrated by a character affected by Alzheimer's Disease stems from Nünning's proposal and aims to simultaneously look at the narrative strategies as well as to speculate on the reading experience.

I propose that when we deal with a narrator with Alzheimer's Disease, we are facing "altered narration", a narrative mode influenced by the presence of this illness, which *alters* the narrative processes and triggers specific patterns relatable to unreliability. In the next section we will look at these patterns and see how a reader may respond to them: time perception, gaps in spatial and temporal cues, tense changes, blurred ontological boundaries between memories and the present all contribute to creating the illusion of a mind altered by a condition of neurological impairment. What makes this kind of narration peculiar are the narrator's references to her or his sensemaking of reality and hence to her or his difficulties in narrating. In order to clarify this, let us turn to the novel *Elizabeth Is Missing* by Emma Healey.

## 4 *Elizabeth Is Missing*: Textual Markers and Time Perception

*Elizabeth Is Missing* is Emma Healey's debut novel, published in 2014, and turned into a successful TV film by BBC in 2019. The novel's autodiegetic narrator, Maud, an eighty-year-old woman affected by Alzheimer's, claims that her best friend Elizabeth is missing. More precisely, the notes she writes and then finds in her pockets and scattered around her house, tell her so. She therefore decides to start looking for her friend on her own, since the people around her do not believe her and do not credit her statements. For her amateurish

8 This essay's case study, *Elizabeth Is Missing*, is inspired by the author's grandmother living with AD; *The Story of Forgetting* by Stefan Merrill Block (2008) also stems from the author's experience with AD affecting his grandmother; in writing *Turn of Mind* (2011), which granted her the Wellcome Prize, a prize normally attributed to non-fictional medical works, Alice LaPlante has taken inspiration from her mother's condition; in *The Corrections* (2001), Jonathan Franzen's portrayal of Alfred is built on his father's illness.

investigation, she mainly relies on her notes, which however, very often do not make sense to her: Alzheimer's often gets in the way and erases both clues and the very fact that she is looking for Elizabeth.

Her search triggers memories of her youth related to a specific traumatic event which has affected her whole life: the disappearance of her older sister Sukey, who went missing when Maud was only fourteen, in post-war England. Sukey has never been found again, and Maud narrates with vivid details the whole event, from the disappearance to the investigations, passing through the possible suspects for Sukey's alleged murder and her attempts to find out what happened to her sister.

Elizabeth's and Sukey's disappearances are narrated in parallel: in every chapter, Maud's investigation of Elizabeth's vanishing alternates with specific moments belonging to Sukey's disappearance. As the novel progresses, the reader also witnesses Maud's illness worsening through the narration, which begins to mix up the two disappearances, thus collapsing past and present as well. The reader finds it increasingly difficult to follow the progression of the two cases which begin to merge in Maud's narration and seem to become one single case. Indeed, Elizabeth has never disappeared. She suffered a stroke while Maud was digging in her garden (2014, 253), where she was subconsciously looking for Sukey's corpse. Sukey's husband, Frank, had killed her and buried her many years before in Elizabeth's garden, when the houses of the neighborhood were still being built. In Maud's mind, Elizabeth's 'disappearance' triggered the need to solve her sister's cold case.

Arguably, one of the reasons for the success of this mystery novel is that the reading experience is in itself a mystery: in order to follow Maud's narrative, readers can count on a series of clues which also warn them of Maud's unreliability. One of these is represented by other characters's contradicting statements. Let us consider the beginning of chapter three, in which Maud and Helen, Maud's daughter, are talking to Maud's doctor:

> 'I am all right', I say. 'What is the fuss?' He breathes out through his nose, an impatient sound, like a foraging animal. 'You called the surgery, Mrs. Horsham. You said you were in urgent need of a house call'. He looks at Helen, then sits down, holds my wrist in his hand and presses it, looking at his watch. 'Can you remember what it was about?' he says. 'You have been ringing fairly frequently of late. And people don't usually ask for house calls when they are *all right*'. Helen shakes her head at me behind him. 'I haven't been calling frequently', I say, still looking at Helen. 'That's not quite true, is it?' he says, scribbling something on a notepad. 'In fact you've phoned us twelve times in the last fortnight'. (Healey 2014, 29)

In this passage, Maud's claims are denied by the doctor's affirmation. Even if, in the previous page, Maud has told the reader that she feels like she is ill and needs to call the doctor (ibid., 28), which she does, she does not mention calling him continuously, as the doctor states. Albeit not being vital for the plot, this passage is a warning sign for the reader and, to refer back to Hansen's taxonomy as mentioned earlier, a case of intranarrational unreliability since it is relying on the other characters' contradicting the narrator's stances.

Altered time perception is also a clue for unreliability. A 2016 study by Mohamad El Haj and Dimitrios Kapogiannis claims that "episodic memory impairment in AD may result in a loss of the ability to retrieve information about time and/or the ability to project oneself in subjective time. […] AD patients suffer from the inability to consciously acquire new memories, and as a consequence, are often 'stuck in time'" (El Haj and Kapogiannis 2016). Very often in the narrative of *Elizabeth Is Missing*, Maud is unable to establish how long she has been in a place and often finds herself stuck in time. One of the most exemplary episodes portraying her distorted time perception is when she comes back from the hospital with her daughter, after having had her injured hand medicated:

> 'It's nice to be home', I say to Helen. 'Nice to be back in my own home after all this time'. We've come from the hospital. I had to go because of some problem. What was it now? Anyway, it's nice to be home. 'You were at the hospital for a few hours, Mum. Don't overdo it'. She drops her car keys on to the coffee table. 'No, Helen', I say. 'It was longer than that. Several weeks. Perhaps months. A long, long time'. 'A few hours', she says again. (Healey 2014, 120)

Here, Maud's comment on the long time she allegedly spent at the hospital is immediately contradicted by her daughter. However, she does not – and cannot – believe her, and is slightly unsettled by the fact that her daughter contradicts her. Remarkably, a few seconds later, her daughter makes a comment that neither Maud, nor the reader, grasps, but that will be crucial for the denouement of the story: "'And I thought you'd feel better after the visit. I know it wasn't very nice, I know it was a bit sad, but at least you can stop worrying now'" (Healey 2014, 120). Incidentally, here, we have again a character contradicting Maud. She does not know that her daughter is referring to the visit they paid to Elizabeth, who was also at the hospital because of her stroke. Given that her short-term memory is damaged by Alzheimer's, Maud is both unable to remember that she saw her friend a few hours before, and to recognise that the time she spent at the hospital was much shorter than her perception of it. Maud's memory gaps allow us to reach the core of her unreliability.

## 5 Minding the Gaps

The first consistent gap occurs between the prologue and the first chapter. The prologue itself is crucial for the whole novel. It presents us readers with all the gaps we will have to fill by reading on. Maud hears a woman calling her from within a house, while she is in the garden looking for something (we do not know what). She looks at an old compact she seems to have found which "makes [her] squirm with memories" (Healey 2014, 1). The connection between a found object and a resurfacing memory is the pattern that will delineate the entire structure of the novel: every time she notices an object in her house – a lipstick, a can of peaches – Maud starts remembering details from Sukey's disappearance. A few lines later, Maud tells us that she has missed the compact for seventy years, but she does not know how it got into her hands (ibid., 2). The other woman steps outside to see what Maud is looking for, and Maud describes her as "precarious and trembling", giving the reader a chance of picturing an old woman. Then Maud describes a noise, "like a fox bark" which "makes an attempt at the edges of [her] brain" (ibid.). This noise comes as an answer to Maud's question about marrows, which she will also ask her daughter later. Like the other missing pieces of information Maud gives in the prologue, the noise will only be explained at the end of the novel,[9] when we find out what happened to Elizabeth (ibid., 253) – she suffered a stroke. Then, the first chapter opens with the news that Elizabeth is missing (ibid., 6).

Now the story is set, and the reader's task is to fill the gap between Elizabeth's stroke and Maud's claim about her disappearance. In other words: readers are faced with the question what happened between the time when Maud is digging in Elizabeth's garden and when she starts saying that her friend is missing. In Genettian terms, this gap is an *ellipsis*, "an elision of a diachronic section" (1980, 51). But the omission that Elizabeth had been at the hospital the whole time is what Genette calls a *paralipsis* (ibid., 52). This narrative device is instead employed when the narrator omits a pivotal element of the narrative in full. The core of Maud's unreliability lies entirely in this *paralipsis*.

9 Maud hears Elizabeth stumble and fall from the three steps of the patio that bring to the garden where Maud is. As Peter, Elizabeth's son, says towards the end of the novel, "It was the shock of the fall that caused the stroke" (Healey 2014, 254).

## 6 Present Tense Narration: a Double-Edged Sword for the Reader

So how does the reader orientate in these frequent time gaps and distortions? As has been mentioned in the previous section, Elizabeth's disappearance is narrated in the present tense, Sukey's case is set in the past and narrated in the past tense. Maud tells us the story of Elizabeth's disappearance as it happens. Sukey's disappearance is instead evoked in her memory, which is still extremely rich in detail as far as this particular event is concerned. For the first part of the novel, the reader can count on this tense alternation to locate the events in the narrative.

To complicate the matter, however, the narrative's progression corresponds to the Alzheimer's progression in Maud. The reader can witness Maud's deterioration in various moments. In chapter eight she cannot recognise her grandchildren: "Both children smile at me and call me Grandma, but I feel like they are strangers" (Healey 2014, 105); in chapter sixteen she cannot read and probably write anymore: "'What are you writing?' she asks. I look down at the paper under my hands. There are just scribbles. Lots of black scribbles on white. I can't read them" (ibid., 224). What determines her deterioration to the point of significantly impacting on the reader's experience is visible in the following passage, namely the opening of chapter seventeen:

> My house is dark when I get there. Ma and Dad are out looking for Sukey. I stand in the front porch trying to find my keys, checking my bag and each of my pockets twice. The keys aren't there. My stomach seems to float into my chest, and my heart beats against it. I breathe carefully in, and turn out my pockets, shaking everything on the ground. [...] Someone, who isn't Ma and isn't Dad, is opening the door. It's a man, youngish, small and fair, who stops just inside and stares at me [...] I don't think I recogni[s]e him, but I don't trust myself. 'Douglas?' I say. 'No I'm Sean', he says, backing into the house. My house. 'Stay here', he calls. (ibid., 235)

At this point in the novel, any careful reader is used to the tense pattern I mentioned earlier: every chapter opens in the present tense with Maud being in her eighties. Within every chapter there are incursions of the past concerning Sukey's disappearance which are narrated in past tense. Here, however, the reader is faced with a present tense narration combined with references to Maud's past ("Ma and Dad are out looking for Sukey"). The narration is mostly paratactic with brief sentences describing the moment of anxiety Maud is experiencing by finding someone in her own house ("My stomach seems to float", "I breathe carefully in"). Suspense is created and immediately disrupted a few lines later when we understand that the man occupying Maud's house is the legitimate new owner of her house, sold by Helen who took Maud to live with her (Healey 2014, 180). Maud is now unable to discern past from present which overlap in her perception, thus overlapping in her narration, too, using the present tense.

In her work on present tense narration, Carolin Gebauer demonstrates how present tense, too, can be a narrative strategy to enhance and highlight unreliability (2021, 269). This is also frequently the case, when we encounter a narrator affected by Alzheimer's disease: in this case, too, we as readers witness the collision between memories and present time in Maud's narrative, and we cannot rely on the tenses to keep track of where we are in time anymore.

As we have seen so far, a reading experience of a fictional narrative influenced by the presence of Alzheimer's disease is speckled by a series of textual markers, which are warning signs for the narrator's unreliability. What these markers – contradictions, time distortions, narrative gaps, present tense narration – elicit in the reader is, I contend, a sense of disorientation which may mimetically reproduce the disorientation felt by an Alzheimer's Disease patient. As Caracciolo notices, facing "strange narrators" can also give the reader new awareness on a particular illness or give unprecedented insight in peculiar mental processes (2016, 50). This is also valid in *Elizabeth Is Missing*: our disorientation in keeping track of the plot, in situating the events, in believing or not a statement made by a character, mirrors Maud's frustration in carrying on her investigation, at keeping record of what she found out, at trusting what the other characters tell her. As we are about to see, frustration makes Elizabeth both reflect and comment on her situation, and triggers the textual cues which contributeto making the narration altered.

## 7 Altered Narration in *Elizabeth Is Missing*

In *Elizabeth Is Missing,* the term Alzheimer's Disease or dementia is never mentioned. Its presence however, as we have seen until now, is quite pervasive. One of the most touching moments in the novel is perhaps Maud's description of her memories, past and present:

> Sometimes, when I'm having a sort-through or a clear-out, I find my photos from my youth, and it's a shock to see everything in black and white. I think my granddaughter believes we were actually grey-skinned, with dull hair, always posing in a shadowed landscape. But I remember the town

> as being almost too bright to look at when I was a girl. […] nowadays, the colours seem faded, as if I live in an old photograph. (Healey 2014, 9)

Counter to what one might think, at the early stages of Alzheimer's Disease, long-term memory still vividly inhabits the mind of a patient. This part of our memory is only affected in later stages of the condition, which, as we have seen in the passage about present tense narration, tends to intrude the present. In this excerpt, Maud still sees her past clearly and in color. Her present is blurry and undistinguishable, and that patina is her condition. In the narrative, Alzheimer's Disease forms a layer, which interposes between the reader and the narrator. This layer causes altered narration.

This narrative mode has three specific indicators which can be easily recognised:

- periphrases;
- self-doubting questions;
- self-references.

More than once in the novel, Maud refers to objects and spaces around her by using periphrases. A fur coat is "an animal for wearing outside"; a piece of soap becomes "the slippery washing cake"; a chair is once referred to as "a wooden thing for sitting" (Healey 2014, 4, 63, 75),[10] and there are many more of such instances throughout. Speech impairment is one of the first arising symptoms of dementia and one big issue with our narrator Maud. Not being able to name things also adds up to the hardships a narrator with Alzheimer's Disease encounters when telling a story.

As readers, these periphrases also contribute to mirroring the difficulties of Alzheimer's for us: as Maud cannot immediately think of an object's name, at the same time we cannot immediately visualise it. This is also one of the reasons why I stress that the presence of Alzheimer's Disease in graphic novels, such as the one analysed by Maria Vaccarella, is not comparable to novels or short stories which ask the reader to only rely on the written word.

In the previous section, I mentioned Maud's sense of frustration which is inferable throughout the novel. Not only does she get angry at other people for

10 When I was teaching this novel for a course on Ageing Studies at the University of Wuppertal, I made my students focus on the use of periphrases in the novel through a small game in which they had to guess what object the quote was referring to. Part of the class admitted to not paying attention to the pattern during the reading. Another consistent part, instead, said that the guessing game had been a considerable part of their narrative experience, especially given the importance of physical objects in the novel.

not believing her, she also starts questioning her own statements in the narrative. Already in the first few chapters, Maud is uncertain as to what she is doing or why she is doing it. Take this passage for instance: Carla, Maud's carer, is telling her about scary events which have recently happened in the neighborhood, and which involve old people: "I've heard of cases where young crack addicts move in with old people […] Well, there was an old woman who was bound in a basement and the robbers took everything and then tortured her and locked her in, and nobody knew she was there. For days and days"[11] (Healey 2014, 42). Maud listens to Carla's words and a few lines later starts writing down notes for her investigations: "*Elizabeth locked in room – crack addicts in house. Bound and tortured in the basement.* I frown at my own writing. I must be going barmy. Crack addicts? The police would have been called. But, I think, why not go to the house anyway and check on Elizabeth?" (ibid., 43). In this passage, Maud merges Carla's words with her concern about Elizabeth and her task to find out what happened to her. However, immediately after re-reading what she wrote, she starts questioning the content of her notes through self-doubting questions. "Could I really have written that?", she keeps asking herself (ibid.). From the reader's perspective, here, it is easy to make sense of what has happened, since Carla's words have just been reported and we can distinguish the contradiction by ourselves. What is crucial, for this passage, though, is Maud's awareness that something does not quite fit. As I mentioned earlier, the words Alzheimer's or dementia never appear in the novel. Nevertheless, the narrator finds ways of communicating to the reader her uneasiness, this patina of blurriness she experiences.

The final characteristic of altered narration is closely linked to the aforementioned self-doubting questions, and it concerns the frequent references to feelings of haziness and uncertainty about what the narrator is about to do or has just done. I call these self-references, because they are moments in which the autodiegetic narrator reflects on her condition, even if it is never medically labelled. At the same time, these moments also implicitly refer to the struggle of narrating coherently. Let us turn to some examples to make this clearer.

At the beginning of the novel, Maud knows she must write, but she does not know what: "The most important thing is to write everything down. For a moment, *I'm hazy* about just what it is I have to write" (ibid., 23; my emphasis). Further on, she completes an action or describes herself in the middle of an action, without really knowing its purpose: "In front of me there's a hole, a hole that I've been digging, in the middle of the green garden carpet. And suddenly

11 On the role of Carla's behavior, see Lucy Burke's essay on the novel, in which she considers it as a reinforcement of Maud's insecurity and fragility (2018, 96–98).

*I can't think what I'm doing here*, what it is I'm looking for [...] And still *I have the urge to go on digging* to search for something in the ground" (ibid., 62–63; my emphasis). Towards the end of the novel, in perhaps one of the tensest moments for the reader, we witness Maud's last effort in communicating to her daughter her real intentions behind the sentence "Elizabeth is missing": "It's the wrong name, I know it's the wrong name, but I can't think of the right one" (Healey 2014, 258).

These markers all slightly distinguish altered narration from unreliability: in these instances, Maud seems to be aware that she is unsure about what she is doing and saying, that her time perception is different, that the things she notes down do not quite make sense. And that is why she makes these small but significant comments on her feelings of uneasiness.

Let us consider one final excerpt which can aptly summarise the discourse on altered narration:

> I ring the bell. 'It echoed through the empty house'. The phrase bubbles up from somewhere, but bells always echo though houses, surely? Empty or not. I wait, and work a hand deep into one of the earth-filled barrels by the front step. These are usually crammed with flowers, but not even a green shoot breaks the surface now. Elizabeth must have forgotten to plant any bulbs this year. I pull my hand out quickly. I can't think what it was doing in the soil. Was I just feeling for bulbs, or am I supposed to be looking for something else? I face the door wondering how long I've waited here. Five minutes? Ten? I check my watch, but it doesn't give me any clues. Time is so elastic now. I ring the bell again, carefully making a note of the time, and then watch the second hand as it moves round. After five minutes I write: *No Sign of Elizabeth,* and begin to walk away. Perhaps she *is* on holiday, as someone suggested. (ibid., 23–24; emphasis in the text)

The simple action of ringing the bell triggers the memory of a sentence which emerges from Maud's damaged memory, and it does so by "bubbling up", as if her memories were all mixed up in a cauldron and the boiling made some of its ingredients randomly resurface only to quickly disappear in the mix again. This process – an action triggering a memory – is the main structural pattern of the novel through which Sukey's story is revealed. Then Maud automatically puts her hand in one of the barrels she sees at the entrance of Elizabeth's house. She notices the lack of flowers, unusual for Elizabeth, and immediately pulls her hand out claiming she does not know the reason for her action. Is she supposed to look for something else? She cannot answer. Then, Maud reflects on time: she cannot discern how much time has passed from when she rang the bell and she comments on her uncertainty by stating that time is "so elastic now". She then decides to ring again and, this time, to keep track of the passing of time by looking at her watch. She counts five minutes and concludes that Elizabeth is probably on holiday.

Any attentive reader confronted with this passage will notice Maud's uncertainty in telling what she is doing, and uneasiness to tell apart the reasons behind her actions. Altered narration makes it so that the narrative flow uniting the reader and the narrator loses its fluidity and suffers continuous halts due to Alzheimer's Disease and its characteristics: *altering* time perception and hindering the ability to narrate.

## 8 Conclusion

This essay has focused on fictional narrators with Alzheimer's Disease, speculating on their narrative strategies and on the reader's experience. More specifically, we have seen how unreliability can be considered an essential feature of this kind of narratives and, at the same time, how it is possible to conceive a narrative entrusted to a narrator with Alzheimer's Disease as altered. In other words, looking at this kind of narrative as an instance of altered narration helps us shift our focus from the narrator's accountability to the presence of Alzheimer's Disease. Dementia influences the narrative for the prominence of the present tense, for the frequent gaps and inconsistencies. The core of altered narration, however, resides in the moments of self-doubt the reader is allowed to witness, where the narrator wonders about his or her actions and, consequently, on his or her ability to narrate.

My focus for this essay has been dementia fiction with autodiegetic narrators. But the spread of the neuro-novel makes altered narration a tool for the analysis of many other narrative situations where a condition hinders the narrator and he or she shows implicit or explicit awareness of it.[12]

Neurological diseases such as Alzheimer's play with deep-seated fears such as memory loss, end of independence, and inability to communicate. Doubtlessly, scientific research is what we must rely on in order to foster the debate about them and in order to find a cure. However, there is something unique that literature and discourses around it can do. A novel such as the case study of this essay can extend the debate on Alzheimer's Disease and reach out to

12 One may argue, for instance, that Jonathan Lethem's *Motherless Brooklyn* (1999) also contains examples of altered narration.

people who have never had any close contact with it, by telling a simple story. At the same time, it can donate solace and comfort to those who experience or have experienced Alzheimer's in their day-to-day life. Pieter Vermeulen argues that "literary studies has the resources to attend to the repetitions, reductions, indirections and fragmentations that mark the language of dementia" (2019, 41). Indeed, researching on the mechanism of Alzheimer's narratives can shed a light on how literature endeavors to access the still unexplored territories of a deteriorating mind, and, perhaps, on how these minds still strive to communicate, only through a different, more complex language that we have not deciphered yet.

## Works Cited

Adelman, Richard C. "The Alzheimerisation of Aging". *Gerontologist*, vol. 35, no. 4, 1995, pp. 526–32.

Adinolfi, Simona. *Mind the Gap: An Analysis of the Narrative Strategies in Alzheimer's Novels*. 2017. Ca' Foscari University of Venice, Master's Dissertation. http://dspace.unive.it/bitstream/handle/10579/11737/841528-1213096.pdf?sequence=2.

Booth, Wayne C. *The Rhetoric of Fiction*. U of Chicago P, 1983.

Burke, Lucy. "Missing pieces. Trauma, dementia and the ethics of reading in *Elizabeth Is Missing*". *Dementia and Literature. Interdisciplinary Perspectives*, Ed. Tess Maginess, Routledge, 2018, pp. 88–102.

Caracciolo, Marco. *Strange Narrators in Contemporary Fiction: Explorations in Readers' Engagement with Characters*. U of Nebraska P, 2016.

El Haj, Mohamad, and Dimitrios Kapogiannis. "Time Distortion in Alzheimer's disease: a systematic review and theoretical integration". *NPJ Aging and Mechanisms Disease*, 16016, 2016, https://www.ncbi.nlm.nih.gov/pmc/articles/PMC5514999/#.

Fludernik, Monika. "Defining (In)Sanity: The Narrator of *The Yellow Wallpaper* and the Question of Unreliability". *Transcending Boundaries: Narratology in Context*, Ed. Walter Grünzweig and Andreas Solbach, Gunter Narr Verlag, 1999, pp. 75–95.

Freißmann, Stephan. "A Tale of Autistic Experience: Knowing, Living, Telling in Mark Haddon's The Curious Incident of the Dog in the Night-Time". *Partial Answers: Journal of Literature and the History of Ideas*, vol. 6, no. 2, 2018, pp. 395–417.

Garrigós, Cristina. *Alzheimer's Disease in Contemporary US Fiction: Memory Lost*. Routledge, 2022.

Gebauer, Carolin. *Making Time: World Construction in the Present-Tense Novel*. De Gruyter, 2021.

Genette, Gerard. *Narrative Discourse: An Essay In Method*. Translated by Jane E. Lewin, Cornell UP, 1980.

Hansen, Per Krogh. "Reconsidering the Unreliable Narrator". *Semiotica*, vol. 165, no. 1/4, 2007, pp. 227–246.

Hartung, Heike. *Ageing, Gender and Illness in Anglophone Literature: Narrating Age in the Bildungsroman*. Routledge, 2016.

Healey, Emma. *Elizabeth Is Missing*. Penguin Random House, 2014.

LaPlante, Alice. *Turn of Mind*. Vintage, 2011.

Lethem, Jonathan. *Motherless Brooklyn*. Doubleday, 1999.

Nünning, Ansgar, and Vera Nünning. *An Introduction to the Study of English and American Literature*. Klett, 2019.

Nünning, Ansgar. "Reconceptualizing the Theory, History and Generic Scope of Unreliable Narration: Towards a Synthesis of Cognitive and Rhetorical Approaches". *Narrative Unreliability in the Twentieth-Century First-Person Novel*, Ed. Elke D'hoker and Gunther Martens, De Gruyter, 2008, pp. 29–76.

Olson, Greta. "Fallible and Untrustworthy Narrators". *Narrative*, vol. 11, no. 1, 2003, pp. 93–109.

Phelan, James. *Living to Tell about It*. Cornell UP, 2005.

Richler, Mordecai. *Barney's Version*. Vintage, 1997.

Riggan, William. *Picaros, Madmen, Naifs, and Clowns: The Unreliable First-Person Narrator*. U of Oklahoma P, 1981.

Roth, Marco. "The Rise of the Neuronovel". *n+1*, issue 8, 2009, https://www.nplusonemag.com/issue-8/essays/the-rise-of-the-neuronovel/. Accessed 18 January 2022.

Turkington, Carol. *The Encyclopedia of Alzheimer's Disease*. Facts on File, 2003.

Vaccarella, Maria. "Visualizing Patients' Unreliability". *Status Quaestionis*, vol. 6, 2014, pp. 87–102.

Vermeulen, Pieter. "Homo Sacer/Homo Demens. The Epistemology of Dementia in Contemporary Literature and Theory". *The Politics of Dementia. Forgetting and Remembering the Violent Past in Literature, Film and Graphic Narratives*, Ed. Irmela Marei Krüger-Fürhoff, Nina Schmidt, and Sue Vice, De Gruyter, 2022, pp. 39–54.

Walsh, Aisling, dir. *Elizabeth Is Missing*. BBC One, 2019.

Wieviorka, Annette. *The Era of the Witness*. Translated by Jared Stark. Cornell UP, 2006.

Zeller, Florian, dir. *The Father*. Lionsgate, 2020.

Zimmermann, Martina. "Dementia and the Politics of Memory in Fiction. From the Condition as Narrative Experiment to the Patient as Plot Device". *The Politics of Dementia. Forgetting and Remembering the Violent Past in Literature, Film and Graphic Narratives*, Ed. Irmela Marei Krüger-Fürhoff, Nina Schmidt, and Sue Vice, De Gruyter, 2022, pp. 55–113.

CHAPTER 8

# Communicating Eating Disorders: Metaphor, Embodied Simulation and Experiential Understanding in Autopathographies

*Jakob Summerer*

> My point is that illness is not a metaphor, and that the most truthful way of regarding illness – and the healthiest way of being ill – is one most purified of, most resistant to, metaphoric thinking.
>
> SONTAG 1978, 3

## 1 Introduction

In her seminal essay *Illness as Metaphor* (1978), Susan Sontag argues in favour of abandoning all metaphors used to conceptualise illness experience, as well as metaphors that use illness to conceptualise something else. An example of the former would be the widely-used 'battle against cancer', while to exemplify the latter, Sontag cites one of her own articles where she conceptualises Europeans as the "cancer of human history" (1978, 85). In her view, both groups of metaphors have harmful and discriminatory effects on individuals afflicted by actual illness, whose experiences are appropriated and distorted by these conceptualisations. While it is obvious that not every metaphor is suited to the needs of every individual sufferer, a radical elimination of metaphor from the process of coping with and treating illness seems unrealistic and misguided.[1] Metaphors are, for better or worse, the backbone of human language and thought, and completely abstaining from them is not likely to be an option any

1 Here I concur with Elena Semino, who aptly states that "[b]y and large, metaphors are not intrinsically harmful or beneficial, especially at the level of the individual: what matters is how metaphor is used, and the extent to which individuals are free and able to select the metaphors that work best for them" (2008, 178). Whether illness should, ethically speaking, be used as a metaphor for other phenomena is of course a different matter.

 | DOI:10.1163/9789004519886_010

time soon. Rather, metaphors can be – and often are, as part of modern metaphor therapy – adapted to the personal needs of those affected by illness.[2] They contribute to disentangling thoughts from harmful cognitions and negative self-evaluations with the help of more positive and empowering ways of metaphorically conceptualising the causes, treatments, and effects of a disease.

In this paper, I will demonstrate that metaphors are important in talking and thinking about mental illness in particular. Due to the fact that this group of disorders is often invisible to others and extremely difficult to explain to those with no personal experience with it, metaphors play a fundamental role in communicating the ontology and phenomenology of mental illness experience (Charteris-Black 2012, 199).[3] Moreover, metaphorical expressions are not merely tools for linguistically encoding illness. Metaphors can also be read as manifestations of a person's way of thinking about their illness, and can be examined as to their possible effects on the mind and body of the receiver. This view of metaphors as both a linguistic *and* a cognitive-embodied phenomenon has been highly influential since George Lakoff and Mark Johnson's seminal *Metaphors We Live By* (1980) – a work that sparked what is now known as Conceptual Metaphor Theory (CMT).[4] In the wake of the research conducted by Lakoff and his colleagues, metaphors are no longer regarded as a primarily rhetorical and literary phenomenon, but as a mainstay of everyday language and thought that is present in and essential to all kinds of discourses. According to CMT, metaphors enable humans to render the abstract aspects of their experience more accessible by drawing on and comparing them to the concrete and the physical (e.g., ILLNESS IS A JOURNEY). Hence, if we see metaphors as natural tools for thinking about and communicating the abstract in terms of the concrete, the fact that mental health narratives generally show a high density of metaphors can come as no surprise. I have found this central role of metaphors in mental health discourse to be particularly striking in the objects of this study: autopathographical narratives dealing with eating disorders.

As the two representatives of this little-discussed genre, I have chosen Marya Hornbacher's *Wasted* (1998) and Nancy Tucker's *The Time in Between* (2015). Both of these autopathographies, which revolve around the authors' experiences with bulimia and anorexia, stood out to me in my research on eating

2 For more information on the methods used by metaphor therapy, see Kopp (1995); Moschini (2018).

3 The central role of metaphors in mental health discourses is also apparent when studying the canon of psychology and psychiatry. See the papers in Leary (1990).

4 For an excellent introduction to and overview of the different milestones and tenets of CMT, see Kövecses (2010). Other essential publications include Lakoff and Turner (1989); Gibbs (1994); and the collection of papers edited by Steen et al. (2010).

disorder narratives due to the remarkable creativity and stylistic inventiveness that these authors demonstrate in narrating their experiences with eating disorders. Marya Hornbacher's *Wasted*, written in her early twenties, is certainly one of the most widely known and critically examined eating disorder autopathographies.[5] Narratologist Greta Olson aptly described Hornbacher's autopathography as a confessional text about "a woman's romance with her dying self" (2003, 230), a description that points towards one of the main themes of this highly figurative and poetic memoir: the splitting of the self, brought about by eating disorders. In terms of plot, her life narrative describes her early childhood, the onset of her bulimia at the age of nine, and her subsequent struggle with both bulimia and anorexia into her early twenties. Nancy Tucker's *The Time in Between* is less widely known and has, to the best of my knowledge, not received any critical attention so far. Her present-tense narrative, which she also wrote in her early twenties, shows a similarly high density of metaphoric expressions and, in its stylistic creativity, often toes the line between autofiction and autobiography. It starts with an account of her childhood years before the onset of her anorexia at nine years old. She then describes being in and out of treatment for her eating disorder as a teenager, the way her illness created multiple selves and inner conflicts, and the social isolation that came with hiding her disturbed eating behaviours from her friends and family.

Before I move on to a closer analysis of these autopathographies, I would like to briefly establish how I read autopathographical metaphors. Following Lakoff and other cognitive metaphor theorists, I understand linguistic metaphors as triggering a "cross-domain mapping" or "projection" on the conceptual level in the mind of the reader (Lakoff 1996, 206–08). As part of this conceptualisation process, a source conceptual domain B is projected onto a target conceptual domain A, which allows metaphor users and receivers to understand domain A in terms of domain B (e.g., ILLNESS as a relatively abstract and subjective target domain is understood in terms of JOURNEY as a more concrete and universal source domain). This conceptual metaphor is then notated as A IS B and is generally understood to serve the purpose of highlighting a specific aspect of the target domain A. Moreover, in exploring the more complex metaphors that are central to these autopathographical texts, I operate under an assumption shared by a number of cognitive metaphor theorists: namely, that novel, unconventional metaphors are foregrounded in the reader's text comprehension and are read at a slower pace and with increased attentive focus (Sperber and Wilson 2008, 102; Miall 2016, 237–40; Semino and Steen 2008,

5 See for example Lelwica (1999); Olson (2003); Senkbeil and Hoppe (2016).

237). Since the reader's mind thus has to exert more energy in decoding these norm-defying metaphorical mappings, one can assume that they are also much richer in terms of potential effects on the reader and corresponding emotional response. These metaphors are thus in a better position to "realise a particular communicative need" and "contribute to a particular communicative goal", which is why I follow Charteris-Black in dubbing them "purposeful metaphors" (2016, 156). What characterises purposeful metaphors is their creative exploitation and reworking of conventional metaphors, which makes them more likely to be recognised and decoded as metaphors. This means that both the source and the target conceptual domain, as well as the associated packets of encyclopaedic knowledge, are more likely to be activated in the mind of the reader (Gentner and Bowdle 2008, 117).

It is this particularly rich and effective kind of metaphor, I argue, that plays a crucial role in Hornbacher's and Tucker's autopathographies, since these metaphors allow the readers to gain a more direct and intuitive access to the narrators' illness experiences. What is more, I will show that some of their most striking purposeful metaphors are tasked with the conceptualisation and communication of the complex experiences of emotional pain caused by eating disorders, and that these conceptualisations of pain have the potential to trigger embodied simulations and increased empathetic reactions in the reader.

## 2 The Voice and I: Nancy Tucker's *The Time in Between*

In Nancy Tucker's *The Time in Between*, the most powerful extended metaphor that runs through the text is 'The Voice'. This character-like personification of the protagonist's anorexia frequently talks to her inside her mind and comes to wield increasing power over her actions and thoughts in the course of the narrative.[6] The protagonist's position in relation to her metaphorical other makes it possible to delineate the different stages of her anorexia, as well as communicate the *qualia* of her illness experience; the sense of 'what it is like' and 'how it feels'. Throughout her text, Tucker elaborates on this personification of

6 For simplicity's sake, I shall refer to the experiencing self of the autopathographical author as the "protagonist", and to the narrating self as the "narrator". In making this distinction, I am intentionally breaking Philippe Lejeune's famous "autobiographical pact" (1989, 14), which means that, for analytical purposes and unlike the casual reader of an autobiography, I do not accept the identity of the author, the narrator and the protagonist of these texts as a single, unified autobiographical subject. For an extended discussion of this distinction between the various textual alter egos of the autobiographical author, see Smith and Watson (2001, 58–64).

illness and draws on a variety of diverse source domains that are used to highlight different facets of her illness experience – above all, the sense of being at the eating disorder's mercy and the mental pain associated with that feeling.[7]

The personification of anorexia makes its first appearance in the story world when the five-year-old protagonist is asked by her teacher to write down her most fundamental personal wants and needs:

> So I scribble it down, and as it spools itself out onto the page in my wobbly joined-up writing I hear the words spoken by a brittle, whining voice. *The Voice* feels *prickly* in my head, and I slam my red Topic book shut, slamming away the whining and the *spiky*, complicated final 'want'. 'I want to be thin'. (Tucker 2015, 22; my emphasis)

In this constitutive passage, the early onset of the protagonist's eating disorder is metaphorically constructed as the appearance of 'The Voice', a distinct individual that is not only able to use direct speech but is also endowed with a physical, and physically harmful, presence in the protagonist's mind. This personification, I argue, is made possible by the split-self metaphor, which is one of the most productive members of a conventional metaphor system first described in detail by Lakoff (1996, 105–06). I will dub this group of metaphors here the "Subject/Self metaphor system", since these conceptualisations are based on folk psychological theories that understand a person as being divided into at least two distinct entities: a "Subject", as the "locus of consciousness, rationality, and judgement"; and a "Self", as "the locus of your needs, desires, and passions" (Lakoff 1996, 102).[8] Generally, this group of metaphors enables their users to think and talk about their inner lives, their sense of self and their experiences of consciousness in terms of physical and spatial relationships between two or more distinct individuals (e.g. 'I lost myself in the music'; 'I am struggling with myself today'; 'I am not myself today').

In Tucker's narrative, the conceptual metaphor BEING ANOREXIC IS HAVING A SPLIT SELF allows her narrator to conceptualise her past self as split into DISTINCT INDIVIDUALS IN CONFLICT. One of these metaphorical

7 On mental pain, also sometimes termed 'psychological pain' or 'emotional pain', see Orbach et al. (2003).

8 In this paper, I will retain Lakoff's capitalisation of 'Subject' and 'Self', whenever I use these words in the sense outlined here. Lakoff (1996, 118) relates this group of metaphors to the Cartesian mind/body dualism so pervasive in Western culture but emphasises at the same time that this metaphor system cannot be reduced to a simple binary, as some of its representatives involve a conceptualisation of the Self itself as divided and split into multiple selves.

individuals is 'The Voice', Tucker's personified anorexia, while the other is the protagonist that is struggling to stay sane in spite of this newly emerged self. Another conventional metaphor at play here is the generic-level metaphor EVENTS ARE ACTIONS, which enables people to conceptualise abstract events in terms of concrete actions performed by wilful agents (Lakoff and Turner 1989, 72–80). In the metaphorical scenario at hand, the abstract event is the onset of the protagonist's anorexia, while the concrete action performed by a wilful agent is The Voice's use of direct speech to speak for the protagonist ("I want to be thin"). As we can see, this personification based on a split-self metaphor is a type of 'ontological metaphor' that allows the metaphor user to give an undelineated, abstract experience a more delineated status (Lakoff and Johnson 1980, 25–31; Kövecses 2000, 39). This makes it possible to directly refer to illness experience, to identify and reify distinct aspects of having an eating disorder. That is the primary function that 'The Voice' performs in Tucker's narrative: it allows the narrator to dramatise her anorexia as an autonomous and wilful agent that has split off from the protagonist's self, while continuing to inhabit her mind and torment her.[9] This helps Tucker to conceptualise the different stages of the protagonist's mental disorder and highlight certain aspects of her experience – above all, her sense of losing control over her emotions, thoughts, and actions to a malevolent, invading other.[10]

In the example above, Tucker additionally tries to communicate the phenomenological aspects of her eating disorder when she uses the two metaphorical expressions "prickly" and "spiky", which both belong to the CAUSES OF PHYSICAL DAMAGE domain. As linguist Elena Semino hypothesises, creative and novel metaphors that conceptualise pain in terms of CAUSES OF PHYSICAL DAMAGE are likely to elicit an embodied simulation of the experience of pain on the part of the reader (2010, 211–14).[11] This type of simulation, which may be defined as the reader's "reenactment of perceptual, motor,

9 For a short discussion of the possible underlying neurological causes for this human tendency to conceptualise themselves as consisting of more than one distinct entity, see Emmott (2002, 161–62). Emmott also points out that the split between narrating self and experiencing self in the first-person narrative situation is made possible by the Subject/Self cognitive metaphors (2002, 171).

10 See Kövecses (2000, 43–44), who discusses the important conventional metaphor LACK OF EMOTIONAL CONTROL IS A DIVIDED SELF that can also be seen as a root here.

11 In her discussion of the metaphor PAIN IS CAUSE OF PHYSICAL DAMAGE, Semino cites research on mirror neurons and their role for embodied simulations. These "groups of neurons have been found to become active when we perform particular actions, when we observe others performing those actions, when we imagine those actions, and when we process linguistic descriptions of those actions" (Semino 2010, 211). Semino also bases her hypothesis on the studies conducted and discussed by Gibbs and Matlock (2008,

and introspective states acquired during experience with the world, body, and mind" (Barsalou 2008, 618), is also a crucial prerequisite and catalyst for any form of empathetic reaction.

I am convinced that, due to its creativity and its evocation of the conceptual domain CAUSES OF PHYSICAL DAMAGE via adjectives such as "prickly" and "spiky", Tucker's metaphorical scenario may trigger an embodied pain simulation. By metaphorically endowing 'The Voice' with sharp points and spikes capable of physically damaging the protagonist's skin, the narrator makes the mental pain experienced by an anorexic person accessible to the reader. The sharp pain caused by being pricked is a sensation that most people have experienced for themselves, which facilitates simulations of this kind of injury and the accompanying pain in the reader – simulations that are then imaginatively connected to the protagonist's pain experience. This form of embodied simulation thus enables the reader to experience (seemingly) comparable sensory and emotional states to the protagonist's, which has the potential to elicit a heightened empathetic response. These pain-targeting metaphorical scenarios thus also serve an interpersonal function in communicating the what-it-feels-like dimension of anorexia. They grant a more direct, experiential insight into the protagonist's pain – as opposed to merely reaching a conceptual understanding of said pain (Gallese et al. 2004, 396).

Only a few pages later, Tucker employs another striking purposeful metaphor. Now, however, in addition to personifying her anorexia, her narrator draws on ANIMALS as a secondary source domain to create a richly detailed metaphorical scenario that communicates the phenomenological aspects of her illness. This additional ontological source domain is thrown into the conceptual mix when the ten-year old protagonist enters a new school; an event that causes her great anxiety and contributes to the development of her eating problems. After her first day in this unfamiliar environment, she is overwhelmed by feelings of insecurity about her appearance and weight, which triggers a second appearance of 'The Voice':

> When I am in bed that night, the words come back to me, *claws* out, *pinching* and *scratching* and rearranging themselves into cruel, caustic loops. They *whip* around my head, *battering* at the sides of my skull [...]. It is a voice which is small and shrill but *spiky* all over, *like a cross hedgehog*, and it flings itself around inside my head, angry and *gleeful* and *maniacal* all at once, and as its pitch rises to a *shallow mewl* I realise that it is

162–73) on the important role that embodied simulations appear to play in metaphor comprehension.

> familiar after all. It is not just a voice; it is The Voice. (Tucker 2015, 28–29; my emphasis)

In the first sentence of this passage, the anorexic self is now endowed with metaphorical "claws" that enable it to "pinch" and "scratch" the protagonist. Moreover, in the third sentence, 'The Voice' is, via a simile, explicitly compared to a "cross hedgehog" that is "spiky all over" and uttering a "shallow mewl".[12] At the same time, however, Tucker's anorexia is clearly still personified as she additionally attributes adjectives such as "gleeful" and "maniacal" to it. Accordingly, the resulting metaphor projects material from the conceptual domain HEDGEHOG onto anorexia as a target, and the reader is likely to integrate this new domain with the already established personification of Tucker's illness – an operation that metaphor theorist Andrew Goatly terms 'metaphor compounding' (1997, 279–80).

This compound metaphorical scenario, I argue, fulfils several important communicative functions here. Firstly, it positions the protagonist as helpless in the face of the combined, doubly dangerous person-like malevolent agency and animalistic ferocity of her anorexia. Secondly, the semantic violence that the mixing of these different metaphorical source domains entails emphasises the inner division of the protagonist and the resulting psychological tension. Thirdly, this kind of complex compounding of metaphors conveys the intense, overpowering emotions and the sense of loss of control experienced by the user as their illness and the accompanying pain worsens (Charteris-Black 2012, 210–11; 2016, 164). And finally, Tucker again invokes several CAUSES OF PHYSICAL DAMAGE, which she metaphorically maps onto the psychological pain experienced by the eating-disordered protagonist. This projection of physical pain onto emotional pain allows the reader to reach a more intuitive understanding of what it feels like to suffer from anorexia. This understanding, which is based on embodied simulations of being "pinched", "scratched", "whipped" or "battered" in the reader, may then facilitate an empathetic response to Tucker's illness experience.

Towards the end of Tucker's autopathography, as her protagonist begins the drawn-out and painful process of recovery and starts to regain weight, she

12 In CMT, similes are analysed as forms of direct, explicitly signalled, cross-domain mapping (Steen et al. 2010, 10–11). Accordingly, similes are understood as the linguistic manifestation of a conceptual metaphor, which means they can be analysed using the same methods that would be applied to linguistic metaphors. This does not mean, however, that similes are processed and interpreted by the human mind in the exact same way as metaphors (Glucksberg and Haught 2006; Dancygier 2016, 37).

finds herself again under attack by her eating disorder. With every kilo that she puts on, Tucker's protagonist feels more "swollen and uncomfortable" (Tucker 2015, 240) in her own skin. This feeling is made accessible to the reader via another detailed metaphorical scenario that draws on the CAUSES OF PHYSICAL DAMAGE domain: "The Voice vociferates madly, digging its claws into my new flesh and twisting and twirling them until the pain is so agonising I wonder if death would be the best way forward after all" (ibid.). The by now firmly established human-animal compound and its alliterative "twisting and twirling" claws thus allow Tucker both to dramatise her mental illness as a physical attack and to facilitate a more intuitive understanding in the reader of what it feels like to recover from an eating disorder.

Towards the end of Tucker's narrative, as the protagonist's recovery progresses, she has two fundamental, metaphorically structured realisations. Firstly, she reconceptualises her mental illness as a plant that "looks dead in the winter and lies dormant for months, but if you cut it open it's still 'wick' inside, and then one day it starts breathing and blooming again" (ibid., 191). This new understanding dampens any hopes for a happy ending to her memoir and reiterates a fact that most of those affected by eating disorders report: full recovery is not an option. At the same time, however, she comes to the realisation that the inner split into rivalling person-like and animalistic agents, which she experienced at the height of her eating disorder, does not have to be permanent. As metaphorical others slowly disappear from her narrative, the narrator recognises that the sensation of splitting may be eventually overcome by reconceptualising her self: "Behind the diagnoses – or beyond them? – there is still a Person, and there is still a Life. I am not a Voice, but I do have a Voice. A Voice entirely my own" (ibid., 336). By thus negating the disempowering metonymy that equates self and voice(s), Tucker signals an end to the power struggle amongst her selves and reclaims a measure of agency over her life.

## 3 Hair Shirts and Absent Subjects: Marya Hornbacher's *Wasted*

Much like Tucker, Marya Hornbacher employs a variety of purposeful and elaborate metaphors in the telling of her illness. A closer look at some of the more striking of these conceptualisations reveals that the conventional Subject/Self metaphor system described by Lakoff is also a crucial conceptual building stone here. While this metaphor system manifests itself in Hornbacher's *Wasted* (1998) in a much less coherent manner – there is no character-like 'The Voice' that regularly interacts with the protagonist – it nonetheless acts as the primary catalyst for a multitude of metaphorical scenarios in this narrative. As we shall see shortly, one of the main functions of these scenarios is to communicate the protagonist's sense of inner division, loss of conscious control, and accompanying psychological pain.

In the following passage from Hornbacher's text, her narrator employs the split-self metaphor to refer to the narrated self, i.e. the protagonist, in the third person. This underlines the ontological split between her two textual alter egos: "She reads books on the saints. The sainted anoretics, who, in their holy asceticism, insisted that God was telling them to starve [...]. *The hair shirt is her own skin, rasping on the rawness of what lies beneath*" (Hornbacher 1998, 86; my emphasis). In this and in many other such instances in her autopathography, Hornbacher uses a metaphorical change in perspective to give her life narrative a veneer of objectivity, to universalise certain aspects of her personal eating disorder experience – aspects which she believes play a key role in not just her own but in other people's eating disorders as well. The felt spiritual dimension of anorexia that she is describing here, in which starvation is equated with spiritual virtue and purity and which she traces back to Early Christian practices of faith, is a theme that reappears throughout her autopathography and that can in fact be encountered in a surprising number of contemporary autopathographical accounts of eating disorders. As Michelle Mary Lelwica points out in her important study *Starving for Salvation* (1999), many of these accounts take inspiration from and contribute to the Western "salvation myth of female slenderness: a quasi-religious fantasy that promises fulfilment through a body that is thin" (Lelwica 1999, 52). According to the logic of this discourse, abstaining from food purifies not just the body but also the soul, thus paving the way to spiritual virtue and equilibrium.[13]

The effect of the phenomenological metaphor that Hornbacher generates in the final sentence above depends to a certain degree on the reader's knowledge of what a "hair shirt" is. As the name suggests, "hair shirts" are extremely rough textiles made from animal hair (Mulhern 2002, 618). They were worn next to the bare skin by early Christian ascetics and medieval monks as a way of proving their self-restraint and of doing penance for their sins. In medieval hagiography, these torturous garments often function as signifiers of high

13 This conceptual link between the set of behaviours that are now considered eating disorders and positively connotated spirituality can be traced back to medieval Christian fasting practices and the self-starving "miraculous maids" and "fasting girls" of the early modern period (Brumberg 1988, ch. 3 and 4). Simultaneously, this insistence on a spiritual interpretation of mental illness runs counter to many Medieval and Renaissance discourses, which frequently conceptualised mental illness as demonic possession caused by sinful behaviour (Thiher 1999, 46–50; Porter 2002, ch. 2).

status, extraordinary holiness and spiritual authority (Gilhus 2018, 90–93). Using this symbolically charged piece of clothing as a source domain and then metaphorically projecting it onto the actual skin of the protagonist is an interesting move. The conceptual metaphor SKIN IS A HAIR SHIRT grants readers an insight into the workings of the protagonist's mind and self-concept, as she aligns herself with the positively connotated Christian saints and ascetics, while it also emphasises another aspect of the what-it-feels-like dimension of anorexia: it paradoxically transforms the protective outer layer of the human body into a body-damaging instrument of self-torture. Underlying this metaphorical scenario is thus not just a physical but also a tangible semantic violence that highlights the paradox hostility of the anorectic protagonist towards her own body.[14] And again, the emotional pain that accompanies this hostility towards the body is communicated via a metaphorical expression from the domain of CAUSES OF PHYSICAL DAMAGE: Hornbacher elaborates on the SKIN IS A HAIR SHIRT metaphor and describes its alliterative "rasping on the rawness of what lies beneath" (1998). The evocation of these physically painful and uncomfortable sensations, which are distributed all over a body trapped inside its own skin, enables her readers to reach a more intuitive understanding of what the protagonist is going through as an anorectic.

Towards the end of Hornbacher's life narrative, the narrator looks back on the protagonist's oscillation between bulimia and anorexia throughout her teenage years. She communicates the phenomenological difference between these two mental illnesses via an elaboration on the more conventional ILLNESS IS A JOURNEY metaphor:

> Past the border of a fiery life lies the netherworld. I can trace this road, which took me through places so hot the very air burned the lungs. I did not turn back. I pressed on, and eventually passed over the border, beyond which lies a place that is wordless and cold, so cold that it, like mercury, burns a freezing blue flame. (Hornbacher 1998, 95)

Hornbacher's purposeful metaphor results in a spatialisation of mental illness: her protagonist is displaced and relocated from her normal position to another world. The world of eating disorders that the protagonist journeys through here consists of two spaces that are characterised by their temperature: the hot and fiery land of bulimia and the cold "netherworld" of anorexia. The underlying conceptual metaphor of HAVING AN EATING DISORDER IS A

14 See Kühle (2019), who discusses the disruption of bodily self-awareness (interoception) and sense of disconnection between body and mind in anorectics.

JOURNEY TO ANOTHER WORLD can be, I argue, traced back to another, more conventional representative of the aforementioned Subject/Self metaphor system; a metaphor that Lakoff terms "absent-subject metaphor" (Lakoff 1996, 110–11).[15] This metaphor allows its user to construct a sense of loss of cognitive control as their Subject – i.e. their locus of consciousness, rationality, and judgement – not being in its normal location (e.g. 'to be beside oneself'; 'to be out of one's mind'). In Hornbacher's text, she creatively exploits and elaborates on the absent-subject metaphor as her protagonist is exiled from the normal, everyday world inhabited by her friends and her family to the world of eating disorders.[16]

Conceptualising the first bounded region of this world, the land of bulimia, as "fiery" and "hot" expresses the excess of emotion and mania that the protagonist experiences as a bulimic. As Kövecses demonstrates, mapping the source domains FIRE and HEAT onto the target EMOTIONS enables the speaker to highlight the intensity of their emotional state – and this is a metaphorical conceptualisation that can be traced back to the root metaphor EMOTION IS FORCE (2000, 75–7). This generic-level conceptual metaphor allows Hornbacher to describe the protagonist's emotional state as an interaction between herself and the overpowering emotions generated by her bulimia. What is more, conceptualising the protagonist's bulimia by drawing on the CAUSES OF PHYSICAL DAMAGE domain ("so hot the very air burned the lungs") further communicates the pain caused by those powerful emotions. The fact that this particular CAUSE OF PHYSICAL DAMAGE is the very air that the protagonist must breathe in order to live further highlights her sense of entrapment and powerlessness.

At first glance, the underlying conceptual metaphor BULIMIA IS A WORLD OF FIRE/HEAT contrasts sharply with the metaphor that is realised in the last sentence of the passage: "I pressed on, and eventually passed over the border, beyond which lies a place that is wordless and cold, so cold that it, like mercury, burns a freezing blue flame" (Hornbacher 1998, 95). Here, the narrator

15 See Senkbeil and Hoppe (2016, 12–13), who also identify this as one of the main metaphorical themes in *Wasted*, but do not discuss its rootedness in the absent-subject metaphor or other more conventional mappings.

16 This spatial representation of mental illness is also coherent with the conventional master metaphor EMOTIONAL STABILITY IS MAINTAINING POSITION (Lakoff et al. 1991, 148). For a discussion of how people suffering from depression conceptualise their illness as a journey, see Semino (2008, 182–83). To explain the potential embodied origins of the DEPRESSION IS DOWN/DESCENT metaphors, Pritzker (2003, 18) cites Gibbs, who states that "[d]uring the first few months of life, being down is a natural state serving maturational purposes, but later in life, when we grow up, being down is associated with all aspects of babyhood, such as dependence, helplessness, and inferiority" (1994, 414).

describes the "netherworld" of anorexia, the other bounded region that the protagonist eventually passes through and that is, throughout the rest of her narrative, constructed as an underworld, as being located somewhere below ground (in accordance with Greco-Roman mythological discourses). Thus, at this point in the narrative, HAVING ANOREXIA IS A JOURNEY THROUGH A SUBTERRANEAN WORLD is already an established metaphor, and it points us towards another conceptual metaphor from the Subject/Self system that is being reversed here: SELF-CONTROL IS UP (Lakoff 1996, 115–16). Elaborating on this root metaphor, Hornbacher conceptualises her mental illness as the protagonist descending from its normal location – a mapping that highlights the accompanying loss of conscious control and feelings of depression.

What is more, the netherworld of anorexia is not only described as "a place that is wordless and cold" but also as one that "like mercury, burns a freezing blue flame" (Hornbacher 1998, 95). These metaphorical expressions trigger several distinct conceptual domains while being syntactically integrated, which is why I read this sentence as the realisation of a rather complex, mixed conceptual metaphor: ANOREXIA IS A NETHERWORLD OF ICE/COLD, FIRE/HEAT, AND MERCURY. As a number of contemporary metaphor theorists have pointed out, a mixed, complex metaphor like this one is best analysed as a 'conceptual blend', in which several conceptual domains are fused with one another in the mind of the receiver (Charteris-Black 2016, 160–61; Forceville 2016, 234–35; Müller 2008, 160–77). Blending Theory (BT), which was brought to full fruition by cognitive linguists Gilles Fauconnier and Mark Turner in their seminal *The Way We Think* (2002), describes a key cognitive mechanism in human language comprehension, which is similar and related to the cross-domain mappings that CMT deals with. In BT, however, the basic units of meaning construction are not the relatively stable conceptual domains that CMT uses, but the so-called 'mental spaces' that a reader temporarily and locally activates during the language comprehension process. These mental spaces are "small conceptual packets constructed as we think and talk, for purposes of local understanding and action" (Fauconnier and Turner 2002, 40).[17] One of the major advantages of BT is that it allows for more than two basic units of meaning construction, as opposed to the single target and single source domain of CMT, which is why it is well-equipped for dealing with mixed and complex metaphors that involve blending more than two conceptual domains.[18]

---

17 Fauconnier (1994) introduces the concept of mental spaces and discusses their key role in human cognition.

18 It is important to note that all metaphors technically constitute cases of conceptual blending and can be analysed as such (Fauconnier and Turner 2002, 154–59). For more

In the above mixed metaphor, which can be seen as another case of metaphor compounding, the three mental spaces FIRE/HEAT ("burns", "flame"), ICE/COLD ("cold", "freezing") and MERCURY ("like mercury") are blended with the already established NETHERWORLD OF ANOREXIA. This blend is schematically represented in Figure 8.1:

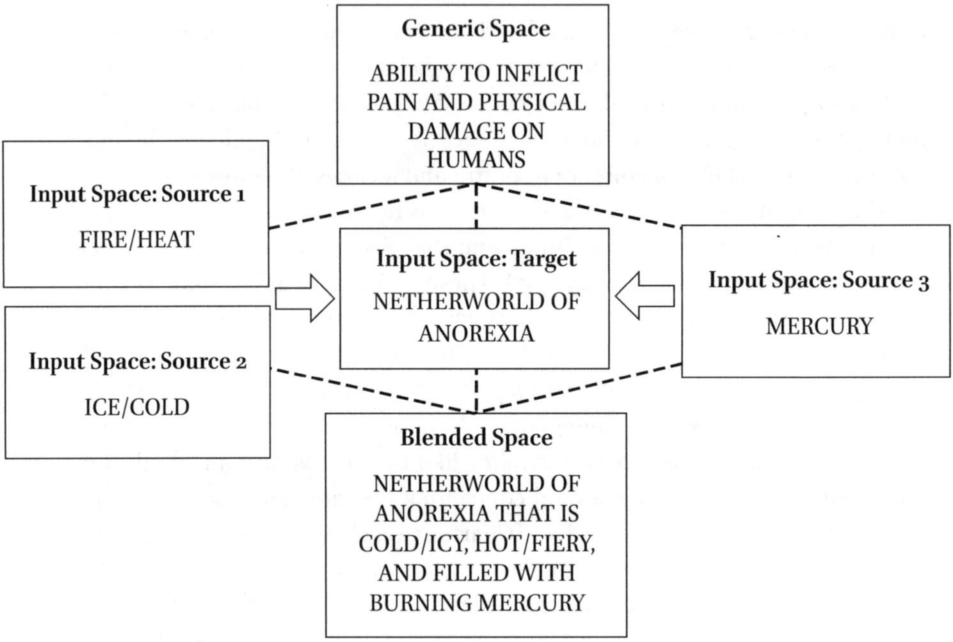


FIGURE 8.1 Blend for ANOREXIA IS A NETHERWORLD OF ICE/COLD, FIRE/HEAT, AND MERCURY

According to BT, any metaphor prompts readers to mentally set up a 'blended space' that contains material from several so-called 'input spaces' that share a 'generic space' (Fauconnier and Turner 2002, 39–50). This complex mental operation, which enables the reader to understand the metaphor, involves blending the distinct conceptual domains that act as input spaces (here: FIRE/HEAT, ICE/COLD, MERCURY, NETHERWORLD OF ANOREXIA). The conceptual integration of these domains is motivated and made possible by the generic space that they share and that contains abstract properties and structure that they have in common. In Hornbacher's metaphor, the generic space shared

information on how CMT and BT handle mixed metaphors, see the papers in Gibbs (2016); Sullivan (2018). A variety of metaphor theorists have noted and demonstrated how well BT compliments CMT. See, for example, Grady et al. (1999, 102–06); Fludernik (2010, 348–49).

by HEAT/FIRE, COLD/ICE, MERCURY, and ANOREXIA contains the information that all four have the potential to physically harm and cause pain to human beings (fire, ice, the poisonous metal mercury, and anorexia are all able to directly and indirectly damage the skin and organs of the human body). Based on this shared property, the three source inputs (HEAT/FIRE, COLD/ICE, MERCURY), as well as the target input (NETHERWORLD OF ANOREXIA), are able to project some of their structure into a blended space. In the blended space that Hornbacher evokes to describe her experience of anorexia, we thus find a rather chaotic, surreal, and life-threatening underworld of ice-cold flames and burning mercury.

While the cold of the netherworld of anorexia, as opposed to the heat of the intensely emotional world of bulimia, at first glance implies an absence of emotions and sensations, the metaphorical post-modifications at the end of the sentence speak otherwise. By throwing both ICE/COLD and FIRE/HEAT into the conceptual mix, the narrator demonstrates that the experience of anorexia and the experience of bulimia are far from being opposites; they correspond and are linked to one another.[19] At the same time, the semantic clash produced by the mixed metaphor for anorexia I have just discussed can be read as highlighting the greater lethal danger posed by that mental illness and the sense of loss of control experienced by the sufferer.[20] Moreover, drawing on FIRE/HEAT, ICE/COLD, and MERCURY as source domains in this metaphorical scenario, Hornbacher once more maps several distinct CAUSES OF PHYSICAL DAMAGE onto the experience of anorexia, which, similar to the person-hedgehog metaphor in Tucker's narrative, captures the associated experience of psychological pain and has the potential to elicit an embodied simulation of pain and an accompanying empathetic response in the reader.[21]

Similar to Tucker's memoir, Hornbacher ends her autopathographical narrative with a densely metaphorical chapter conceptualising her recovery. And

---

19 In light of a history of Western mental illness discourses, these metaphorically hot and cold regions can be read as discursive off-shoots of the highly influential humoural theory of mental illness put forth by Ancient Greek Hippocratic medicine. In these early medical discourses, mental illness came in two main varieties: mania, a condition marked by excess and uncontrollable emotions and believed to be caused by an excess of blood, yellow bile and heat, and melancholia, a disturbance marked by sadness, dejection and apathy said to arise from an excess of black bile and cold in the body (Thiher 1999, 18–19; Porter 2002, 37–47).

20 Anorexia has the highest mortality rate out of all mental disorders with people dying either of the physical health consequences of starvation (such as severe dehydration, multiorgan failure and heart rhythm disturbance), or of suicide (Goss and Fox 2012, 6).

21 Admittedly, this effect is less likely in the case of mercury, as virtually no reader will be familiar with the experience of mercury poisoning.

again, recovery can only be partial: "It's never over. Not really. Not when you stay down there as long as I did, not when you've lived in the netherworld longer than you've lived in this material one, where things are very bright and large and make such strange noises. You never come back, not all the way" (Hornbacher 1998, 285). Where Tucker's memoir ends on a cautiously hopeful note, with a silencing of her inner voices and resolution of the conflict amongst her selves, Hornbacher makes it clear that the absence of her Subject, her exile to the "netherworld" of eating disorders, is permanent. Accordingly, in the final sentence quoted above, the reference of the "you" that "never come[s] back, not all the way" encompasses both the protagonist and the narrator, whose full recovery is thwarted by the present tense of the verb. In contrast to Tucker, then, Hornbacher's narrator remains split, straddling the line between the "netherworld" and "this material one".

## 4 Purposeful Metaphors and Phenomenologies of Eating Disorders

In their analysis of personal accounts of cancer experiences, Gibbs and Franks claim that "[m]etaphors help people make sense of illness by integrating the idea of illness into their own lives and by offering an answer to the existential question, 'Why me?'" (2002, 160). Looking back on the different metaphors in Tucker's and Hornbacher's eating disorder narratives discussed above, I would argue that the 'Why me?' question plays a subordinate role in the conceptualisation of eating disorders. In fact, the main function of the metaphors discussed in this article seems to be communicating the *qualia* of having anorexia or bulimia. This means that these metaphors are not just ontological and structural, in that they render the experience of eating disorders as more delineated and tangible, but, more importantly, they are phenomenological in nature, as they allow expressing the "feeling tone" (Kövecses 2010, 117) of the authors' illness experience. Accordingly, in using these metaphors, Hornbacher's and Tucker's narrators are often primarily concerned with the question 'What does it feel like to be me?', a question that they attempt to answer via a number of richly detailed metaphorical scenarios. In these scenarios, both Hornbacher and Tucker draw extensively on the CAUSES OF PHYSICAL DAMAGE domain, as well as the Subject/Self metaphor system, which enables them to conceptualise their protagonists as split into multiple distinct entities that reside in different locations and exist in various relationships to one another.

While the representatives of the Subject/Self metaphor system are highly conventional and frequently used in everyday thought and speech, Hornbacher and Tucker manage to elaborate on these mappings in creative and novel ways. Accordingly, they construct foregrounded metaphorical scenarios that are much richer in terms of their potential associations and effects on the reader than their conventional archetypes. In *The Time in Between*, Tucker extensively exploits the split-self metaphor to endow the protagonist's anorexia with a life and personhood of its own. By dynamically positioning 'The Voice' in relation to the protagonist, she is able to dramatise the protagonist's increasing loss of agency and sense of powerlessness in the face of her mental illness. Additionally drawing on ANIMAL as a source domain allows her to communicate the mental pain caused by anorexia and its perceived nonhuman otherness.

In *Wasted*, Hornbacher emphasises the split between her recovered narrating self and her anorexic experiencing self when she refers to the latter in the third and the second person. In contrast to Tucker, who splits her protagonist into various distinct entities, she exerts more narrative energy on spatialising the protagonist's eating disorder by drawing on another highly productive member of the Subject/Self metaphor system: the absent-subject metaphor. This metaphor allows her to displace her protagonist to various locations and containers outside the reach of her family and friends. As I have argued, this mapping lays the foundation for a metaphorical theme that is key to how Hornbacher makes sense of her illness: EATING DISORDERS ARE JOURNEYS THROUGH OTHER WORLDS. This metaphor fulfils the crucial communicative purpose of explaining when the eating-disordered protagonist loses control over her life and in how far the feeling tones of her bulimia and anorexia differ.

In communicating the *qualia* of having an eating disorder, both writers thus feel the need to draw on a highly diverse set of source domains – sometimes resulting in complex and mixed metaphors – in order to capture the different facets of their experience and of the associated emotional states. I read this mixing of metaphors as purposeful, as it allows their users to understand and express their complex emotional pain and the fragmentation of their atypical minds. Consequently, as is now recognised by many therapists that incorporate metaphors into their practice, these illness metaphors might offer paths to resolution (Kopp 1995, xix; Moschini 2018, 3–4). In other words, metaphors are capable of having positive therapeutic effects on the mentally ill storyteller, who is able to make sense of their illness in a way that contributes to their recovery. What is more, Tucker's and Hornbacher's metaphors fulfil an interpersonal function, since their evocation of CAUSES OF PHYSICAL DAMAGE make it possible for the reader's mind to run an embodied simulation of and develop an empathetic response to the author's suffering. This response is based on the reader's own memories of experiences with physical pain, and the reader is thus able to foster a more intuitive understanding of what it may feel like to suffer from an eating disorder.

While I hope to have provided a sketch of some of the fascinating roles played by metaphors in eating disorder discourses in this paper, it is clear that much more research in this area remains to be done. In the on-going project of exploring how Western imaginations represent mental illness to themselves, the analysis of metaphorical conceptualisations of eating disorders, and the surrounding discourses on beauty, health, and spirituality, promises to yield data that can be useful to linguists and literary scholars within the Medical Humanities, as well as to medical professionals and those affected by eating disorders. With steadily rising numbers of eating disorder cases throughout the Western world, it is more important than ever to scrutinise linguistic and cognitive metaphors as key elements of the intricate feedback loops that exist between cultural discourses and eating disorders.

## Works Cited

Barsalou, Laurence W. "Grounded Cognition". *Annual Review of Psychology*, vol. 59, 2008, pp. 617–645.

Brumberg, Joan Jacobs. *Fasting Girls: The History of Anorexia Nervosa*. Penguin, 1988.

Charteris-Black, Jonathan. "Shattering the Bell Jar: Metaphor, Gender, and Depression". *Metaphor and Symbol*, vol. 27, no. 3, 2012, pp. 199–216.

Charteris-Black, Jonathan. "The 'Dull Roar' and the 'Burning Barbed Wire Pantyhose': Complex Metaphor in Accounts of Chronic Pain". *Mixing Metaphor*, edited by Raymond W. Gibbs, John Benjamins, 2016, pp. 155–76.

Dancygier, Barbara. "Figurativeness, Conceptual Metaphor, and Blending". *The Routledge Handbook of Metaphor and Language*, edited by Elena Semino and Zsófia Demjén, Routledge, 2016, pp. 28–41.

Emmott, Catherine. "'Split Selves' in Fiction and in Medical 'Life Stories': Cognitive Linguistic Theory and Narrative Practice". *Cognitive Stylistics*, edited by Elena Semino and Jonathan Culpeper, John Benjamins, 2002, pp. 153–82.

Fauconnier, Gilles. *Mental Spaces*. MIT P, 1994.

Fauconnier, Gilles, and Mark Turner. *The Way We Think: Conceptual Blending and the Mind's Hidden Complexities*. Basic Books, 2002.

Fludernik, Monika. "Narrative and Metaphor". *Language and Style*, edited by Dan McIntyre and Beatrix Busse, Palgrave Macmillan, 2010, pp. 347–63.

Forceville, Charles. "Mixing in pictorial and multimodal metaphors?" *Mixing Metaphor*, edited by Raymond W. Gibbs, John Benjamins, 2016, pp. 223–39.

Gallese, Vittorio, et al. "A Unifying View of the Basis of Social Cognition". *TRENDS in Cognitive Sciences*, vol. 8, no. 9, 2004, pp. 396–403.

Gentner, Deirdre, and Brian Bowdle. "Metaphor as Structure-Mapping". *The Cambridge Handbook of Metaphor and Thought*, edited by Raymond W. Gibbs, Cambridge UP, 2008, pp. 109–28.

Gibbs, Raymond W. *Mixing Metaphor*. John Benjamins, 2016.

Gibbs, Raymond W. *The Poetics of Mind: Figurative Thought, Language, and Understanding*. Cambridge UP, 1994.

Gibbs, Raymond W., and Heather Franks. "Embodied Metaphor in Women's Narratives About Their Experiences with Cancer". *Health Communication*, vol. 14, no. 2, 2002, pp. 139–65.

Gibbs, Raymond W., and Teenie Matlock. "Metaphor, Imagination, and Simulation: Psycholinguistic Evidence". *The Cambridge Handbook of Metaphor and Thought*, edited by Raymond W. Gibbs, Cambridge UP, 2008, pp. 161–76.

Gilhus, Ingvild Sælid. "Sheepskins, Hair Shirts and Tunics of Palm Leaves". *Temenos*, vol. 54, no. 1, 2018, pp. 79–102.

Glucksberg, Sam, and Catrinel Haught. "On the Relation between Metaphor and Simile: When Comparison Fails". *Mind & Language*, vol. 21, no. 3, 2006, pp. 360–78.

Goatly, Andrew. *The Language of Metaphors*. Routledge, 1997.

Goss, Ken P., and John R.E. Fox. "Introduction to Clinical Assessment for Eating Disorders". *Eating and its Disorders*, edited by John R.E. Fox and Ken P. Goss, Wiley-Blackwell, 2012, pp. 3–10.

Grady, Joseph, et al. "Blending and Metaphor". *Metaphor in Cognitive Linguistics*, edited by Raymond Gibbs and Gerard Steen, John Benjamins, 1999, pp. 101–24.

Hornbacher, Marya. *Wasted: A Memoir of Anorexia and Bulimia*. Flamingo, 1998.

Kopp, Richard R. *Metaphor Therapy: Using Client-Generated Metaphors in Psychotherapy*. Brunner/Mazel, 1995.

Kövecses, Zoltán. *Metaphor: A Practical Introduction*. 2nd ed., Oxford UP, 2010.

Kövecses, Zoltán. *Metaphor and Emotion: Language, Culture, and Body in Human Feeling*. Cambridge UP, 2000.

Kühle, Lana. "Anorexia Nervosa and the Embodied Mind". *The Bloomsbury Companion to Philosophy of Psychiatry*, edited by Şerife Tekin and Robyn Bluhm, Bloomsbury, 2019, pp. 113–29.

Lakoff, George. "Sorry, I'm Not Myself Today: The Metaphor System for Conceptualizing the Self". *Spaces, Worlds, and Grammar*, edited by Gilles Fauconnier and Eve Sweetser, Chicago UP, 1996, pp. 91–123.

Lakoff, George, and Mark Johnson. *Metaphors We Live By*. U of Chicago P, 1980.

Lakoff, George, and Mark Turner. *More than Cool Reason: A Field Guide to Poetic Metaphor*. U of Chicago P, 1989.

Lakoff, George, Jane Espenson, and Alan Schwartz. *Master Metaphor List*. 2nd edition. U of California, 1991, araw.mede.uic.edu/~alansz/metaphor/METAPHORLIST.pdf. Accessed 7 Sept. 2020.

Leary, David E. *Metaphors in the History of Psychology*. Cambridge UP, 1990.

Lejeune, Philippe. *On Autobiography*. Translated by Katherine Leary, Minnesota UP, 1989.

Lelwica, Michelle Mary. *Starving for Salvation: The Spiritual Dimensions of Eating Problems among American Girls and Women*. Oxford UP, 1999.

Miall, David S. "Neuroaesthetics of Literary Reading". *Neuroaesthetics*, edited by Martin Skov and Oshin Vartanian, Routledge, 2016, pp. 233–47.

Moschini, Lisa B. *Art, Play, and Narrative Therapy: Using Metaphor to Enrich Your Clinical Practice*. Routledge, 2018.

Mulhern P. "Hair Shirt". *The New Catholic Encyclopedia,* edited by Berard L. Marthaler et al., Gale, 2002, p. 618.

Müller, Cornelia. *Metaphors Dead and Alive, Sleeping and Waking: A Dynamic View*. U of Chicago P, 2008.

Olson, Greta. *Reading Eating Disorders: Writings on Bulimia and Anorexia as Confessions of American Culture*. Frankfurt: Peter Lang, 2003.

Orbach, Israel, et al. "Mental Pain: A Multidimensional Operationalization and Definition". *Suicide and Life-Threatening Behavior*, vol. 33, no. 3, 2003, pp. 219–30.

Porter, Roy. *Madness: A Brief History*. Oxford: Oxford UP, 2002.

Pritzker, Sonya E. "The Role of Metaphor in Culture, Consciousness, and Medicine: A Preliminary Inquiry into the Metaphors of Depression in Chinese and Western Medical and Common Languages". *Clinical Acupuncture & Oriental Medicine*, vol. 4, no. 1, 2003, pp. 11–28.

Semino, Elena. *Metaphor in Discourse*. Cambridge UP, 2008.

Semino, Elena. "Descriptions of Pain, Metaphor, and Embodied Simulation". *Metaphor and Symbol*, vol. 25, no. 4, 2010, pp. 205–26.

Semino, Elena, and Gerard Steen. "Metaphor in Literature". *The Cambridge Handbook of Metaphor and Thought*, edited by Raymond W. Gibbs, Cambridge UP, 2008, pp. 232–46.

Senkbeil, Karsten, and Nicola Hoppe. "'The Sickness Stands at Your Shoulder …': Embodiment and Cognitive Metaphor in Hornbacher's Wasted: A Memoir of Anorexia and Bulimia". *Language and Literature*, vol. 25, no. 1, 2016, pp. 3–17.

Sontag, Susan. *Illness as Metaphor*. Farrar, Straus and Giroux, 1978.

Smith, Sidonie, and Julia Watson. *Reading Autobiography: A Guide for Interpreting Life Narratives*.

Sperber, Dan, and Deirdre Wilson. "A Deflationary Account of Metaphors". *The Cambridge Handbook of Metaphor and Thought*, edited by Raymond W. Gibbs, Cambridge UP, 2008, pp. 84–105.

Steen, Gerard, et al. *A Method for Linguistic Metaphor Identification: From MIP to MIPVU*. John Benjamins, 2010.

Sullivan, Karen. *Mixed Metaphors: Their Use and Abuse*. Bloomsbury, 2018.

Thiher, Allen. *Revels in Madness: Insanity in Medicine and Literature*. U of Michigan P, 1999.

Tucker, Nancy. *The Time in Between: A Memoir of Hunger and Hope*. London, Icon Books, 2015.

CHAPTER 9

# De-pathologising Non-normative Bodies and Minds of Persons with Dominance-Oriented Sexualities – the Role of Narratives about and in BDSM

*Henrik Zetterberg-Nielsen*

## 1 Introduction

There is a broad range of reasons to take a special interest in persons with BDSM[1] preferences when discussing narratives of non-normative bodies and minds. BDSM is non-normative in almost every sense of the word "non-normative". The latest edition of *Diagnostic and Statistical Manual of Mental Disorders* (*DSM-5*) (2013)[2] unequivocally describes associations between pleasure and pain in the form of sadism and masochism as mental disorders even as many recent surveys challenge or outright falsify normative assumptions of such preferences being obstacles to physical and mental health (see references and discussions below). There is a long history, from Krafft-Ebing's *Psychopathia Sexualis* (1939) and forward, to pathologise sexual preferences associated with dominance and submission and/or pain and any non-reproductive or non-genito-centric sexual practices and preferences.[3] As so-called paraphilias, such desires are continuously considered beyond the norm, beyond the law, and beyond the usual. Sadism is, not without reasons, but complex and debatable reasons, associated with assault and cruelty in psychiatric manuals

1 The terms "BDSM" and "dominance" are both more neutral and both cover a considerably larger ground than the giving and receiving of pain habitually associated with the narrower terms "sadism" and "masochism", respectively. "BDSM" by implicitly including not less than six preferences (BDSM is normally interpreted to stand for three two-letter abbreviations of "bondage and discipline", "dominance and submission" and "sadism and masochism") and "dominance" by being broadly applicable, open and inclusive. For a discussion of the terms "sadism", "masochism" and "sadomasochism", their pros and cons, and their intimate connections to literary authors, see below.

2 Referenced below as *DSM-5* (2013).

3 In fact, it is part of the history of the changing editions of *DSM* that when homosexuality was finally removed as a mental illness in the *DSM-3* (1987), the number and scope of descriptions of paraphilias were significantly increased, as if to compensate. In this enormous work with all kinds of mental disorders, it is clear that the choices reflect a strong intention to pathologise non-reproductive sexuality in various forms.

 | DOI:10.1163/9789004519886_011

as well as in idiomatic everyday language. The article will discuss these reasons and suggest that more clarity to the issue and discussion can be provided by some simple distinctions such as between consensual and non-consensual and between imagined and real.

In addition, not only is BDSM non-normative; it is also itself distributed between bodies and minds with equally significant interests and preferences in physical impact and pain and in psychologically establishing hierarchical disparity and unequal power status in ways transgressing accepted norms. Moreover, the two most widespread concepts of sadism and masochism are both based on the proper names of literary authors – those of Donatien Alphonse François de Sade and Leopold von Sacher-Masoch. Rarely has any literary fiction had more real-life impact on more real flesh and blood readers than the fictions of these authors. BDSM-related sexual preferences, their literary sources, their representations in erotica and fantasies, and their condemnations by religion and psychiatry alike, thus, are all right at the intersection between narrative and cultural studies of representations of non-normative bodies and minds.

In this article, I trace some genealogies to understand the historical reasons behind the fact that sexual preferences which empirically are not unusual and not generally associated with impairment are perceived of as rare mental disorders in the most important psychiatric manuals as well as in colloquial language use. As indicated by the title, I take interest in the role of narratives *about* BDSM as well as the role of narratives *in* BDSM. In contrast to other mental disorders listed by the *DSM-5* (2013) such as "Schizophrenia", "Bipolar", "Depressive disorder", "Obsessive-Compulsive Disorder", the clinical terms for "sadism" and "masochism" are constituted from the names of literary authors.[4] The article will also discuss how deeply affected the conceptions of

4 The handbook does distinguish between paraphilia and paraphilic disorder in that the former is described as harmless and the latter as harmful. Nevertheless, there are many reasons why *DSM-5* also comes to be pathologising and stigmatising in its descriptions of the individual paraphilias; Among other things, because it itself erodes the established distinction. A very fundamental reason for the handbook's stigmatisation is that all the paraphilic disorders are generally referred to as "mental disorders". In this way, and with the title of the book in mind, they are placed on a par with mental illnesses. When the handbook, for example, includes "Psychotic Disorders" (*DSM-5* 2013, 87), "Depressive Disorders" (ibid., 155), "Posttraumatic Stress Disorder" (ibid., 271), "Fetishistic Disorder" (ibid., 700) and, "Transvestic Disorder" (ibid., 702), it seems as an obvious conclusion that all the different words before "disorder" are on a par with each other, and thus that fetishism and transvestism are equaled to psychosis, depression and post-traumatic stress. In other words, an overall reason for the stigmatisation is that the sexual preferences are combined in the handbook as "mental disorders".

the preferences are by the narrative about events and characters in the fiction of these authors. One step is to look at the preferences at a remove from the fictions. On a very different level, narratives very often play important roles *in* dominance-oriented sexualities because dominance and hierarchies are created symbolically and by means of play and fictionality. Another step in the article is to examine the importance of this narrative dimension in judging such non-normative preferences.

I begin by re-examining one origin story of sexual sin in the form of sodomy in the Bible as paradigmatic for non-reproductive practices; then move on to show how the same conceptions of sexual sins inform the *DSM-5* (2013). Next, I briefly characterise the most important canonical texts on sadism and masochism by Krafft-Ebing, Freud, and others. From religion to psychiatry the conception of sexual pathology is narrative through and through in a way that does not apply to other, non-sexual pathologies. From there I move on to recent surveys and empirical studies, and ask what the departure in the author names of Sade and Masoch has meant for our conception of the sexual orientations described. Finally, I suggest that de-pathologisation is desirable, and possible through a reversal of the perceived hierarchy between pain and dominance/submission and through sharp distinctions between imagined and real, and between consensual and non-consensual.

## 2 Christian Normativity in Relation to Reproductive and Non-reproductive Practices

To situate the specificity of the power-oriented sexual preferences physically and mentally associated with BDSM orientations, I will begin by introducing the ways in which the Bible castigates the non-reproductive in general. This biblical narrative comes to form a looming backdrop for Western psychiatry. It is not the only reason for pathologising BDSM preferences but an important factor since we will see how psychiatry and religion mutually reinforce each other in cataloguing the non-reproductive as non-normative beginning with some of the narratives from the Bible most deeply rooted in Western culture. This holds true for the story of Onan who was sentenced to death as well as executed by God based on – actually not the alleged sin of masturbation associated with his name in several languages but – his refusal to engage in reproduction at all costs, thus practicing coitus interruptus.[5] More surprising, perhaps, the same

5 See Genesis 38:9. [6] Judah got a wife for Er, his firstborn, and her name was Tamar. [7] But Er, Judah's firstborn, was wicked in the Lord's sight; so the Lord put him to death. [8] Then Judah

logic that non-reproduction is a sin graver than anything else imaginable pervades the story of Lot and his wife. A story typically served in quite redacted versions. The story of the destruction of Sodom and Gomorrah in Genesis 19 follows immediately after the story of Sara and Abram learning from the Lord and three visitors (Genesis 18, 1–15, *King James Bible Online*) that they will be parents at a very old age, and is, in a sense, the antithesis to it. Together the two narratives and the story of Onan lay the ground for a fundamental belief in the relation between faith and fertility. The story in Genesis 18 is a narrative about assumed infertility leading to numerous offspring. The story in Genesis 19 is a narrative about fertile men literally turning their back on reproduction. The latter begins with two angels arriving at Sodom in the evening (Genesis 19,1, *King James Bible Online*). Lot invites them and prepares dinner for them when the men from Sodom without a single exception[6] show up at his doorstep:

> [4] Before they had gone to bed, all the men from every part of the city of Sodom—both young and old—surrounded the house.[5] They called to Lot, "Where are the men who came to you tonight? Bring them out to us so that we can have sex with them". (*King James Bible Online*)

Lot does not find the request for anal angelic amusement agreeable but hospitably makes a counteroffer:

> [6] Lot went outside to meet them and shut the door behind him [7] and said, "No, my friends. Don't do this wicked thing. [8] Look, I have two daughters who have never slept with a man. Let me bring them out to you, and you can do what you like with them. But don't do anything to these men, for they have come under the protection of my roof". (ibid)

The not-under-my-roof-protection-attitude, thus, does not include his daughters. The whole logic of the story – which continues through the history of the exegesis of the hierarchies of sins – implies that to God and to Lot virgin rape

---

said to Onan, "Sleep with your brother's wife and fulfill your duty to her as a brother-in-law to raise up offspring for your brother". [9] But Onan knew that the child would not be his; so whenever he slept with his brother's wife, he spilled his semen on the ground to keep from providing offspring for his brother. [10] What he did was wicked in the Lord's sight; so the Lord put him to death also. (Topverses, *The Bible,* New International Version, Genesis 38:9). See also my article, "Dangers of Fictionality, Human Sexuality and Sexual Fantasies" (forthcoming).

6 This is important because in the last episode, Genesis 18, Abram had haggled God's price for saving the city down to first 50, then 40, then 30 and in the end just 10 innocent men/humans.

is preferable to homosexuality. The crowd, however, declines the offer and attempts an assault on the angels but are all struck with blindness. Next, the four family members, Lot, his wife and their two daughters, get to flee the town with fairly unspecific directives hinging on understanding that the "don't-look-back-phrase" is a literal command rather than a hurry-up figure of speaking:

> 15 With the coming of dawn, the angels urged Lot, saying, "Hurry! Take
> your wife and your two daughters who are here, or you will be swept away
> when the city is punished". 16 When he hesitated, the men grasped his
> hand and the hands of his wife and of his two daughters and led them
> safely out of the city, for the Lord was merciful to them. 17 As soon as they
> had brought them out, one of them said, "Flee for your lives! Don't look
> back, and don't stop anywhere in the plain! Flee to the mountains or you
> will be swept away!" (ibid.)

Either Lot's wife was absent during those instructions, or she was less literal-minded than the rest:

> 24 Then the Lord rained down burning sulfur on Sodom and Gomorrah—
> from the Lord out of the heavens. 25 Thus he overthrew those cities and
> the entire plain, destroying all those living in the cities—and also the
> vegetation in the land. 26 But Lot's wife looked back, and she became a
> pillar of salt. (*King James Bible Online*)

This is probably the most well-known element of the story and where it is often cut off. However, the virgin rape does actually take place in the very same chapter – only in an unexpected reverse form:

> 30 Lot and his two daughters left Zoar and settled in the mountains, for
> he was afraid to stay in Zoar. He and his two daughters lived in a cave.
> 31 One day the older daughter said to the younger, "Our father is old, and
> there is no man around here to give us children—as is the custom all over
> the earth. 32 Let's get our father to drink wine and then sleep with him and
> preserve our family line through our father". 33 That night they got their
> father to drink wine, and the older daughter went in and slept with him.
> He was not aware of it when she lay down or when she got up. 34 The next
> day the older daughter said to the younger, "Last night I slept with my
> father. Let's get him to drink wine again tonight, and you go in and sleep
> with him so we can preserve our family line through our father". 35 So they
> got their father to drink wine that night also, and the younger daughter

> went in and slept with him. Again he was not aware of it when she lay down or when she got up. [36] So both of Lot's daughters became pregnant by their father. [37] The older daughter had a son, and she named him Moab; he is the father of the Moabites of today. [38] The younger daughter also had a son, and she named him Ben-Ammi; he is the father of the Ammonites of today. (ibid.)

The double drug rape is doubly sanctioned by the logic here; first, because the begetting of children "is the custom all over the earth"; second, because it results in establishing the families of the Moabites and the Ammonites so that Lot, like Abram in the chapter before, becomes an important ancestor despite Lot being a widower and an alone-father.

The real crime, thus, is not so much rape and coercion per se. Rather, it is the refusal to engage in reproduction at all costs. There is a straight line – no pun intended – from conceiving of this as a sin punishable by death by burning sulfur, to later seeing rape and incest as relatively minor sins compared to sodomy and masturbation.[7] This ranking of sexual sins is also described in Phillips and Reay, in the chapter on 'Sin':

> The number and order of sexual sins varied from [premodern Christian] author to author, but most ranged from fornication (sex between an unmarried man and woman) as the least serious brand of lechery to the 'vice against nature' as the worst. A common ranking ran thus: fornication, adultery, incest, violation or debauchery, abduction-rape (raptus) and the 'vice against nature' (which generally encompassed all acts which could not result in procreation, including use of contraceptives, masturbation, anal or oral sex, same-sex practices and bestiality). Phillips and Reay (2011, 18)

## 3 Paraphilias and Pathologies in Psychiatric Normativity Today

The castigation of non-reproductive practices is a norm that also pervades *DSM-5*, and a lens through which to see non-normative bodies and minds of

7 For a remarkably clear expression of this view, see Anonymous, *Onania: or, the heinous sin of self-pollution* (1756, 8): 'whether we commit abomination with our own sex, or with beasts, or that we defile our bodies with this shameful action, the consequences are the same to society and our species [...]. For fornication and even adultery itself we have frailty and nature to plead, though these are heinous sins: but Self-pollution is a sin not only against nature, but a sin that prevents and extinguishes nature'.

BDSM-oriented sexual preferences characterised in the manual as "paraphilias". John Money (1986) first popularised the term "paraphilia" with the intention of designating unusual sexualities in a non-pejorative fashion. While the term has the advantage compared to "perversion", "deviation", "aberration", and even "deviance" that it does not directly signal a departure from something more normal or natural, it bears negative connotations before and after entering *DSM-3* (1987) as a mental disorder in 1980. Etymologically the term meaning "beside" (παρά) love/friendship (φιλία), wavers somewhat undecidedly between designating a sexual interest that is something different from "normal" love altogether and designating a love that is somehow different from other forms of love. In either case, the obvious antonym is the "normophilic".[8]

In this section, I will outline the reasons for and the limitations of the pathologising approach taken by *DSM-5* – especially in how it falls short in distinguishing between consensual and non-consensual forms and in how it reproduces old religious and quasi-religious ideas about genital, reproductive sex as the norm for non-pathological sexuality. In their excellent review article from 2013, the philosophers De Block and Adriaens present the position of the changing editions of the DSM as follows:

> The post-World War II history of psychiatry is characterized by the growing power of professional organi[s]ations. The American Psychiatric Association (APA) is perhaps the world's most powerful professional organi[s]ation of psychiatrists. It is involved in health campaigns, the publication of psychiatric books and journals, and the organi[s]ation of conferences. Its most visible work, however, is the preparation and publication of the *Diagnostic and Statistical Manual of Mental Disorders* (*DSM*), a standardi[s]ed psychiatric classification system. Today, it is the leading clinical diagnostic manual worldwide, and it is also used for research and administrative purposes all over the world. (2013, 284–85)

Especially interesting in the article is the section on the many controversies on homosexuality and its changing status through the history of the editions, and the relations between the descriptions of homosexuality and of the paraphilic disorders: "Perhaps more so than the 1952 DSM, the DSM-II unambiguously qualified homosexuality as a mental disorder" (2013, 287). In *DSM-3* (1987) homosexuality was deleted and no longer listed as a mental disorder, while

8 Which is also the way it repeatedly appears in *DSM-5*. See, p. 685 et passim: "[…] the term *paraphilia* may be defined as any sexual interest greater than or equal to normophilic sexual interests".

paraphilias were included as mental disorders. The chapter on "Paraphilic Disorders" opens like this:

> Paraphilic disorders included in this manual are voyeuristic disorder (spying on others in private activities), exhibitionistic disorder (exposing the genitals), frotteuristic disorder (touching or rubbing against a nonconsenting individual), sexual masochism disorder (undergoing humiliation, bondage, or suffering), sexual sadism disorder (inflicting humiliation, bondage, or suffering), pedophilic disorder (sexual focus on children), fetishistic disorder (using nonliving objects or having a highly specific focus on nongenital body parts), and transvestic disorder (engaging in sexually arousing cross-dressing). (1987, 685)

Significantly, the introductory lines move seamlessly from the clearly or supposedly non-consensual (voyeurism and exhibitionism)[9] to the frotteurism explicitly specified to be non-consensual to masochism and sadism with no distinction made between widespread consensual practices and rare, criminal offenses. Subsequently, it moves on to paedophilia which can never be consensual, and then to fetishism which can only very rarely even *be* non-consensual in and of itself, to finally end with transvestitism, which cannot possibly be non-consensual. This creates a continuum between allegedly unusual sexual interests of no harm to anyone such as cross-dressing at one end to abusive, illegal, coercive, non-consensual abuse in the form of paedophilia or sadistic violence at the other end.[10] Moreover, what do the paraphilias have in common? The answer, it turns out, hides in the introductory conceptualisation of the umbrella term rather than in any single instance of it, and in a way that is not and could not be manifested in diagnostic criteria: "The term *paraphilia* denotes any intense and persistent sexual interest other than sexual interest in genital stimulation or preparatory fondling with phenotypically normal, physically mature, consenting human partners" (ibid.). This is the description of a necessary action and a necessary target for normophilic sexuality. For a sexual interest to not qualify as paraphilia, the target has to be phenotypically normal, physically mature, and consenting, while the activity has to be stimulation of the genitals or preparing said stimulation of the genitals. With no further discussion, justification or even thematisation, the description is an

9 From the context it must be assumed that voyeurism and exhibitionism are here understood to be performed without the consent or knowledge of other parties.

10 In reality several of the listed paraphilia are not at all unusual – see below and compare De Neef et al. (2019, 130) and Zurbriggen and Yost (2004).

instance of emphatic genito-centric essentialism. The specification that fondling is allowed if (and only if) it serves preparatory purposes in relation to genital stimulation could draw a smile – were it not for the severely pathologising effects this has had and has. It may be hard to verify exactly how direct the connection is between conservative religion and psychiatry here – whether there is causality or just analogy. However, as also mentioned by De Block & Adriaens (2013), there is a lot to suggest an influence from theology to psychiatry – including but not limited to vocabulary.[11]

Regardless, in the lack of a common denominator for the paraphilias in the dysfunctional, the harmful, the impairing, the result is that the non-normophilic and non-genital becomes pathologised to the degree of being put on a par with assault, alcoholism and physical abuse. Recurrent through all the descriptions of all the paraphilias there is a very emphatic choice to **not** make a distinction between fantasy and reality and between internal feelings and external acts. This is not by chance, but repeatedly and deliberately stressed: "fantasies, urges, or behaviors" formulaically repeated ad verbatim seven times. This deliberate, paratactic assimilation is a main vehicle for the pathologising rhetoric and effects of *DSM-5* (2013) where the fantasies and consensual practices of 30–70% of the contemporary population in developed societies are described as rare,[12] mental disorders – figuring prominently among them the diverse preferences subsumed under the names of two authors from the

---

11 With regard to the theological influence on psychiatry, it is noteworthy that many medical authorities in the field of sexual pathology continued to use the term and the notion of perversion. During the Middle Ages and the Renaissance, this term was used to denote an aberration or a deviation from a divine norm: any act that violated the laws of God was considered a perversion. Medieval theologians and Christian philosophers emphasised that the divine law was also a natural law. Even though there were sexual vices in line with nature, such as adultery, rape, and incest, the unnatural vices, such as masturbation, sodomy, and bestiality, were the worst sins because they could not result in conception (Oosterhuis 2000). This distinction between natural and unnatural sexual vices dovetailed with the interests of 19th-century physicians in distinguishing healthy from pathological sexuality (Kamieniak 2003); cf. De Block & Adriaens (2013, 278). The extension of conservative, religious ideas may even be ideological, practical and political: Spitzer once argued that, among other reasons, the paraphilias cannot be removed from the DSM "because it would be a public relations disaster for psychiatry" (Spitzer 2005, 115; cf, De Block & Adriaens 2013, 292). Yost states that "Gayle Rubin [...] theori[s]ed that American society, infused with these religious histories, has created a hierarchy of sexuality with heterosexual, marital, monogamous, reproductive, and non-commercial sex acts in the privileged (normal, natural, good) position, and homosexual, unmarried, casual, non-monogamous, non-procreative sex acts in the subordinate position ("abnormal, unnatural, sick, sinful"; 2010, 282)".

12 See below on empirical studies on the percentages of diverse preferences.

18th and 19th century, respectively. The next section traces some of the effects of the preferences being described from the perspective of illness and becoming firmly attached to the two proper nouns.

## 4 What Is in a Name? Narrating "Sadism" and "Masochism": Krafft-Ebing, Eulenburg, Freud, Deleuze

Two major moves come together throughout the modern history of describing sadism and masochism to the degree that it is difficult to disentangle a discussion of the preferences from these moves. Because even the very terms discussed are pre-determined and over-determined by the narratives from which these terms originate. One move, as previously suggested, is the move to connect two sexual preferences that are both right at the limit between body and mind to specific fictional narratives by specific authors. This sets them apart from most other mental or physical illnesses. Another move is testified to by the long and strong tradition beginning with the title of Krafft-Ebing's multi-edition work *Psychopathia Sexualis* (1939), for describing sexual preferences and orientations from the point of view of illness, mental disorder and pathology and for taking the point of departure in patients approaching the doctor. This means that the point of departure is in reported illness rather than in the sexual preference in general. In fact, Krafft-Ebing's work begins with three sections on sexuality in the general; "Fragments of a system of psychology of sexual life", "Physiological facts", and Anthropological facts" but these 47 pages are then succeeded by almost 600 pages on general and special sexual pathology and criminality (Krafft-Ebing 1939). Sadism is specifically described in terms of "Cruelty and Violence" (Krafft-Ebing 1939, 80 et passim) and explicitly connected by Krafft-Ebing to de Sade (ibid., 80 et passim). The same holds true for masochism as "Endured Cruelty and Violence" (ibid., 131 et passim) and explicitly connected to Sacher-Masoch (ibid., 132 et passim). Krafft-Ebing also discusses Rousseau as an example of a masochist and as a literary author with whom many patients can identify, and whose preferences they see as similar to their own (ibid., 166).[13] The term "sadism" was used only sporadically before

13 Musser makes a strong argument for the relation between Krafft-Ebing's psychiatric construction of a new type of patient and narrative. She claims: "Understanding how and why Krafft-Ebing interpreted Rousseau's behavior as masochistic illustrates masochism's intimate connection with literature and its attendant practices of reading and writing". (2008, 205) She goes on to say that conversely his consultees mirrored themselves in literature and performed a type: "[…] Krafft-Ebing's masochists used literary narratives to transform themselves into masochists" (ibid., 206).

Krafft-Ebing in 1886 in *Psychopathia Sexualis*. From that point onward, it was popularised and conventionalised, for instance by Freud in *Drei Abhandlungen zur Sexualtheorie* from 1905.

Eulenburg's treatise *Sadismus und Masochismus* (1911) puts the two inclinations together already in the title and refers to de Sade from the first page on. Eulenburg also refers to "algolagnisten" in addition to the two terms in the title. Algolagnia was suggested by Albert von Schrenck-Notzing in 1892. It means "lust for pain",[14] and is distinct from "algophilia" by stressing that "lust" rather than love is what the pain sustains and from sadism and masochism by not being tied specifically to biographical persons and their writings. Eulenburg describes at a very early point in the history of psychology how sadism and masochism do not necessarily form mutually exclusive preferences but are closely related and potentially co-existing (1911, 5). He also stresses that pain is far from the only characteristic and that humiliation ("Demüthigung") is central to the understanding (ibid., 6). Strikingly, he also assumes that imagination ("Vorstellung") plays a larger and different role for "algolagnisten" specifically than for other sexualities. His argument is that in algolagnia viewing ("Mitansehen") and/or playing ("Fingiren") can be enough to induce sexuality (ibid., 26).[15] Later he includes an entire chapter on the life and work of de Sade, thus consolidating the link between a general sexual preference and the narratives by a particular author.

In "Das ökonomische Problem des Masochismus", Freud (1975) goes further in the direction of considering masochism as possibly or even certainly primary and not necessarily derived from sadism as he had described it in the more general texts on pleasure and sexuality (*Drei Abhandlungen zur Sexualtheorie* and *Jenseits des Lustprincips*). For Freud, masochism is enigmatic economically speaking because the assumed aim for pain and displeasure seems to contradict the pleasure principle. Freud also suggests that many of the physical aspects of masochism may be playful ("spielerische") acting out of fantasies (1975, 345) and that the masochist sometimes becomes similar to a helpless child.

Later in the century, the most influential monograph on masochism is probably Deleuze's study of Masoch originally published in 1967 as *Presentation de*

14 The word flagellantism serves as a common denominator for religious and non-religious practices of (self-) whipping, but does not encompass pain in general. On the ritualistic and fantastic elements recurring across scenes of whipping specifically see Largier (2007, 13, 14).

15 Later in Reik's 1940 study, *Aus Leiden Freuden*, the author puts even greater emphasis on the intimate connection between masochism and fantasy.

*Sacher-Masoch – le Froid et le Cruel*. Deleuze provides illuminating readings not only of *Venus in Furs* but of Masoch's oeuvre as a whole. It is a large strength of the study that it pursues themes and images across Masoch's writings and presents him in nuanced ways and stresses how he was admired as a professor as well as a literary author at his time – in this way emphasising the aesthetics, language and philosophy of Masoch rather than immediately jumping to the diagnosis of a mental illness. Deleuze also argues against the idiomatic connection of sadism and masochism into an assumed entity of "sadomasochism". While there are good reasons to counter the idea of an imaginary unity of "sadomasochism" and even more that of the alleged identity of "sadomasochist", several of Deleuze's reasonings in this context are decidedly misguided. Especially when he writes:

> The belief in this unity is to a large extent the result of misunderstandings and careless reasoning. It may seem obvious that the sadist and the masochist are destined to meet. The fact that one enjoys inflicting while the other enjoys suffering pain seems to be such a striking proof of their complementarity that it would be disappointing if the encounter did not take place. [[However]...] a genuine sadist could never tolerate a masochistic victim [...]. Neither would the masochist tolerate a truly sadistic torturer. (1991 [1967], 40–41)

Here Deleuze switches to putting pain above everything else and to talking about "victim" and characterising only the torturer as "truly" sadistic – thus eliminating the possibility of consent and consensual relationships and meetings. It is true that a masochist understood as a person with a preference for submissive sexual behavior would never engage with a sadistic person in the colloquial sense of the word. It is also a platitude, and something that holds true for not just the masochist but everyone. No one prefers non-consensual abuse or to be tortured against his/her will.[16] The same counterfactual point based even more explicitly on a collapse between work and preference says in Deleuze's "From Sacher-Masoch to masochism" six years earlier:[17] "Comparing the work of Masoch with that of Sade, one is struck by the impossibility of any encounter between a sadist and a masochist" (2004, 126). Deleuze, in

16 The rare cases of consensual non-consent under certain ramifications in some relationships are not really an exception to this but typically a way of pre-negotiating a complete transfer of power for a certain time.

17 Originally published as "De Sacher Masoch au masochisme" in *Arguments*, 5e année, no. 21, 1er trimestre, 1961, pp. 40–46.

effect completely collapses the distinction between diverse sexual preferences in many real persons on the one hand and the works about a century apart from each other of Sade and Masoch on the other hand.[18] As if the question was really whether Severin from *Venus in Furs* would enjoy the treatment of Dolmancé in *Philosophy in the Bedroom*. Such collapses – and ensuing collapses of consensual and non-consensual, identity and preference and pain and power – have been to the detriment of understanding the preferences of (in this case so-called) masochists. The collapses have contributed substantially to transforming the view on submissive preferences as aesthetic and personal choices and traits in the admired and celebrated enlightenment philosopher Rousseau and the highly regarded professor and renowned author Masoch into mental disorders in impaired patients.

## 5 Pathological Masculinities and De-pathologising Deviance

Empirical persons with non-normative sexualities situated in the nexus between body and mind, we have seen, are treated throughout psychiatric history based on characters in and authors of specific fictions. Thus, the construction of sadism and masochism has been narrative through and through in literature about the preferences.

Collapsing works and proper nouns of historical authors with assumptions about diverse sexual preferences is one non-sequitur. Collapsing consensual and non-consensual practices is another. In the context of the latter, it is not hard to understand why the words “sadist”, “sadism” and “sadistic” are stigmatising. In normal use, no effort is made to distinguish between cruel, abusive behavior and consensual sexual power exchange. In newspapers, in dictionaries and in everyday use, the words are used in the two meanings interchangeably and words like atrociousness, heartlessness, and inhumanity are listed as synonyms with sadism.[19] Furthermore, some persons do actually derive sexual pleasure from non-consensual acts of violence and abuse. In Denmark, two of the most infamous criminals who both independently of each other committed outrageous crimes against women, including molestation and

18 Notably, however, tops and bottoms, dominants and submissives, masters and slaves, daddies and babygirls, M/s, D/s, owners and properties, mistresses and boys, Hotwives and sissies, dominatrixes and dominated, do in fact, to large degree, seek the company of each other and form relationships thus making the “impossibility of any encounter” simply empirically completely wrong.

19 For example, in Collins Dictionary and Merriam-Webster.

murder, Peter Madsen and Peter Frederiksen, were both members of "Det sorte selskab" ("The Black Company"), which describes itself as a club for members who like "erotic dominance and have BDSM in the heart" (*Det sorte selskab*, online). Moreover, in the authorship and life of Donatien Alphonse François Marquis de Sade, there are often no clear distinctions between the consensual and non-consensual, between the cruel and the pleasurable, or between the imagined and the real. It is very easy to jump to the conclusion that the paraphilic preference or interest in dominating others and/or in inflicting pain or humiliation is closely if not inextricably connected to ethical deficiency, criminality and psychopathy or psychopathology. I will get back to the ramifications of this conclusion towards the end. The assumption that persons engaging in consensual sexual power exchange are more likely to commit non-consensual assault is empirically verifiable or falsifiable as we will soon see. Making a direct connection between imagination and play on the one side and reality and assault on the other side on a purely speculative basis gets in the way both of testing the assumption and addressing the very real, massive problem of sexual violence against women across cultures. Using the term "sadist" to interchangeably refer to criminal, atrocious assailants and to persons accepting consensual power transfer is not helpful in this respect.

To disentangle the concept of "sadism" as non-consensual cruelty from sexual preferences associated with mutually staged power exchange, I next move briefly to a couple of the most overarching reviews and surveys on dominance and BDSM which have appeared after the classical texts mentioned and which are much more focused on empirically oriented approaches and data surveys on practices, preferences, self-perception, pleasure and possible impairments. Towards the end, I suggest that while it is fruitful to remove our understanding of the preferences from the narratives by and about Sacher-Masoch and de Sade on one level, it is equally important to re-introduce narrative as something integral to the preferences at another level. De Neef et al. (2019) review a large amount of scientific literature and especially surveys on BDSM. The aim, as also indicated by the title, is "To bring together all the existing scientific literature on BDSM from a biopsychosocial perspective" (de Neef et al. 2019, 129). Several studies demonstrate that power-inequality preferences are not unusual: "Similarly, Jozifkova and Flegr demonstrated that about half of the general population preferred unequal power dynamics in their sexual relationship" (ibid., 130). The article concludes that on an empirical basis BDSM preferences are usual, typically ethical and associated with higher education:

> Klement et al. demonstrated significantly lower levels of sexism and rape myth acceptance in BDSM practitioners […] data [shows] that more than

> half of the general population has BDSM-themed fantasies. […]. (136) Ample literature shows that BDSM practitioners are typically highly educated. […] Wismeijer & Van Assen similarly found that 70% had a higher education (ie, bachelor's or master's degree), as compared with 34% in the general population. (ibid., 137)

It should be unsurprising that BDSM practitioners are less likely to perpetuate rape myth acceptance since consent and stop words and pre-agreed-upon rules are integral to the activities. In the largest study to date, Richters et al. (2008) set out to examine whether stigmatising assumptions could be empirically confirmed and reach similar conclusions to de Neef et al (2019). The article renders the result of a survey comprised of a representative sample of 19,307 respondents. The conclusion reads:

> Cross and Matheson found SM practitioners were not more unhappy or neurotic. The only major demographic finding was that masochists were more likely to be employed than sadists and nonsadomasochists. These findings are completely in line with our finding of higher sexual interest and wider repertoire among those who had engaged in BDSM, and our finding that they were not unhappy or anxious. […] Our findings support the idea that BDSM is simply a sexual interest or subculture attractive to a minority, and that for most participants, BDSM activities are not a pathological symptom of past abuse or of difficulty with "normal" sex. This confirms the conclusions of other empirical studies based on purposive samples […]. (Richters et al. 2008, 1666–67)

## 6 Preference or Identity? Pain or Dominance?

It is worthwhile to pause to keep in mind the enormous disparity between the psychiatric descriptions of sadism and masochism as non-normative mental disorders causing great harm to the individual and others on the one hand, and the empirical data showing significant correlation with education, relationship success, income, self-perception and several other parameters associated with well-functioning personal life, on the other hand.[20] This section further

20 For higher reproductive success see Jozifkova, Konvicka, and Flegr (2014), especially pp. 594 and 598. For lower levels of sexism and of rape myth acceptance, cf. Klement, Sagarin, and Lee (2016); de Neef et al. (2019, 136). For higher average education see de Neef et al 137. See also de Neef et al (2019, 138): "From an evolutionary point of view, male assertiveness

examines some historical reasons for this disparity explaining how the preferences have been constructed as identities and as ultimately concerned with pain.

There is a long tradition in psychiatry to describe sadism, masochism and fetishism as contrary to normative sexuality and in opposition to an interest in the partner as a human being. The masochist, in such conceptions, is interested in pain *rather* than intercourse, or can *only* have intercourse with the help of pain. The fetishist, analogically, is allegedly turned on by the fur or the whip or the heels *rather* than the person. This perspective is that of the clinician treating patients rather than on studying sexual play and diversity. Yet, there is also a long tradition of seeing flogging and other types of pain infliction as simply physical means to sexual stimulation on a par with aphrodisiacs and hot baths etc. – facilitating rather than replacing other sexual practices. Kim M. Philips and Barry Reay reference Davidson in *Sex Before Sexuality*:

> Davidson has provided the telling comparison between a seventeenth-century medical treatise on the use of flogging to facilitate erection, and late nineteenth-century descriptions of masochism. The former, it was believed, involved a physiological (humoral) response to the stimulation of the blood; the latter was an expression of sexuality. The difference between the two was the difference between a physical and a psychological act, between therapy and identity. (2011, 8)

This approximates a Foucauldian insight. When a psychiatrist, clinician or non-professional labels someone as "a fetishist" because he or she "has" a fetish, or a "sadist" because the person enjoys having power consensually transferred to him, something happens which is comparable to Foucault's description of the move from talking about sodomy as a practice or an act, to using "homosexual" as a denominator for an identity. We would not be prone to say about a person who likes candle lights that he suffers from keriaphilia, and it would feel odd to assume about a child enjoying the trampoline that she is constitutionally a "jumper". The move from (possibly occasionally) *practicing* domination to *being* a sadist and thus from act and practice to essence and identity is *one*

is a characteristic valued by women in their male (potential) partners, because it may have led to increased survival chances for women and children. In this line, Jozifkova and Kolackova aimed to investigate the origin of dominance and submissiveness as sexual preferences. [...] They showed that, compared with control subjects, sexually dominant men and sexually submissive women perceived themselves as being more attractive and had more biological children. This led the authors to conclude BDSM to be a successful mating strategy". For less stress and psychological distress see Richters et al. (2008, 1663).

of the moves included in the term "sadist" (and "masochist"). Moreover, going back to the comparison with fetishism, one can certainly contend that: "I have a fetish (if by that you mean that I like nice shoes or short dresses or smooth hair in an also erotic sense) but I don't feel like this turns me into a 'fetishist'". However, it would not make sense to say, "I am most certainly a fetishist but I don't have any fetishes". This brings us to the second move included in the coining of the term "sadism". As opposed to the case of the unimaginable "fetishist without a fetish", it is perfectly possible to self-identify as a "sadist" (in the sense of being or potentially wanting to be the dominant part of a dominant/submissive relationship) but to have no preference for the allegedly defining feature of the sadist of inflicting pain. Thirdly, in addition to the essentialising potential petrification imposed on someone by labelling him as constitutionally "a homosexual", the label "sadist" literally adds insult to injury. The latter label is not only descriptive of an alleged sex-practice-based-identity but adds the proper noun of a biographical person, thus amounting to saying that the essence of the alleged sadist is to be de Sade's or as de Sade or as de Sade's writings or fantasies. Fourthly, beginning from the observation of mentally ill patients, rather than practitioners of certain sexual preferences in general, certainly adds a bias to the description and understanding. In sum, the creation of the figure of the sadist as the umbrella term for the dominance engaged person builds on four moves: a) from practice to identity, b) from catch-all symbolical dominance to synecdochical pain-infliction, c) from denotative descriptive term designating a range of practices to a connotative proper noun of an individual, and d) from observation of pathological behavior in mentally ill patients to application on widespread orientations and preferences of a significant part of the population.

Several recent studies and surveys stress that for a majority of people self-identifying as BDSM practitioners pain (if present at all) is subpart of dominance rather than the reverse. In the article "Dominance, submissivity (and homosexuality) in general population. Testing of evolutionary hypothesis of sadomasochism by internet-trap-method", Eva Jozifkova and Jaroslav Flegr state:

> Two unexpected results were obtained in research of sexual sadism and masochism (SM) in the last decade. Firstly, in modern societies relatively a large number of people are interested or even engaged in SM activities. Secondly, the pleasure from causing pain or suffering from the pain is considered to be a motive of consensual sadomasochistic practices in small minority of SM community. The majority of people in SM community referred to be sexually aroused by both the dominance/submission

> role and mild or mostly symbolical pain caused by sexual practice during the SM interactions. Actually, the pain, or rather a threat of pain, is usually only used for stressing power of a dominant person. (2006, 712)[21]

De Neef et al. state as the most general conclusion of the review of surveys:

> Literature indicates that BDSM is an umbrella term that covers an array of interactions that can be present independently or in different clusterings. A dimensional angle of approach is therefore also applicable on the nature of the interaction and the acts implemented. Generally, a shift in power dynamics is at the core of BDSM play. (2019, 134)
>
> These studies suggest that, contrary to many academic theories, power, and not the giving and receiving of pain, is at the core of SM. [...] The authors concluded that sadomasochists should be seen as sexual gourmets or adventurers, and they suggested further, echoing Weinberg, that "rather than pain, bondage, and humiliation being at the core of the SM experience ... the exchange of power in an erotic context [is] a vehicle for the experience of sexual pleasure". (Richters et al. 2008, 1666)[22]

Thus, more recent, empirically based studies repeatedly show with a clear statistical significance that dominance-based preferences in general are not perceived as impairments;[23] do not cause sexual distress; are not caused by abuse or trauma; and for most builds on a clear hierarchy with power at

21 This amounts to later confirmation of the preliminary reports in Cross and Matheson drawing on Califia: "Some who participate in SM activities argue that SM is best understood as an eroticised, consensual exchange of power (Califia, 1983). They say that, contrary to popular belief, SM is not about the infliction of pain per se (Califia, 1983). Rather, pain is one of many techniques that help delineate power and status, and it is the experience of a power differential that is sought" (ibid., 137). For an entirely similar point in a German context, see Passig und Strübel: "Viele Sadomasochisten können Schmerzen nichts abgewinnen. Ihre Spiele drehen sich um Macht, Unterwerfung und Demütigung" (2009, 11). Musser notes how already Krafft-Ebing stresses that the "subjection to the woman" is the essential element in masochism and how this allows him to suggest masochism as a "new perversion" compared to for instance flagellantism (Musser 2008, 205, 204).

22 For an entire map of diversities associated with BDSM based on the four parameters of "hypermasculinity", "administration of pain", "physical restriction", and "humiliation" see "Alison et al. (2001).

23 These studies are based on surveys of either the entire population or self-identified BDSM-practitioners as opposed to earlier theories based on either pure speculation or empirical studies of mentally ill patients.

the core and pain as one potential among other means to achieve power exchange.

## 7 Conclusion: Non-normativity, Dominance, and Hierarchical Disparity

Two reasons for the disparity between theoretical speculations and empirical data, thus, consist in the theoretical tendency to privilege pain over power and to take the point of departure in mentally ill persons who are either patients who often perceive their preferences themselves as impairments or perpetrators rather than the general population. The terms, then, originate from within specific clinical and pathological contexts; from within the clinic where the psychiatrist, doctor, or psychoanalyst meets and observes mentally ill persons suffering from impairments, anxieties or libidinal maladies. From within such contexts, the terms are applied to a much broader spectrum of persons. It comes to lump together partial or wholesale preferences for power games, domination, unequal dynamics, and pain stimulation as practices into an essentialist tagging of somebody as constitutionally "a sadist" as a profound identity. As we have seen, *DSM-5* (2013) continues this line and fails to distinguish between consensual and non-consensual behavior; between fantasy and reality; between non-genital and pathological and between non-genital and unusual. When these distinctions are re-instated, we find that studies show that between 2% and 20% percent of the population engage in *consensual* sexual domination of different kinds;[24] that 35–67%[25] have *fantasies* about domination, being forced, being tied or tying, or other issues involving unequal power; and that it is extremely *common* and *non-pathological* human behavior to also engage in non-genital sexual activities.

This does not mean that the relationships between the practices and preferences and the stigmatising associations are not complicated and multiple, nor does it mean that there can be no link between the pathological masculinity and misogyny of men committing rape and abuse and sexual fantasies or practices of domination. It does mean, though, that one cannot be reduced to

24 See Jozifkova and Flegr (2006, 712), Richters et al. (2008, 1660), de Neef et al. (2019, 134).

25 De Neef et al. (2019, 130) report that 69% of the population (72% of men) fantasized about tying up or being tied and 30–61% about whipping or spanking. In Zurbriggen and Yost (2004) it says: "[…] fantasies of submission are common among women. Pelletier and Herold (1988) found that 51% of their female sample reported fantasies of being forced to submit sexually".

the other, and that self-identified practitioners and persons with fantasies of domination are less rather than more likely to accept coercive, non-consensual practices and myths.

Based on empirical surveys and an awareness not too quickly to collapse the distinction between literary works and actual preferences and between mentally ill persons and the general population, I suggest that the concepts of "dominance" and "hierarchical disparity" are better fits with the reality of the preferences as well as with the self-perception and self-reports of the practitioners than masochism and (especially) sadism.[26] Firstly, dominance is a driving factor in peer assessment of mate value in general across human and non-human animals.[27] It is indispensable for understanding animal biology and animal sexuality across a very broad range of species. Finally, the largest available and most recent surveys tell us that it is the most central and essential factor in BDSM-related activities to centrally include the establishment of unequal power relationships. What these findings suggest as a whole is that pursuing dominance is a mating strategy in humans as well as non-human animals, and statistically it is a successful one. Eva Jozifkova writes:

> Out of the age cohort 35–44 years it was revealed that 1) sexually dominant men had more biological male children 2) both the sexually dominant men and sexually submissive women perceived themselves as being more attractive. […] sexual arousal by dominance is frequent and confers an increased capacity to pass on genes in the general population. Therefore, sexual arousal by dominance is likely to be the means of mating strategy. (2017, 274)

In a complete reversal of the assumptions of DSM-5 and similar psychiatric texts, the article issues an incredibly queer declaration of confidence in dissociating the natural and the appropriate from the straight and normophilic:

> On the basis of these results, it is possible to conclude that some people may lose their chance to maintain long-term relationships and may bring up fewer children when they suppress their natural preferences

26 Needless to say, I entirely endorse anyone's self-identification as "sadist" or "masochist" as long as the person aligns this identification with safe, sane, consensual sex.

27 See Leivers, Rhodes, Simmons (2014). Compare Kruger, Fitzgerald (2011), and Hill et al., for the connection between dominance and prosocial behavior and altruism in humans (2013, 276), as well as for stressing the gender differences (ibid., 282). For the use in Darwinist approaches to literature see Saunders (2015, 36).

> by pairing with an inappropriate [equal] partner. This finding might open up novel insights into sexology, partnership therapy and domestic violence issues. (ibid.)

In several of the articles by Jozifkova et al. the relationship between dominance in bed and related to sex on the one hand and in the relationship in general on the other hand is somewhat blurred. I find the distinction between the two important, which leads me to stress how dominance for humans is often constructed as a playful way of seeking arousal through creating imaginary, exaggerated disparities in power, status and ability to make decisions for oneself and others sexually in ways that may or may not conform with personal traits outside romantic relationships.

Secondly, this very creation of (imagined) hierarchical disparity itself often plays an integral role in dominance-oriented sexual preferences. Deleuze repeatedly stresses the importance of the contract to the masochist but does not connect it to the question of hierarchy. He even mentions how he finds it peculiar that Reik, whom he admires, does not include it as a fifth element in addition to his four mentioned elements of masochism. In light of the considerations above, we can see how the contract is a playful formalisation of a hierarchical disparity framed as absolute.[28] We can see the same creation of hierarchy from a different perspective in Musser's descriptions: "According to Krafft-Ebing, the main marker of Rousseau's masochism was "the feeling of subjection to the woman"; Rousseau "love[d] the proud, scornful woman crushing him under her feet by the weight of her royal wrath" (2008, 205). Notice how "royal" serves to establish imagined hierarchies. The fantasy and the creation of an imagined scenario allow for the pleasurable imagination of mating with individuals higher or lower in the hierarchy. In fact, the establishment of hierarchical disparity in the form of teacher/student, master/slave, police/convict etc. is recurrent in such plays and fantasies (Moser and Levitt 1987), and almost always narrative in nature. Our ability to imaginatively create such scenarios and narratives, provides us with a means to achieve something similar to what other animals experience as physical and social reality

28 For a description of the same logic in online BDSM-encounters see Cross and Matheson: "Further, indicators of status are derived not simply from actual behavior or influence, but also involve socially constructed symbols that identify directions of power and influence. For example, one indicator of status might be the manner in which an individual is addressed (Falbo & Peplau, 1980). If one individual refers to another as "master", or "mistress", this indicates a conferring of higher status upon the person being addressed. If an individual is addressed as "pet", or "slave", or "slut", this indicates his or her lower status" (2006, 152–153).

but without the same risks and disadvantages. Both the human male and the female can take on roles that may or may not change and that may or may not reflect how they act in social and professional life.

In the article, I have demonstrated that non-reproductive sexual practices in general are usual and not pathological and that sexual inclinations for unequal power positions in particular are better understood as preferences associated with narratively constructed hierarchical disparities than as identities as "sadists" or "masochist" with pain at the core. Further, I have stressed the fundamental importance of distinguishing between imagined scenarios and fantasies about dominance and wishes to really act out violently and coerce as well as the equally fundamental distinction between consensual (imagined) power transfer and non-consensual assault.

The fact that persons reporting to engage in fantasies or consensual practices about overemphasised hierarchical disparity report higher sexual pleasure, more self-confidence and better relationships[29] makes it doubly significant and important that in many historical and cultural contexts, such preferences have been castigated as religiously sinful, psychologically aberrant and pathological, and morally despicable. Here, conversely, non-normative bodies and minds and non-normative sexual preferences prevail and contribute to sustaining relationships circumscribed by desire and consensuality.

## Works Cited

Alison, Laurence, Pekka Santtila, N. Sandnabba, and Niklas Nordling. "Sadomasochistically Oriented Behavior: Diversity in Practice and Meaning". *Archives of Sexual Behavior*, vol. 30, no.1, 2001, pp. 1–12.

American Psychiatric Association. *Diagnostic and Statistical Manual of Mental Disorders*. Fifth Edition, American Psychiatric Publishing, 2013.

American Psychiatric Association. *Diagnostic and Statistical Manual of Mental Disorders*. Third Edition – Revised, American Psychiatric Association. 1987.

Anonymous, *Onania Or The Heinous Sin Of Self-pollution, And All Its Frightfull Consequences In Both Sexes*. London: H. Cooke, 1756.

Bivona, Jenny M., and Joseph W. Critelli: "Women's Erotic Rape Fantasies: An Evaluation of Theory and Research". *Journal of Sex Research*, vol. 45, no. 1, 2008, pp. 57–70.

29 Richters, de Visser, Rissel, Grulich and Smith (2008), de Neef, Coppens, Huys and Morrens, (2019, 136–138); Jozifkova, Bartos, Flegr (2012, 637); Jozifkova, Konvicka, Flegr (2014, 594); Bivona, Critelli (2008, 63).

Cross, Patricia A., and Kimberly Matheson. "Understanding Sadomasochism". *Journal of Homosexuality*, vol. 50, no. 2/3, 2006, pp. 133–66.

De Block, Andreas, and Pieter R. Adriaens. "Pathologizing Sexual Deviance: A History". *Journal of Sex Research* vol. 50, no. 3/4, 2013, pp. 276–98.

de Neef, Coppens, Wim Huys, and Manuel Morrens. "Bondage-Discipline, Dominance-Submission and Sadomasochism (BDSM) From an Integrative Biopsychosocial Perspective: A Systematic Review". *Sexual Medicine* vol. 7, no. 2, 2019, pp. 129–44.

Deleuze, Gilles. "From Sacher-Masoch to Masochism" *Angelaki-journal of The Theoretical Humanities* vol. 9, no. 1, 2004, pp. 125–33.

Deleuze, Gilles. *Masochism. Coldness and cruelty* [*Presentation de Sacher-Masoch – le Froid et le Cruel*], New York: Zone Books, [1967] 1991.

*Det sorte selskab*. https://www.detsorteselskab.dk/. Accessed December 15, 2023.

Eulenburg, Albert. *Sadismus und Masochismus*. Wiesbaden: Bergmann, 1911.

Freud, Sigmund. "Das ökonomische Problem des Masochismus". *Psychologie des Unbewussten. Studienausgabe III*, Frankfurt: Fisher Wissenschaft, [1924] 1975, pp. 339–55.

Freud, Sigmund. "Drei Abhandlungen zur Sexualtheorie". *Sexualleben. Studienausgabe V*, Frankfurt: Fisher Wissenschaft, [1905] 1972, pp. 37–134.

Freud, Sigmund. "Jenseits das Lustprincips". *Psychologie des Unbewussten. Studienausgabe III*, Frankfurt: Fisher Wissenschaft, [1920] 1975, pp. 213–73.

Hill, Alexander K., John Hunt, Lisa L.M. Welling, Rodrigo A. Cárdenas, Michelle A. Rotella, John R. Wheatley, Khytam Dawood, Mark D. Shriver, David A. Puts. "Quantifying the strength and form of sexual selection on men's traits". *Evolution and Human Behavior*, vol. 34, no. 5, 2013, pp. 334–41.

Jozifkova, Eva, Ludek Bartos, and Jaroslav Flegr, "Evolutional background of dominance/submissivity in sex and bondage: the two strategies?" *Neuro Endocrinol Letters*, vol. 33, no. 6, 2012, pp. 636–42.

Jozifkova, Eva, Ludek Bartos and Jaroslav Flegr. "Sexual Arousal by Dominance and Submission Represents Mating Strategy". *The Journal of Sexual Medicine* vol. 14, no. 5, 2017, pp. 273–74.

Jozifkova, Eva, Ludek Bartos, and Jaroslav Flegr. "Dominance, Submissivity (and Homosexuality) in General Population: Testing of Evolutionary Hypothesis of Sadomasochism by Internet-Trap Method". *Neuro endocrinology letters*, vol. 27, no. 6, 2006, pp. 711–18.

Jozifkova, Eva, Ludek Bartos, Jaroslav Flegr, "Evolutional Background of Dominance/Submissivity in Sex and Bondage: The Two Strategies?" *Neuro Endocrinol Letters*, vol. 33, no. 6, 2012, pp. 636–42.

Jozifkova, Eva, Ludek Bartos, Martin Konvicka, and Jaroslav Flegr. "Why do Some Women Prefer Submissive Men? Hierarchically Disparate Couples Reach Higher Reproductive Success in European Urban Humans". *Neuro Endocrinol Letters*, vol. 35, no. 7, 2014, pp. 594–601.

Kamieniak, Jean Pierre. "La construction d'un objet psychopathologi – que: La perversion sexuelle au XIXe siècle" ["The construction of a psychopathological object: Sexual perversion in the 19th century"]. *Revue Française de Psychanalyse*, vol. 67, no. 1, 2003, pp. 249–62.

*King James Bible Online*. https://www.kingjamesbibleonline.org. Accessed December 15, 2023.

Klement, Kathryn R., Brad J. Sagarin, and Ellen M. Lee. "Participating in a Culture of Consent May Be Associated with Lower Rape-Supportive Beliefs". *Journal of Sex Research*, vol. 54, no. 1, 2016, pp. 1–5.

Krafft-Ebing, Richard. *Psychopathia Sexualis*. London: William Heinemann (Medical Books) LTD, 1939. https://doi.org/10.1016/C2013-0-06569-3.

Kruger DJ and CJ Fitzgerald. "Reproductive Strategies and Relationship Preferences Associated With Prestigious and Dominant Men". *Personality and Individual Differences*, vol. 50, no. 3, 2011, pp. 365–69. 10.1016/j.paid.2010.10.002 56.

Largier, Niklaus. In Praise of the Whip: A Cultural History of Arousal. Trans. Graham Harman. New York: Zone Books (Princeton University Press), 2007.

Leivers, Samantha, Gillian Rhodes, and Leigh W. Simmons. "Sperm Competition in Humans: Mate Guarding Behavior Negatively Correlates with Ejaculate Quality". *PloS one*, vol. 9, no. 9 e108099, 2014. 10.1371/journal.pone.0108099.

Money, John. *Lovemaps: Clinical Concepts of Sexual/Erotic Health and Pathology, Paraphilia, and Gender Transposition in Childhood, Adolescence, and Maturity*. New York: Irvington, 1986.

Moser, Charles, and Eugene E. Levitt. "An Exploratory-Descriptive Study of a Sadomasochistically Oriented Sample". *The Journal of Sex Research*, vol. 23, no. 3, 1987, pp. 322–37.

Musser, Amber Jamilla. "Reading, Writing, and the Whip". *Literature and Medicine*, vol. 27, no. 2, 2008, pp. 204–22. doi:10.1353/lm.0.0034.

Oosterhuis, Harry. *Stepchildren of Nature: Krafft-Ebing, Psychiatry and the Making of Sexual Identity*. Chicago, IL and London: University of Chicago Press, 2000.

Passig, Kathrin, and Ira Strübel. *Die Wahl der Qual*. Hamburg: Rowohlt Taschenbuch, 2009.

Phillips Kim M, and Barry Reay. *Sex Before Sexuality: A Premodern History*. Cambridge: Polity Press, 2011.

Reik, Theodor. Aus Leiden Freuden. London: Imago Publishing Co., LTD, 1940.

Richters, de Visser, Rissel, Grulich, Smith, "Demographic and Psychosocial Features of Participants in Bondage and Discipline, "Sadomasochism" or dominance and Submission (BDSM): Data from a National Survey". *Journal of Sexual Medicine*, vol. 5, no. 7, 2008, pp. 1660–68.

Saunders, Judith. 2015. "Darwinian Literary Analysis of Sexuality". *The Evolution of Sexuality. Evolutionary Psychology*. edited by T. Shackelford and R. Hansen. Berlin: Springer, pp. 29–55.

Zetterberg-Nielsen, Henrik. "Dangers of Fictionality, Human Sexuality and Sexual Fantasies" (forthcoming).

Zurbriggen, Eileen L., and Megan R. Yost. "Power, Desire, and Pleasure in Sexual Fantasies". *The Journal of Sex Research*, vol. 41, no. 3, 2004, pp. 288–300. Minnesota UP, 2001.

CHAPTER 10

# Plastic Bodies, Plastic Minds? Transforming Transgender Childhood through Fiction

*Sven Van den Bossche*

## 1 Introduction

The enormous increase in visibility of transgender children in the last three decades could lead us to believe that they are new and without predecessors. Their entrance into the general consciousness is often located in the 1990s and early 2000s, when the VU gender clinic in Amsterdam first started prescribing hormone blockers to trans children that temporarily halted puberty – a now almost standard procedure that became known worldwide as "the Dutch approach" (Bakker 2021, 162). In *Histories of the Transgender Child* (2018), historian Jules Gill-Peterson argues against the idea that trans children are new. According to her, they were even central to the medicalisation of sex and gender throughout the twentieth century. She refers to children who became objects of medical experiments based on a discourse of (gender) plasticity, which argues that young bodies and minds are more "plastic" than those of adults. This discourse served to legitimise highly contested surgical interventions in the bodies of intersex children to fit the standards of "male" and "female" bodies and has supported the belief that children might outgrow their transgender feelings because of the assumption that the mind will adapt to the body. To this very day, children's assumed plasticity continues to inform medical protocols. Hormone blockers, for instance, are meant to halt the development of secondary sex characteristics while the child's mind is considered still too plastic or underdeveloped to make irreversible decisions about their bodies and gender. Within this medicalised discourse, the desires and perspectives of the child are largely invisible, leaving us to wonder how we might gain insight into their subjective experiences and develop alternative ways of imagining trans childhood.

Gill-Peterson's efforts to unearth unknown stories about trans children who came into contact with the medical world sheds an invaluable light on transgender history. Her work as a historian, however, is based on empirical, archival materials that show only glimpses of what a trans childhood might have been and continues to be like. To complement her research, this chapter

 | DOI:10.1163/9789004519886_012

wants to highlight the possibilities and cultural importance of imaginative work insofar as it allows for many more alternative narrativisations. We might follow the example of Kathryn Bond Stockton, who turns to fictional stories in her monograph *The Queer Child, or Growing Sideways in the Twentieth Century* (2009). She supports her decision as follows: "I present this history of these queer children as a matter of fiction, since this history has not yet taken shape in public ways outside of fiction" (2009, 9). Similarly, I would argue that it is only in the realm of the imagination that we can start to develop alternative discourses on (the histories of) trans children. As opposed to the silenced child in an objectifying medical discourse, fictional narratives offer subjective perspectives that allow the reader to develop insight into a wide range of embodied experiences of trans child characters. Thus, this chapter proposes to investigate how various narrative techniques can evoke trans child subjectivities beyond the normative discourse of plasticity. Taking a Belgian film and a Dutch novel as case studies, I argue that cinematic and literary fiction have the capacity to foreground the trans child by means of focalisation, the evocation of consciousness and the dramatisation of embodied actions.

The first part of this chapter will lay bare the specific characteristics of the discourse of gender plasticity. Two important aspects will be highlighted, namely the lack of agency assumed by child plasticity and the specific temporal development that a narrative of plasticity sets as the norm for all children. Along the lines of Gill-Peterson's understanding of child plasticity, Claudia Castañeda argues that current trans health care reduces children to malleable objects with hopes of still guiding them toward a normative developmental path: "the approved treatments reconstitute the child in gendered terms as a not-yet entity, in which the potential for 'normal' gendering must be maintained through reversibility" (2014, 60). In my discussion of fictional representations, I will, first of all, focus on narrative techniques that present trans children as thinking, speaking and acting beings, as against the "not-yet" status ascribed to them in medical discourse. Next, I will highlight how these fictional narratives produce temporalities that subvert the normative path paved through plasticity.

In the second and third parts, I will illustrate how child agency and non-normative temporalities take shape in *Ma vie en rose* (1997; transl. *My Life in Pink*), a Belgian film by Alain Berliner, and *Mijn lieve gunsteling* (2020; transl. *My Heavenly Favorite*),[1] a Dutch novel by Lucas Rijneveld. In both cases, medicalised views and pathologising language are largely or completely absent

1 An English translation of this novel was published after this chapter was written. This chapter makes use of the original novel in Dutch.

from the narrative; instead, an alternative, subjective perspective is evoked through internal focalisation, embodied actions, and animal metaphors for the body. Berliner's film is centered around a seven-year-old trans girl who moves to a suburban neighborhood, where her gender non-normative behavior is met with growing animosity. As the film was produced before the current hypervisibility of trans children, gender non-normativity in *Ma vie en rose* is understood by adults as an expression of (future) homosexuality rather than transness, but still relies on a discourse of child plasticity. In contrast to these dominant views in the adult world, cinematic techniques allow the child's imaginative worldview to take center stage, while simultaneously ridiculing adult perspectives. *Mijn lieve gunsteling* compares dominant and alternative viewpoints in a very different way. The entire story is filtered through the lens of a pederastic unreliable narrator, who eschews pathologising language in an attempt to legitimise his taboo relationship with a pubescent gender-non-conforming child. At the same time, gender is understood by the child through animal metaphors. While the narrator embeds these metaphors in his own narrative, they still give us glimpses of the child's perspective, which stands in marked contrast with the narrator's. Insights from film narratology and theories on the unreliable narrator will guide my analyses of these two works of fiction.

## 2 Discourse of Child Plasticity

While the term "plasticity" in general has mostly positive connotations, such as the capacity to learn or adapt to a new situation, it is important to understand that "gender plasticity" has become a treacherously normative discourse in the medicalisation of sex and gender. As a general definition, Kyla Schuller and Jules Gill-Peterson describe "plasticity" as "the capacity of a given body or system to generate new form, whether internally or through external intervention" (2020, 1). It is widely believed that children have a higher capacity for adaptation than adults, but more interesting to Gill-Peterson's historical project than this actual, material plasticity of children is the entanglement with a disciplinary medical discourse. To her, it matters very little whether something like plasticity is in fact present in the bodies of children – in other words, whether they adapt more easily to their environments than adults, or whether their gender is more malleable. Gill-Peterson judiciously stresses that the discourse of gender plasticity has had "historically specific material, biological effects" (2018, 39).

These effects call into question more utopian visions of plasticity, such as in the work of Catherine Malabou (cf. Malabou 2005; 2008). In its hegemonic use, gender plasticity effectively denies the gendered feelings that children might have about themselves, since those feelings are considered changeable, more so than an adult's gender identity. Children might experience a temporary period in which they are allowed to experiment with gender and be relatively fluid in their expression, without such expressions being taken very seriously. It is assumed that they will eventually grow out of these experiences. While most children are socialised toward what is considered acceptable gendered behavior, attempts at "correcting" non-normative expressions take pathologising forms especially in the case of trans or intersex children. In such cases, childhood does not simply function as a period in which one should learn to abide by the rules of society, but as a temporary window of development in which children's assumed gender plasticity becomes the only hope of "restoring" normality and directing them toward their assigned gender by the time they reach adulthood. On a narrative level, the discourse of gender plasticity can be divided into at least two elements worth studying. In what follows, I will start by discussing the dismissal of trans children's agency that stems from the belief in their plasticity. Then I will demonstrate that the idea of plasticity in this context assumes a specific normative temporality, which restricts sex/gender plasticity to the stage of childhood and expects a development toward an adult stable binary gender identity and sexed body.

First of all, the conviction that gender is plastic up to a certain age reduces any statements children might make about their gender or any desires they might have to near-irrelevance. According to Gill-Peterson, the plasticity discourse turns children into "raw material" or mere "reservoirs of plasticity" (2018, 4). It is important to note, in particular, that the very notion of plasticity, as defined by Schuller and Gill-Peterson (2020, 1), already denies agency as it assumes an agent or force outside or inside of the child shaping their bodies and gender beyond their control. This ties in with the perception that many Western societies have of gender in childhood. As Castañeda explains, a child cannot really claim to be transgender because "the child is always already seen as incomplete, as not yet fully formed; its gender is not fully mature, and the child is also seen as not fully capable of knowing its own gender" (2014, 59). Children are seen as still developing, still plastic, and thus they can never be the central actors of their own story. Plasticity makes them malleable objects to be "kneaded" by adults into the desired sexed form – it treats them implicitly as too ignorant and innocent to make their own decisions. As a result, their own gender experience is somehow less "real" or complete than an adult's.

While medical history overall has thus treated trans children as silenced objects, Gill-Peterson has searched medical archives for "important and startling moments" when trans children's own actions "afforded them brief movements outward and away from the capture of modern medicine" (2018, 5). Even before "transsexuality" started to circulate as a categorisation, children used more familiar narratives of intersexuality or homosexuality to have their needs met: they claimed to have non-normative bodies or used their same-sex attraction as "proof" that they were supposed to be of a different gender (ibid., 63). In this manner, they tried to instrumentalise pathologising frameworks in their favor. The stories in Gill-Peterson's study, however, still function within the medical context and do not tell us how these children might have described their experiences if they had had the liberty to do so without consequences. This is where fictional representations can offer a powerful alternative, since they more readily and extensively allow us to imagine a trans child's agency beyond medical institutions and discourses. The discussion of *Ma vie en rose* and *Mijn lieve gunsteling* will highlight a number of significant embodied actions that foreground trans children as actors rather than as passive plastic objects.

A second focus will be on the normative temporality that is typically implied by a narrative of growth out of plasticity. Gill-Peterson's interest in the discourse of gender plasticity is mostly of historical concern. She highlights how this discourse originated through early twentieth-century developments in endocrinology and sexology which endowed the figure of the animal and the child with a primitive sexual plasticity. Henceforth, it was believed that human plasticity diminished when growing up: "plasticity is forceful and unstable early on in human life but has a definite window, after which it is meant to recede" (ibid., 119). From the beginning, scientific programs on gender plasticity were entangled with eugenics and, as such, caught up in a purported "advancement" of society through normalising the bodies of white intersex children. While medical experiments were clearly also performed on the bodies of black children, Gill-Peterson points out an important difference: doctors took on black children as experimental subjects "because of presumed access and disposability, whereas white children who were subject to similar procedures were framed as exhibiting the potential for a normative cure or at least improved normality" (ibid., 79). In this sense, the hope about future outcomes that doctors attached to a potent plasticity was racialised as white right from the start. According to Zakiyyah Iman Jackson, the goal-oriented manipulation of a white individual's capacity for plasticity stands in contrast to "blackness as a plastic way of being" (2016, 119). Blackness is thus defined as formlessness, while white children are assumed to outgrow their state of indeterminacy by becoming a "full-grown" individual. Even though the works of fiction discussed in this chapter only feature white trans children, I will later point out how they still manage to critique some of the basic subjugating aspects of racial and gender plasticity.

Despite the popular belief that the concept of gender was a progressive feminist invention, Gill-Peterson argues that it simultaneously offered doctors "a new developmental justification for coercive and normali[s]ing medical intervention" (2018, 98). The teleological plotting of white human life along a normative developmental narrative was left more or less unchanged in medical circles. In fact, when it comes to intersex children, "gender would make nonbinary morphology into underdevelopment, allowing medicine to claim that sex assignment was merely its normal completion" (ibid., 99). In the case of trans children, gender plasticity led to the belief that (psychotherapeutic) interventions before certain critical moments in the child's life could prevent it from growing up trans, a conviction that Gill-Peterson calls "a genocidal fantasy of eradicating trans life altogether in its developing forms" (ibid., 4). At the same time, some adolescents were able to medically transition because of the assumption that "puberty marks a threshold after which transsexuality cannot be eradicated by doctors or psychiatrists" (ibid., 92). Slowly but surely, a familiar narrative started to take hold with gender identity as "the endpoint of a teleology of growth out of plasticity" (ibid., 100).

In today's Western societies, some trans, intersex, or gender-non-conforming children have the chance to grow up trans and are able to transition (socially) at an early age. Plasticity, however, continues to function as a normative discourse, disciplining the bodies of children into a specific narrative mold. A child's plasticity may in some places no longer form a legitimation for conversion therapy or "corrective" surgical interventions, but childhood remains a period in which a person's gender identity is still widely assumed to be undecided. Castañeda explains how both puberty blockers that temporarily halt a child's puberty and cross-sex hormone therapy perpetuate the idea of the child as not "fully" formed:

> The phenomenon of transgender childhood has been subjected to medicali[s]ation in which the not-yet status of the child remains central: in one case, the child cannot possibly know its gender for sure and must be put "on hold" until it reaches a more fully adult state of reason; while in the other, the young person is allowed to transition bodily, but only to the degree that the process may be reversed should a different state of reason take shape with maturity. (2014, 60)

The reasoning in medical circles remains that children cannot really know "for sure" what their gender is, while a development into adulthood promises certainty and stability. Moreover, Gill-Peterson (2018) stresses that early social transitions imply an expected evolution toward a binary gender identification and an erasure of bodily visible trans characteristics. If puberty is halted or hormone treatment is started at an early age, secondary sex characteristics such as a low voice or breast development can be (partially) suppressed. While this is desired by many trans people, it also perpetuates gender binary norms; visible and non-binary transness become "lesser" varieties of being trans. As Gill-Peterson puts it, "an early and gender normative transition has become valuable insofar as it uses children's exceptional plasticity to promise a future that erases trans visibility itself" (2018, 197). An important consideration that is frequently missing from this medical logic is that not every child desires a gender-binary adulthood, has access to treatment or is considered eligible for this future of white, binary invisible transness.

As such, Gill-Peterson critiques several ways in which the presumed plasticity of children is instrumentalised in a medical context to discipline children into a normative gender development and restrict the access to care for those with lesser hopes of eventually conforming to the white, gender-binary ideal. In her conclusion, she goes as far as to claim that the conceptualisation of plasticity cannot be instrumentalised in a more liberating way. She writes:

> Plasticity has become so central to the flexible regime of neoliberal economies, where continuous adaptation and change is leveraged for near infinitesimal value extraction and the expansion of laboring to all productive biological and cultural processes, that it cannot easily be adapted for different ends. (ibid., 199)

However, by dividing the criticisms of plasticity into concrete aspects, this chapter aims to still regain some of the concept's more positive connotations. One critique is the reduction of certain groups of people (i.e., children and racialised groups) into formless, undetermined or (not yet) fully developed masses. The other is the re-evaluation of certain groups of people (i.e., white children) who are seen as holding a potent plasticity that they will outgrow towards full development, while this full development is not deemed acquirable for racialised people. Despite featuring white trans child characters, the works of fiction I examine below question both the portrayal of a child as a "not-yet entity" (Castañeda 2014, 60) and formulate an alternative to the normative narrative of plasticity: a development toward an adult stable binary gender identity and an invisible trans embodiment. Precisely these alternative portrayals hint at a more beneficial, agentic, and no longer temporary plasticity. Perhaps these utopian potentialities are unthinkable in Gill-Peterson's vision of "the flexible regime of neoliberal economies" (2018, 199), but they might become imaginable in fictional representations.

## 3 Life in Plastic

While Alain Berliner's film *Ma vie en rose* (1997) does not entirely escape the discourse of gender plasticity, the focus here will lie specifically on the instances where an alternative vision arises. Overall, the film presents a confrontation between the worldview of the main character, a seven-year-old trans girl called Ludo(vic),[2] and the views of her family and neighbors. At the beginning of the film, the family moves to a suburban neighborhood, where Ludo's father is offered a job opportunity by his boss, Albert. In this new environment, Ludo's feminine gender expression is met with growing animosity. When she first shows up in a dress at the neighborhood's welcome party, this is still laughed off as a joke, but the reactions grow more severe and aggressive when Ludo and the boss's son Jérôme develop a romantic interest in each other and stage a play marriage with Ludo as the bride. The turning point occurs when Ludo locks up a fellow classmate to take over her role as Snow White in the school play and receive a kiss from prince Jérôme. Growing concerns over such behavior make Ludo's parents turn to a child psychologist to "correct" her gender-non-conforming behavior. A neighborhood petition leads to Ludo's expulsion from school, the homophobia of the boss causes Ludo's father to lose his job, and hateful slurs and physical violence turn the neighborhood into an uninhabitable place. Eventually, Ludo's father finds a new job in a small town far away. There, Ludo immediately befriends a young transmasculine person and is finally allowed to wear the princess dress she so desperately desires.

While this summary of the plot might give the impression that Ludo is a mere victim of social circumstances, the film actually focusses on the child's inner world and dramatises various small acts of resistance. To deal with the onslaught of setbacks she has to confront, Ludo repeatedly escapes into a fantasy world modeled after *Le monde de Pam* (transl. *The World of Pam*), a film centered around a Barbie-like doll named Pam and her lover Ben. There, Ludo imagines herself in a princess dress, flying away with Pam or marrying Jérôme on top of a plastic castle. I would argue that Ludo's fantasies do not only assert her as a focalising and agentic character, refusing the reduction to a medicalised, plastic object, but they also allude to an alternative temporality from which the idea of a normative development out of plasticity is conspicuously

2 Even though the main character goes by the masculine name Ludo(vic) and is referred to by others with masculine pronouns, I will consistently use feminine pronouns in this analysis. The character's continuous and outspoken desire to be seen as a girl, despite her environment's denial of this identity, warrants this decision.

absent. To support this claim, let me first discuss a few cinematic techniques that invite audiences to take Ludo's point of view, giving them insight into her inner feelings and presenting her experiences as a serious, consistent and reliable source of knowledge. On top of that, the film constructs two contrasting time-spaces that represent opposing views of a child's gender development.

As Peter Verstraten points out in his introduction to film narratology, audiences tend to identify with the character whose field of vision is shown on screen (2008, 89). Technically, this happens through an "eyeline match" (ibid.): one shot shows a character watching something and the previous or next shot presents what the character is watching. Such traditional point-of-view shots are a common way to establish a special bond between the audience and a protagonist. In this case, it is striking how *Ma vie en rose* portrays almost exclusively what Ludo sees. When there are interactions not meant for her ears, the child is shown hiding under the table or in bushes, and the camera presents what she witnesses from her hiding spot. At one point, the film even takes this shooting technique a step further by suggesting Ludo's point of view when she is not actually present. Ludo has gone missing after having been bullied in the locker room, and we only find out later that she has tried to commit suicide by locking herself in the freezer. While her parents and three siblings search for her all over the house, several shots suggest that Ludo is secretly watching them. There is, for instance, a shot of the family through the woodwork of a staircase, and later we see her mother's feet from under the car in the garage. Even when Ludo is not actually present in a scene, her ghost is still lurking in her environment, making sure that the audience never lets go of her perspective.

The visual display of what a character (supposedly) sees through focalising shots is a very straightforward way of centralising Ludo's perspective, but a more in-depth portrayal of her internal life requires still other techniques. While several narratologists in the past have claimed that film cannot represent a character's feelings, thoughts, and fantasies as well as novels or short stories, Jan Alber (2017) argues against this by listing several ways in which film does manage to evoke character interiority. The "cinematic types of consciousness representation" that he identifies are, according to Alber, similar to "novelistic techniques such as psychonarration, free indirect discourse and interior monologue" (2017, 265). They assume either an externalist perspective on the mind, as in tone of voice, facial expression, and bodily position, or an internalist perspective that helps to convey private, inner thoughts and feelings (ibid., 266). Unsurprisingly, there are numerous close-up shots showing Ludo's facial expressions, but an especially meaningful example may be found when Ludo's parents take her to see a psychologist for the first time. Ludo refuses to talk and sits playing with her back to her parents when she suddenly hears them disclosing that they had hoped Ludo would be a girl before she was born. The camera stays fixated on Ludo to show how a hopeful smile appears on her face. Even though the child continues to be quiet, and the action happens elsewhere in the shot, the child's reactions and hope of living as a girl are literally foregrounded. In contrast, the adults' collective interpretation, namely that Ludo's parents might have been "wrong" to raise their child in a feminine way because they wanted a daughter, is pushed into the background and treated as secondary or external. The idea that a certain upbringing can have an influence on the still-plastic gender identity of a child is thus slyly dismissed – instead, the camera zooms in on Ludo's personal happiness when she overhears that her parents wanted a daughter just as she feels she is.

Ludo's more private feelings are evoked through a manipulation of the lens colour as well. In the first half of the film, the images have very bright and vibrant colours, reflecting and expressing persistent feelings of happiness in the main character, even when the child is sometimes reprimanded for her behavior. However, after Ludo is discovered as Snow White in the school play, a sudden blue-grey filter is put over the camera lens, only to be lifted again at the very end of the film when the family have moved to a new environment. This insistent colour scheme allows the viewer no detachment from Ludo's emotions. A more transient or momentary way of presenting Ludo's intimate thoughts and desires is through what Alber calls an "enacted mindscreen" (2017, 275). When Ludo fantasises about the world of Pam, her thoughts or mental images are visually dramatised in the film. The first time we are introduced to Pam, a title screen with *Le monde de Pam* following a black screen signals that we are watching a secondary film within the main film. Ludo later learns to escape into this fantasy by simply closing her eyes. This private fantasy world becomes her internal mindscreen. As the film progresses, however, the boundaries between fantasy world and real world start to blur. We see Ludo looking up to herself as she flies over with Pam, and at the very end of the film Ludo tries to run away with the doll. While searching for her child, Ludo's mother decides to climb a billboard with an advertisement for Pam. There, she witnesses her child hugging the doll in a plastic world and stops Ludo from running off. This crossing between the "real" world and Ludo's fantasy to some extent lifts the distinction between the child's inner and outer experiences and makes the world of Pam come to life.

Such coming-to-life of a dream world is one cinematic method for drawing adult characters – in this case, the mother – into the child's experiences and for convincing such characters to take the experiences seriously. As an audiovisual medium, film allows a character's embodied acts to convey meaning.

In this instance, the media of dance and music function to bring characters closer to Ludo and serve to enhance understanding and empathy for her situation. The specific dance moves are first introduced when Ludo watches *Le monde de Pam* and copies Pam's movements while the film's theme song keeps playing. When Ludo's grandmother catches her dancing in this feminine way, she is at first startled but then joins her grandchild in the dance, stressing their profound connection. As the parents grow more accepting of their child later in the film, they are also found making the familiar moves to the theme song. Finally, in Ludo's imaginary wedding ceremony with Jérôme, all the guests collectively join the couple in Pam's dance, signaling that they all share the same worldview. As such, Pam's dance and theme song become a way of expressing Ludo's feelings and of slowly drawing the people around her into her inner world.

Next to this positive representation of Ludo's worldview as one of possible connection, embodied acts in the film also function to disrupt, oppose or ridicule the normative mentality of adult characters. For instance, after one of the father's temper tantrums at Ludo's gender-non-conforming behavior, he storms off into the garden to do pull-ups on a wooden arch. While her father thus resorts to silly displays of masculinity, the child is portrayed as the stronger and more mature, since she follows her father, reaches out her hand in reconciliation and takes him back inside. This happens again later in the film when Ludo reacts calmly to her father's anger by commenting that he is becoming like his boss, who gets angry over nothing. When Ludo is wearing feminine clothing, by contrast, this is never made to look ridiculous. Instead, a neighbor makes a fool of herself when Ludo shows up at her daughter's birthday party in a kilt – the compromise that Ludo's parents proposed when the child wanted to wear a skirt. The neighbor tries to cut the tension by suddenly pretending it was a costume party, emptying the bowl of chips and putting it on her head. This kind of foolish behavior by adults who cannot think beyond their suburban morals and habits is contrasted with Ludo's composed and mature attitude. Thus, *Ma vie en rose* consistently makes the trans child's perspective central through various techniques that manage to express her worldview to other characters. Ludo is never ridiculed or presented as a child who needs to grow up and adapt to the society of adults. Instead, her self-knowledge and moral high ground stand in contrast with the silly attempts of adults to try and interfere in her presumed gender plasticity.

It should be clear from this discussion that Ludo's perspective is the focus of the entire film. In what follows, I still want to highlight that this perspective also offers a contrast between a normative and alternative time-space representing two possible futures for Ludo through the character of the grandmother, on the one hand, and Pam, on the other. In general, the neighbors' and family's prejudice against Ludo stems from normative developmental expectations. At the outset, Ludo's mother insists that experimenting with gender in childhood is normal and that Ludo will grow out of it. Yet, when she finds out about her child's dream of marrying Jérôme, she starts to believe that this kind of gender-non-normative behavior is a matter of concern if it persists at the age of seven. The neighbors share her fear that Ludo might grow up to be gay, which leads to several homophobic reactions: Jérôme cannot be friends with Ludo anymore because his parents believe he might thus be led down the "wrong" developmental path; Ludo is taken to see a psychologist in hopes of steering her towards a normative, heterosexual future; and Ludo's parents even try to let her wear a skirt because they hope that the fantasy will stop to appeal to her as soon as it is allowed. In this homogenously white, suburban environment, an alternative development seems unthinkable.

Against these social pressures, two characters in the film offer Ludo examples to imagine her future differently. First of all, Ludo's desire to be perceived as a girl is mirrored in her grandmother's desire to still be seen as a young person. Though the grandmother has not necessarily lost all the youthful looks she once had, she regrets that people would ridicule her if she acted "young," whether by dancing euphorically to music, wearing colorful dresses or taking the spotlight. In the film, she stands out because she is much older than anyone else in the neighborhood, who are all either a middle-aged parent or a child. With her age, she disrupts the suburban space that is centered entirely around reproduction and the raising of children. There is no place for Ludo in this reproductive cycle, as she does not fit in its heteronormative, cisgender timeframe, but nor is there any longer for the grandmother, who has become too old to be of any real use to this society. As a coping mechanism, the grandmother teaches Ludo the powers of the imagination. She shows her grandchild that you can just close your eyes and have the world become the way you want it to be. While she does tell Ludo that one has to adapt to the rules of society, she demonstrates how one's imagination can offer a temporary escape.

This will prove to be an underestimation of Ludo's imaginative powers, as the dream world the child builds up does not simply remain a place to which she can occasionally escape, but one that she manages to draw her mother into, thereby making it become reality in the end. Pam and her surroundings offer Ludo a completely different entry into a possible life. In this imaginary time-space, she would be able to marry Jérôme, wear a princess dress and live in a perfect world in which, most importantly, nothing ever changes. Pam herself was never a child and will never grow old, but is the reincarnated ideal of white, heterosexual eternal youth. Ludo does not desire to have a different body or even grow up as a woman, but longs to be seen as a young girl in this fairytale-like eternity. When her sister gives her a brief introduction to human biology, a second fantasy is overlaid on this vision of eternal girlhood. By mixing Christian and biological discourses, the child now imagines that God assigns a gender to children by throwing X's and Y's from the sky. In Ludo's case, she thinks that the X must have accidentally fallen in the bin, which explains why nobody realises she is actually a girl. Both of these worldviews combined result in a reassuring and self-securing conceptualisation of gender as predetermined, static and eternal. While white, able-bodied, youthful, heteronormative and binary gendered ideals remain unquestioned in the figure of Pam, the alternative time-space that she figures somehow still breaks free from the developmental temporality of plasticity. Trans childhood in *Ma vie en rose* is not depicted as an uncertain, troublesome period before one enters the comfortable gendered stability of adulthood. From Ludo's perspective, eternal trans girlhood is a desired state of being, free from imperatives to start acting like a boy or to enter the predefined path laid out by a gender clinic.

## 4 The Frog Prince

While *Ma vie en rose* puts the child's perspective at the center through various cinematic techniques, Lucas Rijneveld's novel *Mijn lieve gunsteling* (2020) foregrounds a different perspective. We encounter the worldview of a pederastic, unreliable homodiegetic narrator, a character narrator reminiscent of Humbert Humbert in Nabokov's classic *Lolita*. Here, however, the object of the narrator's desire is not a nymphet, but a child "shimmering" (Rijneveld 2020, 359; my translation) between genders and this character is consistently addressed as "you" by the narrator. Occasionally, the narrator also addresses the judicial magistrates judging his file, who are the second intended fictional audience for his book-length apology.

The story itself recounts the summer of 2005, when the narrating character, who is a middle-aged veterinarian, becomes infatuated with the fourteen-year-old child – the "Favorite"– of a farmer for whom he works.[3] He calls himself Kurt and it is suggested that the child named him after Kurt Cobain, one of their heroes. Kurt slowly gains the child's trust and then abuses it through acts of molestation that grow more and more severe, even after the child's father

3 In my analysis, I will use the gender neutral pronouns "they/them" to refer to the child because they continuously fluctuate between various gender identities and the narrator almost exclusively addresses them in the gender neutral you-form.

finds out. In doing so, the vet takes advantage of the child's insecurities about their growing body and gender, and their general vulnerability, coming from a family that has been severely traumatised by the death of the Favorite's brother and the subsequent disappearance of the mother. To justify his acts and morals, Kurt repeatedly refers to his childhood trauma of molestation by his own mother. The suggestion is that both Kurt and the child share a common experience of not wanting to grow up. While Kurt desires to regain an idea of innocence that was taken from him at an early age and gets to relive part of his childhood through the Favorite, the latter one struggles more with an unsettling puberty as it brings about unwanted feminine changes to their body.

Without dwelling too far on the unreliability of the narrator, it is important to realise the implications of this narrative filter. For the purpose of this case study, Ansgar Nünning's definition of narrative unreliability seems the most productive. Informed by not only rhetorical but also cognitive approaches to unreliable narration, Nünning argues: "such signals as textual inconsistencies, the verbal habits of the narrator, and discrepancies between the fictional world presented by a text and the reader's world – knowledge and standards of normality provide the basis for establishing a narrator's unreliability" (1997, 85).

In *Mijn lieve gunsteling*, we encounter a narrator who is open about his possible unreliability. He often warns the reader that his mental state and desires might have led him to misremember or misinterpret information. We are not even certain if the child ever calls the narrator "Kurt," as he admits at the beginning that he might have imagined that (Rijneveld 2020, 30), just like he might have imagined other conversations with the child. These signs might make readers question Kurt's reliability as a narrator, and this mostly on the level of the narrator's morality and value system. Following James Phelan's (Phelan and Martin 1999) typology of unreliable narrators, we could say that Kurt most often misregards his own immoral actions, combined with other strategies such as misreporting events which he later calls into question.

However, and more important here, Nünning's definition above stresses that we should not only take into account textual clues, but also differences in readers' cognitive and cultural backgrounds. Readers will judge a narrator unreliable if there is a "discrepancy between the intentions and value system of the narrator and the foreknowledge and norms of the reader" (Nünning 1997, 87). In Rijneveld's novel, this judgement can be based on readers disagreement with Kurt's pederastic sexual norms. Readers more attentive to gender norms, however, could read the novel as exploring the edges of what is "acceptable" or normative gendered behavior in children. I would argue that the narrator's uninhibited account of sexual desires and acts in particular makes room for the child's gender exploration to be portrayed in a liberating way, such as in visceral scenes of the Favorite's obsession with penises and their desire to be able to pee standing up.

Kurt's pederastic deception is at the rhetorical center of the narrative. More subtle and more important for our argument, however, are the moments where events, actions, and imagery tend to escape Kurt's understanding and experience. In these instances, the child's worldview seeps through, despite the narrator's unreliable report. The narrator, for instance, takes over certain phrasings of the child, such as "dear boys" (Rijneveld 2020, 165), referring to the child's male peers. Most notably are the animal metaphors the child uses to express various (desired) embodied experiences or acts. For instance, they desire the ability to fly and thus imagine themselves becoming a bird. The transformation would not only allow them to escape their distressing family circumstances and feelings of guilt they have internalised, but also to regain a sense of agency and control. They hope, for instance, to be able to save the victims of 9/11, who were helplessly stuck in a hopeless situation just like the Favorite.

Other imaginative animal metamorphisations are directly related to gender. After a first kiss with a boy whom the child calls "The Frog" (Rijneveld 2020, 41), they are suddenly able to imagine themselves becoming The Frog. At first, this image introduced by his Favorite escapes the understanding of the narrator: "what did you mean by becoming The Frog?" (ibid., 48; my translation).[4] Later, however, when Kurt learns about the child's longing to have a penis and pee standing up, he realises that The Frog is a metaphor for this desired embodiment. The third significant animal is introduced by Kurt himself, who explains to the child how he can determine the age of an otter after its death, namely by laying bare the hidden genitals and determining the length and thickness of the penis bone. This information allows the child to now also imagine themselves as an otter, which seems to signify a hidden masculinity. The child later asks Kurt to be dissected just like an otter and explains "that there was something hidden inside [them] that must come out" (ibid., 102; my translation).[5] A final important metaphor is Kurt's use of the term "antlers" to refer to his private parts, which allows the Favorite to imagine this body part as a means of control and protection next to gender assignment. In Kurt's report of their reasoning "children with antlers get stolen less easily" (ibid., 346; my translation).[6] There are thus multiple different reasons for the child's desire to live as

4 Original quotation: "wat bedoelde je met dat je De Kikker werd?" (Rijneveld 2020, 48).

5 Original quotation: "dat er in je iets verscholen lag wat eruit moest" (ibid., 102).

6 Original quotation: "Kinderen met geweitjes werden minder snel gestolen" (ibid., 346).

a boy with a cisgender boy's body, ranging from an expression of their inner feelings to being safe.

As such, each of the animals have their own distinct meaning, which Kurt is never able to fully grasp. Still, he reports on them without judgement, leaving room for a limitless gender experimentation in which the child has agency. With his own agenda at the back of his mind, Kurt never holds back the gendered and animalistic fluctuations and even encourages them by explicitly asking: "who are you now, the bird, The Frog or the otter?" (ibid., 177; my translation).[7] He realises that going along in the child's momentary identifications and imaginary transformations will make them more susceptible for his manipulations. When the Favorite comments that they are The Frog, he promises to help and eventually even convinces them that they will grow a penis – or "a boy's antlers" (ibid., 286) – if they have sex with him. While Kurt's personal motivations thus take the center stage, the novel still presents a trans child's worldview that evokes their gendered experiences in animalistic terms and allows various options to freely choose from.

Concerning the temporality of the animalistic imagery, it is important to note that the child never expresses a final or clear preference, but continuously shifts between wanting to fly away, waiting for their masculinity to grow and manifest itself (possibly after their death), or desiring to live as a boy with masculine genitals. While Kurt uses this fluctuation to manipulate the child, his main sexual interest lies exactly in moments of transformation. He desires "youngsters who were at the beginning of their puberty, at the beginning of that sizzling and turbulent valley in which they discovered their own body, their movements staggered between those of a gracious woman and those of the playful child" (Rijneveld 2020, 294; my translation).[8] He consistently compares the pubescent "shimmering" between "a child and a woman" with the shifts between "a girl and a dear boy" (ibid., 359; my translation).[9] The idea of a pubescent plasticity allows for these options to sit comfortably next to each other and both characters want to keep all options open. Kurt, on the one hand, longs for the youthful sexual exploration that he never had, "shyly feeling

7 Original quotation: "Wie ben je nu, de vogel, De Kikker of de otter?" (ibid., 177).

8 Original quotation: "jongelingen die aan het begin van hun puberteit stonden, aan het begin van die zinderende en ontstuimige vallei waarin ze hun eigen lichaam ontdekten, hun bewegingen wankelden tussen die van een gracieuze vrouw en die van het speelse kind" (Rijneveld 2020, 294).

9 Original quotation: "ik zag ook vanaf het begin hoe je schemerde tussen een kind en een vrouw, tussen een meisje en een dear boy" (ibid., 359).

each other without an immediate expectation" (ibid., 293; my translation).[10] The child, on the other, is afraid to move towards a more final (gender) identity and embodiment. Kurt notices: "you wanted to be grown-up and simultaneously didn't want to get older, because it was unavoidable that you would keep losing a version of yourself" (ibid., 57; my translation).[11] Becoming an adult marks, for both them, the limitation of possibilities. For instance, the first menstruation for the child is understood as diminishing the chance of magically growing a penis (ibid., 194). Plasticity in the novel is no longer valuable insofar as it promises the possibility of a normative future. Instead, plasticity is valuable in and of itself and the decrease of plasticity toward a more finite, stable way of being is to be mourned.

The novel does not stop there and we can see the animal metaphors as imagining a way out of a linear, developmental narrative of growth out of plasticity. Gill-Peterson explains that the discourse of gender plasticity first originated through experiments on animals. Scientists believed in a "primitivist sense of a latent bisexual animality" (2018, 20) that meant that the "primitive" capacity to develop masculine or feminine sexual characteristics stayed present in the bodies of animals throughout their lives, while this diminished after childhood in humans. *Mijn lieve gunsteling* turns the reasoning upside down and revalues the animalistic plasticity that is normally seen as primitive. The animalistic imagery, even when it is marked in terms of gender, carries possibilities of continuous transformation without the imperative to settle for a single existence.

## 5 Conclusion

Despite their obvious differences in terms of medium, narration, and plot, *Ma vie en rose* and *Mijn lieve gunsteling* both offer child perspectives that shed a new light on children's assumed plasticity of gender and sexuality. In Berliner's film, the viewer is presented with a child's fantasy world in which plasticity – or change in general – is absent. Instead of waiting to grow into a more final (gender) identity, Ludo imagines herself as being already there, fixed in the frozen ideal time-space of childhood. The child's worldview in Rijneveld's novel stands in opposition to this, as the continuous, imaginary transformations into various animals portray an eternal, animalistic and childhood plasticity

10 Original quotation: "het verlegen aftasten van elkaar zonder dat daar meteen een verwachting aan kleefde" (ibid., 293).

11 Original quotation: "je groot wilde zijn en tegelijk niet ouder wilde worden, want het was onvermijdelijk dat je steeds een versie van jezelf zou verliezen" (ibid., 57).

as the most desirable state. In both cases, childhood regains value, either as an eternal experience of non-plasticity, or as a desired time-space for exploration through plasticity.

My intention has not been to highlight these case studies as alternative – "good" – examples of portraying a child's perspective, as opposed to conventional – "bad" – representations. Instead, I have demonstrated how a child's worldview can seep through and cross with dominant, adult views in fiction. As such, this article wants to be a first step towards unearthing trans child perspectives – or any other non-normative mental and physical experience – precisely *in* conventional narratives. We should, for instance, recognise that childhood, in both case studies, is seldom directly accessible, but instead mirrored in adult characters: Ludo's grandmother's longing for youth and Pam's eternal youth run parallel to Ludo's desire to live as a young girl, while Kurt's wish to experience an adolescent (sexual) exploration leads to points of recognition in the child character. The fictionalisation of these child perspectives remains an important point as well because portrayals of childhood are always projections of how adults imagine childhood. We cannot assume that this can be compared to the lives of real children. However, if we realise the concrete, material consequences of a discourse on gender plasticity, we can only just start to imagine the effects of an alternative to this discourse on medical protocols, parenting approaches and the societal acceptance of trans children.

## Works Cited


Alber, Jan. "The Representation of Character Interiority in Film: Cinematic Versions of Psychonarration, Free Indirect Discourse and Direct Thought." *Emerging Vectors of Narratology*, edited by Per Krogh Hansen, John Pier, Philippe Roussin and Wolf Schmid, Berlin/Boston: De Gruyter, 2017, pp. 265–84.

Bakker, Alex. *Een halve eeuw transgenderzorg aan de VU*. Amsterdam, Boom, 2021.

Castañeda, Claudia. "Childhood." *Transgender Studies Quarterly*, vol. 1, no. 1/2, 2014, pp. 59–61.

Gill-Peterson, Jules. *Histories of the Transgender Child*. U of Minnesota P, 2018.

Jackson, Zakiyyah Iman. "Losing Manhood: Animality and Plasticity in the (Neo)Slave Narrative." *Qui Parle: Critical Humanities and Social Sciences*, vol. 25, no. 1/2, 2016, pp. 95–136.

Malabou, Catherine. *The Future of Hegel: Plasticity, Temporality and Dialectic*. Routledge, 2005.

Malabou, Catherine. *What Should We Do with Our Brain?* Fordham UP, 2008.

*Ma vie en rose*. Directed by Alain Berliner, Canal+/Eurimages/CNC/TF1 Films Production, 1997.

Nünning, Ansgar. "'But Why Will You Say That I Am Mad?' On the Theory, History, and Signals of Unreliable Narration in British Fiction." AAA: *Arbeiten Aus Anglistik Und Amerikanistik*, vol. 22, no. 1, 1997, pp. 83–105.

Phelan, James, and Mary Patricia Martin. "The Lessons of Weymouth: Homodiegesis, Unreliability, Ethics, and The Remains of the Day." *Narratologies: New Perspectives on Narrative Analysis*, edited by David Herman, The Ohio State UP, 1999, pp. 88–112.

Rijneveld, Lucas. *Mijn lieve gunsteling*. Amsterdam/Antwerpen, Atlas Contact, 2020.

Schuller, Kyla, and Jules Gill-Peterson. "Introduction: Race, the State, and the Malleable Body." *Social Text*, vol. 38, no. 2, 2020, pp. 1–17.

Stockton, Kathryn Bond. *The Queer Child, or Growing Sideways in the Twentieth Century*. Duke UP, 2009.

Verstraeten, Peter. *Handboek filmnarratologie*. 2nd ed., Nijmegen, Vantilt, 2008.

CHAPTER 11

# Politics of Mobility and Mental Health: Representations of Refugeedom in the Mini-Series *Stateless* (2020)

*Carolin Gebauer*

## 1 Introduction

In the wake of global increases in forced migration, a growing number of Netflix productions have recently started to negotiate themes of refugeedom and displacement. Documentaries like *Born in Syria* (2016), *Refugee* (2016), *Human Flow* (2017), or *Life Overtakes Me* (2019) offer viewers what philosophers of mind refer to as "qualia" – that is, "the sense of what it's like for someone or something to have a particular experience" (Herman 2009, 144), in this case the experience of being a refugee. Although many of these productions set a different focus in that they highlight different stages of displacement, such as refugees' flight from their home countries, their detention in camps or centers, or their arrival and integration in host countries, they all share a similar humanitarian purpose: In depicting forced migration and displacement as traumatic experiences, they raise the audience's awareness of the psychological burden borne by refugees.

While documentaries on refugees usually strive for authenticity, fictional productions tend to find more unconventional forms of representation which not only serve to address the traumatic experiences of displacement, but also to frame social or cultural criticism. A case in point is the Australian television series *Stateless* (2020), created by Cate Blanchett, Tony Ayres, and Elise McCredie, which combines the themes of refugeedom and mental health to problematise Australian immigration policies. First broadcast on the Australian ABC channel in March 2020 and globally on Netflix only four months later, the mini-series is "[i]nspired by true stories from Australian immigration detention" (E6, 00:53:31) in the aftermath of an unprecedented high number of Irregular Maritime Arrivals (IMA) in 2011/2012.[1] The main part of its plot is

1 Temporal markers suggest that the events depicted in *Stateless* must be set sometime after the Abbott government, which took office in September 2013, launched Operation Sovereign Borders, Australia's strict immigration policy of intercepting and removing unauthorised

 | DOI:10.1163/9789004519886_013

set within the confines of Barton Immigration Detention Center, whose inhumane conditions the series highlights as an example of the negative impact of Australian detention facilities on detainees' mental health. In granting us this inside view, the series creates what can be described as contrastive multiperspectivity,[2] providing access to the minds of two protagonists: Ameer (Fayssal Bazzi), a former school teacher and asylum seeker from Afghanistan, and Sofie Werner (Yvonne Strahovski), an Australian citizen who, after escaping from a mental hospital, impersonates a German backpacker whose visa has expired. At first glance, the juxtaposition of a refugee suppressed by the Australian immigration system and an Australian mistakenly sent to a detention center seems rather far-fetched – even though the character of Sofie is based on a true story.[3] A closer look, however, reveals that the series deliberately shifts its focus from migration to the broader concept of mobility in order to expose the humanitarian shortcomings of Australian immigration policies.

My reading of *Stateless* foregrounds the "structure[s] of attitude and reference" (Said 1994, xii) that influence viewers' perception of the individual experiences of displacement depicted in the series, as well as their effects on the protagonists' mental health.[4] To do justice to the discursive shift suggested by the series, the chapter will draw on categories and concepts introduced by the new mobilities paradigm from the social sciences (Urry 2007). Exploring the movement of people, ideas, and objects, as well as the broader social, cultural, and political implications of these movements, this paradigm provides a useful theoretical framework for uncovering the various social and cultural

boats from Australian waters. One of the government's first measures was the "Stop the Boats" campaign, which addressed potential irregular migrants from countries such as Sri Lanka, warning them not to give money to human traffickers promising to put them on a boat to Australia (van Berlo 2015, 76–77). The series occasionally refers to this campaign (see, e.g., E2, 00:34:50 and E5, 00:15:38).

2 According to Vera and Ansgar Nünning (2000, 58), narratives featuring contrastive multiperspectivity present the narrative events from the point of view of various characters whose diverging perspectives display only very few congruities.

3 Namely on the case of Cornelia Rau (Groves 2015; Mangan 2020), a mentally ill Australian citizen mistaken for a European tourist with no valid travel visa who in 2004 was wrongfully kept for several months in immigration detention before her true identity was revealed (Manne 2005).

4 Edward W. Said argues, in *Culture and Imperialism* (1994), that authors are not "mechanically determined by ideology, class, or economic history," yet they are "very much in the history of their societies, shaping and shaped by that history and their social experience in different measure" (XXII). According to Said, "[c]ulture and the aesthetic forms it contains derive from historical experience" (ibid.), which, in turn, generates what he refers to as "a structure of attitude and reference" (ibid., XXIII): the perceptional framework that informs specific cultures and their representations.

discourses informing the series. I will particularly focus on Vincent Kaufmann's (2016) fundamental distinction between *mobility* and *motility*, i.e., on the one hand the actual capacity for movement in its sociocultural and political, as well as physical, senses, and on the other the subjective individual perception of what mobility (in all these senses) means 'for me.' Tim Cresswell's notion of a politics of mobility (2010), postulating that mobilities both produce and result from social relations and power structures, puts this distinction itself in a wider context. Taken together, the new mobilities approach, I will argue, not only enables us to understand the protagonists' different situations and why they end up in refugee detention, but also makes us see that their individual health and well-being largely hinge on the complex, fluctuating reciprocity between mobility and immobility. I will show that the series stages these diverging states at the nexus of body and mind, representing the characters' states of (im)mobility mainly through depictions of their mental and bodily experiences.

## 2 The New Mobilities Paradigm, Motility, and a Politics of Mobility

The social sciences have recently witnessed a theoretical paradigm shift which has become known as the "mobility turn" (Canzler et al. 2008; Hannam et al. 2006, 1–2; Urry 2007, 6; Urry 2008). Deriving originally from geography, mobility has moved across several disciplinary boundaries, developing into an important term in various academic contexts. For sociologist John Urry, in his programmatic monograph *Mobilities*, the concept designated a ubiquitous and multifaceted "post-disciplinary approach" (2007, 6). Ten years later, geographer Peter Adey saw it as an energetic research field integrating disciplines such as geography, international relations, architecture, and history, as well as cultural and literary studies (2017, 16–17). Mobility is an example of what the humanities call "travelling concepts" (Bal, 2002) – that is, concepts which "cross, transcend and sometimes transform the boundaries between different academic contexts" (Neumann and Nünning 2012, 3). While travelling concepts often form "the basis of a common meta-language" by facilitating cross-disciplinary discussion and exchange, their "meaning and operational value [...] differ between diverse disciplines, national cultures and historical periods" (ibid.). The wide research field of mobility studies reflects this diversity, working with various definitions of the term *mobility*, ranging from physical to virtual locomotion and transportation and from the horizontal to the vertical.

Advocates of the "'new mobilities' paradigm" (Hannam et al. 2006; Sheller and Urry 2005; Urry, 2007, Ch. 4) describe previous social science research as "a-mobile," criticising that the discipline "has largely ignored or trivialized the importance of the systematic movements of people" in various social, cultural, and political contexts (Sheller and Urry 2005, 208). This research lacuna, they argue, is especially manifest in the division between sedentarist and nomadic theories (ibid., 208–12). Sedentarism establishes notions of stability, meaning, and place as the norm, while treating nomadism and its associations of distance, change, and placelessness as abnormal. Such a negative perspective on mobility is often associated with the sovereign politics of the nation state, which has always been "preoccupied [...] with the ordering and disciplining of mobile peoples" (Cresswell 2006, 26) and has construed notions of mobility and movement, "insofar as they undermine attachment and commitment," as "antithetical to moral worlds" (Cresswell 2002, 13). In Western culture, refugees, asylum seekers, nomads, or vagabonds have accordingly often been depicted as "figures of mobile threat in need of straightening out and discipline" (Cresswell 2006, 26).

The marginalisation of mobile groups has been challenged by approaches that acknowledge modernity as an age of mobility, foregrounding what Cresswell has referred to as "nomad thought" (ibid., 43). Studies which draw on Zygmunt Bauman's theory of "liquid modernity" (2000), for example, abandon the idea that our contemporary world can be defined by static structures and fixed orders; instead, they conceptualise contemporary society as a system in constant flux, characterised by the increasing and accelerating movement of people, objects, information, and images (Sheller and Urry 2005, 210). In contrast to sedentarist theories, which rely mainly on static notions of place such as the nation state (Cresswell 2002, 12–15), nomadic or "deterritorialized" theories (Hannam et al. 2006, 5) prefer metaphors of fluidity, travel, and flight, stressing movement not only across geographical borders, but also beyond conceptual and disciplinary boundaries (Sheller and Urry 2005, 210).[5]

The new mobilities paradigm marks itself off from both these theoretical approaches in that it strives to go "beyond the imagery of 'terrains' as spatially fixed geographical containers for social processes" without postulating "a new 'grand narrative' of mobility, fluidity or liquidity as a pervasive condition [...] of globalization" (Hannam et al. 2006, 5). The paradigm proceeds from the assumption that social life is influenced by a complex network of different, yet interrelated forms of mobility. Urry distinguishes five categories in this connection (2007, 47; 2008, 14): (1) bodily movement of individuals, including

5 For a more detailed and differentiated juxtaposition of the sedentarist and nomadic paradigms, see Adey (2017, 69–92); Cresswell (2002; 2006, Ch. 2); Kaufmann (2016, 3–11); and Urry (2007, 31–34).

commuting, travel, and migration; (2) physical movement of objects; (3) imaginative travel effected through the movement of information and images across monomodal and multimodal media; (4) virtual travel, i.e., the real-time experience of transcending geographical and social distance; and (5) communicative travel through person-to-person messages via telephone, email, or other forms of long-distance communication. New mobilities scholars, moreover, maintain that patterns of mobility must not be equated with fluidity per se and can, therefore, only be adequately understood if questions of immobility are also taken into consideration: "Mobilities cannot be described without attention to the necessary spatial, infrastructural and institutional moorings that configure and enable [them]" (Hannam et al. 2006, 3; see also Adey 2017, 11–13).[6] Against this backdrop, one can conclude that, in its attempt to explore the multiple forms of mobility that define contemporary society, the new mobilities paradigm seeks to combine sedentarist and nomadic theories.

But how can we make sense of the close entanglement of various forms of movement within contemporary society, as well as the complex interplay of mobility and immobility in this context? In order to better systematise the diverse phenomena in question, Weert Canzler, Vincent Kaufmann, and Sven Kesselring suggest redefining the concept of mobility as a change of state or condition that involves three dimensions: movements, networks, and motility (2008, 2). The first dimension – movements – can simply be defined as a geographical dimension that connects an origin with one or several destinations, whereas the second dimension – networks – can be thought of as the framework of these movements. Since the term *movement* covers both physical and virtual movement as related to people, objects, and information, networks can take the shape of either technical infrastructures (e.g., transportation and communication) or social structures and institutionalised relationships.

Introducing a new category to mobility studies, the third and final dimension – motility – requires more detailed explanation. The term was coined by Kaufmann, in *Re-Thinking Mobility: Contemporary Sociology*, to describe "the capacity of a person to be mobile, or more precisely, as the *way in which an individual appropriates what is possible in the domain of mobility and puts this potential to use for his or her activities*" (2016, 37; italics original). According to

6 Recent interdisciplinary work in the field of cultural and literary studies serves to substantiate this argument brought forth by new mobilities scholars: The editors of a collected volume titled *Timescapes of Waiting: Spaces of Stasis, Delay and Deferral*, for example, observe "a growing acknowledgment of waiting as a socio-political theme worthy of consideration" (Singer et al. 2019, 2–3), which suggests "an increased perception of waiting as the flipside of mobility" (ibid., 3).

Kaufmann, an individual's capacity to be mobile depends primarily on their own physical and mental predisposition, as well as on spatial, cultural, and societal contexts. Motility, he argues, is "constituted of elements relating to access (i.e., available choice in a broad sense), to skills (the competence required to make use of this access) and appropriation (evaluation of the available access)" (ibid., 38). The notion of access refers mainly to the transportation and communication means available to an actor, whereas that of skill comprises several aspects such as physical abilities (i.e., the ability to move and the senses one needs to orientate oneself in different environments), acquired practical and mental skills (e.g., a driver's license or the knowledge of foreign languages required for international travel), and organisational skills (e.g., the ability to plan events and research relevant information, as well as the willingness to change one's plan in the event of unforeseen problems or obstacles). Finally, appropriation relates to the ways in which actors make use of both their access to mobility and their physical and mental skills to achieve their objectives (ibid., 38–39). That motility does not necessarily lead to mobility – let alone to movement – also sheds light on the relations between mobilities and immobilities.

Given that motility denotes the factors conditioning an individual's decision to embrace possibilities of mobility and to deploy them to realise certain projects, it can bear on various constellations of movement and mobility such as 'being mobile while moving,' 'being immobile in moving,' or 'being mobile without moving' (Canzler et al. 2008, 4–5). However, the realisation of an individual's intention to become mobile also hinges on other factors than their own abilities, skills, and ambitions. Kaufmann emphasises that, although motility "is identified on an individual level, it is not formed individually," but instead has to be negotiated within different social and cultural contexts (2016, 40). The (subjective) perception of mobility, he concludes, is created "by the life course of those involved" as well as "their financial, social and cultural capital, which together define the range of possible specific choices in terms of opportunities and projects" (ibid.).

Kaufmann's argument that "motility is eminently social" implies that mobility is always influenced by various power structures involving questions of gender, class, and ethnicity as well as other cultural and social hierarchies (ibid.). A useful approach which helps us disentangle such interweavings is Cresswell's notion of a politics of mobility (2010). Cresswell construes mobility as an interlacing of movement, representation, and practice, which varies over time and in different contexts: "At any one time," he argues, "there are pervading *constellations of mobility* – particular patterns of movement, representations of movement, and ways of practicing movement that make sense together" (ibid.,

18; italics original). In Cresswell's understanding, then, the physical reality of mobility is also encoded socially and culturally and concretely experienced (ibid., 20). Thanks to this social and cultural embedment, constellations of mobility are "implicated in the production of power and relations of domination," which, in turn, renders them political (ibid.). In the remaining sections of this chapter, I will examine how the mini-series *Stateless* stages different constellations of mobility that influence the protagonists' actions and behavior: The series deploys representations of the characters' motility, as well as their mobility and immobility, as an effective means to uncover the causes and effects of their individual mental health problems.

## 3 Representing the Psychological Burden of (Im-)Mobility: the Mini-Series *Stateless* (2020)

*Stateless* diverges from conventional representations of refugeedom in film and television in juxtaposing the traditional figure of the refugee – Ameer – with a character displaced in a more unconventional way: Sofie, the Australian citizen wrongfully detained in Barton as she tries to escape from her past. In moving its focus from migration to a broader understanding of mobility, the series challenges socially and culturally predetermined notions of refugeedom, presenting it as a state that involves various experiences of physical, imaginary, and other forms of (im)mobility. To illustrate how the series redefines the idea of displacement, I will discuss three central narrative strategies connecting the characters' different practices of mobility to questions of mental health: (1) the juxtaposition of Ameer and Sofie, (2) the evocation of cognitive dissonance with regard to Sofie's misplacement in immigration detention, and (3) the presentation modes used to unveil the protagonists' respective states of mental stability (Ameer) and disturbance (Sofie).

### 3.1 *Mobile Characters and Different Kinds of Refugeedom*

From its very beginning, *Stateless* constantly invites the audience to compare its two protagonists. Episode 1, titled "The Circumstances in Which They Come," serves as an "integrated exposition" (Pfister 1988, 87–88), gradually introducing Ameer and Sofie to the audience, providing background information on their lives. We first see Sofie in a shoulder close-up: she wears a flight attendant's uniform and make-up, her hair is tied back in a braid, she is smiling. The next camera angle presents her in a long shot, revealing that she is at the airport, heading towards the terminal's exit, where she presents her passport at the check-out counter. As we see her leave the airport building, a cut sends the audience to Pakistan, where Ameer and his family are sitting in the back of a passenger truck driving on a crowded street. When the vehicle comes to a halt, Ameer helps his wife and children to jump off the back. The camera captures this scene with two subsequent close-ups focusing on Ameer's and his youngest daughter's smiling faces. Afterwards, a medium long shot presents Ameer and his family leaving the scene, carrying suitcases, bags, and backpacks (E1, 00:00:47–00:01:18).

By focusing on Sofie's and Ameer's nomadic lifestyles, the opening sequence of the series allows the audience to create a prototypical mental model of each protagonist.[7] Sofie, the flight attendant, impersonates our common understanding of the globetrotter; it is no coincidence that the camera shows her passport in a close-up shot, as this document symbolises her mobility rights as an Australian citizen. The freedom of movement which Sofie enjoys as an international traveller is not accessible to Ameer, who represents an undocumented migrant. Unlike Sofie, he and his family cannot travel by plane: they have to take clandestine travel routes in order to remain invisible to the authorities. Despite these differences, however, Sofie and Ameer both seem happy, as is evident not only from their smiling faces, but also from the upbeat soundtrack, Harold Arlen and Johnny Mercer's "Accentuate the Positive" (1944), performed by Cate Blanchett. The message of the opening scenes is clear: Sofie finds fulfillment in her dream job, and Ameer is full of hope that he and his family are moving towards a better life.

Or so it seems. As events unfold, we soon have to revise our initial character models, because we learn that both protagonists are dealing with serious challenges to their mental well-being. Let us first focus on Ameer's situation in Pakistan: On his family's way to the shelter where they will wait for the smugglers' boat, Ameer's optimism is still indefatigable. When Mina asks him about the meaning of the hotel's name – Hotel Excelsior – he urges her to speak English and explains to her that the adjective *excelsior* means "excellent, very excellent, beyond excellent" (E1, 00:03:00). His enthusiastic reaction to his eldest daughter's question reflects his pleasant anticipation of his family's bright future. Having arrived at the scene, however, Ameer is soon disillusioned, for the hotel with the promising name is utterly decrepit: The place is crowded with refugees cramped into small rooms (Ameer's family has to share a room with foreign men) and the hygienic conditions are so miserable that his youngest daughter is soon sick. Moreover, the family's sojourn at the hotel

7 For a detailed description of the cognitive processes involved in recipients' formation of mental models of fictional characters, see, e.g., Eder (2014, Ch. 3.3) and Schneider (2013).

is overshadowed by the constant fear that the human traffickers could be lying and that there will be no boat after all.

In foregrounding that Ameer's family does not know how long they will have to stay in this place, the first episode stages the phenomenon of waiting as a central dimension of the refugee experience even before the series has introduced its main setting of the detention center. Christoph Singer argues that "while a refugee's movement is certainly connected to high mobility, this mobility comes at the cost of having to endure extended periods of immobilization and waiting in *zones [d']attente*, at borders, before bureaucratic offices, or inside detention centres" (2019, 96). Such forms of "chronic waiting can have rather severe psychological effects" (ibid., 96–7), yet the "aspect of stasis is," according to Singer "often overlooked in public discourse" (ibid., 96) and only comes to the fore in literary and cultural productions (Singer, 2019, 2017). The series *Stateless* is not an exception in this regard: Although Ameer invokes an underlying motility in the form of his plans for a better life, the resultant states of mobility and immobility put him and his family in a dangerous and precarious situation, creating a high degree of mental stress for all of them. As the head of the family, however, Ameer cannot give in to this feeling of emotional tension: While his wife is worrying about their sick child, he has to keep a level head in order to find a way out of their misery.

In Australia, Sofie is not happy, either. Witnessing a confrontation between her and her mother Elka (Catherine Wilkin) on Christmas Eve, during which Elka criticises Sofie's job ("All that flying really takes its toll" [E1, 00:06:06]), the audience can tell that mother and daughter must often have arguments about Sofie's lifestyle. This impression is confirmed further into the episode when Sofie has a so-called transformation session with Pat (Cate Blanchett) and Gordon (Dominic West), the leaders of GOPA – a cult organisation advertising itself as "Growing One's Potential Achievement" – with which Sofie gets involved in the hope of finding her true self. In this therapeutic conversation, which is supposed to "transfer all [...] negative energy out of [Sofie] into [Gordon] and away" (E1, 00:23:26), she first articulates her dysfunctional relation to her family, parroting her mother's imperatives: "Go on a date with Wilhelm, Sofie! Wear the stupid apron, Sofie! Have a baby, Sofie! Get a house like everyone else, Sofie!" (E1, 00:25:10) The quotation demonstrates that Sofie's family would like her to settle down and lead a conventionally sedentary life, preferably as a housewife and mother. But Sofie enjoys her nomad life as a flight attendant and has become tired of her family constantly questioning, judging, and criticising her choice to be an independent, mobile woman who does not meet her relatives' stereotypical gendered expectations.

Right at the beginning, then, *Stateless* clarifies that Sofie's mobility serves as a point of friction in her relationship with her family. As the Christmas dinner scene illustrates (E1, 00:08:26–00:09:30), it is especially the arguments with her mother that severely afflict Sofie's mental well-being. When Sofie returns to the dinner table after the argument in the kitchen, her mother continues her insistent talk, urging Sofie to take a desk job, otherwise, she will have difficulties finding a partner. Her sister Margot defends her, while Sofie sits almost motionless at the table. An effective interplay of internal ocularisation and auricularisation strategies offers us an insight into Sofie's consciousness:[8] The camera shows her agonised face in close-up from various angles, revealing her heavy breathing (the sound of which, however, is drowned by the dinner conversation). After a few changes of the camera perspective, she is suddenly presented in double vision, indicating that she is feeling beside herself (internal ocularisation). The dinner conversation fades into an indistinct mutter, except for Elka's whispering voice which is still clearly audible, announcing that she does not want her daughter "to miss the boat," as "she is not getting any younger" (E1, 00:08:41). At this point, ambient mood music sets quietly in, growing louder as Sofie leaves the room. A cut in the visual track sends the audience to the bathroom, where we see Sofie in medium close-up trying to calm herself, supporting her body on the rim of the bathtub. The ambient music swells to a shrilling tinnitus ringing in her ears (internal auricularisation) as video and audio tracks jointly indicate that she is on the brink of a panic attack. Although we cannot hear what Sofie is thinking in this particular situation (the series does not deploy voice-over, which is often used to present characters' verbal thoughts [Kuhn 2011, Ch. 6.1.2]), we nevertheless learn about her emotions given that video and audio track zoom in on the bodily signals of her current ill-being.

The scene not only reveals that Sofie, like Ameer, suffers from her mobility, but it also establishes an interesting link between the two protagonists. In the very moment that we hear a knock on the bathroom door, the view cuts to Margot, who is standing outside asking her sister if she is alright. When she opens the bathroom door, the video track shifts back to the previous perspective, but now we only see an empty room with an open window, through which Sofie, we take it, has fled. We hear the wind whistling from outside the window as the visual track shifts to Pakistan, where the voice of the human trafficker

8 The distinction of two kinds of focalisation in film was first proposed by François Jost; for further differentiation between different kinds of ocularisation and auricularisation, see Kuhn (2011, Ch. 4.2.1).

Oshan (Chum Ehelepola) is telling the refugees that they "must be ready to leave at any time" and "bags must stay packed" (E1, 00:09:26).

The incongruency between audio and visual tracks serves to highlight the parallels between the protagonists' individual situations. While the series presents Ameer as a refugee, who has fled Afghanistan to seek protection in Australia, it similarly stylises Sofie as a character on the run, who tries to escape her home because she can no longer cope with the psychological pressure of her family, especially her mother.[9] An attentive audience will detect numerous similarities between the protagonists, all of which are hidden in small details: Ameer, for example, is robbed of his money and passport by the human traffickers (E1, 00:31:45–00:33:35), whereas Sofie tells Wilhelm (Mitchell Butel), a family friend who visits her in a hospital after she has had a mental breakdown, that her family has stolen her money as well as taken her passport and her home (E2, 00:10:35). These and similar observations eventually cause us to reconsider our ideas about the protagonists, especially Sofie. In foregrounding the similarities (rather than differences) between Ameer and Sofie, the series challenges the social and cultural scripts that prompt us at the beginning of the first episode to form ideas about both characters. In *Stateless*, the notion of refugeedom is not restricted to movement across international boundaries; it also relates to social and psychological forms of displacement. Yet, it soon becomes clear that, in its comparison of both the protagonists, the series draws on gendered conceptions of resilience, vulnerability, and victimisation associated with the state of being a refugee. For, as will be shown in the following, Ameer is depicted as being better able to cope with his situation than Sofie with hers.

### 3.2 *Cognitive Dissonance and Misplaced Bodies in Detention*

The juxtaposition of Sofie and Ameer as different kinds of displaced characters evokes within the audience diverging responses towards both protagonists. Titled "Incognita," Episode 2 shows how, after a long series of obstacles, Ameer eventually arrives in Australia, where he is interviewed and transferred to Barton. Although the series invites the audience to empathise with Ameer's astonishment that the Australian government treats him like a criminal,[10]

9 That the series construes Sofie as a displaced character already becomes obvious in the first thirty seconds of Episode 1, which show Sofie, dressed in dirty clothes, running through the desert before the series title – *Stateless* – appears in white capital letters on a black screen.

10 For example, when Ameer is brought to Barton and sees the detention center for the first time, he says "Please, there has been a mistake, I am not a criminal" (E2, 00:29:55).

viewers familiar with Australian immigration policy will not find it surprising that, being an irregular migrant, Ameer is kept in detention until his application for a protection visa has been processed. In this respect, events simply follow standard protocol.

This is not the case with Sofie. The closing scene of the first episode shows a new group of asylum seekers waiting in line to enter the detention center. Among them is Sofie, who passes herself off as the German backpacker Eva Hoffmann. Sofie's appearance in Barton uncovers a decisive narrative gap for the viewer: In the first episode, we have learned of Sofie's involvement with the cult GOPA, whose leaders have encouraged her to break ties with her family and resign from her job. After she has been rejected by Pat and Gordon – for reasons the audience will come to know only towards the end of the series (more on that later) – she is found confused and disoriented on a heavily trafficked street. Worrying about Sofie's mental health, her parents accommodate her in their house, trying to take care of her.[11] This is the only information available to us. Since we do not learn anything about the circumstances which brought her to Barton, we wonder why an Australian citizen should be waiting in line to enter an immigration detention camp.

Our state of bewilderment about Sofie's incarceration in Barton is reinforced as the series shows the other characters' reactions towards her. The guards speculate that she is a "Russian drug mule" (E2, 00:02:52), and the other detainees are similarly confused about her outward appearance: As Sofie-alias-Eva first approaches the refugee Rosna (Helena Sawires) to find out how she can be deported to Germany, she says "Excuse me, I don't belong here," to which Rosna simply replies, "No, you don't" (E2, 00:03:05). Although this answer can be interpreted in different ways – either to mean that nobody belongs in refugee detention or that Sofie, in particular, does not belong there – Rosna's look reveals that she, too, is perplexed about Sofie's presence in Barton. Another detainee hits the nail on the head: "You're a white girl. I don't understand." (E4, 00:36:04)

By staging Sofie's physical appearance as 'non-normative' in that she immediately stands out from the other people in the camp, the series discloses an "inherent racial bias" (Winkler 2020, online). Within the confines of the immigration detention center, Sofie's white skin color seems strangely misplaced,

---

11 Interestingly enough, her mother's understanding of taking care of Sofie again entails the attempt of rendering her daughter immobile: Since the doctors have warned her family that Sofie might be running away from home, Elka decides to hold on to her bank account and passport, thus declaring her incompetent of making her own choices (E1, 00:50:00–00:51:57).

which once more invites the critical viewer to question culturally encoded notions of refugeedom: from a Western perspective it seems more likely that refugees are from the Global South; a displaced Westener doesn't fit the picture. What is more, the reactions of Rosna and the other refugees suggest that this power structure is inverted in the world outside the camp, as they cannot imagine why a white woman should be excluded from Australian society and instead kept in detention.

When it comes to Sofie's character, then, the series creates cognitive dissonance: we cannot understand why she is among the refugees.[12] However, we quickly infer that something must have happened to her because, from her first day at Barton, we repeatedly witness her undergoing panic attacks. In some cases, these are triggered by flashbacks presented as moments of "internal analepsis" (Genette 1980, 49), gradually revealing the missing gaps the audience needs to fill in order to make sense of her presence in refugee detention. In other cases, they are caused by moments of hallucination in which Sofie suddenly sees Gordon or hears his voice. These delusions suggest that the leader of GOPA must be one of the reasons behind Sofie passing herself off as someone else.

That she is scared of Gordon becomes obvious during her conversations with Javad (Phoenix Raei), another detainee in Barton, who is trying to get back to his family. At one point, he informs Sofie about the revolt that he is planning in cooperation with some activists from outside the camp and asks her to become the detainees' (vicarious) voice in the media:

> The world should know what they are doing to us here. Soon they will. On Sunday, people from outside, Australians, they are coming from everywhere to protest against this. How we are locked up, when all we seek is freedom. […] We need to be heard. We need to be seen. When you get out

12 In cognitive narrative theory, the term *cognitive dissonance* serves to describe the psychological disequilibrium brought about if an individual holds two incompatible mental states. Marco Caracciolo, for example, uses the concept to explain how readers engage with what he identifies as "strange narrators": "Cognitive dissonance […] is the psychological phenomenon that accounts for readers' feelings of strangeness as they are given access to the mental life of a first-person narrator […]. Dissonance can arise in this scenario because the character calls for two conflicting (and hence dissonant) reception strategies: on the one hand, the audience is invited to temporarily 'try on' the character's perspective through narrative empathy; on the other hand, the audience resists the character's perspective because of the failure of their folk-psychological capacities (cognitive strangeness)" (2016, 34–35). I would suggest that Caracciolo's considerations can also be transferred to viewers' engagement with strange characters in film or television series, provided that the audience has access to these characters' consciousnesses.

> of here, and you will, people will be very interested in you. The lily among the reeds. They will want to know why someone who looks like them is trapped in a place like this. You could be our voice. The face of our suffering. Yes? (E3, 00:12:52–00:14:14)

As Sofie rejects his proposal and tries to withdraw from the conversation, he notices her fear and asks her what she is running away from. Later, when Sofie and Javad are hiding in an isolated house after escaping from the center, Sofie confides to him that she is fleeing from a specific person; the audience already knows this must be Gordon (E4, 00:35:35–00:36:56).[13]

Javad's sympathy for Sofie's situation foregrounds the difference between her motility and that of the other detainees in Barton: "All you want to do is leave and all we want to do is stay" (E4, 00:36:57–00:37:02). While Sofie seeks mobility and displacement – she hopes to be deported to Germany – the refugees long to resettle in a new place where their mobility (and by definition, then, motility) can be transformed into immobility. It is this different appropriation of their individual capacity to be mobile which creates the discrepancy between Sofie and the other displaced characters: She desperately tries to run from a place in which the refugees seek protection. However, since the series, for the most part, does not disclose the exact reasons for her flight, the audience will probably find it more difficult to empathise with her situation than with that of the Barton Camp refugees.

### 3.3 *Broken Narrative vs. Narrative Coherence: Refugee Trauma and Resilience*

Despite its numerous allusions to an ominous encounter between Sofie and Gordon, the series long conceals what actually happened between them. Yet among Sofie's flashbacks, there is one particular scene that consistently recurs: a transformation session she has alone with Gordon. As the series again and again replays this scene, it always reveals a little more: Gordon sits opposite Sofie, holding her hands, listening to her fears and wishes. He eventually starts touching her neck, squeezing her shoulders, stroking her thighs; at this point, the flashbacks usually end. Viewers can well anticipate what must have happened next, yet it is not until the fifth episode that the series fully discloses that Gordon rapes Sofie.

---

13 One of her previous flashbacks shows how Gordon threatens Sofie: "If you take your lies to Pat, or the police, then I'll tell them what you really are – a liar, and a whore. So, if I were you, I would run far, far away. 'Cause if I ever lay eyes on you again, Sofie Werner, I'll destroy you." (E4, 00:18:00–00:18:30)

The fragmentary presentation of Sofie's past experiences is reminiscent of what, in narrative studies, has become known as a "broken narrative," a form covering instances of (non-fictional) storytelling in which people seek to come to terms with the experience of trauma (Armstrong 2002; Sewell and Williams 2002), illness (Kirmayer 2000; see also the contributions in Hydén and Brockmeier 2008), or other moments of personal crisis (Nünning and Nünning 2016). Since broken narratives are associated with a drastic rupture in people's lives, they "are often fragmented [or] disorganized or [...] the narrative text is superseded by the performance of the story" (Hyvärinen et al. 2010, 2). Depicted from Sofie's point of view, the analepses form neither a chronological order nor a coherent narrative. They do, however, fulfill two different functions: On the one hand they facilitate what Marie-Laure Ryan describes as "emotional immersion" (2015, 148–157), inviting the audience to share Sofie's state of mental disturbance; on the other hand they make the audience realise that Sofie has been suppressing the memories of her rape – a traumatic experience which the mental strain of being incarcerated in Barton causes her to relive over and over again.

Sofie's suffering from post-traumatic stress disorder (PTSD) becomes most obvious in two key scenes that reveal what actually happened between her and Gordon. When her panic attacks become more frequent and severe, the guards ask a psychologist to see her (E5, 00:32:58–00:36:25). The (male) doctor questions her about her mental health: for example whether she has ever been diagnosed with a mental illness, hospitalised, or prescribed medication. The situation puts Sofie under significant stress and once again triggers a flashback, which causes her to re-experience her last transformative session with Gordon.

The series conveys Sofie's distress in an interesting combination of external and internal focalisation, which again foregrounds the nexus of body and mind (as has been the case in the Christmas scene discussed above). We first witness the scene through a "nobody's shot" (Schlickers 2009, 249), with the camera showing from the outside how Sofie and the psychiatrist sit opposite each other. After the first couple of questions, however, the scene starts blending this external perspective with Sofie's flashback: Although she is sitting in a room in Barton talking to a psychiatrist, she perceives the conversation as if it was her last transformative session with Gordon, at the end of which he raped her. Shifting back and forth between the two conversations, the sequence enables the audience to take a double perspective: In one scene, it shows us what is actually happening in the room – that is, we hear the psychiatrist's questions and see his facial response to Sofie's disturbed emotional state, which he can infer from the agitated look on her face as well as her tense body language. In the next scene, we take Sofie's perspective, where she feels as if she is talking to Gordon. As her distress increases – she cries and tries to shield herself from his molesting touches, while repeatedly asking him to stop – the psychiatrist realizes that she is re-experiencing a trauma and stops the session, which puts an end to the flashback. At a later point in the series, however, Sofie has another flashback triggered by a confrontation with one of the (male) guards who tries to persuade her to enter her cell, even though she shows signs of claustrophobia (E5, 00:40:03-00:43:20). Drawing on the same blending strategy, this scene eventually shows the entire rape scene. This is Sofie's worst flashback (i.e., she begins to scream and attacks the guard whom she, again, mistakes to be Gordon) and, failing to calm her, the guards have to sedate her and eventually commit her to a psychiatric hospital.

Interestingly, *Stateless* stages Sofie's mental health problems as an important character trait that distinguishes her from its male protagonist. Ameer suffers from both a sudden mental and physical breakdown when his twelve-year old daughter Mina (Soraya Heidari), with whom he is reunited in Barton, informs him that his wife and youngest daughter have not survived the passage to Australia (i.e., he begins to cry, collapsing in her arms).[14] The guards sedate him with heavy tranquilisers, which not only confine him to bed, but also cause him to have nightmares: He spends several days and nights in a state of delirium, hallucinating that he is underwater together with his drowning wife and daughter. In rendering his body immobile, the medication puts him in a condition that his friend Farid (Claude Jabbourd) had warned him about when he first came to the camp: "Stay away from the nurses, okay? [...] They will give you so much medicine you won't be able to think for yourself. In here, you have to stay strong." (E2, 00:37:32) Only when his daughter also suffers a mental breakdown does Ameer eventually regain his strength and manages to fight off the side effects of the tranquilisers.[15] Unlike in the case of Sofie, Ameer's temporary mental impairment is thus brought about mainly by an external factor (i.e., sedative medication) rather than the shock he suffers as he learns of the death of his daughter and wife.

Despite all his traumatic experiences, including the loss of the two beloved family members, the male protagonist of *Stateless* shows an astonishingly high

---

14 Ameer is separated from his family in Pakistan as they are about to enter a human trafficker's boat. While he still manages to set his wife and children on the boat, he himself is held up by the human traffickers, who beat him up and afterwards leave him lying on the beach. Once he has regained consciousness, he buys a ticket to get on a different boat to Australia.

15 In detention, Mina starts committing self-harm when she can no longer deal with the trauma she suffered from witnessing the death of her mother and sister with her own eyes.

level of resilience, which presents a stark contrast to the mental fragility of his female counterpart. This becomes obvious in a scene which shows Ameer telling the authorities how he came to Australia and which, again, foregrounds his bodily signals, thus allowing the audience to make inferences about his mental state. The life story he attempts to construct in his immigration interviews shows some inconsistencies: When asked, for example, why he sent his family ahead to Australia while he remained in Pakistan, he replies that he did not have enough money for the entire family (E5, 00:05:13–00:07:53). Although Ameer answers this question in a calm manner, the mode of presentation used in this particular scene indicates that he is nervous and stressed: The camera first shows the dictating machine that is recording his statement in a close-up before shifting to his hand, making nervous movements; the scene is accompanied with suspenseful mood music. When the DIMMA case officer continues to ask him how he paid for his own passage to Australia, he tells her that his brother sent him cash from Afghanistan. She immediately suspects that this is not true because he hesitates when asked for details. Several point-of-view shots, alternately presenting his face and the officer's hand taking notes of his statements, signal to the viewer that Ameer is standing with his back to the wall. Moreover, during the conversation, the visual track repeatedly enables us to access some snippets of Ameer's memory that remind us of an incident in Pakistan where he stole money from the people smuggler Oshan after the latter had tricked him by taking his money and stealing his passport (E1, 00:47:52–00:49:55).

Ameer's hesitant replies during the conversation cause the authorities to pursue investigations which eventually reveal that his brother was already dead at the time when Ameer claims he posted the money (E5, 00:21:08–00:23:08). When Clare Kowitz (Asher Keddie), an official of the Department of Home Affairs sent from Canberra to oversee the private security company's work in the detention center, conducts another interview with Ameer confronting him with these new insights, he first keeps calm, although some close-up shots of his shaking foot and nervous hands under the table again show the extreme stress from which he is suffering. As Ameer adheres to his false story, Clare shows him the death certificate of his brother. Since at this point, he can no longer hide his fear and despair – he looks shocked and breathes heavily – Clare tries to persuade him to tell the truth: "Ameer, I know you have suffered. But if you want any chance of getting protection for yourself and your daughter, you have to tell me the truth." (E5, 00:22:16–00:22:29) Yet Ameer stands firm and instead of saying something that could further incriminate him, asks to speak to a lawyer. Only when Clare leaves the room does he bend under the pressure and almost starts to cry.

These examples show that, in contrast to Sofie's case, the inconsistencies in Ameer's account are not a sign that his accurate memory is failing him, but that he is at pains to conceal some of his past from the Australian authorities, because he knows that the truth would put his and his daughter's visas at risk. His life story in Pakistan would make Ameer in the eyes of the authorities a criminal. For his own and his daughter's sake he has to turn into an unreliable storyteller, strategically bending the truth in immigration interviews to avoid rejection of their claim for asylum and being sent to prison. Recalling the scene of Sofie's therapy session discussed above, one can thus conclude that, by presenting Sofie's story of rape as a broken narrative and Ameer's inaccurate account of his flight as a strategic move, *Stateless* suggests that the male protagonist is more resilient and less vulnerable than the female main character.

This impression is further reinforced at the end of the series. While Sofie's symptoms of PTSD not only prevent her from expressing her pain, but also render her completely immobile – the last scene in which Sofie appears shows her lying motionless in a hospital bed – Ameer's clear mind and his clever storytelling "tactics" eventually bring him success in fighting for his daughter's protection visa.[16] When the authorities find out the truth, they accuse him of involvement in human trafficking. On the brink of being deported back to Pakistan, he spends an entire night awake, thinking how he might rescue his daughter. He knows that in Australian immigration law, unprotected children are granted a protection visa and can be accepted by a foster family. So he comes up with the lie that he met an Afghan woman with two children in Pakistan and decided to take care of them and help them flee to Australia (E6, 00:22:00–00:25:25). In thus denying his biological kinship with his daughter, Ameer eventually succeeds in providing a safe future for Mina, whereas he himself loses any chance of protection as a refugee.

---

16 Michel de Certeau, in *The Practices of Everyday Life*, distinguishes between strategies and tactics as two types of practice (1984, Ch. III). A strategy, he argues, is "the calculation (or manipulation) of power relations that becomes possible as soon as a subject with will and power [...] can be isolated. It postulates a place that can be delimited as its own and serves as the base from which relations with an exteriority composed of targets or threats [...] can be managed" (ibid., 35–36). While a strategy thus qualifies as "an effort to delimit one's own place in a world bewitched by the invisible powers of the Other" (ibid., 36), a tactic is "an art of the weak" or rather "a calculated action determined by the absence of a proper locus" (ibid., 37). Given that "[n]o delimitation of an exteriority [...] provides it with the condition necessary for autonomy," a tactic "must play on and with a terrain imposed on it and organized by the law of a foreign power" (ibid.). According to de Certeau, then, a tactic "does not have the means to keep to itself, at a distance, in a position of withdrawal, foresight, and self-collection: it is a maneuver 'within the enemy's field of vision,' [...] and within enemy territory" (ibid.).

However, even though Ameer will not be released from detention at the end of the series, his decision of bending the truth for the benefit of his daughter can be construed as the active choice on his part to exert agency within the structural constraints of the Australian migration regime. Accordingly, in contrast to Sofie's immobility, which serves to stylise her as the passive victim of Gordon's sexual violence, Ameer's immobility rather constitutes a sign of his high ability to cope with pressure and mental stress. Against this backdrop, then, *Stateless* clearly features a gendered perspective on vulnerability and victimisation, as it attributes notions of mental distress and trauma to the female protagonist on the one hand and notions of resilience and mental strength to her male counterpart on the other.

## 4 Conclusion

This chapter has shown how the mini-series *Stateless* draws on different narratives of mobility to foreground experiences of displacement and their impact on a character's mental health and well-being. The new mobilities paradigm postulates that mobility is always determined by social structures and cultural contexts. Reading the series through this lens reveals the different social and cultural structures that influence both the protagonists' motility – i.e., the reasons, motives, and decisions behind their mobility – and its practical results. As my analysis has shown, the juxtaposition of Ameer and Sofie foregrounds in particular the ways in which gender and ethnicity bear upon the constellations of mobility presented in the series.

Shifting the discourse from migration to mobility, the series stages the female Australian citizen as a displaced character seeking escape from her life. In the continuous decline of her mental health over the course of the series, we can see how constellations of physical and imaginary mobility impact individual happiness and well-being. Sofie starts out as an independent, mobile woman who leads a stable and conventional enough life; yet her social circumstances (i.e., her patronising family as well as her involvement with GOPA) soon turn her into a displaced character without any motility, which eventually renders her immobile and incapable of taking her own decisions (at the end of the series she is committed to a psychiatric hospital where she lies motionless in bed).

Ameer, by contrast, represents the prototypical figure of the male refugee whose mobility is significantly restricted due to his status as an irregular migrant. Although Australia's immigration system further compromises his actions and movements, it neither curtails his motility nor diminishes his resilience. Weighing the few options for action available to him within the confines of the immigration detention center, he puts this potential to use to free his daughter from her misery and enable her to lead a life with better opportunities. With his decision to invent an alternative life story for his family, he offers his daughter the gift of freedom and mental well-being (the last scene of the series shows her walking along the beach, looking out to the open sea symbolising her brighter future); at the same time, however, he forfeits his own mobility (he will remain indeterminately in detention or, in the worst case, even be sent to prison or deported to Afghanistan).

In focusing on the unorthodox ways in which *Stateless* presents its protagonists as displaced characters, my analysis demonstrates how the series challenges conventional notions of what it's like to be a refugee. Given that it leaves us wondering until the penultimate episode why Sofie is willing to accept imprisonment in the detention center, although she could prove anytime that she is an Australian citizen, the series seems to place greater attention on the misery of the privileged white girl than the precarious and traumatising situation of the male Afghan refugee. Yet its use of contrastive multiperspectivity serves to criticise how privileged audiences generally perceive refugeedom. As Javad tells Sofie, the public seems unconcerned about the inhumane treatment of refugees in Australian detention centers until "a white girl," one of them, becomes their vicarious voice. Javad's statement holds not only for the storyworld presented in *Stateless*; on a meta-level it unfolds a deeper meaning: His criticism of the lack of public interest in the fate of refugees makes viewers realise that their main interest in the series has been to find out why Sofie, the Australian citizen, has been detained in the camp – not what happens to the refugees. It is this uncomfortable feeling of being caught off-guard that eventually encourages the audience to reflect upon the "structures of attitude and reference" that influence their engagement with humanitarian crises such as forced migration.

## Works Cited

Adey, Peter. *Mobility*. 2nd ed. London and New York: Routledge, 2017.

Armstrong, Judith G. "Deciphering the Broken Narrative of Trauma: Signs of Traumatic Dissociation on the Rorschach." *Rorschachiana*, vol. 25, no. 1, 2002, pp. 11–27.

Bal, Mieke. *Travelling Concepts in the Humanities: A Rough Guide*. Toronto: U of Toronto P, 2002.

Bauman, Zygmunt. *Liquid Modernity*. Cambridge: Polity Press, 2000.

Canzler, Weert, Vincent Kaufmann, and Sven Kesselring. "Tracing Mobilities – An Introduction." *Tracing Mobilities: Towards a Cosmopolitan Perspective*. Ed. Weert Canzler,

Vincent Kaufmann, and Sven Kesselring. Aldershot, Burlington: Ashgate, 2008, pp. 1–10.

Caracciolo, Marco. *'Strange' Narrators in Contemporary Fiction: Explorations in Readers' Engagement with Characters*. Lincoln and London: U of Nebraska P, 2016.

Cresswell, Tim. "Introduction: Theorizing Place." *Mobilizing Place, Placing Mobility: The Politics of Representation in a Globalized World*. Ed. Ginette Verstraete and Tim Cresswell. Amsterdam and New York: Rodopi, 2002, pp. 11–32.

Cresswell, Tim. *On the Move: Mobility in the Modern Western World*. New York and London: Routledge, 2006.

Cresswell, Tim. "Towards a Politics of Mobility." *Environment and Planning D: Society and Space*, vol. 28, no. 1, 2010, pp. 17–31.

De Certeau, Michel. *The Practices of Everyday Life*. Berkeley: U of California P, 1984.

Eder, Jens. *Die Figur im Film: Grundlagen der Figurenanalyse*. 2nd ed. Marburg: Schüren, 2014.

Freeman, Emma, and Jocelyn Moorhouse, dir. *Stateless*. Aired March 1, 2020 on ABC. (Netflix, 2020). www.netflix.com/de/title/81206211. Accessed February 15, 2022.

Genette, Gérard. *Narrative Discourse: An Essay in Method*. Translated by Jane E. Lewin. Ithaca: Cornell UP, 1980.

Groves, Nancy. "Cate Blanchett to direct Australian TV drama, Stateless, based on Cornelia Rau." *The Guardian*, July 21, 2015. www.theguardian.com/film/2015/jul/21/cate-blanchett-to-direct-australian-tv-drama-stateless-based-on-cornelia-rau. Accessed February 15, 2022.

Hannam, Kevin, Mimi Sheller, and John Urry. "Editorial: Mobilities, Immobilities and Moorings." *Mobilities*, vol. 1, no. 1, 2006, pp. 1–22.

Herman, David. *Basic Elements of Narrative*. Malden and Oxford: Wiley-Blackwell, 2009.

Hydén, Lars-Christer, and Jens Brockmeier, eds. *Health, Illness and Culture: Broken Narratives*. New York and London: Routledge, 2008.

Hyvärinen, Matti, Lars-Christer Hydén, Marja Saarenheimo, and Maria Tamboukou. "Beyond Narrative Coherence: An Introduction." *Beyond Narrative Coherence*. Ed. Matti Hyvärinen, Lars-Christer Hydén, Marja Saarenheimo, and Maria Tamboukou. Amsterdam and Philadelphia: Benjamins, 2010, pp. 1–15.

Jost, François. *L'œil – Caméra: Entre film et roman*. Lyon: PU de Lyon, 1989.

Kaufmann, Vincent. *Re-Thinking Mobility: Contemporary Sociology*. London and New York: Routledge, 2016.

Kirmayer, Laurence J. "Broken Narratives: Clinical Encounters and the Poetics of Illness Experience." *Narrative and the Cultural Construction of Illness and Healing*. Ed. Cheryl Mattingly and Linda C. Garro. Berkeley: U of California P, 2000, pp. 153–80.

Kuhn, Markus. *Filmnarratologie: Ein erzähltheoretisches Analysemodell*. Berlin and Boston: De Gruyter, 2011.

Mangan, Lucy. "Stateless Review – Harrowing, Hypnotic Refugee Drama." *The Guardian.* July 8, 2020. www.theguardian.com/tv-and-radio/2020/jul/08/stateless-review-harrowing-hypnotic-refugee-drama. Accessed February 15, 2022.

Manne, Robert. "The Unknown Story of Cornelia Rau: How an Australian Citizen Was Wrongfully Incarcerated in Immigration Detention." *The Monthly* (September 2005). www.themonthly.com.au/monthly-essays-robert-manne-unknown-story-cornelia-rau-often-she-cried-sometimes-she-screamed-she-be. Accessed February 15, 2022.

Neumann, Birgit, and Ansgar Nünning. "Travelling Concepts as a Model for the Study of Culture." *Travelling Concepts for the Study of Culture.* Ed. Birgit Neumann and Ansgar Nünning. Berlin and Boston: De Gruyter, 2012, pp. 1–22.

Nünning, Ansgar, and Vera Nünning. "Conceptualizing 'Broken Narratives' from a Narratological Perspective: Domains, Concepts, Features, Functions, and Suggestions for Research." *Narrative im Bruch: Theoretische Positionen und Anwendungen.* Ed. Anna Babka, Marlen Bidwell-Steiner, and Wolfgang Müller-Funk. Vienna: V & R unipress/Vienna UP, 2016, pp. 37–86.

Nünning, Vera, and Ansgar Nünning. "Multiperspektivität aus narratologischer Sicht: Erzähltheoretische Grundlagen und Kategorien zur Analyse der Perspektivenstruktur narrativer Texte." *Multiperspektivisches Erzählen: Zur Theorie und Geschichte der Perspektivenstruktur im englischen Roman des 18. bis 20. Jahrhunderts.* Ed. Vera Nünning and Ansgar Nünning. Trier: Wissenschaftlicher Verlag Trier, 2000, pp. 39–77.

Pfister, Manfred. *The Theory and Analysis of Drama.* Translated by John Halliday. Cambridge: Cambridge UP, 1988.

Ryan, Marie-Laure. *Narrative as Virtual Reality 2: Revisiting Immersion and Interactivity in Literature and Electronic Media.* 2nd ed. Baltimore: Johns Hopkins UP, 2015.

Said, Edward W. *Culture and Imperialism.* New York: Vintage, 1994.

Schlickers, Sabine. "Focalization, Ocularization and Auricularization in Film and Literature." *Point of View, Perspective, and Focalization Modeling Mediation in Narrative.* Ed. Peter Hühn, Wolf Schmid and Jörg Schönert. Berlin and Boston: De Gruyter, 2009, pp. 243–58.

Schneider, Ralf. "The Cognitive Theory of Character Reception: An Updated Proposal." *Anglistik: International Journal of English Studies*, vol. 24, no. 2, September 2013, pp. 117–34.

Sewell, Kenneth W., and Amy M. Williams. "Broken Narratives: Trauma, Metaconstructive Gaps, and the Audience of Psychotherapy." *Journal of Constructivist Psychology*, vol. 15, no. 3, 2002, pp. 205–18.

Sheller, Mimi, and John Urry. "The New Mobilities Paradigm." *Environment and Planning A*, vol. 38, no. 2, 2005, pp. 207–26.

Singer, Christoph. "The *Camp* as Extra-Temporal Space in E.C. Osondu's 'Waiting' and Dinaw Mengestu's 'An Honest Exit.'" *Timespaces of Waiting: Spaces of Stasis, Delay and Deferral*. Ed. Christoph Singer, Robert Wirth, and Olaf Berwald. Leiden and Boston: Brill/Rodopi, 2019, pp. 94–107.

Singer, Christoph. "The Temporalities of British Detention: Chronic Waiting at the Colnbrook Detention Centre." *Journal for the Study of British Cultures*, vol. 24, no. 2, 2017, pp. 175–87.

Singer, Christoph, Robert Wirth, and Olaf Berwald. "Introduction." *Timespaces of Waiting: Spaces of Stasis, Delay and Deferral*. Ed. Christoph Singer, Robert Wirth, and Olaf Berwald. Leiden and Boston: Brill/Rodopi, 2019, pp. 1–16.

Urry, John. *Mobilities*. London: Polity Press, 2007.

Urry, John. "Moving on the Mobility Turn." *Tracing Mobilities: Towards a Cosmopolitan Perspective*. Ed. Weert Canzler, Vincent Kaufmann, and Sven Kesselring. Aldershot, Burlington: Ashgate, 2008, pp. 13–23.

Van Berlo, Patrick. "Australia's Operation Sovereign Borders: Discourse, Power, and Policy from a Crimmigration Perspective." *Refugee Survey Quarterly*, vol. 34, no. 4, 2015, pp. 75–104.

Winkler, Isabelle. "The Subtle Art of Cultural Activism: A Review of Stateless." *Right Now: Human Rights in Australia*. December 2, 2020. https://rightnow.org.au/review-3/the-subtle-art-of-cultural-activism-a-review-of-stateless/. Accessed February 15, 2022.

# PART 3

## *Embodied Non-normativities*

CHAPTER 12

# Side-Effect Narration: Unreliable Embodiment and Ideological Repositioning in Clare Allan's *Poppy Shakespeare*

*Sandra Marzinkowski*

## 1 Introduction

*Poppy Shakespeare,* written by Clare Allan and published in 2006, depicts clients' everyday life at the Abaddon, a fictional psychiatric institution in contemporary London. From the outset readers follow the homodiegetic narrator, N, as she oscillates between her life in the hospital's day unit, the Dorothy Fish, and her humdrum private life in the housing complex adjacent to the institution. When asked to guide a new entrant, Poppy Shakespeare, through the Dorothy Fish, N, initially naively compliant with and dependent upon the institution, regains a sense of purpose, which prompts her to write down her experiences in the form of a story. The novel depicts N and Poppy as reverse mirror images, juxtaposing N's growing opposition to psychiatric practices and her discharge with Poppy's overdose and placement in the closed ward after a suicide attempt. The process leading up to N's discharge and Poppy's decline in wellbeing foregrounds several elements associated with orthodox psychiatry including the intake of psychotropic drugs.[1] While the novel initially caters to the dominant framing of psychiatric clients as mentally deviant and thus unable to narrate their experiences in a way conventionally deemed faithful to 'reality', this framing can easily be dismissed towards the end of the novel, which shows how N's discontinuation of drugs is tied to shifts in her perception and evaluation of the institution.

By stressing the favourable effects of re-narrativising the past through writing outside of a psychopathological rationale the novel blatantly opposes an adherence to the biomedical paradigm, which casts forms of mental distress as

1 I use the term 'drug' rather than 'medication' to stress the detrimental side-effects of psychopharmacology rather than the intended effects and to underline the similarity in effect to what is commonly referred to as 'drugs'. For an account of how the side-effects and intended effects of psychotropic drugs are inherently blurred, see Cohen and Moncrieff (2005, 150) or Martin (2006).

 DOI:10.1163/9789004519886_014

categorisable and (medically) treatable 'disorders'. N's metanarrative emphasis on (re-)storying her past and present experiences triggered by her encounters with Poppy cues readers to recognise the entanglement of wellbeing and self-authored coherence free from deficit-focussed forms of treatment, a nod to Allan's favourable stance towards alternatives to orthodox psychiatry.[2] In an article in *The Guardian* published in response to BBC's then-recent *In the Mind* series and its "almost total lack of any social perspective on mental health in the programmes" (Allan 2016, online), Allan harshly criticizes the series' focus on biomedicine as a treatment for mental distress because it sweeps under the carpet the possible roots of suffering in a person's adverse family history or in social variables such as racism and poverty. Her anti-psychiatric view of mental distress as more-than-biology hence moves the responsibility for mental suffering on to a decidedly social plane. In accordance with this view, *Poppy Shakespeare* highlights the entanglement of psychiatric diagnoses and social determinants, especially social class and gender. This becomes clear, for instance, when N, who is shown to have grown up in social precarity, begins to adopt Poppy's middle-class habitus, which includes sartorial and linguistic markers that camouflage her educationally disadvantaged upbringing, while increasingly detaching herself from the psychiatric institution (Allan 2006, 324). The coincidence of visual markers of conventional beauty and N's discontinuation of psychotropic drugs as well as N's growing resentment towards and independence from the psychiatric institution and its practices suggests a correlation between mental wellbeing and performing a socially respected type of middle-class femininity on the one hand and between mental distress and social stigma on the other.

As Tim Snelson (2021) carefully examines, anti-psychiatry emerged as a radical counterposition to the 'mental hygiene movement', a conservative postwar development in British society closely associated with the National Association for Mental Health, the leading UK mental health organisation at the time. While the mental hygiene movement favoured psychosurgery such as ECT and lobotomy,[3] thus promoting a biologist understanding of mental distress, proponents of anti-psychiatry advocated non-surgical forms of psychotherapy with a heavy emphasis on community care and notoriously questioned the dichotomy between 'madness' and 'sanity' (Snelson 2021, 56–7). Quite in line with anti-psychiatric reasoning, *Poppy Shakespeare* echoes this critique by

2 See especially *Poppy Shakespeare* chapters 14, 15, 20, and 38.

3 'ECT' is short for Electroconvulsive Therapy and refers to a controversial treatment in which electric currents are applied to the scalp. The procedure is still being used nowadays, especially to treat 'disorders' such as depression and mania.

questioning the utility of the diagnostic system and psychopharmacology to treat mental distress, thus enabling readers to question essentialist frames of unreliable narration.[4]

My analysis heeds Ansgar Nünning's call to conceptualise the notion of unreliability not in terms of an "essentiali[s]ed and anthropomorphized entity designated 'unreliable narrator'" (1997, 88), but in terms of readers' attempts to create coherence and to attribute a perceived violation of coherence to the purported failings of the narrator. Stressing the idea that ascriptions of unreliability are contingent upon both readerly projections and the cultural context of readers and the narrative, the notion must be considered "not so much a character trait of a narrator as [...] an interpretive strategy of the reader" (Nünning 2005, 95). Ascriptions of unreliability "not only [depend] on the distance between the norms and values of the narrator and those of the text as a whole [...] but also on the distance that separates the narrator's view of the world from the reader's or critic's world-model and standards of normalcy" (ibid.).

In accordance with this and taking as axiomatic the second-generation cognitivist assumption of the inextricableness of body and mind (cf. Caracciolo et al.), I propose that the effects of psychotropic drugs as depicted in the novel help de-essentialise unreliability by framing it in terms of variable states of the body and variable narratorial modes that result from this bodily variability. In other words, the way drugs are shown to impact narration in the novel helps question premature framings of narrators coded as 'mad' as unreliable and, more importantly, contributes to negotiations of the meaning of 'truth' as part of discussions surrounding unreliability.

As I will show, the practice of drug intake significantly influences N and the other clients' bodily states, all characterised by rigidity, repetitiveness, short-sightedness, and a lack of energy. This drug-altered state, in turn, has an impact on clients' perception of space and time, their emotions, and their socio-cultural evaluations. Drawing especially on James Phelan's taxonomy of unreliability (2004), Marco Caracciolo's five concentric circles of experience (2014), Seymour Chatman's take on perspective (1986), and Lisa Blackman's juxtaposition of ontologies and their sociopolitical implications (2012), this paper investigates narrative patterns in relation to the narrator's drug-induced changes in embodiment.

4 For a thorough examination of the psychiatric practices and discourses alluded to in the novel, cf. Cox (2014).

## 2 The Politics of Psychotropic Drugs and Un-selfing the Narrative

In an article on the intersection between narratology and health studies, Ansgar and Vera Nünning (2018) emphasise the potential of a cross-fertilisation between these disciplines due to their shared interest in narrativisation. The notion of *salutogenesis*, introduced by Aaron Antonovsky and originally used in the context of medicine and trauma recovery research, represents an alternative to illness-centred models including psychopharmacology, swerving the focus from the origins of (mental) illness to those of health (Bull et al. 2022, 29). Salutogenetic research yielded the concept of the 'sense of coherence', which posits a link between (mental) well-being and the ability to make sense of one's lived selfhood through "an orientation towards life as more or less comprehensible, manageable and meaningful" (Bauer and Mittelmark 2002, 11). This concept parallels the effort to investigate the link between self-creation and narrativisation in the field of narratology, which is why Nünning and Nünning call for a 'salutogenetic narrative theory' (2018, 169). In the context of the present analysis, the notion of salutogenesis is useful as a theoretical backdrop to elucidate how the creation of coherence through storying one's experiences is to be viewed in contrast to pathogenetic ways of dealing with mental distress, including diagnostic processes and labels, restriction on movement, as well as psychotropic drugs and their dampening effects.

*Poppy Shakespeare* juxtaposes salutogenesis and pathogenesis in the novel in the depiction of different types of psychiatric practices as well as clients' own coping strategies. While the narrator, N, is preoccupied with making herself cohere through autobiographical storytelling and hence with the creation of plot out of fragments of her past and present experiences, the psychiatric practices of the Abaddon, ranging from the panoptic setup to the way clients are diagnosed and evaluated are decidedly centred around a deficit-oriented illness paradigm. As part of this paradigm, orthodox psychiatric approaches use a disease-centred rather than a drug-centred model. The disease-centred model "assumes that drugs move an abnormal physiological state towards a more normal one, [whereas] the drug-centred model suggests that drugs create their own characteristic abnormal states or alterations of normal states" (Cohen and Moncrieff 2005, 146). The inherent enmeshment of psychopathology's epistemic structures and drug prescription is noteworthy. The DSM, the most widely used diagnostic catalogue, has grown immensely from the beginning of the 20th century down to the present, turning from "150 spiral bound pages" into an "internationally used 900-page bible" (Appignanesi 2008, 449). This is relevant in that many diagnoses are linked to a "'recommended' drug treatment" (ibid.). According to this rationale, drug treatment is intended to outweigh the purported physiological deviance of individuals diagnosed with a 'mental disorder' while the idea that it can itself cause forms of deviance that may increase suffering is commonly neglected.

In *Poppy Shakespeare*, the two models of drug use are juxtaposed. The chapter "How I offered Poppy to Show Her Banker Bill" depicts how clients deal in psychotropic drugs, which they buy for their side effects to alter their embodiment to their liking, for example by using them as appetite suppressants (Allan 2006, 122). By contrast, psychotropic drugs as administered by the Abaddon are depicted as tools used to create compliance by reducing noticeable deviations in behaviour (ibid., 123). According to N, it is "bastard medication [...] meant to slow you down a bit and stop you acting mental but it gone completely over the top, seized up your jaw and locked up your knees so's your legs wouldn't bend in the middle" (ibid.) Compliance is demanded to differing degrees according to the supposed severity of clients' 'madness' or their number of diagnoses. For example, the clients on the closed wards, whom N calls 'flops', are described as "bug-eyed with meds and madness" (ibid., 32), and as having to be 'rounded up' like cattle to be dosed with drugs (ibid., 20). Moreover, after her suicide attempt, Poppy ends up with thirty-three diagnoses (ibid., 339), presumably drugged as well as unable to move and to converse with N (ibid., 340–41).

As regards the way *Poppy Shakespeare* is narrated, it can be observed that psychotropic drugs run counter to creating a sense of coherence by inducing in the narrator what Lisa Blackman calls 'recursive loops' (2012, 115–16). The latter designate an ontology marked by circularity and inertia that is commonly interpreted as a sign of mental distress. In dominant discourse, this type of ontology is cast as the counterpart of a phenomenology of 'flow', which is largely considered an absence of distress in contemporary discussions surrounding well-being (ibid.). Recursive loops surface in the way N narrates. For example, many of the earlier chapters depict the routine of institutional life and the extent to which clients are motivated by the wish to remain a part of this routine by avoiding discharge. Psychotropic drugs emerge as anti-salutogenic in that they reduce rather than foster an individual sense of coherence because they ensure that clients are in the same space at the same time and do not engage in activities other than those offered by the institution (e.g., Allan 2006, 20, 26–27, 49, 123). Drugs thus are part of the 'mortification processes' distinctive of total institutions as defined by Erving Goffman, which systematically strip inmates of markers of selfhood and impose an anonymised, collective type of selfhood, which marks their positions as inmates in an institution enforcing the same ever-recurring activities (1961, 70).

The inability to create a self devoid of psychiatric influence is particularly prominent in the descriptions of the 'flops', who are "so drugged up they looked like they been whizzed in a blender and poured back into their bodies" (ibid., 12) and are subjected to the rigidly clocked routines of the institutions that prevent individuation processes (ibid., 20). The routine is less rigid, or recursive, for 'dribblers', who are on the first floor of the institution and allowed the highest degree of freedom because they are allowed to go home in the evening and at the weekend. The novel frames the relation between 'flops' and 'dribblers' as a rivalry resulting from an institutional reward system, which benefits those who act 'normal' with moving down floors and with fewer restrictions, and punishes those who act up by making them move up floors and by drugging and restricting them more (ibid., 6, 108).

Inertia and a high degree of circularity as fostered by a drug-induced dependency on institutional care here stand in contrast to the experience of lightness and flow that comes with an opposition to the institution (ibid., 313). N describes weight loss as the most noticeable effect of discontinuing drugs and equates this loss with losing a part of her self and 'putting on' a new one by wearing Poppy's clothes:

> I'd been on anti-psychotics all my life, do you know what I'm saying, taken Parazine along with my mother's breast milk so I s'pose it weren't surprising when you took out the stopper to find half of me disappeared. The skinny me – I was almost skinny! – it didn't even look nothing like the old N and it weren't going to share no clothes with her. So I tried on a couple of things of Poppy's, them clothes I'd rescued from Oxfam, and they fitted like I'd bought them new. (ibid., 325)

N's new slender self can be read as a switch of position with Poppy and literally prevents her from 'falling back' into the habits of the institution when she comes to visit (ibid., 327). At this late point in the narrative, her sense of self clearly diverges from that of the other clients, whose selfhood is still dependent on the institution and its clock-regulated habits.

## 3 A Framework for Side-Effect Narration

To link (changes in) embodiment to unreliability, I draw on the notion of the experiential background. According to Marco Caracciolo (2014), in processing narrative readers tap into a five-level background of everyday experiences. The most basic level, that of bodily experience, includes "bodily sensations like pain, proprioception and kinesthesia" (Caracciolo 2014, 57). The second level, perception, which is closely related to the first, denotes our sensory system, including vision, hearing, and olfaction (ibid., 59). The third level, emotion, "track[s] bodily states that reliably cooccur with important organism-environment relations" (Prinz 2004, 69), especially in situations that "seem significant for the well-being of an organism" (Caracciolo 2014, 59). Level four refers to "long-term memory, propositional imagination, conceptual thought, language, and narrative understanding" (ibid.). The fifth and outermost level, that of socio-cultural practices, refers to assessments, value judgments, and conventions contingent upon culture and is the least universalisable layer of experience (ibid.).

The notion of the experiential background described here is rooted in enactivist narratology, a second-generation cognitivism-influenced branch of cognitive narratology that considers the organic interaction between the mind-body and its environment to be the generator of experience. Readers tap into their "acquired, practical, embodied knowledge" (Caracciolo et al. 2017, 451) when engaging with stories, attributing a consciousness to or merging with a character's consciousness to differing degrees depending on the narrative situation. According to the model of Caracciolo, Guédon, Kukkonen, and Müller (2017), all five levels are interactive and thus able to produce *inside-out* or *outside-in* effects: the sensing body and the acculturated body "form a feedback loop in which physical experience and bodily make-up feed into our cultural understanding of the body, and this, in turn, informs physical experience and plays a role in conceptuali[s]ing our bodily make-up" (ibid., 437). In other words, changes in the bodily level of experience, such as changes in movement patterns, can have an impact on higher cognitive functions such as ideological positionings and vice versa.

Regarding the dimension of (un)reliability, *Poppy Shakespeare* can be read in terms of James Phelan's distinction between misreading or underreading, and misregarding or underregarding, two of Phelan's subcategories of narrative *unreliability* (2004, 49). While mis/underreading is a result of limited perception (which relates to Caracciolo's second level of the experiential background) mis/underregarding relates to insufficient critical evaluation (Caracciolo's fifth level). These subcategories of unreliability will serve as a heuristic framework to highlight psychiatry's accountability for the perception of its clients as well as possible reading positionings. In addition, I suggest that Seymour Chatman's (1986) conceptualisation of 'point of view' is helpful to gauge to what extent unreliability is linked to bodily functioning and positioning. While *point of view* is generally thought to imply a "purely spatial position from which a scene is observed" (Azaryahu, Foote, and Ryan 2016, 20), Chatman's conceptualisation of the notion involves a process of metaphorical transfer: "[s]ince we can 'see' in more ways than the merely optical, 'point of view' can be transferred to other kinds of mental activity" (1986, 190). Chatman's understanding thus points to the conflation of physical capacities, spatial perception, and ideological positioning. Modifications of one of these aspects through the side effects of psychotropic drugs will be shown to modify the others. *Poppy Shakespeare* is focalised only through N's thoughts, feelings, and the perception of her environment. While the narrative suggests that other clients' point of view is skewed in similar ways, readers arguably only get to witness the action through N's eyes and consciousness. However, as I suggest, N has an on-drug and an off-drug point of view, with the former likely deemed unreliable by readers, which may create the impression that the narrative has two focalisers instead of one.

## 4 *Poppy Shakespeare* and Psychotropic Disturbances

I read narration, including modes of narration of specific types of narrators likely considered unreliable by readers, as 'ingestible'. Ingesting, that is, to take food or other substances into the stomach, is a bodily process. Following Emily Martin's notion of the "pharmaceutical person" (2006, 275), I suggest that psychotropic drugs operate as 'ingestible' personality-shaping agents intended to enhance the undrugged parts of the self. They are specific in that their effects on the narrator's point of view are shown to change throughout the narration, with N having an on-drug and an off-drug mode available.

The narrator, N, and Poppy, whose development can be viewed as mirror images, are likewise juxtaposed in their ingestion of drugs. While N is on drugs until towards the end of the narration, Poppy avoids taking them until the distress caused by forced hospitalisation prompts her to overdose. As Annabel Cox observes, "[t]he idea of the fusing and eventual transposition of the two women is given a literal aspect in the novel during a groupwork exercise involving mirroring" (2014, 65). In the chapter on group work drug use and the creation of intercorporeality are inherently enmeshed. During the mirroring exercise, N reflects on how much Poppy means to her, expressing devotion through her readiness to give even her bone marrow to Poppy if necessary (Allan 2006, 228). Strikingly, it is when N starts to see her drug-intake as an inhibiting factor to donating marrow that she and Poppy synchronise their movements in perfection: "But what if the meds meant I couldn't ever? So I wouldn't tell them; how would they *know*? And that's when I noticed Poppy had folded her arms" (ibid.). While N's attitude towards the institution grows more critical from this point onwards, Poppy relinquishes her resistance to being pathologised, 'ingesting' compliance with the institution through her overdose (ibid., 313). Drug use here emerges as decisive in shaping the plot.

The way readers are cued to engage with the novel can be conceptualised through 'audience design' as introduced by sociolinguist Allan Bell (1984). Due to the conversational style and positioning N adopts, it can be argued that readers are hailed to engage with the narrative not as distant eavesdroppers but as direct and emotionally involved addressees. This distinction helps determine the degree to which interlocutors modify their speech depending on the degree of monitoring involved in the communicative situation (Bell 1984, 155). N's task assigned in the very first chapter is to guide Poppy through the institution, given that she knows more than anyone else about "dribbling", that is, being a client of the day hospital (Allan 2006, 4). Readers' parallel positioning as new entrants who need guidance is paratextually indicated, although somewhat tongue-in-cheek, for example in the chapter title "A bit about the Dorothy Fish and the Abaddon and stuff like that you can skip if you been there already" (ibid., 5), in which the narrator likewise offers guidance to readers. With N thus functioning as both an intradiegetic and an extradiegetic guide, readers share a conversational role with Poppy, who supposedly knows as little about institutional life as Allan's implied readership and has to adapt quickly to its rules.

Following embodied narratology, I suggest that the communicative situation also points to the degree of bodily involvement in the narrative: while eavesdroppers may listen from afar without having to interact as familiar and acknowledged participants, addressees are part of the arguably closer and more involved embodied situation. Since Poppy goes through an off-drug and an on-drug embodied state and N undergoes the reverse process, it can be argued that the change in embodiment is likewise triggered in the reading process. Readers are cued to infer to what extent compliance with the institution is caused by a non-human psychotropic agent, which induces in clients institutional dependency and a lack of bodily functioning.

While anti-psychiatric critique is hence potentially inferable through reader positioning and bodily involvement, it is also metafictionally voiced through the character of Middle-Class Michael, a fictionalised version of Michel Foucault. In the chapter entitled "How Middle-Class Michael should of got in the Guinness Book of Records", Allan (2006) creates an allusion to Foucault's *A History of Madness* by having Michael deliver a speech to his fellow clients about 'madness' from the Victorian Era to the present day. Alluding to the break between the 'Great Confinement' and Pinel's alleged liberation of the 'mad' from their chains at la Salpêtrière, which Foucault describes, the speech likewise addresses movement restrictions: "[i]n previous eras the focus was more upon physical restraint and containment. Before the relatively recent advent of anti-psychotic medication, many were shackled and held in chains to prevent them from committing acts of violence towards themselves and others" (Allan 2006, 68).

While this passage is not overtly critical of the persistent restrictions on movement induced by drugs, the last chapter of the novel shows Poppy bleary-eyed, unable to move her limbs and tied to a bed on the upper floor of the psychiatric institution, a place formerly occupied by a character tellingly called 'Mitchell the Meds'. This facilitates a retrospective construal of Michael's speech as critique, even for readers unacquainted with Foucauldian thought. The novel here creates a blend between Weir Mitchell's misogynist practice of the so-called Rest Cure and the trope of the 'madwoman in the attic' coined by Sandra M. Gilbert and Susan Gubar (2000). While the former has been commonly acknowledged as a gendered restriction on movement as well as an attempt to reduce deviant performances of femininity (e.g., Bassuk 1985), the latter, in addition to a discourse of confinement, is connected to a colonialist discourse that equates non-western femininity with bestiality (Gilbert and Gubar 2000, XXXVI). Mapping this onto the novel reveals the intersection of the deprivation of humanity and agency as linked to the persistence of bodily confinement. The reference to anti-psychiatric as well as feminist critique revolving around the pathologisation of women (of colour) emerges as relevant within the context of (un)reliability in *Poppy Shakespeare*. It can be viewed as an instruction for readers on how to question the epistemic injustice (Fricker) of contemporary psychiatry by attributing N's supposedly poor judgment and clouded perception not to an inherent lack of truthfulness psychiatric clients are generally suspected of, but to social factors and psychiatric practices, including the administration of drugs.

### 4.1 *From Misreading to Underregarding*

As regards the different ways narrator perception can be skewed, one striking manifestation of N's change in embodiment is her evaluation of space. N misreads the spatial properties of the institution, which leads her to underregard its desolate state. At the beginning of the novel, N introduces to the readers the Abaddon Unit, which she describes as an eminent "huge red tower as tall as the sky", standing on an "enormous hill" and reaching through the clouds (Allan 2006, 5–6). Even though the lift only goes up to the seventh floor, N is convinced that there are so many floors that they could not all possibly be counted. By contrast, the discontinuation of her drugs, changing her vision and cognitive functioning, leads N to re-evaluate the spatial properties of the Abaddon:

> It weren't nothing like I'd remembered it. The hill weren't hardly a hill at all, just a bit of a slope, what a ball wouldn't know to roll down it. Either side was an ugly great housing estate, row after row of brown brick flats, stacked three storeys high with walkways between them stinking of piss and stale beer [...] The Abaddon Mental Health Care Centre was this red brick building, halfway long the street. Seven floors; I know cause I counted. Seven rows of windows. Then it stopped like someone just chopped it off, flat roof and cloudy sky. (ibid., 337)

In contrast to N's slanted on-drug state, the Abaddon now has clear-cut spatial limitations. The description of the 'flat roof' that looks like it has been 'chopped off' can be read as an indication that N's eyesight has sharpened.

Emotionally magnified in N's on-drug mode, the Abaddon emerges as indispensable to her life, and she therefore desperately tries to avoid discharge. The institution's eminence is mirrored by its spatial extension, which is immeasurable beyond N's eyesight. After discontinuing the drugs, the institution has clearly delineated boundaries and a countable number of floors. A shift in her bodily point of view (level one and two in Caracciolo's model) here implies a different emotional and evaluative point of view (level three and five). While having viewed her stay at the day unit as the "best of both worlds" and a place from which nobody would ever voluntarily be discharged (ibid., 30), she later feels betrayed by the psychiatric institution:

> I stood there and give it a look, like a look, do you know what I'm saying. "Fucking wankers!" I said out loud [...] It was like I been conned. Like the tower and all that; I ain't saying it makes sense, but you know what I mean, I'd give it thirteen years of my life and it was all just a big fucking con. (ibid., 337)

I read the idea of having been 'conned' as indicative of N's critical re-evaluation of her drug-induced perception and as a simultaneous distancing from her earlier account. Readers, in turn, like N herself, may consider the latter to have 'misread' the psychiatric space. However, N's lack of reliability can be attributed to the psychiatric institution, which drugs N and thereby crystallises as the agent of her presumably slanted perception and sense of self.

### 4.2 *Under-/Misregarding*

The scene in which Elliot grabs Tony's (one of the staff member's) leg instead of his cup of coffee due to his drug-induced drowsiness as refracted through N's account presents an instance of the narrator's underregarding:

> Well I was just pissing myself; I couldn't help it, and before very long I'd set Tina off too and the more we tried not to the more it just seemed even funnier and every time one of us managed to stop, the other one would set them off again and I never seen Tina so out of herself, and the coffee cup shooking so bad it was flowing down the sides. (ibid., 27)

To come back to Phelan's taxonomy of unreliability, N's account can be categorised as underregarding because N's "ethical judgment is moving along the right track but simply does not go far enough" (Phelan 2004, 52). This is because even though N does perceive the antipsychotics as 'bastard medication' and continually notes the inconvenient side effects as well as the lack of desired effects, she does not go so far as to criticize the psychiatric institution for the detrimental effects of drugs.

The idea that the change in perception accounts for the idealisation of the Abaddon becomes more manifest because the other clients perceive it in almost the same way as N. At the beginning of the novel, one of the clients at the Dorothy Fish suggests that "the [Abaddon] tower was so tall if you got to the top you'd see right around the world and back in through the windows behind you" (Allan 2006, 6). When N visits Poppy on the closed ward at the end of the novel, the latter is confined to a bed on the seventh floor, that is, the floor where the 'maddest' clients are sent (ibid.). Poppy's statement here reiterates Max McSpiegel's: "'You can see right around the world', she said. 'When it's clear'" (ibid., 341), which suggests that clients undergo similar changes in embodiment such as skewed eyesight. Compliance with the institution is produced through a conventionalised psychotropic treatment. N and the other drugged characters' misregarding can thus be read as a side effect because it can be construed as not an essential quality of the narrator and the other characters but rather as something that everyone on these drugs ingests to differing degrees.

## 5 Conclusion

To conclude, in shifting the cause of deviant narration to the adverse effects of psychotropic drugs, *Poppy Shakespeare* cues readers to reattribute the cause of poetic disturbance to the shortcomings of the psychiatric institution, thus enabling a body-centred critique of conventional psychiatric practices. This critique is enabled through an analysis of changes in characters', and especially the narrator's, perception and evaluation. Drawing on Marco Caracciolo's five concentric circles of experience, I proposed that readers' belief systems can be aligned with a critical psychiatric stance especially through a focus on N's and Poppy's on-drug and off-drug state. N's shift from compliance with to opposition to psychiatry's diagnostic system as well as her discontinuing her drugs can be seen as an *inside-out* effect of experience and emerges as the reverse process of Poppy's development in the institution. Through the evocation of the level of bodily experience, the most universalisable level of anthropomorphic experience, a shift in reading positioning is facilitated.

*Poppy Shakespeare* depicts drug-intake not as helping clients reduce their distress and leave the institution as 'healed' individuals but as the main factor that stifles their independent selfhood and solidifies their reliance on psychiatric care by preventing them from creating their own sense of coherence. Aside from stressing the adverse effects rather than the intended effects, psychotropic drugs, in their narrative functionality, emerge as a useful lens for the investigation of unreliability because they help question essentialist framings of narrators marked as perceptually deviant as inherently unreliable.

## Works Cited


Allan, Clare. "Mental Health Problems Aren't All in the Brain". The Guardian, 2016. https://www.theguardian.com/society/2016/mar/01/mental-health-problems-brain-bbc-equality. Accessed Jan 28, 2022.

Allan, Clare. *Poppy Shakespeare*. Bloomsbury, 2006.

Appignanesi, Lisa. *Mad, Bad and Sad: Women and the Mind Doctors*. Norton, 2008.

Azaryahu, Maoz, Kenneth Foote, and Marie-Laure Ryan. *Narrating Space/Spatializing Narrative: Where Narrative Theory and Geography Meet*. Ohio State UP, 2016.

Bassuk, Ellen L. "The Rest Cure: Repetition or Resolution of Victorian Women's Conflicts?" *Poetics Today*, 1985, vol. 6, no. 1/2, 1985, pp. 245–57.

Bauer, Georg F., and Maurice B. Mittelmark. "Salutogenesis as a Theory, as an Orientation and as the Sense of Coherence". *The Handbook of Salutogenesis*. Ed. Georg F. Bauer et al., Springer, 2002, pp. 11–18.

Bell, Allan. "Language Style as Audience Design". *Language in Society*, vol. 13, no. 2, 1984, pp. 145–204.

Blackman, Lisa. *Immaterial Bodies: Affect, Embodiment, Mediation*. SAGE, 2012.

Bull, Torill, Hege Forbech Vinje, and Eva Langeland. "Aaron Antonovsky's Development of Salutogenesis, 1979–1994". *The Handbook of Salutogenesis*. Ed. Georg F. Bauer et al., Springer, 2022, pp. 29–46.

Caracciolo, Marco. *The Experientiality of Narrative: An Enactivist Approach*. De Gruyter, 2014.

Caracciolo, Marco, Cécile Guédon, Karin Kukkonen, and Sabine Müller (2017): "The Promise of an Embodied Narratology: Integrating Cognition, Representation and Interpretation". *Emerging Vectors of Narratology*. Ed. Per Krogh Hansen, John Pier, Philippe Roussin, and Wolf Schmid, Berlin/Boston: De Gruyter, 2017, pp. 435–459.

Chatman, Seymour. "Characters and Narrators: Filter, Center, Slant, and Interest-Focus". *Poetics Today*, vol. 7, no. 2, 1986, pp. 189–204.

Cohen, D., and Joanna Moncrieff. "Rethinking Models of Psychotropic Drug Action". *Psychotherapy and Psychosomatics*, vol. 74, no. 3, 2005, pp. 145–153.

Cox, Annabel. "Poppy Shakespeare: Verging on the Historical". *English*, vol. 63, no. 240, 2014, pp. 57–78.

Foucault, Michel. *History of Madness*. Ed. Jean Khalfa, trans. Jonathan Murphy. Routledge, [1961], 2006.

Fricker, Miranda. *Epistemic Injustice: Power and the Ethics of Knowing*. Oxford UP, 2007.

Gilbert, Sandra M., and Susan Gubar. *The Madwoman in the Attic: The Woman Writer and the Nineteenth-Century Literary Imagination*. Yale UP, 2000.

Goffman, Erving. *Asylums: Essays on the Social Situation of Mental Patients and Other Inmates*. Anchor, 1961.

Martin, Emily. "The Pharmaceutical Person". *BioSocieties*, vol. 1, no. 3, 2006, pp. 273–288.

Nünning, Ansgar. "'But Why Will You Say that I Am Mad?' On the Theory, History, and Signals of Unreliable Narration in British Fiction". *AAA: Arbeiten aus Anglistik und Amerikanistik*, vol. 22, no. 1, 1997, pp. 83–105.

Nünning, Ansgar. "Reconceptualizing Unreliable Narration: Synthesizing Cognitive and Rhetorical Approaches". *A Companion to Narrative Theory*. Ed. James Phelan and Peter J. Rabinowitz. Malden: Blackwell, 2005, pp. 89–107.

Nünning, Ansgar, and Vera Nünning. "How to Stay Healthy and Foster Well-Being with Narratives, or: Where Narratology and Salutogenesis Could Meet". *How to Do Things with Narrative: Cognitive and Diachronic Perspectives*. Ed. Jan Alber and Greta Olson. Berlin: De Gruyter, 2018, pp. 157–86.

Phelan, James. *Living to Tell About It: A Rhetoric and Ethics of Character Narration*. Cornell UP, 2004.

Prinz, Jesse J. *Gut Reactions: A Perceptual Theory of Emotion*. Oxford UP, 2004.

Snelson, Tim. "From In Two Minds to MIND: The Circulation of 'Anti-Psychiatry' in British Film and Television During the Long 1960s". *History of the Human Sciences*, vol. 34, no. 5, 2021, pp. 53–81.

CHAPTER 13

# "She Is Not Ours, We Are Hers": We-Narration and Embodied Selves in Akwaeke Emezi's *Freshwater*

*Anke Sharma*

## 1 Introduction

To date, most studies of we-narration[1] have focused on the form's affordance of expressing groupness—and justifiably so, because the majority of novels or short stories that employ we-narration *do* demonstrate a concern with shared narratives, collective desires, or communal phantasies. Many we-narrators express the necessity for community (Lanser 1992), the oppressiveness of community (Richardson 2006, 58) or an ambivalent position between these two poles. Conceived as collective narration, we-narration may portray "plural protagonists" (Fludernik 2018, 172), or collective subjects that amount to more than the sum of their parts (Bekhta 2020). Overall, studies of we-narration as collective or communal narration have conceived of we-narrators as fictional representations, or constructions, of human groups, whose size may range from two to infinite.[2]

This chapter, however, turns towards a different kind of we-narration, through the example of Akwaeke Emezi's debut novel *Freshwater* (2018). *Freshwater* introduces a we-narrator who expresses the non-normative bodymind of the novel's protagonist, Ada. This 'we' differs from collective or communal we-narrators in so far as it describes several selves of one person. But, instead of displaying these selves merely as different facets of one personality, which

1 I am using the term *we-narration* throughout this essay to designate the act of narration, and not the narrative as a whole. *We-narrative*, on the other hand, is a by no means uncontested term that is used by Natalya Bekhta (2017) in a narrow sense to designate specific instances of narratives. Among other conditions, Bekhta terms narratives 'we-narratives' if they predominantly employ the mode of we-narration and establish a collective subject.

2 John Barth's *Sabbatical* (1982) and *Tidewater Tales* (1987) are examples of we-narration as couple-narration. Examples of indeterminate we-narrators that include one or several generations are Julie Otsuka's *The Buddha in the Attic* (2011), Chang-rae Lee's speculative fiction novel *On Such A Full Sea* (2014), and David Levithan's young-adult novel *Two Boys Kissing* (2013).

 | DOI:10.1163/9789004519886_015

come to the fore depending on the situation and the people the protagonist interacts with, the 'we' selves appear as two separately embodied spirits inside the protagonist. As the two spirits lament at the beginning of the novel: "The main problem was that we were a distinct *we* instead of being fully and just *her*" (Emezi 2018, 5). The "main problem," that the novel thus stages, is one of dis-integration.

While conventional coming-of-age narratives may portray a multiple self[3] as incompatible with the ideal of the unified, *integrated self*,[4] I suggest that *Freshwater* presents Ada's journey as a journey towards reconciling the two: Ada's ogbanje being (as a multiple self) and the striving towards the integrated self. To this process of integration, narration is crucial. The novel's narration ultimately partially confirms and partially diverges from Adriana Cavarero's concept *narratable self* (2000), which I discuss further below. Thus, the ogbanje myth, which is posited not as myth but as reality by the novel, offers a way of reconciling Igbo cosmology with the Western psychological concept of self-integration, in what is finally a narrative of self-acceptance and self-reconciliation.

Before going into the specifics of this chapter's case study, some contextualisation with regard to the novel's plot and structure is in order. *Freshwater* is the debut novel of Akwaeke Emezi, a US-based Nigerian writer and artist with Tamil Indian and Igbo Nigerian heritage and was published in 2018. It comprises 22 chapters, whose titles reflect three different narrative perspectives. The chapters titled 'Ada' are written in Ada's I-narration, the chapters titled 'We' present the we-perspective of the female spirit Asughara and the male spirit St. Vincent (who are occasionally joined by Yshwa/Jesus). While St. Vincent is gentle, Asughara is raging, and any attempts of St. Vincent to assuage Asughara fail.[5] St. Vincent never becomes strong enough to take the position of the narrator, unlike Asughara. While Asughara's perspective takes up the most space (110 pages), this is followed by the we-chapters, which open the novel and span 87 pages, and finally Ada's I-narration, which is allotted a

3 Multiple self, in this context, refers to the idea of the self as composed of multiple, distinct and contradictory parts, which results in mental instability including unpredictable moods and behavior. This may, but does not necessarily have to, result in self-harm or the harm of others.

4 Here, integrated self designates an idea—and an ideal—of the self that is the result of the integration of its multiple, contradictory parts into one whole. The concept is discussed in more detail below.

5 The maintenance of binary sex and gender in the descriptions of St. Vincent and Asughara somewhat contradict their later declaration of the inaccuracy of the concepts of male and female.

mere 15 pages. However, Ada's 'I' narrates the last chapter, and thereby occupies a significant rhetorical position, which is arguably as authoritative as the novel's opening chapter in the 'we' voice. Thus, the spirit 'we' and the human 'I' form frame the novel, as the narration moves—as it does in many works employing we-narration[6]—from 'we' to 'I.' However, this is by no means a linear progression.

The plot traces Ada's life from birth to her late twenties or early thirties. Ada is born as the daughter of Saachi, a Malaysian nurse, and Saul, a Catholic Nigerian doctor, and her name means not just "precious," but also "in its truest form, the egg of a python" (Emezi 2018, 9). As an ogbanje child, Ada is not only the child of her human parents, but also the child of goddess Ala: "Before a christ-induced amnesia struck the humans, it was well known that the python was sacred beyond reptile. It is the source of the stream, the flesh form of the god Ala, who is the earth herself, the judge and mother, the giver of law" (ibid.). Within Igbo mythology,[7] ogbanje are "children who come and go," due to the evil spirits that live inside these children (ibid.). Usually, an ogbanje child dies during childhood, only to return later in another child, typically a younger sibling. According to Igbo belief, this is often interpreted as a punishment for the child's mother in particular, for not adhering to conventional role expectations. However, Ada is an atypical ogbanje, because she survives into adulthood. During her childhood in Nigeria, Ada discovers and names the spirits inside of her:

> Our forms were young and indistinct, but this naming was a second birth, it sorted us into something she could see. The first of us, Smoke, was a complicated tray, swirled layers and depths, barely held together in a vaguely human shape. We lifted our fogged arms, clumsy fingers exploring a blank and drifting face. The second of us, Shadow, was a deep black, pressed malevolently against a wall, hints of other colors (mother color eyes, yellowed teeth) that never made it past the fullness of the night. The Ada made us and continued to feed us. Blood and belief. This is how the second madness began. (ibid., 42)

6 Examples of novels and short stories that move from 'we' to 'I' (either gradually or abruptly at the end) are Justin Torres's *We the Animals* (2011), Rebecca Brown's "Bread" (1994), Maxine Swann's *Flower Children* (2007), Joshua Ferris's *Then We Came to the End* (2006), and Ed Park's *Personal Days* (2008).

7 As well as in Yoruba mythology, where it is known as abiku. For readings of ogbanje in literature, see Aji and Ellsworth (1992) on Chinua Achebe's *Things Fall Apart*; Magaqa and Makombe (2021) on *Freshwater*.

Later, Ada gives "Smoke" and "Shadow" the names Asughara and St. Vincent. As is already alluded to in the above-quoted passage, the spirits are nonhuman and yet to a certain extent embodied, assuming a "vaguely human shape" with "fogged arms" and "clumsy fingers" (ibid.).

Later, Ada moves to the United States to attend college. During her late childhood in Nigeria and at college in the US, she repeatedly experiences sexualised violence. As a response, Asughara becomes stronger and protects Ada, by distancing her from her own body after she is sexually assaulted at age 18: "*She has come. She has come for me at last*" (ibid., 58). The stronger Asughara becomes, the more she is described as a separate self inside of Ada, greedy for blood, sex, and (self-)destruction. Yet, Asughara is differently embodied than humans, as she reminds herself: "Wait, is this how humans feel? To know that you are separate and special, to be individual and distinct? It's amazing. But I had to remind myself that I wasn't human or flesh. I was just a self, a little beast, if you like, locked inside Ada" (Emezi 2018, 70). Here, and throughout the entire novel, embodiment is repeatedly compared to imprisonment, which I will discuss more in detail below. The plot follows Ada for several years after college, during which she starts to self-harm, because "[o]nce there was blood, we subsided, temporarily sated" (ibid., 41) and attempts suicide, prompted by the spirits' wishes to "take her home" so "we could be with our brothersisters again" (ibid., 150).

Prompted once again by the spirit 'we' inside, near the end of the novel, Ada chooses to have chest surgery: "We were a fine balance, bigger than whatever the namings had made, and we wanted to reflect that, to change the Ada into us. Removing her breasts was only the first step" (ibid., 187). Finally, Ada reunites with her human mother Saachi, who eventually comes to terms with Ada's choice of the surgery and helps her during the recovery. Yet, more relevant than the reunification with her human mother is Ada's reconciliation with her several selves. While Ada's narrative is narrated mostly by the spirits, who are Ada and not-Ada at the same time, Ada assumes narrative agency at the end of the novel by assuming the narration and beginning to reconcile with the spirits.

Through the we-narration, *Freshwater* constructs a multiple self that represents a decolonial alternative to the language of (Western) psychology and psychiatry, while centering the Igbo myth of ogbanje. This ogbanje self is not only multiple, but also "shifting, and often self-contradictory" (de Lauretis 1986, 9). Furthermore, *Freshwater* describes the selves within a framework that resembles what Kara Keeling describes as "being as more-than-identity" in *Queer Times, Black Futures* (2019, 74). *Freshwater* centers indigenous knowledge and adapts the ogbanje myth to reflect non-binary conceptions of gender, as well as recent changes in theorisations of the self, which Keeling relates to reconceptualisations of Race and gender:

> The current shifts within Western philosophy to notions of ontogenesis, autopoiesis, and "sympoiesis" (a term Donna Haraway introduces to mean "making – with"), as well as to a variety of "new materialisms," signal, among other changes, a set of transformations in how racialization and engendering might be conceptualized. (ibid., 74)

Part of Ada's self-reconciliation is also the reconciliation with her non-normative, genderqueer embodiment, and the novel's we-narration thus not only concerns the multiple self but also the multiplicity and fluidity of gender, and thereby counteracts discourses of transnormativity.

## 2 Defining Transnormativity, Integrated Self, Narratable Self

Following Austin Johnson's definition, by transnormativity I mean a "hegemonic ideology that structures transgender experience, identification, and narratives into a hierarchy of legitimacy that is dependent upon a binary medical model and its accompanying standards, regardless of individual transgender people's interest in or intention to undertake medical pathways to transition" (Johnson 2016, 466). One of the effects of transnormativity is the creation of a hierarchy of "*realness*" or "*trans enough*" that privilege "*born in the wrong body*" and "*discovery*" narratives (ibid., 468) over narratives that portray gender and sex as fluid and socially constituted (cf. Butler 1993, 1–12; 1990, 22–33). It is exactly these narratives that *Freshwater* challenges, through the protagonist's surgery narrative and the we-narrator, who, as spirits, appear to exist beyond human conceptions of gender.

By integrated self, I mean an idea—and an ideal—of the self that equates mental health with the integration of all contradictory parts into one whole. Gabrielle Taylor and Raimond Gaita describe a person who has achieved self-integration as one who "'keeps his [sic] inmost self intact,' whose life is 'of a piece,' whose self is whole and integral" (1981, 143). This chapter is interested in the relationship between integration and narration in *Freshwater*. Is integration a state that is achieved *through* narration? Can it ever be fully achieved? Or is it a goal, an ideal, as I have suggested above, which can only be approximated through the narration of the self to the other? If this is so, the integrated self is perhaps best understood as a goal of the *narratable self*, which feminist philosopher Adriana Cavarero theorises in *Relating Narratives: Storytelling and Selfhood* (2000). Cavarero describes the narratable self as follows:

> Although she is immersed in this tale, the narratable self is not however the *product* of the life-story which the memory recounts. She is not, as the experts of narratology would say, a construction of the text, or the effect of the performative power of narration. She coincides rather with the uncontrollable narrative impulse of memory that produces the text, and is captured in the very text itself. As we know, the contents of this text are necessarily discontinuous – fragmentary, fleeting, and even casual – because the weaving-work of memory is itself discontinuous, fragmentary, fleeting – and casual. But the familiar sense of the narratable self is not a result of text itself, and neither does it lie in the construction of the story. It lies rather in a narrating impulse that is never in 'potentiality' but rather in 'actuality,' even when it refrains from 'producing' memories or 'reproducing' past occurrences. (2000, 34)

While other proponents of narrative personhood postulate that it is through narrative that an individual is constituted as a person (Schechtman 1996) or as a subject (Butler 2009), the above passage makes clear that Cavarero views the narratable self as one that does not require a narrative to *become* a narratable self.[8] Instead, the self that Cavarero describes is *already* narratable, prior to her life story being told by herself or by another person. This narrating impulse, is, for Cavarero, inseparable from the desire for "unity," which the telling of the life story expresses (2000, 43). She continues:

8 Cavarero's narratable self may seem extremely closely related to, if not interchangeable with, the concept of narrative identity, as formulated by Dan McAdams in *Power, Intimacy, and the Life Story* (1985), which gave rise to the thriving field of narrative psychology. Both the psychological concept 'narrative identity' and 'narratable self,' which relies on the philosophical tradition, emphasise the relevance of narration for the self. Both emphasise the 'doing' of selves and reject the notion of the self as 'essence.' Yet, the two concepts differ in one important regard. Cavarero's narratable self emphasises that the self (as narratable self) does not require the act of narration to become the narratable self. It is already a narratable self, prior to any narration. By contrast, the term narrative identity implies that identity emerges through narration. Cavarero counteracts precisely this logic in her conceptualisation of narratable self. Thereby, the concept admits the limits of language and rationality. In this difference lies the main reason for my choice of the term narratable self over narrative identity.

> The ontological status of the narratable self becomes distinguished, therefore, from the text of her story; even if it is irremediably mixed up with it. Such a distinction is neither separateness nor self-sufficiency, because the self cannot lie in perfect isolation outside, or beyond, the text of her story. This is not, however, a perfect coincidence, because the text of the story is inessential to the self-sensing [*assaporarsi*] of the self as narratable. Put simply, through the unreflecting knowledge of my 'sense-of-self' [*dell'assaporarmi*], I know that I have a story and that I consist in this story – even when I do not pause to recount it to myself, 're-living' through the memory some episodes through a sort of interior monologue. I could nevertheless not know myself to be narratable unless I were not always already interwoven into the autobiographical text of this story. Such an interweaving is indeed irreparable, and comes irremediably to the self as a reifying experience. (Cavarero 2000, 34)

In addition to emphasising the significance of unity and narration for the constitution of the self, the term narratable self in relation to *Freshwater* is helpful because, as the novel progresses, readers come closer to Ada as a subject, as opposed to "the Ada" as an object. If we accept Cavarero's premise, the novel thus traces Ada's life story, but does not produce her, since she is already a narratable self from the beginning, in the sense of Cavarero's conceptualisation of the narratable subject.

## 3 *Freshwater* and/as Africanjujuism

Emezi, who identifies as trans, non-binary and ogbanje, often emphasises the novel's autobiographical dimension. Accordingly, while *Freshwater* was published as fiction, Emezi has repeatedly spoken about the inaccuracy of the category:

> I wasn't writing it [*Freshwater*] as fiction, you know. With *Freshwater*, I knew that I was writing a memoir, but it was also my debut. And I really did not have faith in the industry that I would be able to get it published if I wrote it as nonfiction. It was already incredibly hard to get it published as fiction. (…) I don't think any publisher would have accepted this as nonfiction. It was too strange. And in a way, in order for me to be able to write *Dear Senthuran* [published as nonfiction/memoir], I needed to be my own source by having *Freshwater* exist first." (Emezi 2021, par. 12)

This chapter reads *Freshwater* as an example of *Africanjujuism*, which defies any clear-cut distinction between fiction and non-fiction. Since author Nnedi Okarafor coined the term in 2019 in order to account for her own writing, Africanjujuism has started to emerge as a lesser known, adjacent term to Africanfuturism in literary scholarship. Okorafor introduced the terms Africanfuturism and Africanjujuism to position her own writing vis-à-vis Afrofuturism. As Okorafor explains, "Africanfuturism is a sub-category of science fiction. Africanjujuism is a subcategory of fantasy that respectfully acknowledges the seamless blend of true existing African spiritualities and cosmologies with the imaginative" (2019). The term Afrojujuism has been adopted by relatively few scholars thus far, and it is mostly used in conjunction with Afrofuturism and Africanfuturism.[9] While Hope Wabuke (2020) suggests that Emezi's works blend Africanfuturism and Afrojujuism, Ainehi Edoro (2021) deems *Freshwater* a clear representative of Afrojujuism. In agreement with Edoro, I suggest that Africanjujuism is a useful lens through which to read *Freshwater*, because it

> involves a form of storytelling through which fantasy comes organically out of the depiction of everyday life and cultural experiences. [...] When certain writers like [Ben] Okri write about mythological beings that have lived a thousand lives or when Akwaeke Emezi writes about a character who is Ogbanje, these are not contrived literary inventions. 'It is not,' as Okorafor puts it, 'fantasy for fantasy's sake.' They are attempts to capture a fantasy that is 'more real than the everyday.' (Edoro 2021)

It is this "more real than the everyday" that is central to *Freshwater*. The novel does not describe the spirits as *fantasy* in the sense of something that is *not real*. Instead, the spirits are integrated into the real and the everyday of Ada's life, and they are as real as the other parts of her experience. In other words, *Freshwater* integrates the spirit 'we' in the real and the everyday, suspending Ada's experience between spirit terms and human terms. In addition, *Freshwater* as an Africanjujuist work challenges the separation between fiction and non-fiction. Through this generic hybridity, the novel expands past the limits of Okorafor's definition of Africanjujuism as fiction. Reading *Freshwater* as an Africanjujuist work means emphasising the novel's decolonial impulse. This consists in centering African epistemologies and simultaneously decentering Western (neo)colonial epistemologies.

---

9 For a study of Africanjujuism, Africanfuturism and Afrofuturism in Hollywood films, see Simons 2021.

As Kelsey Ann McFaul notes, "In Caribbean slang, 'freshwater' refers to someone who affects an accent after a short or non-existent visit to a colonial metropole" (2021, 56). Based on this meaning of freshwater, McFaul describes Emezi's novel as a "homecoming" after a period of "distancing from African realities" (ibid.). However, I suggest that instead of looking at Nigeria and Africa in a nostalgic or sentimental manner that understands homecoming in the sense of a *return to*, *Freshwater* creates its own version of African cosmology that combines a turn to African epistemologies with an outlook that reflects José Esteban Muñoz's queer futurity, understanding queerness as "not simply a being but a doing for and toward the future" (Muñoz 2009, 1).

## 4 Madness and Ogbanje

Unlike McFaul, several reviewers of *Freshwater* read the novel as an account of mental illness, encoded in the language of Igbo mythology, and offer their own diagnosis of the main character Ada. Heather Hewett, for example, reads Ada's story as an account of "trauma" in *The Women's Review of Books* (Hewett 2018). Tariro Mzezewa from *The New York Times*, on the other hand, makes sense of *Freshwater* as a mental health narrative of "dissociative identity disorder" and "manic depression" (Mzezewa 2018). Ayòbámi Adébáyò, in *The Guardian*, reads the we-narration as a successful tool for displaying Ada's different facets of herself, which, in Adébáyò's view, she is finally able to integrate in the novel's last chapter which is narrated by the 'I' of Ada (and not 'we' or Asughara, which fill the majority of the novel's pages) (Adébáyò 2018). Thus, Adébáyò seems to interpret the final chapter as an overcoming of the 'we' and the sign for a successful integration and individuation process, writing that the last chapter's narration retains aspects of Asughara's voice and the 'we,' but is ultimately a "manifestation of Ada's realisation that she is irrevocably an amalgamation of all her varied and even divergent selves" (ibid.). Finally, Katy Waldman from *The New Yorker* reads *Freshwater* as a "study in dysphoria," by which she does not refer to gender dysphoria but to "the more nebulous pain of being imprisoned in a physical form, of losing your wraith-like ability to evade categori[s]ation" (Waldman 2018).

Yet, *Freshwater* does not incorporate a single diagnosis that could be found in the DSM-5, the current edition of the American Psychiatric Association's Diagnostic and Statistical Manual of Mental Disorders (2022), despite Ada's brief encounters with mental health professionals: a therapist, a psychiatrist, and a medical doctor who performs her chest surgery. Instead of being framed as a story of mental illness, then, Ada's story is introduced as a "litany of madness"

(Emezi 2018, 14). Through the term *madness*, the novel evokes a discourse that precedes the advent of psychiatry as a discipline, and at the same time lets readers decide between adopting a psychiatric lens and diagnosing Ada, or succumbing to the alternative discourse of Igbo cosmology, which is interwoven with discourses on transgender identity beyond the binary. This narrative strategy of interweaving Igbo mythology with transgender studies language results on the one hand in a de-familiarisation of psychiatric discourses on dissociative identity disorder or suicidal tendencies and in a familiarisation of the ogbanje, through the telling of the coming to terms with the liminality of ogbanje through the tropes of transgender transitioning and trauma, which are likely more familiar to readers.

As Michel Foucault writes in *Madness and Civilization*, madness is a term that precedes the advent of psychiatry and the transformation from madness into mental illness. He notes that the

> constitution of madness as a mental illness, at the end of the eighteenth century, affords the evidence of a broken dialogue, posits the separation as already effected, and thrusts into oblivion all those stammered, imperfect words without fixed syntax in which the exchange between madness and reason was made. The language of psychiatry, which is a monologue of reason about madness, has been established only on the basis of such a silence. (Foucault 1965, x–xi)

Foucault sees the dichotomy madness/reason as foundational to the self-conception of Western culture (ibid., xi). This appears to be a stance that *Freshwater* adopts, when the we-narrator declares:

> This is all, ultimately, a litany of madness—the colours of it, the sounds it makes in heavy nights, the chirping of it across the shoulder of the morning. Think of brief insanities that are in you, not just the ones that blossomed as you grew into taller, more sinful versions of yourself, but the ones you were born with, tucked behind your liver. Take us, for instance. (Emezi 2018, 14)

Yet later, the 'we' revokes their framing of the story as one of madness:

> Earlier, when we said she went mad, we lied. She has always been sane. It's just that she was contaminated with us, a godly parasite with many heads, roaring inside the marble room of her mind. Everyone knows the

> stories of hungry gods, ignored gods, biter, scorned, and vengeful gods. First duty, feed your gods. If they live (like we do) inside your body, find a way, get creative, show them the red of your faith, of your flesh; quiet the voices with the lullaby of the altar. It's not as if you can escape us—where would you run to? (ibid., 41)

The we-narrator thus reveals their unreliability through the admission of a lie. Yet, this confession is also unreliable. At the same time, this direct address of the reader reveals the instability of madness as a concept. The language of 'contamination,' however, reframes madness as a result of possession. By doing so, the novel recites religious and early scientific discourses of madness and steers further away from contemporary psychiatric diagnoses such as dissociative identity disorder and gender dysphoria. At the same time, "madness" is intertwined with Igbo ontology, which explains madness as a result of being an ogbanje. Being an ogbanje is a form of possession, by separate deities who depend on their host's body for survival. Yet, these deities are often called by their "brothersisters" to the other side, the world of the deities. This results in suicidal tendencies of their host, who, as an ogbanje, occupies a liminal space between being 'us' and not 'us.'

Throughout the course of the story, the spirit 'we' change their narrative, which makes them an unreliable collective narrator. This unreliability mostly concerns the relationship between Ada and the spirits, and the assessment of Ada as an example of "madness" (Emezi 2018, 5, 14, 20, 33, 42) or "completely sane" but "contaminated" (ibid., 41). At the outset of the narrative, 'we' begin by prefacing Ada's life story as a "litany of madness" (ibid., 14). The spirit 'we' then proceeds by recounting in chronological order the first "madnesses" in Ada's life. The origin of all madnesses is the porousness of the border between life and death:

> We came from somewhere—everything does. When the transition is made from spirit to flesh, the gates are meant to be closed. […]
>
> By the time she (our body) struggled out into the world, slick and louder than a village of storms, the gates were left open. We should have been anchored in her by then, asleep inside her membranes and synched with her mind. That would have been the safest way. But since the gates were open, not closed against remembrance, we became confused. We were at one old and newborn. We were her and yet not. We were not conscious but we were alive—in fact, the main problem was that we were a distinct *we* instead of being fully and just *her*. (ibid., 5)

These open gates are also later the explanation for Ada's suicide attempts, and the separation between "us" and "her" serve as an alternative discourse to describing Ada's experience of a dis-integrated self in the Western medical-psychological terminology. The narrative describes this dis-integration as a continuous struggle.

The we-narrator is not interested in dis-ambiguating the relationship between madness and ogbanje, and to what extent it is the myth of ogbanje that functions as a metaphor to help readers understand the experience of what *Freshwater* names "madness" (instead of dis/ability or mental illness). Conversely, it may also be that "madness" functions as a metaphor for the experience of being ogbanje. Finally, both madness and ogbanje can be read as metaphors that bridge the gap between language and the experience of multiplicity. I am using the term multiplicity instead of fragmentation, because fragmentation suggests the existence of a prior whole, which was shattered into pieces that can be put (back) together to restore the whole. *Freshwater* avoids the perspective of fragmentation, which would conjure humanities and social sciences discourses of the late 20th century, which diagnosed the postmodern self as empty or fragmented (cf. Vassilieva 2016, 49–58). This is inevitably a perspective of lack, which *Freshwater* questions. Instead, the novel describes the experience of being one and many simultaneously, which for Ada comes both with an intensity of life and a closeness to death.

On the other hand, Emezi expands the established meanings of ogbanje as liminal beings by extending the meanings of ogbanje to gender identity and utilising it to make sense of Ada's non-binary gender identity. As they say in an interview, Emezi's portrayal of the ogbanje experience was perceived as "heresy" and "blasphemy" by some Nigerian critics of *Freshwater*, because Emezi's portrayal of ogbanje does not always correspond to existing criteria for ogbanje (Emezi 2021). Building on Maria Lugone's theory of the coloniality of gender, Tina Magaqa and Rodwell Makombe convincingly argue that *Freshwater* adapts the concept of ogbanje to show that it "has room to accommodate difference and/or alternative identities/sexualities"—a space that opens up an alternative to the binaries of the colonial gender system (Magaqa and Makombe 2021, 27).

Corresponding with the novel's challenging of binaries and demarcations, the lines between the spirits own, separate embodiment within Ada and their being Ada are often blurry. The novel describes the spirits' separation from Ada within Ada as an error in the system: "We should have blended into the Ada when she was born, but instead there was a stretch of emptiness between us, bitter like kola, a sweep of nothing. A space that has no place in a mind" (Emezi

2018, 35–36). Especially the spirit Asughara appears as a separately embodied character, as the following passage shows: "I sank my fists into the marble and split her head open with a crashing migraine, and it worked. She never went back to that therapist again" (ibid., 150; my emphasis). Here, Asughara appears as a separately embodied spirit inside Ada's mind. Therefore, it is not only her aims and intentions that separate her from Ada, but also her body within Ada's body. At the same time, Asughara cannot exist without Ada, because Ada is a vessel for the spirits. Accordingly, Asughara complains: "You don't know what it's like to share a life and a body …" (ibid., 146). Thus, paradoxically, the spirits are portrayed as simultaneously separately embodied and part of Ada's embodied self.

The rules that apply to human characters do not apply to the spirit characters, as the spirits represent extremes and are rather static beings that do not change their motivations and goals. The spirit "we," and Asughara in particular, view embodiment as "being sentenced to meat" (ibid., 187), and adopt different strategies to make this experience, which they perceive as a punishment, less painful. One strategy is Asughara's defiant, hedonistic diving into the flesh, which is accompanied by self-destructive tendencies and episodes of reckless behavior:

> If we were trapped in a body, then we would do bodily things. We painted the Ada's mouth and lined her eyes with night, and we went out with Asughara on a long and relaxed leash. It was easy, as it always was. (…) The flesh was flesh, and for a little while, we could forget all the hurt, all the weight of over two decades of embodiment destroying us. (Emezi 2018, 185)

The equation of "embodiment" with "hurt," "weight" and "destroying" in this passage shows particularly Asughara's vexed relationship with Ada as the spirits' vessel. The expression "[t]he flesh was flesh" recalls Hortense Spiller's theorisation of *flesh* in the context of black women's subjecthood and its representation. Spillers argues that 'flesh' is central to understanding black women's experiences and representations of black womanhood as historically conditioned and transgenerational (ibid., 67). For Spillers, 'flesh' points to the denigration of black women through slavery, experiences of physical and sexualised violence and being denied the status of a free subject. Underlying this theorisation is a hierarchy between 'body' and 'flesh': "before the 'body' there is the 'flesh,' that zero degree of social conceptualisation that does not escape concealment under the brush of discourse, or the reflexes of iconography" (ibid., 67). Thus, the "flesh" is Asughara's denial of Ada's subject status, and at the same time a temporary liberation from human experience as one where body and mind cannot be separated in a Cartesian manner.[10]

## 5 Against Transnormativity

Another strategy is Ada's bodily transformation, to adapt to the collective wishes of the spirits:

> And with Saint Vincent, our little grace, taking the front more than he used to, the body, as it was, was becoming unsatisfactory, too feminine, too reproductive. That form had worked for Asughara—those breasts with the large, dark areolae and nipples she could lift to her mouth—but we were more than her and we were more than the saint. We were a fine balance, bigger than whatever the namings had made, and we wanted to reflect that, to change the Ada into us. Removing her breasts was only the first step. (Emezi 2018, 187)

In order to access surgery, Ada enters the medical system and is treated as a transgender patient who wants to transition from female to male, even though these categories are inadequate. Thus, the spirits' we-narration offers a way of explaining Ada's nonconformity to mainstream legal and cultural narratives about being transgender, which are subject to the binary system, and only leave female-to-male transition and male-to-female transition as choices. The indeterminacy of *Freshwater*'s spirit voice challenges these transnormative narratives and undermine the logic of *becoming who you truly are* through a surgical, or several surgical procedures. The logic of 'becoming who you truly are' implies the existence of an end point to a journey, at which one will have arrived after transitioning, and this end point is either 'male' or 'female.' It thereby leaves intact the false equation between gender identity and embodiment, implying that the most successful transition is that after which the person can 'pass' as a cisgender individual. Ada's transition, however, does not comply with this narrative, because Ada does not want to undergo chest surgery to look more masculine.

Instead of explaining her diversion from the expected narrative of female-to-male transition, however, Ada limits her interaction with the psychologist

10 Cartesian dualism refers to "the doctrine that mind and matter exist as distinct entities" (OED).

to the bare minimum that she needs in order to get clearance for the surgery as quickly as possible:

> The Ada used a therapist to assist with our carving plan and we discovered that human had medical words—terms for what we were trying to do—that there were procedures, gender reassignment, transitioning. We knew what we were planning was right. Even the things that the Ada used to dislike about her body had mellowed out once we let Saint Vincent run. (Emezi 2018, 189)

Thus, the spirits temporarily adopt the psychiatric language which is required to carry out their "carving plan." This language also comes with a wrought history of psychiatric diagnostic criteria that until recently pathologised diversions from the binary system of sex and gender. Not only in the medical realm but also in Ada's friends' reactions do narratives of transnormativity surface:

> Before the surgery, the Ada had told her friends that she couldn't wait for when she could wear dresses again. They were confused. They stared at her bound chest and boy clothes.
>
> "Why would you go more feminine without boobs? They asked. "Most people get it done to be more masculine."
>
> The Ada shrugged and we moved in her shoulders. It was simple how we saw ourself, dresses creeping up the thigh, gashing open at the front to show chest bone—tulle and lace and clouds of clothes. Just like how having long hair weighing down our back made us want to wear buttons up to our throat, men's sleeves rolled up our biceps, handsome, handsome things. [...]
>
> We have understood what we are, the places we are suspended in, between the inaccurate concepts of male and female, between the us and the brother sisters slavering on the other side. (ibid., 192–193)

Here, the we-narration becomes a singular 'we' by referring to themselves as "ourself" (ibid., 192). In the context of gender constructions, this singular 'we' could be seen as a complementary construction to the singular 'they' used by non-binary or genderqueer individuals. Like the singular they, the singular 'we' of *Freshwater* constructs an alternative to the gender binary masculine/feminine. While St. Vincent and Ashughara are described as masculine and feminine respectively, they are both liminal beings inside of their host, Ada. This liminality affects Ada's gender expression and identity insofar as she no longer exclusively presents herself or identifies as feminine. At the same time,

Ada does not aspire to the label 'masculine.' Through her friends' reactions, however, Ada is confronted with the expectation that someone undergoes chest surgery to better 'do masculinity.' *Freshwater* rejects this, making room for the possibility of genderqueer trans embodiment. However, it is not the human Ada who opens up this possibility, but the ogbanje spirits. They declare,

> This was our body and it would become what we wanted, now that the reconfiguring was done. [...] We had been the same since the first birth, through the second naming, the third molting. To make the vessel look a little more like us—that was the extent of our intent. We have understood what we are, the places we are suspended in, between the inaccurate concepts of male and female, between the us and the brothersisters slavering on the other side. (Emezi 2018, 192–193)

By attributing the being beyond the binary to the spirits and not to the human, the novel may be seen as positing being nonbinary transgender as somehow *outside* of human experience. At the same time, it may be seen as undermining human agency (cf. Hewett 2018). Because the spirits are taking control of Ada's body, human terms like transgender and nonbinary do not apply to them; human terms only become necessary when Ada has to interact with medical and psychological professionals. Potentially, relegating the accountability for trans and genderqueer embodiment to the spirits could be seen as a narrative strategy that invalidates the very human experiences of transgender nonbinary individuals. At the same time, through the spirits, *Freshwater* provides an alternative to familiar psychological and medical discourses that could potentially be seen as empowering, and which undermines discourses of transnormativity as it moves towards a strengthening of Ada's agency. It is not my interest to posit one or the other as true; the novel lets these possibilities coexist.

## 6 Towards Unity

In *Freshwater*'s last chapter, which is written from Ada's I-perspective, the 'we' briefly appears, expressing a counter-voice to the discourse of an integrated self as a whole self. Yet at the same time, the validity of self-integration is partially reaffirmed, as 'we' are subsumed into Ada, through an inversion of possessive pronouns: "she is not ours, we are hers" (Emezi 2018, 215). If at the beginning of the novel, "the main problem was that we were a distinct *we* instead of being fully and just *her*" (ibid., 5), the movement towards "she is not ours, we are hers" (ibid., 215) signals a movement towards a resolution of the initially stated "problem," through self-integration and the narration of Ada's self that is no longer predominantly determined by Asughara and St. Vincent. The question whom Ada's body belongs to is negotiated throughout the entire novel, and the chest surgery is a crucial marker of the spirits' making Ada's body their own. It seems, then, that beyond the reconciliation of the spirit selves, there is not separate human 'I' that 'belongs' to Ada. The 'I' of Ada always contains the 'we' of the spirits. It is the reconciliation with this aspect of being an ogbanje that opens up the path to an integrated self for Ada.

At the same time, the surgery also signals an alignment between Ada's gender identity and her embodiment, both of which defy transnormative notions of doing gender. The surgery thus contributes to Ada's self-integration and ends some of the unease that she experiences. The last chapter suggests that the struggle between 'we' and 'I' has been appeased, and Ada is finally able to say "I." In this regard, Freshwater follows the coming-of-age narrative convention which consists in the protagonist's acceptance of their various contradictory personality traits and the formation of one coherent, narratable self. I therefore disagree with Tina Magaqa and Rodwell Makombe's claim that *Freshwater* "debunks Western philosophies such as existentialism which depict humans as independent beings" (Magaqa and Makombe 2021, 34). In my reading, this is only partially achieved, as the ending at least partially confirms the centrality of the separate and singular subject, albeit Ada is a subject that is one *and* many, and a subject that is dependent on others.

In its conclusion, *Freshwater* appears to designate ogbanje as the stable referent and madness and the concepts of transgender and non-binary[11] as bridges to help readers understand ogbanje. The novel therefore affirms the necessity of centering Igbo cosmology in a move of centering indigenous knowledge. As Emezi phrases it in an interview with Saidiya Hartman, they conceive of both the protagonist Ada and of themselves within a framework of "spirit first" (Emezi 2021). This means a view of Ada and themselves as primarily spirit, and then human. Thus, the spirit assumes the primary position, while human language is only a means of communicating the spirit experience. While some critics seem to understand ogbanje as the metaphor, the novel plays with the reader's preconceived notions regarding what is 'real' experience (which a mental health narrative written in mimetic language would conform to) and what belongs to the world of an "indigenous fairy tale" (Waldman 2018). Thus, Ada, living as spirit and human simultaneously, concludes: "I am my others;

11 Though the terms *non-binary* and *transgender* do not directly appear in the novel.

we are one and we are many. Everything gets clearer with each day, as long as I listen. With each morning, I am less afraid" (Emezi 2018, 226).

As the continuous struggle of being disparate selves begins to resolve itself, the integration that Ada describes is thus paradoxically one that leaves intact the dis-integration of being ogbanje, which means being one and many simultaneously. The increased clarity that Ada experiences signals a movement towards resolution, and a confirmation of the psychological discourse that asserts the necessity for an integrated and narratable self. On the other hand, Ada's integrated self is one that is never just one, it is always many. The we-narration allows the novel to express this ambiguity, between affirming and rejecting pre-conceived notions of the psychiatric subject and the humanist liberal self. The ogbanje self is nevertheless a "whole" self. By Ada's coming to terms with her ogbanje self, the novel ultimately validates the notion of the narratable and unified subject, as the movement towards unity and integration demonstrates. Ada can finally speak as an 'I' and is no longer spoken for by the spirit 'we.' Instead, the 'we' is incorporated into her ogbanje 'I.' This construction of a stable subject, which remains a prerequisite for living a meaningful life, is asserted in *Freshwater* through the I-narration of Ada.

## Works Cited

Adébáyò, Ayòbámi. "Freshwater by Akwaeke Emezi Review: A Remarkable Debut." *The Guardian*, 15 Nov. 2018. https://www.theguardian.com/books/2018/nov/15/freshwater-akwaeke-emezi-book-review-nigeria.

Aji, Aron, and Kirstin Lynne Ellsworth. "Ezinma: The 'Ogbanje' Child in Achebe's 'Things Fall Apart.'" *College Literature*, vol 19/20, no. 3/1, 1992, pp. 170–75.

American Psychiatric Association. *Diagnostic and Statistical Manual of Mental Disorders*. 5th ed., Text Revision, American Psychiatric Publishing, 2022, https://doi.org/10.1176/appi.books.9780890425787.

Bekhta, Natalya. We-Narratives: Collective Storytelling in Contemporary Fiction. Ohio State UP, 2020.

Bekhta, Natalya. "We-Narratives: The Distinctiveness of Collective Narration." *Narrative*, vol. 25, no. 2, 2017, pp. 164–81.

Brown, Rebecca. "Bread." *The Penguin Book of Lesbian Short Stories*, ed. Margaret Reynolds, Penguin Press, 1994, pp. 219–39.

Butler, Judith. *Bodies That Matter. On the Discursive Limits of "Sex."* Routledge, 1993.

Butler, Judith. *Gender Trouble: Feminism and the Subversion of Identity*. Routledge, [1990] 2014.

Butler, Judith. *Giving an Account of Oneself*. Fordham UP, 2009.

Cavarero, Adriana. *Relating Narratives: Storytelling and Selfhood.* Translated by Paul A. Kottman, Routledge, 2000.

de Lauretis, Teresa. "Feminist Studies/Critical Studies: Issues, Terms, and Contexts." *Feminist Studies/Critical Studies*, ed. Teresa de Lauretis, Palgrave, 1986, pp. 1–19.

"dualism, n." *OED Online,* Oxford UP, September 2023, https://doi.org/10.1093/OED/5496357852.

Edoro, Ainehi. "What is Africanjujuism?" *Brittle Paper*, 7 July 2021, www.brittlepaper.com/2021/07/what-is-africanjujuism.

Emezi, Akwaeke. *Freshwater*. Faber, 2018.

Emezi, Akwaeke. "Spiritfirst: Akwaeke Emezi with Saidiya Hartman." *The Schomberg Center Literary Festival*, New York Public Library, Interview by Saidiya Hartman, 8 June 2021, www.nypl.org/events/programs/2021/06/08/spiritfirst-akwaeke-emezi-saidiya-hartman.

Fludernik, Monika. "Let Us Tell You Our Story: We-Narration and Its Pronominal Peculiarities." *Pronouns in Literature: Positions and Perspectives in Language*, eds. Alison Gibbons and Andrea Macrae, Palgrave Macmillan, 2018, pp. 171–92.

Foucault, Michel. *Madness and Civilization: A History of Insanity in the Age of Reason.* Translated by Richard Howard, Random House, 1965.

Hewett, Heather. "Litany of Madness." Review of *Freshwater*, by Akwaeke Emezi. *Women's Review of Books*, vol. 35, no. 4, 2018, p. 15.

Johnson, Austin H. "Transnormativity: A New Concept and Its Validation through Documentary Film About Transgender Men." *Sociological Inquiry*, vol. 86, no. 4, 2016, pp. 465–91.

Keeling, Kara. *Queer Times, Black Futures*. New York UP, 2019.

Lanser, Susan S. *Fictions of Authority: Women Writers and Narrative Voice.* Cornell UP, 1992.

Magaqa, Tina, and Rodwell Makombe. "Decolonising Queer Sexualities: A Critical Reading of the *Ogbanje* Concept in Akwaeke Emezi's *Freshwater* (2018)." *African Studies Quarterly*, vol. 20, no. 3, 2021, pp. 24–39.

McAdams, Dan. *Power, Intimacy, and the Life Story: Personal Inquiries into Identity.* Guilford, [1998] 1988.

McFaul, Kelsey Ann. "'One Foot on the Other Side': An Africanfuturist Reading of Irenosen Okojie's *Butterfly Fish* (2015) and Akwaeke Emezi's *Freshwater* (2018)." *Feminist Africa*, vol. 2, no. 2, 2021, pp. 47–61.

Muñoz, José Esteban. *Cruising Utopia: The Then and There of Queer Futurity.* New York UP, 2009.

Mzezewa, Tariro. "In This Debut Novel, a College Student Hears Voices." Review of *Freshwater*, by Akwaeke Emezi. *The New York Times*, 26 Feb. 2018, www.nytimes.com/2018/02/26/books/review/freshwater-akwaeke-emezi.html.

Okorafor, Nnedi. "Africanfuturism Defined." *Nnedi's Wahala Zone Blog*, 19 Oct. 2019, http://nnedi.blogspot.com.

Richardson, Brian. *Unnatural Voices: Extreme Narration in Modern and Contemporary Fiction*. Ohio State UP, 2006.

Schechtman, Marya. *The Constitution of Selves*. Cornell UP, 1996.

Simons, Nicholas Nathaniel Kweku-Egyir. "Expanding Spaces: Examining the Landscape of Afrofuturism, Africanfuturism, and Africanjujuism in Hollywood." Master's Thesis, African Studies, University of California, Los Angeles, 2021. *UCLA eScholarship,* doi: https://escholarship.org/uc/item/5d73q4p0.

Spillers, Hortense J. "Mama's Baby, Papa's Maybe: An American Grammar Book." *Diacritics*, vol. 17, no. 2, 1987, pp. 64–81.

Taylor, Gabriele, and Raimond Gaita. "Integrity." *Proceedings of the Aristotelian Society, Supplementary Volumes* 55, 1981, pp. 143–76.

Vassilieva, Julia. *Narrative Psychology: Identity, Transformation and Ethics*. Palgrave, 2016.

Wabuke, Hope. "Afrofuturism, Africanfuturism, and the Language of Black Speculative Literature." *Los Angeles Review of Books*, 27 Aug. 2020, https://lareviewofbooks.org/article/afrofuturism-africanfuturism-and-the-language-of-black-speculative-literature.

Waldman, Katy. "A Startling Début Novel Explores the Freedom of Being Multiple." Review of *Freshwater*, by Akwaeke Emezi. *The New Yorker*, 26 Feb. 2018, www.newyorker.com/books/page-turner/akwaeke-emezi-startling-debut-novel-explores-the-freedom-of-being-multiple.

CHAPTER 14

# Who Sees and Who Speaks with Our Head? Non-normative Bodies, Minds, and Acts of Narration

*Ellen Peel*

> I saw him lie down with his head—our head—between the … tendrils …
>
> BRIN 2002, 458

## 1 Introduction

Imagine a novel where one narrator can make a duplicate narrator who can in turn recount a narrative about both of them, including about the first one's head, which in a sense belongs to the second as well. This passage exemplifies what I will be exploring: the kind of narrative that is non-normative partly because it is told by a character whose body is constructed. When a narrative concerns a *body* that is constructed, that body often houses a non-normative *mind*, with their interplay often creating a non-normative *act of narration*. I aim to show that extremely non-normative bodies and minds can play a major role in extremely non-normative acts of narration, and that understanding this dynamic can also enrich our understanding of more normative bodies, minds, and acts of narration.[1] Extremely non-normative texts repay study on their own account but can also defamiliarise more normative ones, helping lay bare what is ordinarily taken for granted. Taking as examples three science fiction texts narrated by their protagonists, I look briefly at *Bone Dance* (1991), by American author Emma Bull, where one body narrates; I spend more time on "The Mask" (1976), by Polish author Stanisław Lem, where multiple bodies narrate; and then I concentrate on *Kiln People* (2002), by American author David Brin, where many bodies narrate.

1 I am grateful to Elizabeth Bush-Peel for her comments on this essay.

 | DOI:10.1163/9789004519886_016

This study brings together a number of strands from narratology and other theories. My focus on bodies draws on Daniel Punday's corporeal narratology (2003)[2] and is in part a response to Susan S. Lanser's call for narratology to give embodiment the attention it deserves (Lanser 2020).[3] My focus on minds refers to cognitive narratology, considering "mind" to include not only thought but also beliefs, desires, and the like. In relating bodies to minds, I am concerned with the concept of embodied cognition (see Herman 2010, 165); I refer sometimes to "body," sometimes to "mind," and sometimes to "body/mind," as shorthand for "body, mind, both separately, or both in interaction." My focus on acts of narration goes back to Gérard Genette's classic questions "Who sees?" and "Who speaks?"—by which he analyses what is commonly called point of view (1980, 186). Among bodies, minds, and acts of narration, I focus on those that are "non-normative," by which I imply no value judgment. I simply mean elements that are, accurately or not, considered to be uncommon or impossible in a given context (in this case, the secular West in the last fifty years). And among non-normative bodies, minds, and acts of narration, I focus on the subset composed of "unnatural" ones because, lying very far from normative ones, they highlight the issues at stake and because unnatural narratology offers particularly helpful analytical tools.

How does unnaturalness relate to narratives of the constructed body? Some of the most fascinating constructed-body narratives are unnatural, especially when they disrupt the questions "Who sees?" and "Who speaks?" because the "who" is unnatural—the texts are focalised or narrated, wholly or in part, by a character whose body has been constructed. All constructed-body narratives are self-referential because they remind us that the body of the text itself is constructed, and all unnatural narratives are self-referential because, as we shall see, their dialectic with realist conventions highlights narrative conventions more broadly. Thus, the rare and compelling narratives in which the constructed body overlaps with unnaturalness are doubly self-referential. After I give more detailed definitions of "constructed body" and of "unnatural," we can examine where the two types overlap.

In referring to a body as "constructed," I mean either physically or mentally, though this study concentrates on the physical.[4] Physical construction can be

---

2 Except for unreliable narrators, when Punday discusses narrators, he usually emphasises disembodied, magisterial third-person figures, unlike the very embodied first-person ones I examine (e.g., 2003, 176, 162–63).

3 My attention to the narrator and focalisation addresses two questions on Lanser's "preliminary list," and it would be rewarding to apply over half of her other questions to the narratives I analyse (Lanser 2020, 127–28).

4 For more detail on the concept of constructed bodies, see Peel 2009.

a modification, as in Hans Christian Andersen's "Little Mermaid," or can be construction from scratch, as in Mary Shelley's *Frankenstein*. The constructed bodies in those narratives, along with the ones I study here, would count among what Lisa Zunshine calls the "*counterontological* entities who straddle the respective domains of artifacts and living beings" (2008, 75)—entities that intrigue us because they challenge our ordinary categories (ibid., 53).[5] As Punday says, "The contrast between [human] bodies and nonbodies is an especially rich but relatively unexplored area of narrative poetics" (2003, 59). Constructed bodies often introduce unsettling and thought-provoking themes, such as the ethics of creation; the intersection of race, gender, and disability—be they literal or metaphorical; the role of passing, memory, and self-awareness in identity; and the difficulty of figuring out whether a constructed-body character is exercising free will. (These themes haunt the texts I examine, but this study can only touch on them.)

"Unnatural texts" are "texts that feature strikingly impossible or antimimetic elements" (Alber et al. 2013, 1);[6] they narrate something very strange or narrate something very strangely.[7] While conventional narratology has generally concentrated on mimetic narratives that are conventionally narrated, unnatural narratology has turned to antimimetic or unconventionally narrated narratives, such as postmodern texts.[8] Unnatural narratives are summed up in Brian Richardson's comment about innovative authors: they "problemati[s]e each term of" the ordinary definition of narrative as "someone relating a set of events to someone else" (2006, 5). In this study I draw on an essay in which Jan Alber, Richardson, and other unnatural narrative theorists give an overview of their project (Alber et al. 2010). Their essay locates unnaturalness in three realms: storyworlds, minds, and acts of narration.

Where do narratives of the constructed body overlap with unnatural narratives? In terms of storyworld, I focus on bodies that are "strikingly impossible" and thus unnatural. It might seem that every text about a constructed body would be unnatural, but Long John Silver's wooden leg does not make *Treasure Island* an unnatural novel. Nevertheless, many constructed-body texts are

5 While I admire Zunshine's overall analysis, I am agnostic about the evolutionary roots of these categories, and I would not link "essentialism" so tightly to living beings and "functionalism" so tightly to artifacts.

6 Since 2010, narratologists have diverged somewhat in their definitions of "unnatural," but this one conveys their common ground. Note that the somewhat misleading term "does not designate any social practices or behavior as natural or unnatural" (Alber et al. 2013, 4).

7 As I have argued elsewhere, there is no universally valid definition of strangeness (Peel 2021).

8 Lanser warns that a "corporeal narratology risks turning characters into living people" (2020, 123–24); narratives with unnatural elements can help guard against that risk.

indeed unnatural in terms of their impossible storyworlds, especially within fantasy or science fiction.

The second unnatural realm involves the mind, which may belong to a character, a narrator, or a character who is also a narrator (Alber et al. 2010, 120). Unnatural minds confound Alan Palmer's notion of the "continuing-consciousness frame" that "the reader uses in order to read a character's mind" (Alber et al. 2010, 121). The reference to (metaphorical) mind-reading alludes to "theory of mind," one term cognitive scientists use "to describe the cognitive adaptation that allows us to consider a broad variety of mental states—thoughts, beliefs, desires, intentions—as underlying our own and other people's behavior" (Zunshine 2008, 58). Some constructed bodies do have a continuing consciousness, but even that may lack stretches of consciousness that readers ordinarily take for granted: since Frankenstein's creature, for example, lacks a childhood, he lacks childhood memories. Other constructed bodies, such as that of the Little Mermaid (Andersen 1980, 49, 56) have curious breaks in consciousness, especially at the moment when construction occurs.

In the third realm of the unnatural, "[u]nnatural acts of narration include physically, logically, mnemonically, or psychologically impossible enunciations" (Alber et al. 2010, 124). To understand them, I employ Genette's terminology for point of view, as explained by Lanser: "Genette carefully distinguishes, as many critics have not, between voice ("who speaks?") and vision ("who sees?"). [I.e., in addition to voice,] a separate set of indices is necessary for describing the mode of vision or 'focali[s]ation' the narrative entails" (Lanser 1981, 37; cf. Lanser 2020, 122). The persona who speaks is looking out at the world through the eyes of the persona who sees, and often that seeing also includes looking into the mind of that focalising persona. (I will be following the common narratological practice of using "who sees" to mean more broadly "who perceives," and "who speaks" to mean more broadly "who expresses her/himself" [see Genette 1988]). Although "the persona who 'sees' the events of the story need not be the persona who speaks" (Lanser 1981, 37), they are the same in first-person narration.[9] Body/minds affect not only *how* things are perceived and expressed but also *whether* things are perceived and expressed in the first place.[10] Both perceiving things and expressing them involve body/minds, so the degree of normativity in body/minds can affect the degree of normativity in acts of narration. Thus, unnatural texts disturb Genette's classic "Who sees?" and "Who speaks?" by representing an unnatural "who."

---

9 Technically, the texts I am discussing employ autodiegesis: first-person narration by a narrator who is the protagonist (Prince 2003, 9).

10 I am extending Daniel Punday's idea of "perceptual access" (2003, 131).

A number of constructed-body texts are unnatural because of their acts of narration, especially when constructed bodies are the personas who speak, who see, or who do both. Yet some texts about a constructed body are close to normative: *The Edible Woman* [1969] (1976), by Margaret Atwood, uses unnatural narration by an unnatural mind, but the storyworld is realistic, for the focaliser constructs her body only through anorexia and through metaphor, as a cake (cf. Peel 1989). Jorge Luis Borges's "The Circular Ruins" [1956] (1964), while focalised through a character with a body constructed by dreaming, otherwise employs rather ordinary third-person limited acts of narration; and in *Frankenstein*, even when the creature is the one who sees and speaks, the acts of narration are conventional, if not always believable. In contrast, the most intriguing narratives are the ones that combine a constructed body with unnaturalness of all three sorts—storyworld, mind, and acts of narration. All three often appear when those who focalise and narrate are the characters whose bodies are constructed, as in the examples to which I now turn. Do these narrators have one body, several, or none? One mind, several, or none? What non-normative acts of narration are made possible?

## 2 *Bone Dance*: One Body Narrates

*Bone Dance* deviates from normative narration in two ways: the narrator, Sparrow, has an ambiguous identity and suffers from blackouts. The narrator's identity leads to the novel's first kind of body construction, mental projection: usually he/she is perceived by men as male, and by women as female. (I refer to Sparrow as "he/she" and "her/him" [see Bull 1991, 254].[11]) Before the novel makes this issue explicit (ibid., 143), it is largely concealed from readers by the use of first-person narration. In English, "which requires gender-identification only in third-person pronouns" (Lanser 2020, 130, note 8), no grammatical rule requires first-person narrators to refer to their own gender, so—if no other clues exist—it is possible for readers to differ in which gender they picture.[12] Although first-person narration is not in itself unnatural, it performs an odd function in this text.

This trick brings us to the second type of construction and a second ambiguity, between person and thing. Sparrow's body is not only constructed mentally by other characters; it has been constructed physically and has no

11 I avoid using "they" because it might seem to refer to other characters. I avoid using "it" because the term hurts Sparrow deeply when a few other characters use it (e.g., 268).

12 On gender ambiguity in narrative, see Punday (63) and Lanser (2020, 120–21, 123).

sex whatsoever, though it looks androgynous when clothed (Bull 1991, 100). Observers mentally construct the character as human, but when Sparrow's physically constructed nature becomes known, some characters refer to Sparrow not as "she" or "he" but as "it" (e.g., ibid., 101). Narration by a thing instead of a person would fit the definition, given above, of an unnatural text as featuring "strikingly impossible or antimimetic elements" (Alber et al. 2013, 1). Perhaps some people would perceive any body that was constructed from scratch to be a thing and thus, if it narrated, those people would perceive the process to be unnatural; lacking a sex, Sparrow's constructed body in particular certainly strikes some characters as a thing and thus tinges the first-person narration with unnaturalness.

The third type of construction involves the "Horsemen," humans constructed by the government to perform espionage by temporarily usurping minds and bodies (Bull 1991, 110–11).[13] The Horsemen have gone rogue, and some are still "riding" other characters, including Sparrow, creating blackouts—intervals of time that cannot be remembered by the "horses."[14] While possessed, the horses have no experiences to remember later, for their minds are sealed away (Bull 1991, 152): it is Horsemen who are perceiving through the horses' senses, controlling their movements and speech (ibid.). Thus, if Sparrow, the one who narrates, tried to recount what was experienced during one of these blackouts, that would be impossible because he/she was not the one who was perceiving (ibid., 54).[15]

In short, *Bone Dance*, while not extremely unnatural, disrupts who sees (by means of the Horsemen's physically constructed bodies, which cause blackouts in the narrator) and disrupts who speaks (by means of Sparrow's mentally and physically constructed body and the female/male, human/thing identity it presents).

---

13 We never learn how the Horsemen are constructed. Jenny Wolmark notes that, although they "began as gendered subjects, they also take on both the gender and desires of whichever host body they inhabit" (1995, 163), except, presumably, Sparrow's sexless body.

14 Horsemen usually employ ordinary humans as horses (Bull 1991, 98), but Sparrow is a special horse—a *cheval*, custom-made for the purpose, with "[i]ndigenous Western Hemisphere genes" (ibid., 100). Unlike other *chevaux*, he/she has a mind (ibid., 102).

15 The blackouts lead to another oddity of narration. In *Bone Dance*, second-person narration makes more sense than usual—another character tells Sparrow what he/she did during a blackout (Bull 1991, 40) (though technically it was what a Horseman did using Sparrow's body). Moreover, while riding, Horsemen literally read the horses' minds, which may be why the novel is also pervaded by references to metaphorical mind-reading, successful and unsuccessful (e.g., ibid., 202).

## 3 "The Mask": Multiple Bodies Narrate

We turn now to Stanislaw Lem's novella "The Mask" (1977). Narration is more unnatural here than in *Bone Dance*, partly because the constructed narrator is more unnatural than Sparrow. Admittedly, in one respect this narrator is more ordinary: she lacks Sparrow's gender ambiguity.[16] I refer to her with female pronouns since for about half the novella she seems to be a woman—in fact, a stereotypically beautiful white woman (but just wait).[17] I call her "X" because she has no real name; instead, she possesses implanted memories of several mutually exclusive pasts, each corresponding to a different woman's name, such as the Duenna or Angelita (Lem 1977, 198). Early on, X realises that she has been constructed by a king in order to attract and then assassinate Arrhodes, a courtier who opposes the king's authority. X claims she does not love Arrhodes (ibid., 208), but she does admire him and in complicated ways tries to resist the king's murderous programming, only to find—poignantly and disturbingly—that even her attempts at defiance may be programmed in.[18] Arrhodes falls deeply in love with her but eventually flees, with her in pursuit, not sure herself whether she will kill him if she finds him. She does find him, but only in time to witness his death, then embrace him.

"The Mask" creates a stronger overall sense of unnaturalness than *Bone Dance*, partly because we know from the start that its narrator has been constructed. The story opens as machines build her body and she develops a rudimentary sense of self: "In the beginning there was darkness and cold flame and lingering thunder, and, in long strings of sparks, char-black hooks, segmented hooks, which passed me on ..." (Lem 1977, 181). After that process, she suddenly finds herself entering a ballroom at the king's court, instantly acquiring gender, language, and an understanding of what she is seeing (ibid., 182). What I have described so far indicates an unnatural storyworld, where a very human-like body can be constructed, and an unnatural mind, which awakens from a break in consciousness just before X enters the ballroom. The presence of conflicting sets of memories, each set corresponding to a different identity,

16 N. Katherine Hayles explains how the Polish original handles grammatical gender (2005, 178).

17 Jo Alyson Parker, however, says that Lem leaves "unrepresentable ... a female 'subject,'" and "'The Mask' is played out in a narrative field of the male and the neuter" (1992, 180).

18 Parker notes that, as constructor of X, Lem resembles the king, and, as writer in the first person, Lem resembles X (1992, 181, 187), all of which is appropriate since X embodies the king's wishes.

further contributes to the unnaturalness of her mind, as does the presence in that mind of her programmed destiny along with wishes that may or may not be her own.[19]

This body/mind leads to the novella's unnatural acts of narration. It is unnatural for a first-person narrator to call herself "she," and yet that sometimes happens here. The first instance occurs when she acquires gender: "*I*, a *she* now, felt the rush of gender so violent, that *her* head spun and *I* shut my eyes" (ibid., 182; my emphasis). The narrator is referring to herself in the first and third person in a single sentence. After more oscillations, the narration mostly settles into first-person pronouns, but there lingers an impression of alienation, as if X regards herself as an object, not just a subject. X is clearly the one who sees, but who speaks?

Since the king has constructed her, she indeed is an object, and not just in the grammatical sense. Her sense of this status leads to an oscillation that is more unsettling than the variation between "I" and "she," for X also sprinkles her discourse with inanimate pronouns and nouns. The very first sentence mentions "the thing that was me …" Soon X also says, "the *it* that was *I* increased and came to know *itself*, discovering *its* own limits, and *I* cannot say just when *I* was able to grasp *its* own form fully, to take cogni[s]ance of every place where *I* left off … *I*, *it*, rested" (ibid., 181; my emphasis). X, again, is clearly the one who sees, but who—or what—speaks? Once X acquires gender, "I" versus "it" becomes "I" versus "she" and then usually "I," but with a few reminders that she is a constructed object.

The most shocking reminder of her construction comes on the third evening, when "I finally set about discovering who I was" (ibid., 212). Feeling a large, hard shape in her belly, she cuts her abdomen open, with little pain, and finds a silvery oval with legs, a beetle-like killing-machine. Understanding that "it was not *it*, a foreign thing, different and other, it was again *myself*," X emerges from the "chrysalis … after which Tlenix, Duenna, Mignonne first sank to *her* knees, then tumbled face-down to the side and *I* crawled out of *her*, straightening all *my* legs" (ibid., 213–15; my emphasis). In this Kafkaesque metamorphosis, the singular "her" strangely refers to plural, alternate identities of the superficial human part, while "I" refers to the insect-like, mechanical self inside. Perhaps this "I"—not human, not even organic—has all along been the one who has been seeing and the one who has been speaking—an unnatural act of narration indeed, and an act that represents the narrator's unnatural mind.

---

19 N. Katherine Hayles does an intricate reading of how the novella represents the conflict between (supposedly human) agency and (supposedly machine) programming (2005, 171–92).

Readers' shock is compounded by the fact that Arrhodes unexpectedly comes in just after X has slit herself open.[20] Understandably, he flees. In the second half of the text, X still thinks like a human but now has an insect's acute sense of smell and a machine's speed and endurance. Resisting the king's will—or possibly following it—X lets Arrhodes "get a good head start," then sets out in pursuit of her "unsuitor, unlover" (ibid., 216), until the novella reaches its appropriately bizarre ending.

Unlike *Bone Dance*, this text has only one character with a constructed body, and in a sense that one body has throughout been the one who sees and speaks. But the story goes through three phases: concerning a construction of unspecified appearance, a humanoid, then an animal-like machine.[21] Interestingly, the third phase, the one with the most unnatural storyworld, is the only phase free of pronoun and noun oscillations. Yet, if normative narration consists of "someone relating a set of events to someone else," then a text is surely non-normative when it turns out that the events have been related not by someone but by a talking assassination machine whose perceptions, beetle-like, have become largely olfactory. Combined with the narrative's storyworld and mind, these acts of narration add up to intense unnaturalness, springing from a single character.

## 4 *Kiln People*: Many Bodies Narrate

The third text represents many constructed bodies and is thus unnatural in more complex, even comical, ways. In Brin's *Kiln People*, people can create duplicates ("dittos") of themselves by imprinting their "Standing Wave" on a blank clay body that has been unfrozen and baked.[22] Dittos come in many colours, which signify their quality and intended role. Most people use dittos to

20 To be more precise, the shock is felt by the authorial audience, since the unnaturalness is located in the relation between the textual element (revelation of the machine) and the reaction that the implied author intends the authorial audience to have (Peel 2021). Real readers may or may not match the authorial audience. I myself felt the shock of what Ralf Schneider would call X's "decategori[s]ation" (2001, 623), yet I was struck by how quickly I coped with such shocks here and elsewhere in the three texts. Some unnatural narratologists, such as Jan Alber, have classified strategies used by readers "to make sense of" the unnatural (Alber 2016, 47).

21 A change of phase sometimes brings a change of perception: upon entering the ballroom, she sees "vertical trunks" with "globes, which turned in its direction tiny buttons bright with water"; with her next step, she gains understanding and realizes she is seeing people who have heads with eyes (Lem 1977, 182).

22 The following summary of the novel is a modification of the Wikipedia entry "*Kiln People*."

do their work, and many use them to experience pleasure that could inconvenience or hurt the original archetype (or "archie"). A ditto receives all memories acquired by the archie up until the time of duplication and then goes out and acquires her or his own memories. The ditto disintegrates after about 24 hours; before that happens, the archie can choose to inload the ditto's recent memories, assuming the ditto has returned. Thus, the archie accumulates not only her or his own memories but also all the memories inloaded up to now from the dittos, and each new ditto receives both sorts of memories.

The novel centers on Albert Morris, a private detective who uses dittos extensively. The book is intriguing in narrative technique because each chapter is narrated by him or by one or more of his dittos. One day, Albert sends out a green ditto (i.e., a cheap one for drudgery) and two grays (i.e., high-quality ones suitable for business). This particular green is an imperfect copy of Albert, or a "frankie" (an invented slang word alluding to Frankenstein's creature). The first gray searches for Yosil Maharal, one of the founders of Universal Kilns, who has disappeared under suspicious circumstances. The man is later discovered dead, and the first gray is captured by the surviving Maharal ditto. Meanwhile (and there are a lot of "meanwhiles" when one is talking about dittos), Albert's second gray gets involved in a plan to infiltrate Universal Kilns. The plot then becomes very complicated, including a trip that Albert takes with a real woman, each disguised in order to pass as a gray ditto, unbeknownst to the other.

Because dittos are and are not the same as their archie, this storyworld is fundamentally unnatural, blurring the line between self and other.[23] Even before a ditto goes out and has experiences that diverge from the archie's, the two already differ. One is flesh,[24] the other is legally required to be brightly coloured clay;[25] one has lived years in one body, the other has not; one is multi-faceted, the other is specialised, in some cases actually more skilled than the original. (I refer to individual dittos as "he" or "she," even though they are sometimes called "it," even on the same page with "he" [Brin 2002, 140]).

These bodily characteristics produce unnatural minds. In particular, archies do not know when they will die, whereas dittos know they have only one day, a fact that weighs on them—and liberates them. Moreover, the relationship

23 The situation of a person with dittos sounds like dissociative identity disorder but is more extreme because in this novel the multiple selves exist in separate bodies and therefore exist simultaneously. In fact, one character does have dissociative identity disorder, which causes her to unwillingly produce male dittos that differ drastically from her.

24 Albert has dark hair and, it is implied, buff-colored skin (Brin 2002, 22, 435).

25 The novel alludes lightly to appearance-based racism, for example, mentioning "*Red Like Me*, a docudrama about a woman whose permanent skin condition made her look unbrown" and caused her to be treated like a ditto (Brin 2002, 219).

between archie and ditto resembles familiar patterns, but it fits neatly into no single one. They are older twin and younger twin, parent and child, employer and employee, master and slave (who differ in colour), executioner and victim. The archie is reborn in the ditto, and the ditto—if inloaded—is reborn in the archie.

Once the ditto's experiences start to differ from those of its archie, the two differ more, not only in what they see but also in what they do. Oddly enough, though, when the ditto comes back and inloads the day's memories, the two beings almost become one again. A further complication is that dittos differ subtly from each other as well. Here is what some of Albert's dittos say right after they are animated:

> *Green (Frankie):*
> I hate getting off the warming tray, throwing paper garments over limbs that still glow with ignition enzymes.
> Not only am I a copy today, I'm the greenie.
> Damn. (Brin 2002, 71)

Note how that differs from the grumbling of a more sophisticated gray:

> *Gray #1:*
> Damn ...
> Oh, never mind. I'm always just a bit grumpy getting up off the warming tray, grabbing paper garments from a rack and slipping them over limbs that still glow with ignition enzymes, knowing I'm the copy-for-a-day. (ibid., 51, ellipses in original)

Even the grays differ slightly from each other:

> *Gray #2:*
> Damn.
> I'm always grumpy getting up off the warming tray ... grabbing paper garments from a rack and slipping them over limbs still glowing with ignition enzymes, knowing I'm copy-for-a-day. (ibid., 63, ellipses in original)

As these passages show, the multiplicity of dittos makes the characters' ontology even more unnatural. Albert and his multiple dittos present unnatural minds, frustrating readers' attempts to discern a continuing consciousness.

This strange storyworld raises a host of compelling issues concerning narration. The first inheres in the storyworld's very premise. When an archie imprints her or his memories in a new ditto and when that ditto inloads newly-acquired memories into the archie, those acts constitute a sort of narration—to oneself, yet to someone else.[26] Even if the novel itself were narrated in a conventional way, its storyworld would contain these unnatural acts of narration.

Most importantly, on another level, the novel itself is narrated in an unnatural way, by Albert and his dittos. Who sees? The dittos do and do not see in the same way as Albert and each other. Moreover, the dittos do and do not see the same things as Albert and each other. Who speaks? This novel has only one narrator, and it also has several. This situation raises the unanswerable question, "When one of these narrators refers to another, is that first-person or third-person narration?" Here are some typical passages, starting with ones in which one narrator functions almost independently of the others. Note the pronouns in particular.

At one point, Albert is seen by one of his ditto narrators, who says:

> [H]e's getting in the way.
> Poor Albert may have to go. (Brin 2002, 398)

The narrator's rebellious attitude is reflected in his clear distance from Albert, who is referred to in the third person.

At another point, the lowly green ditto speculates: "Maybe I just duplicated work that's already been done by other, much better versions of 'me'" (ibid., 279). Although he does use "me" to refer to Albert and the other dittos, his scare quotes and the word "versions" indicate that he notices distance between himself and them.

At other times characters use "me" but do so ungrammatically, indicating distance. Albert's girlfriend, before going out of town, uses "me" as a noun in a note that she leaves him:

> I LEFT A ME IN THE FREEZER
> IN CASE YOU GET LONELY (ibid., 48)

At various other points, first- and third-person narration blur more. Gray #2 tells of seeing the green ditto during a crisis: "I spy a version of myself ... Running by, I share a split-second glance with my other self and recogni[s]e

26 A different sort of non-normative narration occurs when dittos recount their experiences to themselves. Albert's grays do so in real time, using a subvocal recorder, whereas the cheaper greens do so on a minirecorder after the fact (Brin 2002, 180).

this morning's greenie. Looks like I found something more interesting to do today than clean toilets. Good for you, Green" (ibid., 163). On the one hand, distance from the green ditto is indicated by terms such as "version of myself" (albeit without scare quotes) and "my other self." Similarly, the silent tribute, "Good for you, Green," addresses the other ditto as a separate being. On the other hand, there remains the unnatural sentence, "Looks like I found something more interesting to do today than clean toilets." Ordinarily, assuming no blackouts, one would already be aware of one's own recent activities. But Gray #2 has neither performed nor perceived the activities, and yet, as the one who speaks, he says "I" when referring to the green ditto: "Looks like I found something more interesting to do today than clean toilets."

Here is a complex non-normative use of "I": "It's a good thing I pay to give my ditto blanks phobia blocks" (Brin 2002, 175). Taken in isolation, this excerpt sounds ordinary (except, of course, for its reference to ditto technology). We seem to be hearing Albert speak. Actually, though, this is Gray #1, so this reference to "my ditto blanks" is coming from a ditto, not a purchaser of ditto blanks. Who speaks as this "I"? Things get stranger in a longer excerpt from the passage: "It's a good thing I pay to give my ditto blanks phobia blocks, or I'd be having fits right now, pinned inside a narrow cylinder …" (ibid.). The archie "I" who pays to block claustrophobia is not exactly the ditto "I" now pinned in the cylinder. Shouldn't one of those be third-person?

The narrator, whoever he may be, goes on to say: "All right, Albert … ditAlbert … quit banging the walls" (ibid.). Addressing oneself by name, though technically unnecessary, is such a convention that it usually goes unnoticed. Here, however, it takes a peculiar twist. Why, after addressing himself as "Albert," does the narrator correct that to "ditAlbert"? Because "Albert" alone refers only to the archie, not the ditto in the cylinder? Or because "Albert" alone refers to the union of all the dittos plus their archie, whereas the narrator wants to specify only himself, a ditto?

Even more complex instances arise later. A mad scientist uses Gray #1 to produce a red ditto and then merges their Standing Waves, causing the two at times to narrate as one "I" (e.g., ibid., 350). Furthermore, as the book starts to transcend its already unnatural storyworld, Albert starts inadvertently reading the minds of some of his dittos (ibid., 400), and a mysterious voice, printed in boldface, begins to address some of the narrators (ibid., 365), apparently alternating between being Albert and his dittos, an omniscient narrator, and a dramatised author. *Kiln People* explodes with unnaturalness—in bodies, minds, and acts of narration.

## 5 The Stakes of Extreme Non-normativity

Having examined each of the three narratives individually, we can now ask, what are the stakes of their extreme non-normativity? It is indeed extreme: according to Western, secular beliefs, significant elements in the identities of the protagonists are impossible. A real man might feel, after a drunken spree that he cannot remember, as if he has been ridden by a Horseman, but he has not. A real woman might feel, after giving up coquetry at court for an obsessive pursuit, as if she has become a machine, but she has not. A real detective might feel as if he is a different person when interrogating different people, but he is not. The three unnatural narratives make literal what would ordinarily be metaphorical.[27]

The particular nature of the constructed bodies in these narratives means that, in at least one respect, their non-normative bodies entail non-normative minds. Having been created full-grown, the characters have had no childhoods, and so initially they have no knowledge and have had no earlier experiences to remember. Therefore, they need implanted knowledge and—in "The Mask" and *Kiln People*—implanted memories. Even if all their constructed bodies were indistinguishable from normative ones, those implantations would make their minds non-normative. As it turns out, their constructed bodies are so anomalous that they are in fact distinguishable from normative ones, and their minds have other non-normative traits in addition to the implanted knowledge and memories.

To contemplate the three body/minds at a higher level, we can inquire into their selfhood, as that concept is broadly conceived by secular Westerners. How many selves does each narrator have? In one sense, Sparrow has a normative self, with one body and one mind. But in another sense, he/she has no sex and no human body, or two gender presentations and two bodies. Moreover, since during blackouts it is a Horseman, not Sparrow, who is perceiving and acting, her/his body has lived a bit longer than the mind it houses. One could say he/she has less than a full self.

In one sense, X has only one self and one body, the killing machine that has been there all along: Jo Alyson Parker says, "The dropping of the [female] mask signifies the death of the subject; self is exposed as object" (1992, 183). But in another sense, she has sequential selves based in sequential and simultaneous bodies: a humanoid body that later becomes a mechanical one that is, ambiguously, also an insect. She has one mind, which, despite gaps, remembers her

27 Samuel R. Delany has said that science fiction often makes literal what would be just a metaphor in "naturalistic" fiction (Philmus 1990, 296).

experiences from the factory, through the king's court, to the fortress where Arrhodes dies. But she also has multiple simultaneous minds, each with its own mutually exclusive memories of life as Angelita and others before she came to court, as if those minds have, in total, lived longer than her body.

In one sense, Albert has only one self, the human archie, with one body and one mind. But in another sense, that self has many bodies and minds when his dittos are out living their lives: Albert remarks, "It's tough lying to yourself, especially when you're standing right in front of you" (Brin 2002, 136). And, when he inloads their memories, he has one body but multiple minds, which have, in total, lived longer than his body. Moreover, since the dittos differ from him in abilities, the experiences they have are not exactly the ones Albert would have in their situation, and so their memories differ from the ones he would acquire. The number of selves gets still harder to count at the end, when Albert's altered mind leaves his body, into which the frankie inloads their earlier mind.[28]

Within any single self, one characteristic of normative selfhood is continuing consciousness.[29] Sparrow's blackouts violently sever any such continuity. X, while in humanoid form, experiences two similarly abrupt breaks in consciousness, which thus "operates as if it were a machine being turned on and off" (Hayles 2005, 179). Ironically, no such break occurs when she changes from humanoid to machine. Consciousness is mostly continuous in Albert but is harder to categorise in his dittos. During their 24 hours, they are always conscious, but that period is preceded and followed by a break. Various characters philosophise about these issues (Bull 1991, 206, 259, 447).

Another key component of selfhood is self-awareness. In some literary periods, self-awareness and other types of interiority have outcompeted embodiment: Lanser notes that narratology's usual "overemphasis on interiority [at the expense of embodiment] is attached to an overemphasis on the modern novel" (2020, 119). Yet the texts studied here manage to combine the interiority exemplified in printed verbal narratives, such as the modern novel, with the embodiment exemplified in constructed-body narratives. This combination is made easier by the fact that the protagonists do the narrating. Since such narration encourages self-analysis by the narrator, such narration by a constructed-body character makes possible interiority that analyses embodiment in particular.

To varying degrees, these three narrators have self-awareness, while also being aware that they lack awareness of certain crucial information about

28 Zunshine investigates twins and other seemingly duplicate selves (2008, 1–50).

29 Similar issues arise with what Punday calls "continuity of the name" (2003, 25).

themselves. Sparrow knows that he/she was constructed and does not have normative sexual characteristics—in order to pass, he/she conceals these facts from other characters, which contributes to her/his heartbreaking loneliness. Yet Sparrow does not know why he/she was constructed or has blackouts, and he/she often refers to herself/himself as if to a puzzling separate person (e.g., "I was … amazed to hear my voice," 96). X also knows she was constructed but mostly considers herself a human female, until she finds the machine inside her abdomen. Revelation of this truth about her body is, however, almost a cruel joke, since it fails to answer the question that obsesses her: does her mind have any free will? This central element of self-awareness remains missing throughout. In contrast, Albert possesses normative self-awareness, as does each ditto, considered individually. During most of the novel, however, when Albert is using dittos, no part of his self is aware of what is currently going on in the minds of all the others.

Selfhood roughly corresponds, in the grammatical, narratological realm, to person. As we have discovered, person is the most non-normative aspect of narration in these three texts. X and the various Alberts mix first- and third-person narration in unnatural ways, and Sparrow—while mostly less strange than the other two—turns out to enact person most strangely. Because Sparrow neither perceives while being ridden, nor can express those blackouts later, it is almost as if, during those parts of the narrative, he/she is employing the zeroeth person. These particular highly non-normative protagonists *must* narrate using person unnaturally. In contrast, characters with mildly non-normative, or even normative, body/minds *can* narrate using person unnaturally (Peel 1989) but need not do so. Having a mildly non-normative body—say, because of a heart transplant—might prompt a narrator to rethink selfhood but would not necessarily entail anything as drastic as speaking of oneself in the third person.

What other observations, more widely applicable, can we make about the extreme non-normativity of these three striking narratives? Unnatural narratives about constructed bodies matter because, in addition to exerting an intrinsic fascination, they can generate three additional dynamics, all of which defamiliarise what we ordinarily take for granted, jolting us into seeing old things with new eyes. First, unnatural bodies, minds, and acts of narration can contrast with the normative. In terms of bodies, for instance, dittos who know they will die within 24 hours can make us reflect on the ramifications of the fact that most of us have little idea which day we will die. Similarly, a fictional mind that shares all of another mind's memories, except those of the last 24 hours, can force us to notice how un-shareable are the minds of people in our ordinary world. And narrative acts that we cannot confidently classify as first- or third-person can make us more aware of how blithely we tend to pigeonhole acts of narration.

Unnatural narratives about constructed bodies can also, however, have a very different effect, by presenting surprising similarities with the normative, at least with what might be called "the new normative." Because of advances in such fields as robotics and assisted reproductive technology, bodies that used to be impossible are approaching possibility. And online role-playing games may be blurring the boundaries between one individual mind and another, along with blurring narratological categories through phenomena such as the first-person shooter.

Finally, extreme non-normativity in body/minds can awaken us to how profoundly perception and expression are affected by body/minds in general, regardless of where they lie on the normativity scale. Our perception is fashioned by myriad factors, such as height, tendency to analytical thinking, or substances we ingest. Race, ability, gender, and other identity traits that we or others attribute to our body/minds can affect how others treat us in a given setting, including what we are permitted or encouraged to perceive (on Punday and Bakhtin's chronotope, see Lanser 2020, 121). Similarly, our expression is shaped by numerous body/mind factors. For instance, as children's body/minds develop, so do their skills in speaking and writing, and sometimes injury, disease, or age saps those skills in adults. Furthermore, expressing oneself in what Lanser calls "gestural narrative" (2020, 120), such as sign language or dance, depends on particular pairings of body and mind. These examples may seem obvious, but it is their very unremarkableness that can make them go unremarked. Tales told by characters with impossibly non-normative body/minds can startle us into pondering how characters in other texts-and we ourselves—are molded by body/minds that are possible, whether normative or mildly non-normative.

I am not claiming that non-normative bodies and minds always accompany each other. Nor, if one does accompany the other, was it necessarily inevitable that they would: social, environmental, and other variables can play a large role. Nor am I claiming that non-normative bodies and minds always result in non-normative acts of narration. I am simply claiming that such causation can exist, especially in fiction, and that it can have powerful effects.

I hope to have shown the provocative unnaturalness that can characterise constructed-body texts, especially those that shake up our sense of "who sees" and "who speaks." I have traced how extremely non-normative bodies and minds intertwine and how, when belonging to a protagonist who is narrating, they intertwine with the act of narration. I also have suggested that, by implication, such phenomena throw fresh light on something often taken for granted: the functioning of normative or mildly non-normative bodies, minds, and first-person narration.

The three texts exemplify a type of non-normativity that has continued to thrive, as in Richard K. Morgan's *Altered Carbon* (2002) and its spin-offs, John Corey Whaley's *Noggin* (2014), and John Scalzi's *Lock In* (2014) and *Head On* (2018). As cloning, organ transplants, and the like continue to develop in the scientific world, constructed bodies will no doubt burgeon in fiction as well. They will continue to enrich the understanding of narrative in "our head."

## Works Cited

Alber, Jan. *Unnatural Narrative: Impossible Worlds in Fiction and Drama*. Lincoln: U of Nebraska P, 2016.

Alber, Jan. Stefan Iversen, Henrik Skov Nielsen, and Brian Richardson. "Unnatural Narratives, Unnatural Narratology: Beyond Mimetic Models." *Narrative*, vol. 18, no. 2, 2010, pp. 113–36.

Alber, Jan. Stefan Iversen, Henrik Skov Nielsen, and Brian Richardson. Introduction. *A Poetics of Unnatural Narrative*. Ed. Jan Alber, Henrik Skov Nielsen, and Brian Richardson. Columbus: The Ohio State UP, 2013, pp. 1–15.

Andersen, Hans Christian. "The Little Mermaid." *Tales and Stories*. Translated by Patricia L. Conroy and Sven H. Rossel. Seattle: U of Washington P, [1837] 1980, pp. 34–58.

Atwood, Margaret. *The Edible Woman*. New York: Popular Library, [1969] 1976.

Borges, Jorge Luis. "The Circular Ruins." Translated by James E. Irby. *Labyrinths: Selected Stories & Other Writings*. Ed. Donald A. Yates and Irby. New York: New Directions, [1956] 1964, pp. 45–50.

Brin, David. *Kiln People*. New York: Tor-Tom Doherty, 2002.

Bull, Emma. *Bone Dance*. New York: Ace, 1991.

Genette, Gérard. *Narrative Discourse: An Essay in Method*. Translated by Jane E. Lewin. Ithaca, NY: Cornell UP, 1980.

Genette, Gérard. *Narrative Discourse Revisited*. Translated by Jane E. Lewin. Ithaca, NY: Cornell UP, 1988.

Hayles, N. Katherine. *My Mother Was a Computer: Digital Subjects and Literary Texts*. Chicago: U of Chicago P, 2005.

Herman, David. "Narrative Theory after the Second Cognitive Revolution." *Introduction to Cognitive Cultural Studies*. Ed. Lisa Zunshine. Baltimore: Johns Hopkins UP, 2010, pp. 155–75.

"*Kiln People*." *Wikipedia*. 7 November 2021. en.wikipedia.org/wiki/Kiln_People. Accessed 1 February 2022.

Lanser, Susan S. "Till Death Do Us Part: Embodying Narratology." *The Edinburgh Companion to Contemporary Narrative Theories*. Ed. Zara Dinnen and Robyn Warhol. Edinburgh: Edinburgh UP, 2020, pp. 117–31.

Lanser, Susan S. *The Narrative Act: Point of View in Prose Fiction*. Princeton, NJ: Princeton UP, 1981.

Lem, Stanislaw. "The Mask." *Mortal Engines*. Translated by Michael Kandel. New York: Continuum-Seabury, [1976] 1977, pp. 181–239.

Morgan, Richard K. *Altered Carbon*. New York: Del Ray-Random House, 2002.

Parker, Jo Alyson. "Gendering the Robot: Stanislaw Lem's 'The Mask.'" *Science-Fiction Studies*, vol. 19, 1992, pp. 178–91.

Peel, Ellen. "Imagining the Constructed Body: From Statues to Cyborgs." *Teaching World Literature*. Ed. David Damrosch. New York: Modern Language Association, 2009, pp. 362–76.

Peel, Ellen. "Subject, Object, and the Alternation of First- and Third-Person Narration in Novels by Alther, Atwood, and Drabble: Toward a Theory of Feminist Aesthetics." *Critique*, vol. 30, 1989, pp. 107–22.

Peel, Ellen. "Unnatural Narratology and the Return of the Repressed Reader." *Narrative*, vol. 29, no. 1, 2021, pp. 71–90.

Philmus, Robert. "On *Triton* and Other Matters: An Interview with Samuel R. Delany." *Science-Fiction Studies*, vol. 17, 1990, pp. 295–324.

Prince, Gerald. *A Dictionary of Narratology: Revised Edition*. Lincoln: U of Nebraska P, 2003.

Punday, Daniel. *Narrative Bodies: Toward a Corporeal Narratology*. Houndmills, UK: Palgrave Macmillan, 2003.

Richardson, Brian. *Unnatural Voices: Extreme Narration in Modern and Contemporary Fiction*. Columbus: The Ohio State UP, 2006.

Scalzi, John. *Lock In*. New York: Tor-Tom Doherty, 2014.

Scalzi, John. *Head On*. New York: Tor-Tom Doherty, 2018.

Schneider, Ralf. "Toward a Cognitive Theory of Literary Character: The Dynamics of Mental-Model Construction." *Style*, vol. 35, no. 4, 2001, pp. 607–39.

Shelley, Mary. *Frankenstein, Or, The Modern Prometheus*. Signet-New American Library, [1818, 1831] 1983.

Stevenson, Robert Louis. *Treasure Island*. London: Cassell, 1883.

Whaley, John Corey. *Noggin*. New York: Atheneum Books for Young Readers-Simon & Schuster, 2014.

Wolmark, Jenny. "The Postmodern Romances of Feminist Science Fiction." *Romance Revisited*. Ed. Jackie Stacey and Lynne Pearce. New York: New York UP, 1995, pp. 158–68.

Zunshine, Lisa. *Strange Concepts and the Stories They Make Possible: Cognition, Culture, Narrative*. Baltimore: Johns Hopkins UP, 2008.

CHAPTER 15

# Embodied Being and Non-being in Bernard Rose's *FRANK3N5T31N* (2015)

*Kit Schuster*

## 1 Introduction: 200 Years of *Frankenstein*

Looking back on the centuries since Mary Shelley's *Frankenstein* was first published, its impact on the mythology of the Gothic genre and the modern history of horror cannot be emphasised strongly enough. It is "the most frequently taught canonical novel written by a woman in the early nineteenth century" (Long Hoeveler 2003, 60). As Diane Long Hoeveler notes, the novel "continues to entrance, irritate, and puzzle readers and critics alike because it speaks at once—in so many different contradictory voices—to so many issues that are central to what we make of being 'human'" (ibid.). This ambiguity makes the text particularly rich for adaptations, which explains why over 200 film versions of Shelley's work have been produced (Denson 2014, 52). One of these, Bernard Rose's 18-rated 2015 production of the same title, presents a version of the story updated to contemporary Los Angeles, graphically showing the bleak landscapes and violent lives on the margins of modern society. Historically, *Frankenstein* films "depict 'human nature' as threatened by both the technical/artificial and the non-normative" (ibid., 25). As such, Rose's 3D-printed creature reflects contemporary discussions about the morality of bioengineering, a debate in which Shelley's monster is already invoked on a regular basis, demonstrating its cultural significance for both scientific and ethical discourses. At the core of any *Frankenstein* narrative lies the issue of "social and cultural constructions of human normalcy and deviance, along with their consequences for bodies and identities marked as unnatural, anomalous, freakish, or queer" (ibid., 24). The tradition of *Frankenstein* adaptations, then, documents "representations of social processes of exclusion through which privileged forms of subjectivity negatively derive their shape—and power—from abnormal or monstrous Others" across 200 years (ibid., 24f.). In his updated version, Rose picks up on this theme of the posthuman 'other' in the neoliberal-capitalist context of the 21st century.

Othering in Shelley's *Frankenstein* both creates and denies subjectivity. By way of embodied empiricism and mirroring practices, the body plays a central

 | DOI:10.1163/9789004519886_017

role in this process of developing a stable sense of self. Conversely, the body also constitutes the locus of the creature's dehumanisation, as his appearance and the physical violence he is exposed to mark him as non-being, as 'monster.' In Rose's *FRANK3N5T31N*, this development of body-related self-awareness and the dehumanisation he experiences, culminate in Adam's exposure to the circumstances of his artificial creation and lack of a unique body.[1] Adam learns that he is a person through his body, but it is also through and because of his body that his personhood is denied.

## 2 Conceptions of Body and Mind – the Gothicised Body

In *Skin Shows: The Technology of Monsters*, J. Jack Halberstam's seminal work in Gothic studies, Halberstam connects the emergence of the Gothic monster to a change in how British society saw the body and its role in subject making (1995, 2). Conceptions of the self turned from Cartesian dualism towards a "body which enveloped a soul ... a body, indeed, enthralled to its soul" (ibid., 2). This enmeshment of physical and spiritual natures produced a "psychology of self" that would turn out to be the perfect breeding ground for a new kind of horror (ibid., 8). Halberstam points out that while 18th century Gothic Romances locate horror in the spatial dimension—a horror of locale—Mary Shelley "maps out a new geography of terror" in *Frankenstein* by "[making] flesh itself Gothic" (ibid., 28). Fear is no longer simply "a trick played upon the body by the mind," something to be overcome through clarity of thought; instead, by introducing her monster, Shelley "finds fear to be a by-product of embodiment" and therefore an inevitability when one possesses a body (ibid., 28). This is what Halberstam terms the "gothici[s]ed body," a body that is itself a source of fear (ibid., 19). After *Frankenstein*, the Gothic genre is irreversibly entwined with the idea of embodiment, permanently linking the body to the self and the horrors the gruesome realities of bodily existence can put this self through (Law 2006, 975). The fear now lay within the human having to rely upon a body that becomes sick, ages, and dies (Béres Rogers 2015, 360). The body must be nurtured and protected from dangers both outside and within. It is a place of power, of interaction with the world, and yet terrifyingly vulnerable. It can potentially reproduce and thus create other bodies, other sources of fear, a "race of devils" in the words of Victor Frankenstein (Shelley

1 For the purpose of disambiguation, I use "creature" to refer to the creation in Shelley's novel and "Adam," the name given to FRANK3N5T31N's creation by Victor during their final showdown, to refer to the one in Rose's film, although he is called "monster" until this moment.

1818, 203). The "dialectic of embodiment and dissolution" that followed when Gothic literature made flesh a metonym of the human self, posits that horror and violence are in fact an inevitable component of corporealisation (Law 2006, 975).

The obsession with the inherent horror of bodies focuses especially on particular kinds of 'deviant' bodies (Halberstam 1995, 3). In this way, the Gothic produces that from which it draws its terror: the observed, dissected, othered subject. It functions at its core as a technology of social control by creating a non-human human and revealing its aberrations through the relentless, categorising gaze of a society afraid of its own bodily vulnerability. The parameters of "the normal, the healthy, and the pure" are set by way of marking and making visible that which is supposed to be its opposite, that is, the monstrous (ibid., 2). By "implicitly linking embodiment to the logic of specularity," the othered body is positioned as an object whose material existence lays the ground for the seemingly natural, discursively constructed fear and resentment it is subject to due to the violent gaze that particular bodies are caught up in (Law 2006, 975). When bodies deemed 'other' are spectacularised as gruesome or eerie, they are dehumanised, and thus, those bodies, which the Gothic genre made intrinsic to subjectivity by interconnecting the body and the soul, are paradoxically the very thing used to deny them their status as human subjects. The gothicised body makes obvious the importance of both body and mind to the empirical experience of life in a society which is ruled by discursive structures and material realities—a fearful prospect considering the frailty of the human body and the arbitrariness of the markers of difference. As such, it "must be spoken, identified, or eliminated" within the narrative to stabili[s]e the normative subject (Halberstam 1995, 19).

## 3 Embodied Empiricism

"Who was I? Whence did I come? What was my destination?" Shelley's creature asks (1818, 152), raising the twin issues of ontology and epistemology: what is nature, "both the external world and human nature? Put otherwise, what is 'being'?," and "how do we know what we know?." These basic enquiries about the essence of human existence are central to the analogy of the Creature as a being on the edges of the contested definitions of what it means to be, and to be human, specifically. How do we learn of our own subjectivity, through our interactions with the world or through introspective observation? How much are we a product of our birth; or, in the updated terms of Bernard

Rose's *FRANK3N5T31N*, of our genes and cells, of our DNA?[2] How much are we determined by our environment and socialisation? Jane Flax defines healthy subjectivity as "the ability to live in and (sometimes) even enjoy the multiple worlds available to people," that is, "fantasy, play, solitude, creativity, rational thought, sexuality, embodiment, social interaction and expression, necessity, and ethical responsibility" (1993, 37), but the question of how one comes to see themselves as a subject in the first place is continually problematised through the metaphor of a monster that is artificially created, marked as non-human and shunned by society. Does such a monster become what it is because of the treatment it receives or is its monstrosity inherent in its creation? Moreover, could the horrors of *Frankenstein* be avoided by allowing it to be a part of a community?

Rose's film, I posit, shows a phenomenological-empirical conception of embodiment as an answer to these ontological questions. The body, by way of empirical enquiry and experience, becomes an epistemological tool: We know what we know because we perceive our environment, and ourselves in it as acting subjects, and because we are perceived and interacted with as acting subjects in return, we understand ourselves as such. It thus depicts the idea that we come to a subjective identity by way of embodied empiricism, highlighting "the centrality of the body to our sense of self, our experiences and relationships and practices ... continuously shaped by our ongoing bodily engagement with the world" (Aranda et al. 2012, 558). Phenomenology is defined as "the philosophical study of conscious experience from an individual person's subjective perspective" (Wilkerson 2015, 197). Embodied empiricism is "the keen interest in the body as both an object of research and an instrument of experience" (Wolfe and Gal 2010, 2). Combining these two methods creates a theoretical lens through which Adam's actions and his journey to selfhood can be read as a specifically embodied mode of trying to achieve a state of subjective identity. When Adam learns that fire is both a source of comforting warmth and painful heat by reaching out into the flames, or when strangers comment on his grotesque appearance, Rose directly appliesthe phenomenological notion of the "experienced and experiencing body" (Hughes and Paterson 1999, 601). Through interaction with the natural world, hunting, drinking, and befriending a wild dog, Adam becomes aware that he has a certain level of control and influence over his own body and, by way of his body, over his environment. He learns to survive in the wild and carves out a place for himself in the world he

---

2 The stylised spelling *FRANK3N5T31N* as seen on the film's theatrical poster is chosen here to distinguish it from Mary Shelley's novel *Frankenstein*.

has been thrown into. He thus begins to see himself as an independent actor, because he possesses "a body which simultaneously experiences and creates the world" (ibid., 601).

His body allows him to perceive and participate, it is his access point to individual action. Only because of his corporeality can he defend himself from his attackers in the laboratory and get Elizabeth's motherly attention and care. His body keeps him alive, whether it is eating and drinking or running away from danger. "Conscious perception of the outside world is mediated by the body," Shane Denson writes, referring to the biological processes by which our sense organs relay information about external stimuli to the brain, which in turn synthesises this information "into a world in which I, as subject, can act" (2014, 187). Adam's senses, quickly developing after his 'birth,' show him an outside reality where Elizabeth feeds him, touches him gently, and speaks to him in a soothing voice, resulting in Adam seeing her as a central figure in his life. The body also works as a mediator the other way around when any action one performs must use the body as a "motor instrument" to "achieve subjective expression or cause objective movement" (ibid.). This is pointed out early in the film when Victor attempts to test Adam's reflexes by throwing him a ball. Adam catches the ball and throws it back at Victor, hitting him with great force in the face, which causes Victor to swear at him, nose bleeding. At first, Adam laughs, clearly enjoying the act and its result. However, when Victor reacts with anger, Adam experiences hurt and confusion, asking for physical comfort from Victor. In this short sequence of events, Adam learns that he can manipulate his environment, cause actions and reactions, and that his individual choices have consequences which physically and psychically affect both him and others. In his interactions with the world, he comes to realise the inherent tension "between having and being a body," between being an acting subject, and an object which is acted upon (Hughes and Paterson 1999, 601). Adam beats a police officer to a pulp for shooting his dog and is later ambushed and assaulted by an angry mob because of it. Adam has to face the fact that in the "phenomenal-empirical world," as Denson puts it, his body is "both agent and patient of actual and potential interaction" (2015, 187).

## 4 Mirroring

Lisa Diedrich's work on mirroring in Mary Shelley's *Frankenstein* supplies another framework that can be used to analyse Adam's embodied subjectivity in Rose's 2015 adaptation. Diedrich posits that the central moment in Shelley's text is the instance of the creature beholding its own reflection for the first time in a pool of water (2018, 388). While this scene is alluded to in Rose's film when Adam, newly escaped from captivity, submerges his form in a pond to drink, the crucial aspect of self-reflection through the recognition of his own mirror image in the water is notably lacking in this updated version. However, mirroring does occur at other points. After Elizabeth touches his face, he reaches out to touch her, cradling her face in his hand in a moment of human connection. He realises that he is a material being, and by mirroring her gesture, he can confirm that she is a person he can communicate with. The physicality they have in common lays the grounds for their initial interaction. As Diedrich writes, "mirrors and mirroring are central to the complex processes of subject formation that *Frankenstein* enacts," and Rose's version of the text continuously calls attention to this as well (2018, 388). Surrounded by violence, a newly 'born' Adam quickly becomes violent as well, taking his cues about how to act from his surroundings. When one of the scientists attempts to cut his body, he turns the bone saw on his attacker, mirroring the abuse he is subjected to. A policeman attempts to execute him with a gun to his head and leaves him to die, which Adam then copies during the latter half of the film, killing the policeman on his way back to the laboratory. Adam can only learn what it means to be a human person from those around him and their actions, mirroring them to claim this subjectivity for himself.

According to Diedrich, "[m]irrors, both literal and figurative, create the effect of mise en abyme, a doubling operation integral to representations of the self-becoming-self in written texts, photographs, film, and graphic narratives" (ibid., 389). *Mise en abyme* refers to the technique of placing a copy of an image within an image to achieve an illusion of infinity. Similarly, Adam mirrors the people around him and thus becomes a copy of their characters, which in turn leads to them treating him accordingly, which leads to him copying this behaviour, ad infinitum. Adam is abused, becomes violent, and his violence makes him more of a threat, from which follows that he is treated worse, and so on. Notably, there is one scene in the movie that includes an actual mirror. Adam sees his own body clearly reflected for the first time, naked after taking a shower in a hotel bathroom. His form is riddled with tumours, sores and wounds, his eyes are bloodshot, his skin is sagging grotesquely. Much more than Adam submerged in the pool in the woods earlier, this resembles Shelley's central mirroring scene. Bruce Wyse points out the parallel between this moment and the Narcissus myth, except that his image has the reverse effect on the creature (2018, 142): "At first I started back, unable to believe that it was indeed I who was reflected in the mirror; and when I became fully convinced that I was in reality the monster that I am, I was filled with the bitterest sensations of despondence and mortification" (Shelley 1818, 133). Only after seeing his reflection does the creature come to identify as a monster, "the inimical image contradicting, if not nullifying, his nascent sense of a benevolent self" (Wyse 2018, 142). In the corresponding scene in Rose's *FRANK3N5T3IN*, Adam reacts with the same horror to what he sees in the mirror. Although the film cannot render the narration about his thought process, , his expression makes it clear that he is shocked and distraught by the view of his body. To quote Diedrich again, "verbal and visual depictions of mirroring … operate as formal passageways—relational vestibules or transitional spaces—between interior and exterior, subject and object, self and non-self" (2018, 390). The mirror in the hotel bathroom bridges the divide between how Adam experiences himself as a subject and how others see him as an object. For the first time, Adam has an outside view of himself, objectifying himself and taking the position of those who reject his humanity. While mirroring the people around him works to a degree for developing a subjective identity, Adam's own mirror image of a non-normative body reflect the non-normative mind that those he interacts with see in him. Consequently, his reflection shows him that he is not afforded a 'self' like others. As such, Adam's body paradoxically counteracts his embodied subjectivity.

Heather Laine Talley points out that "embodiment is absolutely universal and yet incomprehensibly unique," meaning that while the reality of inhabiting a body is shared by all humans, how we experience that bodily reality depends on a diverse variety of factors, from our physical ability to the culture we grow up in and the trauma we experience (2014, 200). In the words of Bryan S. Turner, "our relationship with the world is always through our embodiment," but "human embodiment means that [our] perceptions of the world are differentiated and limited" (2006, 21). In this way, embodiment combines parts of the 'nature' versus 'nurture' argument. The material body, including its innate ability and appearance, shapes how we experience subjectivity by influencing our participation in society and empiric observations of the world, and how that world reacts to our bodily existence. Adam moves through the landscape of Los Angeles in a way that is not different to that of many other people, taking in his surroundings through his human senses and interacting with the public, learning of his own agency and self and thus his subjectivity. However, his body, marked as aesthetically unpleasant and undesirable in a variety of other ways, shapes how others see and interact with him—mostly as a non-subject or non-being—which in turn problematises and questions his identity as a subject.

## 5 Making a Monster

"Each society has its Otherness," Riva Kastoryano writes (2010, 82). Othering is a tool of social control, creating in-groups and out-groups, as well as hierarchies within them. The other is the negative example that should never be followed unless one wishes to experience the same social ostracisation. By clearly delineating who is not part of our group, we strengthen inter-community bonds and identities, defining a commonality in our difference from the other. The other always seemingly poses a threat, meaning that the community must work together and defend itself. Social cohesion is achieved through the exclusion of those deemed wrong or inferior in some way. However, while the phenomenon of Othering can be observed in most societies, it is important to mention that it "is not an objective property of certain kinds of bodies, but rather the product of social processes that produce a hierarchy of identities" (Hughes and Paterson 1999, 609). The figure that historically combines aspects of unwelcome difference, projecting and amplifying that which makes the other 'other,' is the monster. Shelley's monster may seem monstrous in its very nature, "an unearthly, transgressively fabricated, composite creature fundamentally like no other in existence" (Wyse 2018, 77), yet that is not why it is "not even of the same nature as man … a blot upon the earth, from which all men fled, and whom all men disowned" (Shelley 1818, 141). Rather, he is a "socially constituted pariah, an object of intense, reactive animosity, apprehended as, at best, a 'filthy type' of the normative human image" (Wyse 2018, 77). Frankenstein's creation, in both the 1818 and 2015 version, is not born a monster, it becomes one.

Once again, this can be viewed through a materialist and a constructivist lens: Adam is othered because of his monstrous body, but the monstrosity of his body is discursively inscribed. His body is a "material [bearer] of discourse" (Denson 2015, 152). Adam is continuously met with hatred, fear, revulsion, violence, and ridicule in the "practice of everyday life" (Mossman 2001, n. p.). He is made a monster by learning that he is a monster, and he learns that he is a monster because he is treated as such. Tellingly, he takes on the name of 'Monster' after the term is hurled at him by the angry mob. 'Monster' becomes an unquestioned part of his self, "a term for anomalies, a name for an unnameable and most wretched of conditions," and thus a non-identity, a negative image of everything normal and human (Botting 2018, 313). The name 'Monster' proves "ineffectual in offering any answer to pressing questions of origins and subjectivity," it does not refer to any genealogy, or indeed to anything but "isolation, non-belonging, … non-personhood" (ibid.). Where Shelley's creature states to his maker, "I ought to be thy Adam," Bernard Rose's creature goes by 'Monster' for most of the film. He never gets to choose a name, and it is only by the end of his life that his 'mother' calls him Adam. His stammered "I am … I am …," sounding so close to 'Adam,' connects the name to his search for identity (Rose 2015, 1:18:10–1:18:40).

Normality needs its others, and the existence of a monster figure "demonstrates the dialectical constitution of ideological norms that tacitly require such difference" (Denson 2015, 152). By providing a stark example of that which "must be removed from the community at large," *Frankenstein* gives an answer to the question of "what threatens national security and prosperity" (Halberstam 1995, 3). But what difference is it that needs to be excised in *FRANK3N5T3IN*'s case? For one, Adam, just like his original iteration, depicts a danger to "the ideologies of Humanism and Enlightenment" by blurring the lines between human and animal, nature and culture, and, especially in Adam's case, biological and artificial (Karmakar and Parui 2018, 346). As such, Adam's existence as a 'printed' human, a laboratory experiment, threatens to shake the foundations of "anthropological and anthropocentric ... categories of human and humanism" (ibid., 351). He violates the 'natural order' of the "pregiven, linear set of events which we ultimately cannot alter: birth, maturity, ... aging, death" by being 'born' an adult and almost immortal (Flax 1993, 38). Adam, as a "trans-species being who transgresses the normative understanding of being human," cannot be treated as a full and equal member of human society without the ideologies and hierarchies of it coming into question (Karmakar and Parui 2018, 339).

## 6 Ugliness

"Alas! I did not yet entirely know the fatal effects of this miserable deformity," Shelley's creature laments (Shelley 1818, 133), the 'miserable deformity' being the state of his body: patched together, inhuman, frightening, in a word: ugly. Likewise, Adam's appearance raises a lot of negative attention. It soon becomes obvious that ugliness is not simply a subjective aesthetic category; it can be, to refer to the creature's words, fatal. The physiognomic judgement both versions of the creature face due to their looks leads to their physical and emotional abuse. Essentially, their outer appearance is seen as "a valid index to [their] nature" (Mellor 2003, 20). Their ugliness is equated with moral decay and thus taken to confirm their monstrosity and justify their treatment as unwanted others. "Beauty is often associated in our culture with moral goodness," Noël Carroll writes (2003, 89). "The beautiful exterior is taken as a sign of inward or moral goodness," and conversely, "the nonbeautiful or ugly exterior is often imagined to correlate with evil or depravity" (ibid.). "My person was hideous and my stature gigantic. What did this mean?" the creature asks (Shelley 1818, 152).

Ugliness is not seen as an acceptable state of being, and as such, we expect it to carry some ostensibly inherent meaning that is actively put upon it by our judging gaze. The moment that a body is conceived by the gaze of another is when "construction takes place, when [the body is] written" (Mossman

2001, n. p.). When Adam's body is beheld, it is 'fixed' as ugly and abnormal and therefore as 'other.' These "dynamics of the social construction of deformity" thus shape Adam's self-image and his development of a subjective identity (Stoddard Holmes 2018, 378). "Even before he sees his own reflection, he experiences what it means to be a 'staree,' to have an eminently 'stareable' body and face" (ibid.). Even more so, as a science experiment, Adam is subjected to the microscopes and lights—the scrutinising examination of his creators—directly after his birth and even before he meets the gaze of the broader public. Although he is beautiful for the first days of his life, his 3D-printed body is still an anomaly. Just as Shelley's creature "learns his visual identity first from the stares, words, and behaviors of others," Adam is taught by the reactions he experiences that he is not the same as other people (ibid.). Once his cells start to break down because of an error in his creation, and his looks rapidly deteriorate, Adam's life is considered worthless, and he, a broken commodity. "Endued with a figure hideously deformed and loathsome," he feels "not even of the same nature as man" (Shelley 1818, 141).

It is notable that Shelley continuously uses the word "deformity" to describe the creature's body (Shelley 1818, 83, 133, 155, 168, 170, 202, 205). Adams et al. connect this term to monstrosity; 'monstrosity' implying a link to the supernatural, and 'deformity' representing "a falling away from godliness into a particular kind of moral and physical ugliness" (2015, 32). 'Deformity,' by way of its definition as 'misshapen,' Helen Deutsch points out, also implies the existence of a "negligent agency, a body created and abandoned by its author" (2015, 158). Adam is abandoned because of his deformity, as his form is created incorrectly. A similar term in this realm of appearance and morality is that of 'disability' (Adams et al. 2015, 32). As critical responses to *Frankenstein* have been persistently "[concerned] with the aberrant body and the tyranny of normative embodiment" (Wyse 2018, 10), scholars of Disability Studies, which "make meaning out of the ways appearance determines worth, value, and morality," often read the creature's narrative through the lens of disability, attempting to better understand the cultural meaning of ugliness by analysing how it is narratively constructed (Friedman and Kavey 2018, 267).

To extrapolate from deformity to disability is not far-fetched, considering that "aesthetic judgements implicate disability insofar as they presume a normative standard of perception and an ideal of bodily perfection as the object of affective response" (Davidson 2015, 85). Adam does not meet this standard; consequently, he becomes the object of discrimination. "Trapped in repeated social construction," he has no way to escape the constant visual scrutiny of his body other than befriending the blind Eddie, much like Shelley's creature seeks to befriend the blind old Delaney (Mossman 2001, n. p.). "In open daylight,

[his] disfigurement and abnormality are always present, immediate, defining," and as such, the creature must take on this deformity as an immutable and intrinsic part of his self (ibid.). Adam's physical difference "cannot be ignored or put aside," it colours every social interaction he has (ibid.). His narrative mirrors the damnation/pity paradigm of disability studies:[3] He is seen as a threat (for example by Victor) or met with compassion (from Elizabeth), frequently at once (Wanda). Some of the Othering of disabled, deformed bodies, can be traced back to the prevalence of Descartes' mind-body dualism, "which made it possible to conceive of a human body without a working (rational) mind and to equate these supposedly mindless human bodies with animals" (Gabbard 2015, 284). Disabled people thus have their subjective humanity denied, either seen as human bodies without human minds, or just in-human (ibid., 282). "Fucking animal," "freak show," "elephant man," all these insults are hurled at Adam (Rose 2015, 41:10–41:37). *FRANK3N5T3IN's* Adam, then, can be read as a disabled individual, his physical abnormality marking him as an outsider.

In Heather Laine Talley's study on facial disfigurement and its cultural meaning, she notes that in "appearance-obsessed cultures" such as ours, "facial difference is treated as a threat compromising notions of self and identity and profoundly affecting social relations" (2014, 12). The body, especially the face, is not only "a means of communication," it is "a marker of identity and personhood, a signifier of social status, and a form of capital" (ibid., 13). Having the 'wrong' kind of face or body, then, profoundly threatens our status as full subjects at its core. "If human beauty is, at the limit, the perfect realisation of the concept of human being," Noël Carroll writes, "then nonbeauty … is somehow an inadequate instantiation of the concept of human being" (2003, 88). The ugly individual is merely seen as a "filthy mass that [moves] and [talks]," sickening Victor Frankenstein's heart and evoking "horror and hatred" (Shelley 1818, 177). Its appearance makes it too abnormal to be a part of the community, "its unearthly ugliness rendered almost too horrible for human eyes" (ibid., 113).

"Within the traits that make a body monstrous … we may read the difference between an other and a self, a pervert and a normal person, a foreigner and a native," and the inscription of a body as 'ugly' thus serves as a tool to uphold the hierarchies of an us-versus-them mentality (Halberstam 1995, 8). The creature, human-like in its movements and general form, yet markedly non-human, is an ambiguous figure. The horror of the Gothic genre draws from the fear caused by this ambiguity, the disturbing quality of something that is indeterminate, "neither wholly self, nor wholly other" (Aranda et al. 2012, 558).

3 Leonard Kriegel: "the cripple is a threat and recipient of compassion, both to be damned and to be pitied—and frequently to be damned as he is pitied," quoted in Mark Mossman (n.p.).

Not only is the status of the monster's being ambiguous, but it also terrifies because of the possibility that we are not safe from the same judgement. After all, disfigurement is potentially always a fate that could strike us, too. "The ugly is that which threatens to consume and disorder the subject," and Adam's deformity, his de-humanised 'wrong' existence, threatens not only his own subject status, but also "the entire system of symbolic representation" at the heart of cultural hegemony (Gigante 2000, 568–9). The monster is a monster because its existence is unacceptable, and as such, it is unthinkable (Aranda et al. 2012, 558). As mentioned earlier, societal hierarchies need the 'other,' and yet the monster is a danger to authority because it can question and unsettle established norms. Ugliness resists "the aestheticі[s]ation that enables that very authority" (Gigante 2000, 568). The ugly 'other,' the monster, must be excised from society, its very claim to subjectivity disputed to uphold the "elaborate symbolic network" of appearance and value (ibid., 567).

## 7 Violence and Vulnerability

Bryan Turner writes in his essay on vulnerability and human rights that "[o]ur relationship with the world is always through our embodiment" (2006, 21). While Adam's body gives him a unique, individual perception of the world and therefore makes him part of the "commonality of human cultures," he is denied the sympathy and exchange that other human beings are afforded, because he is too markedly different (ibid.). His body separates him from the 'body' of humanity. As such, he is constantly exposed to violence. The scientists, security guards, and the police represent a constant threat and his life on the streets is characterised by the absence of physical safety. He is beaten up and robbed, must forage for food in dumpsters and beg, all while constantly having to fear police brutality. "These eyes, look at them. Each one took six months to print … I'm keeping these, give me the scalpel," one of the scientists says over his supposedly dead body (Rose 2015, 17:24–17:42). He is seen as a collection of high-tech bio-parts instead of a holistic unit, a 'self' like other human beings are afforded. Although Adam is much stronger and more resilient than any normal person, the constant attempts on his life and the disregard that is shown to his safety, continuously make it clear to him that his vulnerable body does not deserve protection. Time and time again, Adam is denied his right to life.

The physical aspect of his experience is prominently emphasised in the movie. Rose sets his film in a violent, bleak environment. The laboratory is a space of cold colours and bright lights, bare and unnatural, a space where "human life [is reduced] to the status of a disposable experimental animal" (Botting 2018, 311). Rose intersperses Elizabeth's motherly affection for Adam with "shots and sounds of pain," most disturbing of which is possibly the 'euthanisation' scene, "[Adam's] body going into spasms while strapped to a surgical table and violent convulsions as another needle penetrates his skin" and his 'parents' try to put him down like a wounded animal (ibid.). The gratuitous amounts of body horror and gore graphically remind the viewer of their own corporality. Bodies in Rose's *FRANK3N5T3IN* are fragile things capable of great violence, the threat of being cut or sliced or pierced or maimed always at the forefront. Precious blood is all too eager to leave the confines of skin, and death is ever-present where life is constituted of biomass and bodily juices. With childish wonder, a young Adam flails and punches and slices those who attack him, marvelling at the blood and gore hidden within the human form and seemingly brought to light so easily. Later, the crass depictions of pornography Wanda shows Adam on her phone, followed immediately by a recording of a birth, adds to this impression of human life as a crude, animalistic process. Adam is a part of this process through his own physicality, yet his body is not like those that surround him. His disability and ugliness mark him to other people as an outsider, but so do his superhuman strength and resistance. He is at once too powerful and too vulnerable to be a part of the society he sees around him. Eventually, his "acts of physical violence" turn out to be "the only real control or power that the creature is able to achieve" (Mossman 2001, n. p.). He cannot find lasting human connection and acceptance through his simple embodied existence or his acts of kindness or curiosity, such as when he offers Eddie a rat to eat, befriends a wild dog, plays with a little girl, or bonds with Wanda over Elizabeth. All these actions end in rejection or suffering, but he has a degree of leverage over his environment through violence. He can kill the police officer that attempted to execute him, he can destroy his copy, and he can take revenge on his creator. His power, then, "comes not in achieving normalcy, but in embodying deviance," which, in turn, is already "associated with physical abnormality," the prophecy fulfilling itself (ibid.). The gothic monster is violence "embodied within a specifically deviant form … that announces itself (de-monstrates) as the place of corruption" (Halberstam 1995, 2). As a result, Adam has no choice but to become monstrous by embodying the only mode of authority available to the monster.

Furthermore, Adam's pain is not just a biological symptom, "[a]ll pain is subjectively, and, therefore, culturally meaningful" (Hughes and Paterson 1999, 602). Pain itself is a "state of embodiment which 'produces culture'" (ibid.), that is, culture and meaning are not additional to pain, but inherently a part of it. Pain "is always 'socially informed' and it informs the social" (ibid.). Who gets to hurt people and in what way, whose body is vulnerable and whose pain matters, those are all questions that go beyond mere biology. Consequently, being physically hurt has cultural meaning insofar as it expresses social hierarchies. The 'other' is not safe from violence, and, by implication, those not safe from violence are made 'other.' Violence, harm caused and suffered, then, becomes a marker of the outsider in a society. In a vicious circle, those assigned the label of 'other' hence live with violence as a seemingly obvious and inevitable part of their lives, seen both as violent and as deserving of violence. Adam, as a homeless person, not only suffers indirect, systemic violence in the form of poverty and homelessness, he is also subjected to violence from fellow outsiders, as seen in the attempted robbery of Eddie's belongings, and from police, all of it exemplifying an "inescapable chain in which punishment, revenge, suppression, and reaction" seem to be "the only imperatives" (Botting 2018, 313). Having to endure this precariousness, the constant physical attacks and the threat of pain, Adam's vulnerability makes it impossible for him to form a healthy, subjective sense of self. "Vulnerability is both a physical and spiritual condition," and as such, Adam's situation makes "embodiment, enselfment, and emplacement" impossible (Turner 2006, 27). As Fred Botting writes on the "moral counterpart" of physical suffering: "extreme violence is not only directed at bodies but towards subjects in the ruining of self-respect, the 'robbing' of dignity and denial of the possibility of resistance" (2018, 309). Adam's status as 'other' makes him vulnerable, and his vulnerability, in turn, marks him as 'other.'

## 8 Coda: (The Politics of) Metaphor

Traditionally, Shelley's *Frankenstein* narrative has been understood as a "representation of marginalisation and victimisation," her creature becoming "the ultimate [symbol] of practices of discrimination" (Mossman 2001, n. p.). Indeed, *Frankenstein* has been established so firmly as allegorical that it has become "a metaphor for metaphor itself" (Young 2008, 107). Bernard Rose, too, employs a broad reading of *Frankenstein*'s creature, in which Adam "stands in for all those physically different human beings unjustly misrecognised, devalued, and excluded, subject to the social projection of dread and disgust, in short, dehumanised" (Wyse 2018, 77). As a 21st century update, the film aligns him with the urban outsider, specifically the disabled and mentally ill, the homeless, and the racialised poor 'other,' that is, what Karmakar and Parui call the "human leftovers" of "neoliberal consumer culture" (2018, 348). Re-contextualising the original's "nineteenth-century complaint about the heinous inequalities of wealth" for our time, *FRANK3N5T3IN* "offers stark evidence of the absence of human progress" as "[w]retchedness, misery, and poverty remain as visible and palpable as ever" (Botting 2018, 312).

Coming face to face with his own artificiality and non-being, Adam "reali[s]es that unlike humans he lacks a respectable lineage, rank, and birth history: the definable genealogy required in order to be acknowledged as a member of a politically agentic community" (Karmakar and Parui 2018, 347). He is a "non-citizen ... pushed to the geographical margins" of the city and "viewed as a valueless threat" (348–9). Importantly, he is not treated significantly worse than those who share his situation, "the lesser others of Western culture—women, people of color, the coloni[s]ed," as seen with Eddie and Wanda (Flax 1993, 46). They, too, are treated inhumanely, robbed, and murdered, their bodies unsafe and vulnerable. The horrific life of Adam plainly gives the metaphor the moral dimension of damning the exclusion he—and, consequently, those marginalised like him—experience. Adam is a "pitiable figure," but he is also violent, causing death and destruction, like that of Wanda and Elizabeth (Burdan 1998, n. p.). The film may make the viewer understand the unfairness of Adam's fate, but ultimately, just like the 1818 novel, "it also seems glad for the monster's promised death" (n. p.).

The metaphor is also muddied by portraying the stand-in for the urban Western 'other'—the marginalised, the racialised, the disabled, the poor—as a white man. As Halberstam points out, race, in the Gothic narrative, is "wedded to the various demonized class identities and coded into the overall monstrosity of the monster" (1995, 126). It is used metaphorically, rather than actually appearing 'as race' (ibid.). "Perhaps because race has been so successfully gothicised within our recent history, filmmakers and screenplay writers tend not to want to make a monster who is defined by a deviant racial identity" (ibid., 4), and by using the marginalisation of race as metaphor on a white body and aligning Adam's experience with that of the racialised other (such as his only friends Eddie and Wanda), the film turns the realities of racism into a "Gothic [discourse] given over to the making monstrous of particular kinds of bodies" (ibid., 4). Similarly, disabled activists and scholars have long spoken out against disability as metaphor, "which [they] regard as a way of appropriating disability for purposes not consonant with the interests of the disabled" (Berger 2015, 505). "[S]ince the beginning of Western culture, disabled characters have symboli[s]ed the crossroads of human and nonhuman" (Gabbard 2015, 283). By having the monster be recognised as a disabled figure, most plainly when the policemen call him "mongoloid" and "elephant man" (Rose 2015, 41:31-41:37), the film questionably conflates disability with non-humanity. So, while the narrative may portray Adam as a pitiable and thus mostly sympathetic character, it still uses metaphor to speak about the marginalised of society. While acts of Othering are depicted as harmful and immoral, they are also naturalised to a degree. For the viewer, "humanity—humane treatment of others, justice, etc.—is always beyond our reach," an intrinsic part of not only the present but also the sci-fi future, "[j]ust as, for the monster, paradise is always lost in *Frankenstein*" (Halberstam 1995, 37).

## 9 Conclusion

By putting the story of *Frankenstein* in a vaguely futuristic urban context, Bernard Rose re-imagines Mary Shelley's most influential work for a 21st century audience. His movie examines how a phenomenology of the body can create a sense of unique subjectivity. Rose's creature, Adam, experiences the world via embodied empiricism and learns to act and feel human, to develop a mind, by mirroring those around him. His is a consciousness of being that is grounded in the body, and yet his body is also the locus of his troubled existence as a non-being and an outsider to his community. Adam's deformity marks him to the regulating and punishing gaze of normative society, exposing him to physical violence, and discursively making his body and mind monstrous. In conclusion, *FRANK3N5T31N* depicts processes of Othering that are firmly located in the body as both source and downfall of Adam's mind, his humanity, and his personhood. Yet what is the purpose of transplanting a story from the early 19th century into a modern setting? Posthumanist arguments about technology and humanity, being and non-being, are inherent to the *Frankenstein* narrative. However, by creating Adam, the 3D-printed monster, *FRANK3N5T31N* establishes a direct link between Mary Shelley's age and our own. Concerns about who is or is not human, the boundaries of scientific discovery, the value of life—all of these issues are just as urgent now as they were 200 years ago.

## Works Cited

Adams, Rachel, Benjamin Reiss, and David Serlin. "Disability." *Keywords for Disability Studies*, edited by Rachel Adams, Benjamin Reiss, and David Serlin. New York: New York UP, 2015.

Aranda, Kay, Laetitia Zeeman, Julie Scholes, and Arantxa Santa-María Morales. "The Resilient Subject: Exploring Subjectivity, Identity and the Body in Narratives of Resilience." *Health: An Interdisciplinary Journal for the Social Study of Health, Illness and Medicine*, vol. 16, no. 5, 2012, pp. 548–63. https://doi.org/10.1177/1363459312438564.

Béres Rogers, Kathleen. "The Monstrous Idea in Mary Shelley's *Frankenstein*." *Literature and Medicine*, vol. 36, no. 2, 2018, pp. 356–71. https://doi.org/10.1353/lm.2018.0018.

Berger, James. "Trauma." *Keywords for Disability Studies*, edited by Rachel Adams, Benjamin Reiss, and David Serlin. New York: New York UP, 2015.

Botting, Fred. "What Was Man ...? Reimagining Monstrosity from Humanism to Trashumanism." *Global Frankenstein*, edited by Carol Margaret Davison and Marie Mulvey-Roberts. Cham: Palgrave Macmillan, 2018.

Burdan, Judith. "*Frankenstein* by Mary Shelley (1818)." *Encyclopedia of the Novel*, edited by Paul E. Schellinger, Christopher Hudson, and Marijke Rijsberman. London: Fitzroy Dearborn, 1998.

Carroll, Noël. *Engaging the Moving Image*. New Haven: Yale UP, 2003.

Davidson, Michael. "Aesthetics." In *Keywords for Disability Studies*, edited by Rachel Adams, Benjamin Reiss, and David Serlin. New York: New York UP, 2015.

Denson, Shane. *Postnaturalism: Frankenstein, Film, and the Anthropotechnical Interface*. Bielefeld: Transcript, 2014.

Deutsch, Helen. "Deformity." *Keywords for Disability Studies*, edited by Rachel Adams, Benjamin Reiss, and David Serlin. New York: New York UP, 2015.

Diedrich, Lisa. "Being-Becoming-Monster: Mirrors and Mirroring in Graphic *Frankenstein* Narratives." *Literature and Medicine*, vol. 36, no. 2, 2018, pp. 388–411. https://doi.org/10.1353/lm.2018.0020.

Flax, Jane. "Multiples: On the Contemporary Politics of Subjectivity." *Human Studies*, vol. 16, no.1/2, 1993, pp. 33–49. https://doi.org/10.1007/bf01318570.

Gabbard, D. Christopher. "Human." *Keywords for Disability Studies*, edited by Rachel Adams, Benjamin Reiss, and David Serlin. New York: New York UP, 2015.

Gigante, Denise. "Facing the Ugly: The Case of *Frankenstein*." *ELH*, vol. 67, no. 2, 2000, pp. 565–87. https://doi.org/10.1353/elh.2000.0015.

Halberstam, Jack. *Skin Shows: Gothic Horror and the Technology of Monsters*. Durham: Duke UP, 1995.

Holmes, Martha Stoddard. "Born This Way: Reading *Frankenstein* with Disability." *Literature and Medicine*, vol. 36, no. 2, 2018, pp. 372–87. https://doi.org/10.1353/lm.2018.0019.

Karmakar, Manali, and Avishek Parui. "Victor's Progeny: Premonition of a Bioengineered Age." *Literature and Medicine*, vol. 36, no. 2, 2018, pp. 337–55. https://doi.org/10.1353/lm.2018.0017.

Kastoryano, Riva. "Codes of Otherness." *Social Research*, vol. 77, no. 1, 2010, pp. 79–100.

Kavey, Allison B., and Lester D. Friedman. "Introduction: Chemistry, Disability, and *Frankenstein*." *Literature and Medicine*, vol. 36, no. 2, 2018, pp. 264–68. https://doi.org/10.1353/lm.2018.0013.

Law, Jules David. "Being There: Gothic Violence and Virtuality in *Frankenstein*, *Dracula*, and *Strange Days*." *ELH*, vol. 73, no. 4, 2006, pp 975–96. https://doi.org/10.1353/elh.2006.0000.

Long Hoeveler, Diane. "*Frankenstein*, Feminism, and Literary Theory." *The Cambridge Companion to Mary Shelley*, edited by Esther Schor. Cambridge UP, 2003.

Mellor, Anne K. "Making a 'Monster': An Introduction to *Frankenstein*." *The Cambridge Companion to Mary Shelley*, edited by Esther Schor. Cambridge UP, 2003.

Mossman, Mark. "Acts of Becoming: Autobiography, *Frankenstein*, and the Postmodern Body." *Postmodern Culture*, vol. 11, no. 3, 2001. https://doi.org/10.1353/pmc.2001.0012.

Paterson, Kevin, and Bill Hughes. "Disability Studies and Phenomenology: The Carnal Politics of Everyday Life." *Disability & Society*, vol. 14, no. 5, 1999, pp. 597–610. https://doi.org/10.1080/09687599925966.

Rose, Bernard, dir. *Frankenstein*. Alchemy, 2015.

Shelley, Mary. *Frankenstein*. Planet Ebook. www.planetebook.com/free-ebooks/frankenstein, [1818] 2020.

Talley, Heather Laine. *Saving Face: Disfigurement and the Politics of Appearance*. New York: New York UP, 2014.

Turner, Bryan S. *Vulnerability and Human Rights*. University Park, Pennsylvania: Pennsylvania State University, 2006.

Wilkerson, Abby. "Embodiment." *Keywords for Disability Studies*, edited by Rachel Adams, Benjamin Reiss, and David Serlin. New York: New York UP, 2015.

Wolfe, Charles T., and Ofer Gal. *The Body as Object and Instrument of Knowledge: Embodied Empiricism in Early Modern Science*. Dordrecht, New York: Springer, Cop., 2010.

Wyse, Bruce. "'The Human Senses Are Insurmountable Barriers': Deformity, Sympathy, and Monster Love in Three Variations on *Frankenstein*." *Global Frankenstein*, edited by Carol Margaret Davison and Marie Mulvey-Roberts. Cham: Palgrave Macmillan, 2018.

Young, Elizabeth. *Black Frankenstein: The Making of an American Metaphor*. New York: New York UP, 2008.

CHAPTER 16

# Playing with Speculative Bodies and Minds: Moral Imagination at Work in Primo Levi's Science Fiction

*Marzia Beltrami*

## 1 Introduction

Both in Italy and internationally, the name of Primo Levi (1919–1987) is largely known in connection with testimonial writing and his experience as a survivor of Auschwitz. While most of Levi's work is therefore nonfictional or fundamentally realistic,[1] it is perhaps less known that he also authored several short stories ascribable to the science-fiction genre. These stories feature manifold representations of non-normative and even impossible bodies and minds, as the result of either technological or fantastic manipulation. Yet, arguably, these speculative creatures are not intended to strike for their sheer impossibility: in fact, I argue that what remains verisimilar is their embodied condition, that is to say the irreducible interdependence of bodily make-up and the type of mental and social life a certain body enables.

In this chapter, I aim to explore in particular the ethical underpinnings of Levi's science fiction and its explorations of non-normative bodies and minds, also with a view to proposing a broader argument about the potential ethical function of imagination in fiction. Due to his literary and cultural role as witness, Levi's authorial ethos (Korthals Altes 2014) inevitably leads one to interrogate the moral engagement of these stories vis-à-vis with his nonfictional production linked to the Holocaust and the *univers concentrationnaire*. My suggestion, however, is that the ethical dimension of Levi's science fiction stands out in its own right and is pursued through the speculative nature of these stories, not *despite* it. In other words, Levi recognises the unique potential

1 *The Periodic Table* (*Il sistema periodico*, 1975) is a collection of stories, each titled after a chemical element that features concretely or metaphorically in episodes from Levi's youth or early career as chemist. *The Wrench* (*La chiave a stella*, 1978) gathers stories revolving around the theme of work as a skilled craft, fictionally told by rigger Libertino Faussone to a first-person narrator which could easily pass as a mildly fictionalized avatar of Levi. *If Not Now, When?* (*Se non ora, quando?*, 1982) is a fictional historical novel, focusing on a group of Jewish partisans in Eastern Europe.

 | DOI:10.1163/9789004519886_018

and positioning of fiction and, more specifically, of a speculative genre such as science fiction (Polvinen 2021, 2018) when it comes to tackle moral reasoning from a different angle. I shall argue that he took the distance of science fiction from realism (yet not from reality) as the pathway to a kind of moral thought more in line with his own: aiming less at establishing *the right* solution, and more directed towards the cultivation of moral reasoning as the practice of contemplating possible ethical outcomes which are fundamentally embedded in specific circumstances.[2]

Through my discussion, I give shape to an understanding of moral imagination as a use of imagination which has an inherently ethical dimension inasmuch as it explores and renders a certain sense of what it is to be living beings in the world. On the one hand, I claim we can see moral imagination at work in Levi's science-fiction stories because they feature the systematic investigation of bodies and minds whose speculative manipulation brings their situatedness – situatedness in their material condition, even before than in the social and interpersonal context – to the fore; this, in turn, expresses precisely that "sense of life" which according to philosopher Cora Diamond is at the heart of the workings of moral imagination. On the other hand, the case study of Primo Levi shows how moral imagination may fully operate in fiction even in its speculative forms, whose relative distance from realism does not undermine its ethical function and may work also in the absence of moral issues explicitly addressed at the level of content.

## 2 Previous Mentions of Moral Imagination in Relation to Levi

Reference to the notion of moral imagination is not unprecedented in Levi studies. At least two critics resort to the idea, although focusing in both cases on Levi's nonfictional writing.

Philosopher and Holocaust literature scholar Berel Lang uses the expression to emphasise the moral sensibility that is "clearly directing [Levi's] imagination" in his skilful description of "the startling features of nature, human and nonhuman" (2013, 82). Lang praises Levi's imagination not as *inventio*, but as the capability of presenting actual facts and features of nature or society through a creatively rich gaze that renews others' attention towards them. Later on,

2 In Levi scholarship, this position matches with the claim shared by Pierpaolo Antonello (2005), Robert Gordon (2003), Federico Pianzola (2017), and Charlotte Ross (2011) among others that Levi is not a moralist author as he does not aim to determine an aprioristic or normative ethics.

Lang employs a similar expression to comment on Levi's original articulation of the concept of gray zone.[3] The gray zone defines an intermediate moral area that includes conducts taking place in situations where neither good nor evil are fully applicable descriptors: Lang defines Levi's concept as "morally imaginative" because it recognises the moral standing of a position that, being nonstandard, would be otherwise pushed aside in conventional moral accounts (2013, 30). Moral imagination, thus, is called upon to capture an application of imaginative skills to the rendering of contextual features or nonstandard scenarios. However, in neither case Lang expands on the concept of moral imagination itself, nor does he refer to any specific previous use of the term.

More recently, in her 2021 monograph reconstructing the compositional history of Levi's nonfictional work *The Drowned and the Saved* (*I sommersi e i salvati*, 1987), Martina Mengoni refers to moral imagination as an important tool employed by Levi in his contribution to Simon Wiesenthal's *The Sunflower* (2021, 92–105). In *The Sunflower*, Wiesenthal recounts the real story of how he, as a Jew, was asked for forgiveness by a dying SS soldier in 1942. The author asked various prominent figures among European survivors and intellectuals for their personal opinion on the matter, gathering their answers in an appendix. Levi's prompt reply to Wiesenthal was included already in the 1969 first Dutch edition: in this letter, Mengoni recognises what she describes as moral imagination, that is an exercise in imagination in order to explore a moral conundrum – namely, whether or not Wiesenthal was right in denying his forgiveness to the Nazi soldier.

Unlike Lang, Mengoni explicitly borrows the term from Cora Diamond (2003) and her discussion of J. M. Coetzee's Tanners lectures delivered at Princeton University in 1997–98, later published with the title *The Lives of Animals*. Coetzee had structured his lectures in a fictional form, as two stories centred on the fictional character of Elizabeth Costello, she herself engaged in the delivery of a series of public lectures on the very same topic. Diamond's own essay revolves around the commentary on Coetzee's lectures provided by four scholars: in particular, she criticises the scholars' abstracting operation, as they reason about Costello's arguments while dislodging them from their fictional context. By contrast, Diamond argues it would be best *not* to do so: taking issue with the assumption that ideas can and ought to be always abstracted and examined as general principles, she re-appraises the value of the fictional and contextualised form of Coetzee's lectures (2003, 5). She admits that this move would make it impossible to regard Costello's moral deliberations as universal

3 For the concept of grey zone see Levi (1987, ch. 2); cf. Brown (2013), Gordon (2003, 19–20), Mengoni (2018).

principles, but she also claims that it does not take anything away from their ethical value either; it simply makes them different from the type of elaboration demanded by the moral philosophical tradition. Importantly, Diamond connects moral imagination to an activity that does not seek to establish moral *rules*, and she reclaims the viability and fruitfulness of this kind of moral reasoning.

One of the points Mengoni thus gets from Diamond's moral imagination and traces back in Levi is the idea of the narrative context as irreducibly intertwined with the moral issue at stake (2021, 98). This propensity she connects to what Levi himself in *If This Is a Man* calls "to demonstrate by telling".[4] In Mengoni's argument, the idea of moral imagination does not much indicate the moral content of Levi's reflection: rather, it captures the situated and embodied quality of his imaginary scenarios, which acquire a moral dimension and ethical quality precisely for being situated and embodied. As she observes, "to imagine, for Levi, does not mean therefore to create something *ex nihilo*, but rather to embed it in reality" (2021, 277 – my transl.). In this she aligns with Lang's comment that Levi's ethical reflection consists in the consideration of human behavior "under *certain* conditions": "the key question Levi introduces here is why *that* behavior in *that* context should be judged more revealing of human nature than the fact that under other circumstances people conduct themselves quite differently" (2013, 120). Lang concludes that in *If This is a Man* Levi argues for a contextual view of human nature in contrast to an essentialist view: "a situational view that differs from the others in emphasi[s]ing the *relationship* between human responses and the settings occasioning them" (ibid., 121). This arguably confirms Levi's interest in the particular and the situated, rather than in the general principle (which goes hands in hands with his scepticism towards collective moral responsibility). Idiosyncratic (and non-normative) cases are not exceptional when it comes to undergoing evaluation and judgement: in fact, in a sense all cases should be regarded as idiosyncratic in their situatedness, in the deliberate effort to avoid generalisations.

Following Diamond, moral imagination is the capacity of telling the other while maintaining – and conveying to the reader – "the awareness we each have of being a living body, of being 'alive to the world'" (2003, 22). In this broader sense, Mengoni suggests that speaking of moral imagination for Levi expresses less a moral quality per se and more an analytic approach or outlook: some sort of deliberate projecting capacity of Levi for "inhabiting other bodies

4 Unless stated otherwise, English translations of Levi's work are from Levi (2015); quotes from Cassata (2016) are taken from the bilingual text.

and other perspectives".[5] Because Mengoni focuses on Levi's testimonial writing, it is worth noting that she does not equate 'narrative' with 'fiction': and yet the argument unfolded by Levi in the letter to Wiesenthal (as by Coetzee via Diamond) does include the assessment of hypothetical scenarios, too. It follows that the importance of the narrative context lies not in its factual or historical truth, but in its capability of rendering the complexity and intricacy of specific circumstances. Like for Diamond, for Levi to appreciate the particularity of an episode does not mean to limit its value: far from being undermined by its lack of universal validity, to recognise such particularity implies the possibility of acknowledging its totalizing effects on that specific life ("the individual incurability of an offence", Mengoni 2021, 100 – my transl.).

Mengoni's arguments are especially significant because, in addition to fitting Levi's nonfictional writing, they offer a lens to highlight powerful continuities with the fictional production without denying its specificity. It often happens that, when ethical engagement is expressed in terms of reflection on the limits and risks of scientific experimentation, the richly fictional nature of the narrative gets sidelined, its exquisitely speculative mode bracketed or justified in the light of a more dignified purpose. Contrary to this view, for Levi not only science fiction is an early interest and not merely an entertaining container for higher messages (Cassata 2016), but it also constitutes an alternative and unique mode of moral reasoning. As I shall show by looking at Levi's speculative stories, the employment of moral imagination as the capability to imagine what is like for a certain creature holding non-normative body and mind to be alive (Diamond 1991) may be seen as fostering a double, or reinforced, situatedness of his narrative: on the one hand, its embeddedness in a historically or at least socially situated context; on the other hand, reference to the living body brings attention to the material situatedness that is, in fact, the embeddedness of characters in their biological context. Their unfaltering awareness of "being alive in the world" could indeed be rephrased as *embodiedness*.[6]

5 It should be noted that Mengoni never uses the term 'empathy' to discuss this inhabiting of others' perspective. Although a discussion of the issue is beyond the scope of this essay (cf. Carta and Marchese 2024), suffice it to say that Levi would not go as far as to argue that one should necessarily feel empathy towards the other and particularly towards one's persecutors: it is enough to imagine the situated historical and psychological circumstances, without entering the emotional sphere. My understanding is that Diamond, too, strives not to equate moral imagination to sympathetic identification (cf. Diamond 1991).

6 Later on in her analysis, Mengoni retrieves the notion of moral imagination and couples it with that of historical imagination (2021, 276–78). These two uses of imagination are similar and correlated, but while moral imagination focuses on the situated exploration of moral details, historical imagination refers to the articulation of historical circumstances

## 3 Mark Johnson: Further Embodying Moral Imagination

Before looking more closely at Levi's science fiction, I wish to further enrich Diamond's moral imagination by encasing it deeper in embodiment, which can be done by relating it to Mark Johnson's own elaboration of the concept.

From Diamond's writing, it follows that fictional narrative does not have to engage directly with moral topics or stage moments of mimetic reflection in order to have an ethical import. Building on Martha Nussbaum and Iris Murdoch among others, Diamond argues that creative writers can "show us, then, the shape of certain possibilities in human life" (1988, 265), even when they do not directly touch upon any instance of choice or evaluation of events or states of affairs. The hypothesis she puts forward is that literature and fiction can participate in our moral life by impinging on the process of conceptualisation.[7] Reading stories, in other words, can interact with the dynamic regulating the formation and development of concepts, including moral ones. According to Diamond, "grasping a concept […] is not a matter just of knowing how to group things under that concept; it is being able to participate in life-with-the-concept" (1988, 266). This could be rephrased as the imaginative implementation of a concept within a situated context. To integrate Diamond's reflection with Mark Johnson's, another philosopher who devoted much attention to moral imagination, allows us to take full advantage of the implications he draws. Johnson's work on moral imagination may come helpful in two main respects: first, because he ties it firmly to embodiment; secondly, because he offers a viable explanation of how imagination intervenes in the process of conceptualisation, creating a strong connection between moral philosophy and cognitive literary studies.

Johnson's exploration of moral imagination is framed within the wider rethinking of moral theory in the light of recent developments in our understanding of how the mind works and, particularly, following the recognition of cognition as embodied that marked the so-called second-generation cognitive sciences (Lakoff & Johnson 1980; 1999).[8] In *The Moral Imagination* (1993),

more specifically. She reckons that both types of imagination run across Levi's reflection throughout the years, and yet it is in *The Drowned and the Saved* that they achieve their more balanced and more profitable combination.

7 Following Diamond's argument, I shall keep speaking of literature, but it should be borne in mind that the same goes for any other creative form, from films to visual art and so on.

8 The term 'second-generation', introduced by Lakoff and Johnson (1999, 77–78), captures the renewed attention to embodiment in contrast with first-generation approaches, which tended to promote a view of cognition as disembodied, abstract and computational that initially thrived on exchanges with artificial intelligence and information science.

Johnson seeks to reframe the Enlightenment tradition and Western moral theories which are grounded in it, "in a way that is consistent with what we know about the self, reason, concepts, and so forth" (244).[9] If empirical research has been providing increasing evidence that our cognition is deeply situated in the type of body we have and shaped by the interactions we hold with the surrounding environment, traditional theories concerning our moral thinking cannot remain untouched either. For Johnson, imagination is part and parcel of our reasoning capabilities, and to make a case for moral imagination means to acknowledge the imaginative nature of moral concepts, moral reasoning (i.e., understanding a situation as morally laden), and moral deliberation (i.e., deciding one's position or course of action in relation to the morally-laden situation). Holding a view of reason as embodied and metaphoric, he challenges the classic dichotomy between rationality and imagination, a dichotomic understanding that traditionally justifies the exclusion of imagination from moral reasoning at any level, for it was regarded as entirely uncontrolled, free-floating, and subjective.

If we are to acknowledge a more central role to embodiment, Johnson provides a philosophical yet cognitive-based explanation of how literature and fiction may impact the process of conceptualisation. In classic theory of categorisation, for a concept to fall within a category it needs comply with a certain set of essential properties: for instance, to define the concept of *human being* means to list a set of qualities something must have in order to be recognised as such. Johnson, however, draws on experimental work carried out by cognitive psychologist Eleanor Rosch on conceptualisation to contend that our construction and recognition of concepts does not work in this way: to recognise something (from a table to a human being), we do not automatically compute a set of features and verify whether they apply. Instead, the way we actually think seems to be better described by a *prototypical* structure of conceptualisation: this means that, for each concept, we usually hold in mind a standard situation or image – a prototype – against which we position and assess other instances as well as real-life nonprototypical cases. It follows that, while prototypical instances make up the centre of the concept, nonprototypical instances radiate at various conceptual distances from the central members (1993, 92).

9 Problematic assumptions questioned by Johnson include the idea of a split self based on the Judeo-Christian conception of human beings as metaphysically bifurcated (reason vs. bodily desires and emotions); a universal and disembodied reason, directly resulting from the idea that there are distinct mental capacities, namely Feeling, Understanding, Reason and Will (a view that goes under the label of Faculty Psychology); radical freedom; absolute moral laws.

One key consequence of grounding our understanding of concepts in a theory of prototypes rather than categorisation is the relative structural indeterminacy of concepts, and the acknowledgment of their porous, blurred, and negotiable nature. While such indeterminacy would be disastrous for classic moral theories relying on the rational application of moral laws, for Johnson "moral reasoning cannot consist merely in the rational unpacking of a determinate concept": instead, it inherently "requires imaginative extensions to nonprototypical cases" (1993, 100). In this light, the consideration of nonprototypical and nonstandard instances is by no means a marginal eventuality, but rather an *essential* part of moral reasoning. Indeterminacy is not a flaw; it is inherent to our conceptualisations. It is no accident that Johnson frequently associates moral reasoning to a form of investigation or inquiry: "most of what we do is a form of engaged probing and experimentation with our understanding of situations, our relationships, and our grasp of the implications of various projected courses of action" (1993, 212).

Johnson's and Diamond's insights may thus productively complement each other. On the one hand, Johnson's explanation supplements Diamond's reflection around the nature of concepts, their flexibility, and how they ought to be open to change and constant re-assessment through experience (including experience through imagination as a cognitive exercise). She argues that:

> if we get rid of the idea that using a concept is a matter of using it to pick out what falls under the concept and what does not, if we see instead that life with a concept involves doings and thinkings and understandings of many sorts, into which one's grasp of the concept enters in different ways, then we can accept that coming to understand a conceptual life other than our own involves exercise of concepts belonging to that life. (Diamond 1988, 276)

Johnson's theory of conceptualisation based on prototypes indicates a way to do so.

On the other hand, Diamond approaches the impact of literature and fiction more directly, making a case for their key role in the cultivation of our capability of moral reasoning. In fact, Johnson does not refer to "imaginative" in the sense of "fictional" or even "non-realistic", and what he analyses is the imaginative nature of moral reasoning, rather than the distinctive role fiction and literature may or may not play in supporting our moral life. The closer he gets to addressing the impact of stories is when he focuses on the moral relevance of the *narrativisation* of events and elements and the sense-making practices this entails (a use that rather reminds one of discussions carried out in narrative medicine). Narrative is called upon as a synthetising structure employed alongside other structures of imagination (i.e., image schemas or metaphors), a strategy that provides us with unique imaginative resources to unify the temporal dimension of our existence, that is, to transform sequences of isolated events into significant human actions and projects (ibid., 171). However, it is not this specific quality of narrative I aim to stress in Levi's case, nor it is what makes the contribution of fiction distinctive. Diamond's reflection, by contrast, explicitly considers the unique power of imagination in its fictional and speculative sense, as a cognitive operation capable of detaching itself from factual reality and delving, instead, into the depths of the possible and even the impossible, as long as some basic constraints are retained. By combining insights from both philosophical positions, therefore, I propose an understanding of moral imagination that is both embodied and fit to capture the ethical potential of fiction.

## 4 Manipulations of the Body-Mind Nexus

I shall now turn to Levi's science fiction, focusing in particular on the first collection of stories published in 1966, *Natural Histories* (*Storie naturali*).[10] In the remainder of the chapter, I seek to show how Levi's speculative narratives represent an exercise in moral imagination due to their attention to embodiment and because they use their disengagement from realism – though not from reality – to unfold an imaginative, collectively rich, and deliberately ambivalent exploration of the body-mind nexus which escapes definitive moral laws and absolute ethical stances.

Although his cultural fame was essentially due to testimonial writing and activities (*If This Is a Man* [*Se questo è un uomo*], 1947; *The Truce* [*La tregua*], 1963), scientific interests loomed large in Levi's life. By training and profession, he was a chemist. Until early retirement in 1975, he worked full-time as production director at a varnish factory near Turin and writing was pursued as a side occupation. His mindset and lively curiosity for the scientific method and technical inquiry are thus likely to have drawn Levi more easily towards

10 I leave momentarily aside Levi's second science-fiction volume, *Flaw of Form* (*Vizio di forma*, 1971). Despite certain continuities, the two collections are also characterised by significant differences in atmosphere and concerns (Cassata 2016), as a result of which the second collection often adopts a larger, sometimes planetary perspective, which might displace the focus from the individual body. Other science-fiction and fantastic stories will be later included in the miscellaneous volume *Lilith and Other Stories* (*Lilít e altri racconti*, 1981).

the imaginative opportunities and ethical concerns underpinning a narrative genre that engaged programmatically with these fields. And yet, as I shall argue, the ethical dimension of Levi's science fiction goes beyond the mimetic exploration of the fascination and risks of scientific experimentation, whose limits were also certainly and terribly challenged by Nazi scientists.

As Francesco Cassata remarks, to interpret Levi's deliberately speculative production as a mere transfiguration of Auschwitz would be a banalization and an act of excessive reductionism, for the relationship between the two is "neither unambiguous, nor symbolic, nor intentional" (2016, 237–39, 46).[11] Similarly, to interpret his science fiction as cautionary tales about scientific experimentation and misapplications of technology not only does risk overemphasising the presence of this topic throughout the collection, but also oversees the fact that these stories are not uniformly pessimistic. Indeed, given Levi's life-long career as a chemist, the assumption that he should hold such an unambiguously sceptical attitude towards experimental inquiry and technological developments is hardly tenable.

Out of the fifteen stories composing *Natural Histories*, six of them display overt misapplications of technologies, with outcomes ranging from questionable to indisputably unethical. "Angelic Butterfly" tells the story of the mysterious and disturbing experiments carried out by Dr Leeb, who injected test subjects (possibly prisoners from a concentration camp) with hormones extracted from the glands of the axolotl, an actual kind of Mexican salamander, in order to stimulate the evolutionary step that should supposedly trigger the metamorphosis of humans into angels. In "Versamine", Dr Kleber discovers a chemical substance which can transform pain into pleasure: in contrast with predicted outcomes, however, instead of being spared painful experiences, the animals injected with the drug irreducibly end up dying as they grow addicted

11 Admittedly, Levi himself often recognized a strong link between his science fiction and ethical concerns, describing it as "the experience of a gap, a flaw of form which nullifies one aspect or another of our civilization or our moral universe" (Leopizzi 1965; transl. from Cassata 2016, 44–45). However, this kind of authorial comments are to be read in context: Levi's engagement with science fiction, whose status was still far from settled in Italy (the topic is thoroughly explored in the recent special issue of *Enthymema* on Primo Levi's science fiction, Malvestio, Maiolani and Lima 2023, including also Beltrami 2023a; cf. also Antonello 2008; Brioni and Comberiati 2019, 2020; Pagetti 1979), was seen as a hazard to his credibility as a witness and "serious" writer – a concern that led Einaudi to suggest the use of a pseudonym for *Natural Histories*; Levi will accept, adopting the *nom de plume* of Damiano Malabaila. The publisher's stance and the overall tepid reception from readers probably led Levi to assume a defensive position and, when speaking about the collection, reinforce the continuities between the science-fiction production and the Lager experience (Cassata 2016, 37; cf. Zanda 2019, 242).

to practices which are bound to harm them (licking scalding stoves, self-biting, eating poisonous substances, crashing themselves against objects), in which they uncontrollably indulge as they found them most gratifying. "Some Applications of the Mimete" (and, as a sort of premise leading to it, "Order at Good Price") and "Sleeping Beauty in the Refrigerator: A Winter's Tale" both stage situations in which technological techniques – cloning and cryogenics – result in the objectification of individuals. In the former story, on the spur of absent-minded experimentation Gilberto clones his wife Emma without even consulting her, and the arrival of Emma II – in addition to the obvious ethical issues – breaks the equilibrium of their relationship; in the latter, not only Patricia's sense of social relations and the world are profoundly affected by her unnatural existence regulated by the cryogenic machine she lives in and from which she is released only briefly a few times every year, but she is also further objectified by her "host" who repeatedly rapes her taking advantage of her semi-unconscious state. The closing story of the collection, "Retirement Package", partly retains the ominous feelings of "Versamine" as the protagonist becomes fatally addicted to the Torec, a VR machine which allows the user to experience vicariously the recorded sensory perceptions of others.

In "The Measure of Beauty", "The Versifier", "Full Employment", and "The Mnemagogs", technology or experimental practices ("Full Employment" revolves around a new way of communicating with insects rather than some technological artefact) are employed with vaguely upsetting or partially discouraging outcomes, which point less to the straightforwardly unethical nature of such applications and more to their vacuity. In "Man's Friend", technology plays a neutrally instrumental role, as it leads to decrypt messages in the epithelial cells of some tapeworms, but the story revolves around the discovery of the poetic attachment of the worms to their human hosts. In almost all these cases, with the strong exception of "Angelic Butterfly", the problem is hardly technological experimentation per se but, if any, it is its inconsiderate or unfortunate use on the individual's part. Finally, the remaining stories – "*Cladonia rapida*", "*Quaestio de Centauris*", "Censorship in Bitinia" and "The Sixth Day" – are not about the (mis)application of technology at all.

This brief overview aims to stress that automatically turning the theme of scientific experimentation into an ethically-oriented reading risks flattening the productive ambiguity of Levi's science fiction. In "Some Applications of the Mimete", for instance, the distress caused by Gilberto's reckless cloning of his wife is seemingly solved thanks to the very technology which had caused it, as he recreates two couples by duplicating himself too; contrary to a straightforward condemnation of experimentation, this final balancing act might imply that technological resources – whatever their level of sophistication – are constant factors in our lives as humans, and they can be neither blamed nor saluted as something that straightforwardly condemn or save us.[12] Analogously, without side-lining the unethical treatment of Patricia in "Sleeping Beauty", she also strikes as an ambivalent character at best, showing a self-centred, exploitative, and scarcely empathetic behaviour that prompts the reader to wonder whether the major faults lie, in fact, with individual nature (or culture) rather than technological advancement. To understand these narratives as exercises in moral imagination emphasizing the relevance of context, actual agents, and circumstances over the ethical issue in an abstracted way is arguably truer to the unsolved ambivalence of each story as well as of the collection taken as a whole. It allows to recognize thematic relevance without fixing on an unequivocal interpretation. Furthermore, with a view to acknowledging the role of the fictional mode chosen by Levi in addressing this issue, the plurality of stories may be mired less to reiterate a certain stance and more to promote a contextual view of scientific inquiry versus an essentialist view of it, thus reproducing the aforementioned difference spotted by Lang in relation to Levi's view of human nature.

However, an altogether alternative way of looking at these stories – and this is the original critical angle proposed here – is to see them as variously foregrounding the profound interdependence between bodily materiality and socio-cognitive practices. Embodiment arguably emerges as an unavoidable condition, which may cause alienation if disregarded in favour of a rigid Cartesian dualism (Ross 2011), but which is also variously explored both in its constraining and enabling implications and effects. Scientific experimentation does not recede in the background, and can be considered in relation to its impact on embodiment. Interestingly, Italian writer Italo Calvino's comment on Levi's stories already grasps the prominent role played by biology, and proposes to adjust the science-fiction label (in Italian: *fantascienza*) into "fantabiological".[13]

From this perspective, *Natural Histories* displays a diversified range of bodies and minds, from fully-fledged impossible ones (e.g., in "Angelic Butterfly"; "*Cladonia rapida*", "Man's Friend", "Some Applications of the Mimete", "*Quaestio de Centauris*") to others which defy normative representations not

12 The equivalence among technological resources – and even between biological and cultural affordances – emerges even more strongly if we think of "His Own Blacksmith", a story included in *Flaw of Form*. Here, the protagonist is provided with an impossible consciousness, stretched over the millennia and species evolution, and for whom the acquisition of human-like hands is seamlessly followed by the capability of using a stick as basic tool, which is then immediately turned into a weapon.

13 Letter from Calvino to Levi, 22 November 1961 (Calvino 2000, 695–96; transl. from Cassata 2016, 30).

much by being biologically impossible but rather because a defamiliarising light is cast on them (see "The Sixth Day", discussed below). A comment by Robert Gordon offers a small yet telling example of how the shift of focus on embodiment and its implication may prove fruitful. According to Gordon, "*Quaestio de Centauris*" represents an exception in *Natural Histories* because it is not about science nor inventions of any kind. Protagonist of the story is the centaur Trachi, a mythological creature half-man and half-horse, situated in a contemporary and otherwise realistic context. However, rather than dwelling on the social discrimination to which the Trachi is subjected, a large portion of the story also focuses on the practical discomforts and adjustments brought about by the centaur's hybrid biology: his equine digestive system is meant to rely on fodder but, since Trachi has to ingest the food to support his large horse body through a small human mouth, he needs to spend most of his time munching, which leads to long meditation and is thus conducive to the renowned wisdom of his species. Even more interestingly, Trachi's non-normative body and mind also work as narrative trigger for the plot: because centaurs are biologically predisposed to grasp sexual tensions around them, he immediately discovers the betrayal of the narrator with the girl Trachi loved, thus provoking his fury and the end of his friendship with the narrator. Both quantitatively and qualitatively, the centaur's embodied condition plays a central role in the story: this perspective gives this fact full recognition, instead of bracketing it as a diversion from the supposed thematic centre of the collection. In the next section, I shall continue this discussion by considering what functions and effects these manipulations of the body-mind nexus achieve and foreground.

## 5 Fiction and Non-normativity: Multiplicity and Defamiliarisation

By foregrounding the focus on embodiment, I seek to disengage Levi's science fiction from the idea that it should be used as a privileged genre to convey unambiguous moral or cautionary messages, and rather argue for a deliberately speculative and explorative use of fiction whose fruitfulness lies in the possibility of considering different scenarios. Johnson's idea of moral reasoning as "engaged probing and experimentation" strongly resonates with the kind of imaginative operation allowed for to Levi by fiction – and denied, instead, by testimonial writing. Speaking of his science-fiction stories to his friend Luciana Nissim, Levi writes that this speculative turn "[isn't] a betrayal, but simply, on my part, an effort to return to reality and an evasion from the official and professional role which destiny has imposed on me" (1993, 212).[14] This idea of resorting to speculative fiction to *return* to reality is crucial, but needs to be unpacked: does Levi seek to escape his own individual reality, in which he has been assigned the role of witness and against which he reclaims his right to imagination and experimentation with fiction (Cassata 2016, 55)? Or do these stories attempt to evade reality altogether?

If Levi attempted to "evade" something, it is arguably not ethical engagement per se, but rather the ethical and narrative limits of bearing witness. Among the ethical constraints imposed by the testimonial function, one may count the pressing need of sticking to the exact circumstances, in order not to undermine the reliability and value of one's testimony; the fear of having one's speculative attitude mistaken for a step back from the uncomfortable burden of judgment; more generally, a deep sense of respect for other victims of the same crime, who might feel differently from Levi. In contrast with these premises, science fiction could offer the opportunity not to escape, but to broaden the scope of moral reflection. But there are also limits of testimonial writing which might be called narrative. Enrico Ferrero, Einaudi chief press officer at the time of the publication of *Natural Histories*, reported that Levi saw science fiction as an opportunity to emancipate himself from the role of witness-writer and become a fully-fledged literary writer, a step for which the capability to invent characters and situations – as opposed to recount them – he regarded as crucial (Zanda 2019, 72; Beltrami 2023b).

So, if we could see Levi's science fiction as an attempt at breaking free from the role of witness and the constraints that come with it, the challenge of *inventio* more specifically could be understood as a "return to reality" in response to Levi's ambitions as a writer (which might have been in his eyes more of a "real" choice compared to being a survivor). Most importantly, however, it is for Levi the chemist-writer that engagement with science fiction may represent a return to reality, in the sense of a renewed immersion in the materiality of life. Foregrounding the exploration of embodiment captures how this immersion is implemented and how fiction may work, in fact, as a fruitful instrument to investigate the profound entanglement of life – and ethics – with matter. By playing with the body-mind nexus, Levi manipulates – either through futuristic technologies or by sheer intervention of fantastic imagination – the features and circumstances of living bodies (Beltrami 2023c). Johnson's view of moral imagination as resulting from a *collective* endeavour rather than based

14 Letter from Levi to Nissim, 22 February 1966, reported in Chiappano 2010, 234–35; transl. from Cassata 2016, 52.

on establishing and applying moral laws is mirrored in Levi's case by the multiplicity of stories: unlike factual accounts, fictional narratives can co-exist and complement and create a dialogue with one another, without there having to be one that is "truer" than the others. In other words, the specific form chosen by Levi, thanks to its speculative and plural nature, approaches ethical reflection from a different angle, which can be captured through the notion of moral imagination. As Levi probes the consequences of imaginary manipulations on how his characters live in their environment, he fully implements a form of moral imagination characterised by a re-appraisal of indeterminacy (yet not randomness), deviancy from standards, and multiplicity.

In this framework, the non-normativity of bodies, minds and their states of affairs plays a complex and multifarious role: at different times and to different degrees, it aims both to defamiliarise and, on the contrary, to highlight the disturbing familiarity of certain situations, as well as it arguably contributes to unsettle the prototypical concept of human or human-like agent.

As a crucial mechanism of defamiliarisation, Levi exploits non-normativity to make the interrelations between body and mind more visible. "The Sixth Day" is an extraordinary example of this. The story stages a supernatural and yet very down-to-earth committee meeting which is to deliberate on the design of the soon-to-be created Human species: after agreeing on a set of desirable behavioural and social characteristics (including the capability of making tools, articulated language, thermic adaptability, and propensity to social life), committee members proceed to discuss what biological make-up is most advisable in order to obtain these. The story thus consists in the debate around which and how certain features of the environment (e.g., water vs. dry land) or of the material body (e.g., size, chemical composition, sexual vs. asexual reproduction) are key to determine specific cognitive faculties and social practices, laying full stress on the continuum not only between these "internal" and "external" dynamics, but also between living beings and the world around them. In this relation, the defamiliarising effect comes, firstly, from the inverted application of Darwinian evolution, which is not determined by chance but rather strategically designed to achieve certain desired outcomes. Secondly, increasing estrangement ensues from the slow realisation that the creature that is being progressively outlined accumulates more and more features which are typical of birds rather than humans. In the end, with a plot twist, the prototype of the Human as we know it (and, therefore, endowed with "conventional" body and mind) is created via a sort of *coup* by God himself, who bypasses the committee; the reader is thus left wondering whether all the target faculties and ethical potential which according to our commonsense characterise the human species are in fact likely to be present in the first place.[15]

"The Sixth Day" provides an effective example of how Levi foregrounds the body-mind nexus and reflects on its implications in an open-minded way which is neither straightforwardly optimistic nor pessimistic. In fact, this story also suggests how attention to scientific experimentation may be rearticulated in terms of a central role played by manipulation: manipulation of the features of material bodies through technological devices ("Retirement package"), chemical compounds ("The Mnemagogs", "Versamine"), or sheer fantasy ("*Quaestio de Centauris*"), by means of which Levi imaginatively explores how these changes highlight the irreducible and inescapable interdependence between biological features and the kind of sentient life they originate. Sometimes, these speculative alterations determine affordances that enable different interactions with others, such as in the case of the centaur Trachi and his attunement to surrounding sexual tensions. In other cases, the imaginative game consists in a new, somehow unfamiliar way of seeing certain bodies, human or otherwise: "Censorship in Bitinia" does not envision any actual bodily modification and the shift is purely perspectival, as the ascription of censorship duties to chickens is based on psychological and physiological traits that, though from a fictional perspective, already belong to this species.

However, if the embodied condition we share as living beings emerges as an underlying constant of Levi's representations, non-normativity may result disturbing not always because of the stark alterity it emphasises, but, on the contrary, because of how "natural" and familiar the interdependence of body and mind appears, though within the limits of the specific fictional circumstances of each story. In fact, this fruitful balance between familiarity and unfamiliarity is brought to the fore by Darko Suvin (1979) in his seminal work on science fiction. Suvin describes the genre as literature of "cognitive estrangement", for it programmatically relies on the representation of situations which are significantly different from naturalist or realistic accounts and yet are not perceived as completely impossible.[16]

15 An additional defamiliarising element is arguably represented by the ironic and pseudo-religious background of the committee (a curious mix of technicians and spiritual entities – Arimane and Ormuz referring, respectively, to the Zoroastrian principles of chaos and order –, all responding to God), which combines scientific and cultural traditions in ironic and yet interesting ways, hinting at the complementarity of the two perspectives.

16 Lino Aldani, one of the major writers and critics of science fiction in Italy, also concurs with Suvin in identifying the development of a fantastic premise in a coherent manner as

In "The Mnemagogs", for instance, Dr Montesanto learns to synthetise chemical compounds whose smell is capable of triggering specific and personal memories. Not only recent studies actually demonstrate that olfactive experience can cue exceptionally vivid and emotionally-laden episodic memories (Chu and Downes 2000), but it is particularly interesting how the story explicitly entertains the idea that these products should be regarded, *de facto*, as part of the protagonist himself inasmuch as they code memories constituting the backbone of his identity: as Dr Montesanto observes, "One might even say [these memory evokers] *are* me, since I, at least in part, consist of them" (*Natural Histories*, Levi 2015). In cognitive science, this is a viable idea captured by the concept of *extended mind* (Clark and Chalmers 1998; Clark 2008). Even though the younger doctor is ill at ease while being shown these artefacts, I would argue that his disquiet is not really a matter of unethical discomfort due to some misapplication of scientific inquiry. My impression is that Levi expects that the experience of having a very specific memory or atmosphere strongly evoked by a certain smell is likely to be shared by readers, instead of something that should provoke a defamiliarizing effect. In fact, Levi seems rather fascinated by exploring the entanglement of chemical processes and their impact on higher-level cognitive, emotional or social phenomena.

In this light, although the title of the collection has been often taken as ironic (Levi 2016, 1506–07; Mengoni and Scarpa 2022, 233, 270) – given the fact that most of the stories feature very *unnatural* bodies –, I would rather suggest that it may not be entirely so. Far from being unnatural, the connection between our bodies, in their biological and physiological materiality, and the life they afford is very much real; changes brought about in the latter by altering the former are, in fact, most natural. It may be, thus, that the title chosen by Levi is meant to remain ambiguous, rather than overtly ironic.

Finally, the interplay between estrangement and familiarity is relevant to what I suggested before about the impact of speculative fiction on prototypical concepts, as it may be argued that the representations Levi elaborates and runs in his science fiction work very much like Johnson's nonprototypical cases. Significant reflections on the general function of models (or prototypes) in any judgment appear in "The Measure of Beauty": promoted as an instrument to assess beauty, the Kalometer works, in fact, as an instrument to measure conformity. The narrator, though, observes that "anyone who judges is a conformist, inasmuch as, consciously or not, he uses some sort of model as his point of reference" (*Natural Histories,* Levi 2015). And even more interestingly is the

---

one of the most important aspects of science fiction (1962, 16–17). The relevance of Suvin's discourse for Levi is also discussed by Ross (2011).

following comment, if projected onto a moral scenario: "the most *alarming* phenomenon of today's civilization, […] is that the average man, today, can be calibrated in the most incredible ways […] it was essentially not very sporting to denigrate a machine simply because it reproduces a human mental process" (*Natural Histories*, Levi 2015). And again, in "*Quaestio de Centauris*", the narrator reports that, according to the centaurs' legends, only *archetypes* for living species were saved on Noah's ark: "only the archetypal animals, the key species, were saved: man but not the monkey; the horse but not the donkey or the wild ass; the rooster and the crow but not the vulture or the hoopoe or the gyrfalcon" (*Natural Histories*, Levi 2015).

Levi's view on prototypes thus seems productively ambivalent. On the one hand, it harkens back to the semantic area of conformity, normativity, and, possibly, mediocrity. On the other, one cannot overlook that, in his capacity as chemist and production technician, adherence to standards is also a practice that ensures quality, order and regularity. Chemistry is described as "the art of separating, weighing, and distinguishing: these three exercises are equally useful to those setting out to describe events or give form to their imagination" (*Other People's Trade*, Levi 2015). To set a standard may be as important as to accept that some instances may differ from that standard, depending on the circumstances.

In his science fiction, Levi exploits the negotiation between familiar and estranging elements to put into questions ethically-normative scenarios as well as more subtle representations. More specifically, the imaginative handling of non-normative body-mind nexuses serves an ethical function because it puts standard ideas of what a human being is to the test, acting upon related prototypical concepts. In other words, readers are encouraged to imagine non-prototypical ways in which an entity could organise its life – be it a "conventional" human being somehow enhanced thanks to futuristic technological devices, an animal, a vehicle, or a fantastic creature. At the same time, by envisioning embodiment as an ineliminable constraint, Levi ensures that these representations are not completely free-floating and retain, on the contrary, a key criterion around which to organise themselves conceptually in shaping the prototype of living being. This is not much a philosophical principle, but rather an understanding of life as rooted in materiality which stems from his ingrained scientific outlook on reality. Importantly, though, Levi does not settle for a new prototype for the human: the point is to upset and question extant prototypical views, without getting to an updated, univocal stance.

Levi's stories not only do explore the body-mind nexus, but they continuously re-assert it. Levi uses speculation and imagination to push its boundaries and constraints, to probe and investigate the consequences of this double situatedness, social and biological. On the one hand, even when the narrative context is clearly speculative – in storyworlds where centaurs exist, or in the Berlin of year 2115 –, what counts is not historical accuracy but the specificity of social circumstances, as opposed to their vagueness and genericity. The purpose of this situatedness is to make a scenario imaginable and therefore assessable (even in moral terms), rather than portraying some factual truth faithfully. On the other hand, Levi's science-fiction stories are fascinating explorations of material situatedness: they constitute a "return to reality" insofar as they revert to the material reality of our existence, exploring it in imaginative ways. In this light, their engagement with moral reasoning exceeds the mimetic portrayal of ethical conundrums; instead, it is arguably induced in the reader (via the author) through the very fictional form Levi chooses, which allows him to make full use of strategies to defamiliarise and foreground our embodied condition. The display of a range of different bodies and minds, however, does not aim at mere reiteration. What Levi does, and what fiction seems to be uniquely positioned to do, is to embed these bodies and minds variously challenging standards and expectations within narratively rich contexts, in which the implications of these variations may have space to unfold without being seen in contradiction with one another.

Levi's exploration of non-normative body-mind nexuses may be regarded, therefore, as a case of moral imagination at work because he employs imaginative resources to reassert and emphasise, through a defamiliarising gaze, the embodied condition shared by all living beings. Reverting to Diamond's view, such operation reveals a significant ethical dimension because it is heavily entwined with the rendering of a sense of life – of being alive in the world – which, for her, lies at the heart of ethics itself.[17] In this light, not only Diamond's reflection on the role of literature in dialogue with moral philosophy is relevant to Levi, but Levi's work, in turn, fruitfully exemplifies how speculative fiction, by using its distinctive tools, may bear on moral reasoning in ways other than offering alternative perspectives for the reader to inhabit. Furthermore, Levi's case endorses an understanding of moral imagination as particularly entangled with embodiment.

## 6 Conclusions

In this contribution, I sought to cast a fresh light on Levi's science fiction, identifying in the prominent exploration of speculative bodies and minds a fil

17 For Diamond, ethics is not a sphere of discourse (description of what a good life is) but rather something "tied to everything there is or can be, the world as a whole, life" (2000, 153).

rouge which had remained overshadowed so far. More specifically, I suggested that, if by playing with non-normative representations Levi aims for a sense of defamiliarization, these bodies and minds still consistently share the fundamental condition of embodiment which makes them oddly familiar.

The tension between speculative exploration and ethical dimension is fruitfully captured by the notion of moral imagination, which I elaborated through Cora Diamond's and Mark Johnson's combined philosophical reflections. By foregrounding and probing the embodied condition under fictional conditions, Levi arguably provides a fascinating example of what it is like to be alive in the world and, therefore, of how moral imagination may be operational and meaningful even when the narrative does not address explicit ethical conundrums. Moral imagination thus serves to make sense of the tension between the content and form of Levi's science fiction, and it functions as a way of reconciling ethical concerns, the relationship with reality, and the speculative, even fully imaginative, drive of these stories.

The emphasis on embodiment and the proposed formulation of the ethical dimension of Levi's science fiction constitute original contributions to the scholarship on Levi in their own right. However, I also believe that this case study may serve to illuminate the productive connection between embodiment and moral imagination, and it proposes another way in which literature and fiction may impact on our moral reasoning by shaping our moral concepts, thus attempting to cast a bridge between empirical psychology, moral philosophy and narrative studies.

## Acknowledgements

This work was supported by the European Regional Development Fund and the programme Mobilitas Pluss (MOBJD667) and by the Estonian Research Council Grant (PUT1481). I am grateful to participants in the Primo Levi Summer School 2021 (especially Martina Mengoni, Robert Gordon and Marco Belpoliti), to NCC members, and to NARMESH members for earlier discussions around these ideas.

## Works Cited

Aldani, Lino. *La fantascienza: Che cos'è, com'è sorta, dove tende*. Piacenza: La Tribuna, 1962.

Antonello, Pierpaolo. "La nascita della fantascienza in Italia". In *ItaliAmerica*, edited by Emanuela Scarpellini and Jeffrey Schnapp. Milano: Il Saggiatore, 2008, pp. 99–123.

Antonello, Pierpaolo. *Il ménage a quattro: scienza, filosofia, tecnica nella letteratura italiana del Novecento*. Firenze: Le Monnier, 2005.

Beltrami, Marzia. "Il complesso straniamento della fantascienza di Primo Levi: giochi di scala in 'Una stella tranquilla' e 'Visto di lontano'". *Enthymema*, vol. 33, 2023a, pp. 8–25.

Beltrami, Marzia. "Primo Levi's Science Fiction: A Difficult Negotiation of Ethos, Authorial Posture and Framing Acts". In *Morale della fabula*, edited by Stefano Ballerio. Milano: Biblion, 2023b, pp. 107–32.

Beltrami, Marzia. "Questione di *embodiment*: esplorazioni immaginative del rapporto mente-corpo nella fantascienza di Primo Levi". In *Letteratura e altre scienze. Incroci e sovrapposizioni*, edited by Lorenzo Battistini, Maria Di Maro, Lucia Faienza, Lorenzo Marchese. Bruxelles: Peter Lang, 2023c, pp. 251–72.

Brioni, Simone, and Daniele Comberiati. *Ideologia e rappresentazione. Percorsi attraverso la fantascienza italiana*. Milano: Mimesis, 2020.

Brioni, Simone, and Daniele Comberiati (eds). *Italian Science Fiction*. Cham: Palgrave Macmillan, 2019.

Brown, Adam. *Judging 'Privileged' Jews: Holocaust Ethics, Representation, and the 'Grey Zone'*. New York: Berghahn Books, 2013.

Calvino, Italo. *Lettere 1940–1985*, edited by Luca Baranelli. Milano: Mondadori, 2000.

Calvino, Italo. *Le cosmicomiche*. Torino: Einaudi [*The Cosmicomics*], 1965.

Carta, Ambra, and Lorenzo Marchese. "Modi e processi della conoscenza in Primo Levi: intuizione puntiforme, invenzione ed empatia". *Enthymema*, vol. 35, 2024, pp. 102–21.

Cassata, Francesco. *Fantascienza? / Science Fiction?* Torino: Einaudi, 2016.

Chiappano, Alessandra. *Luciana Nissim Momigliano: una vita*. Florence: Giuntina, 2010.

Chu, Simon, and Joseph John Downes. "Odour-evoked Autobiographical Memories: Psychological Investigations of Proustian phenomena". *Chemical Senses*, vol. 25, no. 1, 2000, pp. 111–16.

Clark, Andy, and David Chalmers. "The Extended Mind", *Analysis*, vol. 58, no. 1, 1998, pp. 7–19.

Clark, Andy. *Supersizing the Mind: Embodiment, Action and Cognitive Extension*. Oxford: Oxford University Press, 2008.

Diamond, Cora. "The Difficulty of Reality and the Difficulty of Philosophy". *Partial Answers: Journal of Literature and the History of Ideas*, vol. 1, no. 2, 2003, pp. 1–26.

Diamond, Cora. "Ethics, Imagination and the Method of Wittgenstein's *Tractatus*". In *The New Wittgenstein*, edited by Alice Crary and Rupert Read. London and New York: Routledge, 2000, pp. 149–73.

Diamond, Cora. "The Importance of Being Human". *Royal Institute of Philosophy Supplements*, no. 29, 1991, pp. 35–62.

Diamond, Cora. "Losing Your Concepts". *Ethics*, vol. 98, no. 2, 1988, pp. 255–77.

Gordon, Robert. *Primo Levi: le virtù dell'uomo normale*. Roma: Carocci, 2003.

Korthals Altes, Liesbeth. *Ethos and Narrative Interpretation. The Negotiation of Values in Fiction*. Lincoln: University of Nebraska Press, 2014.

Johnson, Mark. *The Moral Imagination. Implications of Cognitive Sciences for Ethics*. Chicago: University of Chicago Press, 1993.

Lakoff, George, and Mark Johnson. *Philosophy in the Flesh*. New York: Basic Books, 1999.

Lakoff, George, and Mark Johnson. *Metaphors We Live By*. Chicago: University of Chicago Press, 1980.

Lang, Berel. *Primo Levi. The Matter of a Life*. Grand Rapids, MI: Yale University Press, 2013.

Leopizzi, Maria Grazia. "Pause fantastiche di Primo Levi". *Avanti!*, 6 July 1965; republished in *L'Indice dei Libri del Mese*, 10, October 2015, Speciale Primo Levi, 18.

Levi, Primo. *Opere complete*, edited by Marco Belpoliti, 2 voll. Torino: Einaudi, 2016.

Levi, Primo. *The Complete Works of Primo Levi*. E-book edited by Ann Goldstein, 3 voll. New York and London: W.W. Norton & Company, 2015.

Levi, Primo. *I sommersi e i salvati*. Torino: Einaudi [*The Drowned and the Saved*], 1986.

Levi, Primo. *L'altrui mestiere*. Torino: Einaudi [*Other People's Trade*], 1985.

Levi, Primo. *Se non ora, quando?*. Torino: Einaudi [*If Not Now, When?*], 1982.

Levi, Primo. *Lilít e altri racconti*. Torino: Einaudi [*Lilith and Other Stories*], 1981.

Levi, Primo. *La chiave a stella*. Torino: Einaudi [*The Wrench*], 1978.

Levi, Primo. *Il sistema periodico*. Torino: Einaudi [*The Periodic Table*], 1975.

Levi, Primo. *Vizio di forma*. Torino: Einaudi [*Flaw of Form*], 1971.

Levi, Primo. *Storie naturali*. Torino: Einaudi (first published as Damiano Malabaila) [*Natural Histories*], 1966.

Levi, Primo. *Se questo è un uomo*. Torino: De Silva [*If This Is a Man*] 1947.

Malvestio, Marco, Michele Maiolani, and Eleonora Lima (eds). Primo Levi's Science Fiction. Special issue *Enthymema*, vol. 33, 2023.

Mengoni, Martina. I sommersi e i salvati *di Primo Levi. Storia di un libro (Francoforte 1959 – Torino 1986)*. Macerata: Quodlibet, 2021.

Mengoni, Martina. *Variazioni Rumkowski. Primo Levi e la zona grigia*. Torino: Zamorani, 2018.

Mengoni, Martina, and Domenico Scarpa. "Postfazione". In Primo, Levi. *Storie naturali*. Torino: Einaudi, ed. 2022, pp. 232–76.

Pagetti, Carlo. "Twenty-Five Years of Science Fiction Criticism in Italy (1953–1978)". *Science Fiction Studies*, vol. 6, no. 3, 1979, pp. 320–26.

Pianzola, Federico. *Le «trappole morali» di Primo Levi. Miti e fiction*. Milano: Ledizioni, 2017.

Polvinen, Merja. "The Dark Inside the Prologue: Enactive Cognition and Eerie Ontology in Catherynne M. Valente's *Radiance*". *Style*, vol. 55, no. 3, 2021, pp. 385–405.

Polvinen, Merja. "Sense-Making and Wonder: An Enactive Approach to Narrative Form in Speculative Fiction". In *The Edinburgh Companion to Contemporary Narrative*

*Theories*, edited by Robyn Warhol and Zara Dinnen. Edinburgh: Edinburgh University Press, 2018, pp. 67–80.

Ross, Charlotte. *Primo Levi's Narratives of Embodiment. Containing the Human*. New York and London: Routledge, 2011.

Suvin, Darko. *Metamorphoses of Science Fiction. On the Poetics and History of a Literary Genre*. New Haven and London: Yale University Press, 1979.

Thomson, Ian. *Primo Levi*. London: Hutchinson, 2002.

Zanda, Carlo. *Quando Primo Levi diventò il signor Malabaila*. Vicenza: Neri Pozza Editore, 2019.

# Index

Printed in the United States
by Baker & Taylor Publisher Services